Ethics for Bureaucrats

POLITICAL SCIENCE

A Comprehensive Publication Program

Executive Editor

KENNETH FRIEDMAN
U. S. Department of Energy
Office of the Assistant Secretary
for Conservation and Solar Application
Washington, D.C.

Publications in Political Science

1. Public Administration as a Developing Discipline (in two parts)
   by Robert T. Golembiewski

2. Comparative National Policies on Health Care
   by Milton I. Roemer, M.D.

3. Exclusionary Injustice: The Problem of Illegally Obtained Evidence
   by Steven R. Schlesinger

4. From Contract to Community: Political Theory at the Crossroads
   edited by Fred R. Dallmayr

5. Liberalism and the Modern Polity: Essays in Contemporary
   Political Theory
   edited by Michael J. Gargas McGrath

6. The Politics of the Criminal Justice System:
   An Organizational Analysis
   by Ralph A. Rossum

7. Exploring Competitive Arms Processes:
   Applications of Mathematical Modeling and Computer
   Simulation in Arms Policy Analysis
   edited by W. Ladd Hollist

8. Ethics for Bureaucrats:
   An Essay on Law and Values
   by John A. Rohr

Other volumes in preparation

Developmental Editors

At the birth of societies, the rulers of republics establish institutions; and afterwards the institutions mould the rulers.
Montesquieu

Ethics
for Bureaucrats

An Essay on Law and Values

JOHN A. ROHR
College of Business and Public Service
Governors State University
Park Forest South, Illinois

Foreword by Herbert J. Storing

MARCEL DEKKER, INC.   New York and Basel

Library of Congress Cataloging in Publication Data

Rohr, John Anthony, [Date]
    Ethics for bureaucrats.

    (Political science ; v. 8)
    Includes index.
    1. Civil service ethics. 2. Civil service--United
States. 3. Government executives--United States.
I. Title. II. Series: Political science (New York);
v. 8.
JK468.E7R56   17'.2   78-15327
ISBN 0-8247-6756-X

Grateful acknowledgment is made to the following for permission to quote:
Good Government; America; Political Science Quarterly; Public Admin-
istration Review; Louisiana State University Press, Baton Rouge; The
Macmillan Company, New York; Didactic Systems, Inc., Cranford, N.J.;
Prentice-Hall, Englewood Cliffs, N. J.

MARCEL DEKKER, INC.
270 Madison Avenue, New York, New York 10016

Current printing (last digit):
10 9 8 7 6 5 4 3 2 1

PRINTED IN THE UNITED STATES OF AMERICA

To Kathy

"There lives the dearest freshness deep down things"

Foreword

It is to our credit as students and practitioners of public administration that we have begun to grapple seriously with the long-neglected ethical side of public decision making. Yet it must be conceded that we have not, on the whole, grappled with it very effectively. We tend to focus on narrow, rather legalistic questions involving, for example, codes of ethics or conflict of interest; or we aspire to articulate vast schemes of general ethics or political philosophy or Judeo-Christian tradition. The pleasure of welcoming studies declaring the pertinence to administration of ethical inquiry is alloyed with the sense that most of them miss the mark.

John Rohr avoids the extremes of narrowness and breadth and leads us to the heart of the matter with the simple, profound idea that the most prominent features of the American public administrator's ethical horizon are what Rohr calls the American regime values—the values or ends or goods that the American political system is designed to secure. To this observation, Rohr adds the persuasive argument that excellent access to these regime values is provided by United States Supreme Court opinions. Finally, he shows that what we are looking for—or what we ought to be looking for—are not commands of political or administrative right and wrong but well-grounded, disciplined, illuminating dialogue about the meaning and implications of those great principles to which all Americans give assent.

Having sketched the broad ethical horizon of the American public administrator and having made the case for focusing on American regime values, Rohr goes on to do what he says ought to be done. He provides lengthy extracts of Supreme Court opinions that are especially significant for this purpose. By judicious comment and questions he guides his reader through the opinions and to their implications regarding the pervasive themes of equality, freedom, and property.

This is a book that is meant to be used—and it will be used—by public administrators and prospective public administrators. It will sharpen and deepen their practical grasp on the complex and sometimes ambiguous political principles that provide most of the ethical ground and substance of their work as American public administrators.

Herbert J. Storing

Preface

Perhaps the most pleasant moment in writing a book comes at the end when one reflects upon the generosity, encouragement, and helpful criticism one has received over the years spent in thought, research, reading, conversation, and writing about one's topic. This is especially true when the topic of one's book does not fit neatly into a well-established academic discipline. There is no clearly defined body of knowledge, complete with models and paradigms, to which I could turn when I decided to investigate the question of ethics for bureaucrats.

For this reason I find myself especially indebted to many friends and colleagues who helped me explore the first principles of my topic. I became a bit alarmed when they pointed out that those principles would soon lead me to fields as diverse as philosophy, law, politics, religion, psychology, history, organization theory, and management. So indeed they did, and when, somewhat discouraged, I returned to these colleagues, I found remarkable patience with what I am sure they recognized as very elementary questions.

Consequently, I find genuine satisfaction in following the gracious tradition of acknowledging the contribution of others to whatever merit this book might have. Similarly, I recognize the propriety of granting the customary absolution for the defects in my work to all those mentioned below.

It is a gratitude tempered with great sorrow that I express toward my dear friend and mentor, Herbert J. Storing, who passed away on September 9, 1977. I was honored when he agreed to write the foreword to this book because it was from him that I learned so much about ethics, bureaucrats, law and values. My gratitude to Herbert Storing for so many personal and professional kindnesses is surpassed only by my sense of loss from his premature death at the age of forty-nine. Those who had the good fortune to know him personally will recognize the appropriateness of the words of the Book of Wisdom: "Being perfected in a short time, he fulfilled long years; for his soul was pleasing to the Lord."

It was well over a decade ago when, as a student in Herbert Storing's course on "The American Bureaucracy," I first began to think about the normative implications of the little-lamented demise of the politics-administration dichotomy. In an essay written in the mid-1960s, Storing had maintained that "the civil servant has least understanding of his own doings when he is exercising his highest responsibilities." Just how deeply I was impressed by that insight will become apparent in the pages that follow. Indeed, this entire volume might well be considered an attempt to respond to the challenge implicit in Storing's sound but troubling observation.

Many professors and practitioners of public administration have been most generous in sharing their writings, comments, and criticisms with me. Among these are Robert Biller, Chester Newland, and Ted Thomas of the University of Southern California; Fred Brown, formerly of the same university; Michael Harmon of George Washington University; David K. Hart of the University of Washington; Frank Marini of San Diego State University; Fred Thayer of the University of Pittsburgh; James Childress of Georgetown University; William Harader of Indiana State University; Richard Chapman of the National Academy of Public Administration; William Maher of the Nuclear Regulatory Commission; Donald Murphy of the National Institutes of Health; David Reich of the United States Civil Service Commission; and the late Martin Diamond. Because in Chapter 2, I find myself somewhat at odds with the approaches to ethics advocated by Hart and Harmon, it is only fitting that I should now acknowledge my gratitude to these fine scholars for forcing me to think through the implications of my own position and for educating me on its weak points.

As is so often the case with studies of this nature, substantial institutional support was required to carry on the necessary research. I am happy to acknowledge my thanks to the National Endowment for the Humanities for its generous support. I am also grateful to the National Association of Schools of Public Affairs and Administration for sponsoring me as a NASPAA Fellow during the academic year 1975-1976. I had the good fortune to spend that fellowship year with the General Management Training Center of the United States Civil Service Commission. There I had the challenging responsibility of designing a manual on ethics for the courses conducted by the Training Center. More than a passing word of thanks is due to Wilton H. Dickerson and E. C. Wakham for giving me a remarkably free hand in carrying out my work. Lengthy conversations with Stephen King, also of the General Management Training Center, were particularly helpful and my debt to that brilliant young man is hereby gladly acknowledged.

I am also pleased to acknowledge my appreciation to the graduate students at Governors State University who cooperated so splendidly in experimental courses in which, together, we discussed many of the ideas developed in Chapters 3, 4, and 5. My colleagues at Governors State have always been supportive friends and constructive critics. The comments of Paula Wolff, Michael Cohen, Daniel Bernd, and Carl Stover have been both welcome and incisive. Ruben Austin, Ralph Winston, Virginio Piucci, and Richard Vorwerk provided generous administrative support for my work, and Marsha Doyle prepared the manuscript with characteristic competence and cheerfulness.

My deepest gratitude, however, is reserved for my wife, Kathy, who excels in the most important values and to whom this book is lovingly dedicated.

John A. Rohr

Contents

Ethics for Bureaucrats

Introduction

*We see the wisdom of Solon's remark that no more
good must be attempted than the nation can bear.*
Thomas Jefferson

This book is written for career government managers and for those
aspiring to such careers. It addresses a wide variety of topics—ethics,
bureaucracy, law, and values—but it is education that unifies these dispar-
ate themes and provides the focus of this essay. The educational problems
examined in the pages that follow is how to integrate the study of ethics
into the curricula of schools of public administration and centers for public
management training. A plan for achieving this integration is set forth and
defended on moral, political, and academic grounds.

EXPLAINING TERMS

At the outset, several words that appear frequently in this book will
need a word of explanation. "Education" is used in a broad sense that
includes public management training. Although education and training can
be distinguished both in principle and practice, these distinctions have
little significance for our purposes. For the same reason, references to
"schools of public administration" include public management training
centers. On the few occasions when it is necessary to distinguish between
education and training or schools and centers, these distinctions will be
stated explicitly.

The expression "public management" requires a twofold explanation.
"Public" refers to governmental activities at the federal, state, and local

1

levels.[1] Although the examples and illustrations used in this essay are taken from federal practices, the principles underlying the argument apply to managers in state and local government as well. The term "management" is not used with any specific job description in mind. The federal civil service distinguishes among supervisors, managers, and executives, but experience teaches one not to put too much trust in these categories. Supervisors are often described as "first line," just as managers are often called "mid-level" and executives are said to be found in the cadres of the "supergrades." These terms are helpful, but they are not used with any rigorous consistency either in this book or in the world it describes. The management positions pertinent to the analysis in this book are those in which administrative discretion is exercised in a way that has at least some effect on public policy. Administrative discretion is discussed in Chapter 1.

A "bureaucrat" is a public official hired, retained, and promoted through a merit system. A merit system is contrasted with a patronage system. The latter is a personnel system characterized by political (usually partisan) loyalty, whereas the former purports to be based on achievement. The key point for our purpose is that bureaucrats are neither elected nor politically appointed and that they hold their positions during good behavior or until they reach retirement age. In a word, the bureaucrat is exempt from the discipline of the ballot box.

The primary purpose of defining the bureaucrat in terms of his or her relation to a merit system is to stress his or her independence from the electoral process. "Bureaucrat" is not used in the prejorative sense that suggests bungling inefficiency, red tape, goal displacement, or a variety of other organizational pathologies. The bureaucrat's position is sharply distinguished from that of the elected official, even though, as we shall see below, he or she shares governing power with the elected official. The combination of these two ingredients—governing power and independence from the electorate—presents a significant problem for a democratic society. It is a problem that cannot be answered without a serious look at the ethical norms bureaucrats bring to their governing role.

The word "regime" is not used in the journalistic sense of the "Johnson regime," the "Nixon regime," and so on. Rather it is simply intended as the best English equivalent of what Aristotle meant by a "polity." More specifically by the American "regime," I mean the fundamental political order established by the Constitution of 1789.

"Ethics" is used in a more general sense than one often finds in contemporary discussions of ethical issues such as conflict of interest. This book examines broader questions of moral character that educators once took more seriously than we do today. For the most part, I shall use the words "ethics" and "morals" interchangeably. Although there may be

nuances and shades of meaning that differentiate these words, they are
derived etymologically from Latin and Greek words with the same
meaning. Any distinction that is intended between these words will be
stated expressly.[2]

In discussing ethics in terms of character, our task would be much
simpler if we could make frequent use of the word "virtue," but, unfortunately, that unhappy word has been so degraded that today it is but a sad
and pale reflection of its former self. The Latin word virtus and the Greek
areté meant "excellence." The political life of the regimes of antiquity
aimed at encouraging the development of a certain manifestation of human
excellence. On the few occasions when "virtue" is mentioned in this book,
it is with this vigorous classical model in mind rather than its prudish
descendant.

"Prudence" is another word I would like to use more frequently than I
do but, like "virtue," it too has fallen on hard times. A recent commentary on the attitudes of Harvard law students noted that they looked at the
word in "essentially cost-benefit terms." Their guiding principle was said
to be "prudence rather than ethics."[3] This contrast between prudence and
ethics is an astounding statement. There was a time when prudence, along
with justice, fortitude, and temperance, composed the four cardinal virtues upon which the whole of moral life was thought to depend. In the
medieval world prudence was the virtue that enabled one to apply univers-
alistic moral principles to concrete human situations.[4] I would like to say
that Chapters 3, 4, and 5 of this book provide exercises intended to
develop the virtue of prudence, but, if prudence today is contrasted with
ethics, the word must be used with considerable caution. Apparently,
prudence today suggests a shrewd calculation of one's not so enlightened
self-interest, whereas ethics is reserved for the more rarified atmosphere of absolute principles. Perhaps this explains how temperance, the
erstwhile colleague of prudence, came to mean total abstention and thereby
ended up with just as sorry a fate as prudence. Even more interesting is
that when we look for the absolute principles lodged in the heavenly city of
ethics, we are told that the epistemological crises of modern philosophy
have rendered them obsolete. This is the philosopher's version of
Catch 22.

Perhaps it is instructive that a book on ethics for bureaucrats should
begin with a somewhat querulous effort to explain the problems occasioned
by certain words once commonplace in moral discourse. The sad truth is
that we are unaccustomed to serious moral discussion. We prefer to take
our morals in small doses of slogans, epithets, and invectives. When
Machiavelli told us to look at the way things are and not as they ought to be,
he made us modern men; but in so doing he bequeathed us a sorry legacy
of trained incapacity for sound moral debate.

OUTLINING THE ARGUMENT

This book is not a traditional textbook. Texts can be written only when a field of inquiry is sufficiently developed to have an established literature capable of being ordered, summarized, and presented in a way that is meaningful to the uninitiated. Unfortunately, issues of ethical interest to bureaucrats have by no means reached this degree of development. Indeed, the somewhat informal manner in which the argument of this book is presented—especially in Chapters 3, 4, and 5—is deliberately intended to underscore its tentative character.

Before presenting my argument, it might be helpful to provide in this introduction a brief outline of the plan of this book. Chapter 1 attempts to state the most appropriate starting point for investigating ethics for bureaucrats. Stated briefly, it is that through their administrative discretion bureaucrats, who are nonelected officials, participate in the governing process of a democratic regime. To establish this point it is necessary to review the well-known issues surrounding the origin and decline of the dichotomy of politics and administration. Although this topic will be quite familiar to students of public administration, there are important normative implications of the collapse of the dichotomy that have received little attention in the literature. The normative dimensions of administrative discretion are highlighted in developing the ethical significance of the statement that bureaucrats govern.

Chapter 2 builds on the point that the democratic principle requiring accountability to the people from those who govern applies to bureaucrats as well as to elected officials. But because bureaucrats govern through authority that is discretionary, and because they are not elected, the ordinary means of popular control are inapplicable. To the extent that formal, legal, or institutional controls over the bureaucrat's behavior are either nonexistent or ineffective, bureaucrats have an ethical obligation to respond to the values of the people in whose name they govern. The values in question are not popular whims of the moment but rather constitutional or regime values. This is because the bureaucrat has taken an oath to uphold the Constitution. As far as schools of public administration are concerned, the best educational means for preparing bureaucrats to fulfill this obligation is to use Supreme Court opinions on salient regime values to encourage them to reflect on how those values might best influence their decision making as one who governs.

The remaining chapters support this approach by showing how Supreme Court opinions can enrich ethical reflections. These chapters examine specific regime values—equality, freedom, property—as they have been discussed and debated by the Supreme Court. Although questions of public law are raised, it should be carefully noted that their focus is on law as a symbol of values rather than on law for its own sake. In jurisprudential terms, these chapters highlight the pedagogical aspects of the law—a point developed both in the biblical tradition and in classical antiquity.[5] In these chapters, the bureaucrat is urged to follow Socrates' example of entering into a dialogue with the laws of the city.[6]

In each of these chapters, selections from Supreme Court opinions are given, and value-laden questions based on the opinions are then posed. The questions presented in the text are intended to stimulate lively discussions. It is in these discussions that real learning will take place. That is, the values articulated by the Court will first be clarified, then judged by the reader and finally modified, rejected or appropriated in a personal sense. This is the purpose of the method proposed in this book. It is not intended simply to enumerate a checklist of values for the reader's edification. Its purpose is rather to structure a discussion of moral values along broad, constitutional lines and then, by posing pertinent questions, to encourage the reader to make these broad values more specific by reflecting on just what these values might mean to him or her. When the Court's opinions are studied in a classroom setting, instructors and students will undoubtedly want to add cases and questions of their own, depending on their interests and background.[7]

It should be noted that this book has a very limited purpose. No case is made herein for reorganizing or reforming the bureaucracy in an institutional sense; nor is any case made to hinder such efforts. This book deals only with ethical questions concerning the bureaucracy regardless of how it might be organized, and these questions are limited to ethical problems grounded in whatever discretionary authority bureaucrats might have.

Further, this book deals only with what educational institutions can do about ethics for bureaucrats. I hope I am not betraying any secrets when I say there is precious little that such institutions can do about anything that goes on outside themselves. The little we can do, however, is precious indeed, and we should do it well.

Finally, this book offers an approach to ethics that presupposes a basic decency on the part of bureaucrats and addresses to them an appeal to reflect seriously on the moral dimensions of their discretionary authority. James Madison long ago warned against the inadequacy of appeals to morality.[8] We would be quite foolish to forget all we have learned from the past in our present enthusiasm for the post-Watergate morality. It is as true for us as it was for Madison that in our efforts to promote the common good we ignore the primacy of passion and self-interest only at our peril. Questions of morals must be seen against the broader background of what the centuries have taught us. It was Jefferson who said, "We see the wisdom of Solon's remark that no more good must be attempted than the nation can bear."[9] Without this cautious view of our own moral strengths, discussions of ethics run the risk of either trailing off into trivial happy talk among the superficial or escalating into strident fanaticism among the grave.

FALSE STARTS

To conclude this introduction, several "false starts" in the approach to the study of ethics will be examined. These are approaches that have some merit but, in my opinion, run into such serious difficulties that in the long run they are counterproductive. At the outset it should be clear that these approaches are not being discarded in a rigid or doctrinaire manner. Each of them has considerable educational merit, but what is at issue is their usefulness in yielding a principled rationale to justify a particular method for teaching ethics and their practical effectiveness in helping bureaucrats address ethical problems in their careers. I do not suggest that the considerations listed herein as "false starts" have no place in a course in ethics, but I do question their propriety as the central focus of such a course.

Conflict of Interest

Conflict of interest is such an important ethical issue that the term is fre-quently used as a surrogate for broader questions of ethics in government. Despite the public attention lavished upon conflict of interest, it is not the best starting point for educational purposes. There are three reasons for this. The first is that a serious examination of conflict of interest neces-sarily centers upon technical questions of legal interpretation that hold little promise of generating more substantive considerations. For example, X and Y are partners in a legal firm. X takes a position with the Bureau of Traffic of the Interstate Commerce Commission (ICC). Y is approached by a client whose company is being investigated by that bureau. Can Y take the case? Suppose X works for a different bureau in ICC—for example, the Bureau of Accounts? Does this change make a difference? Suppose the client was being investigated by an entirely different agency — for example, the Antitrust Division of Justice. Could Y then take the case? If Y is permitted to take the case in any of these instances, can X share in the fees the partnership derives from Y's efforts? While these issues are of considerable interest to those involved in such situations, they are, after all, simply questions of positive law that do not—at least in any obvious sense—reach out to broader issues of inherent moral concern.

  The second reason for rejecting conflict of interest as the focus of a study of ethics is related to the legalistic character of this topic. Pre-cisely because conflict of interest is minutely regulated by law, the questions it triggers are necessarily structured in negative terms of administrative sanctions and criminal penalties.[10] The motive of fear of punishment is implicit in any discussion of conflict of interest. While this motive may at times be salutary, it is not a likely staging area for developing a high sense of ethical commitment in the public service.

The third reason for rejecting conflict of interest is that it is not the
sort of issue that is likely to occur on a regular basis in a career as a
public manager. For example, at the beginning of one's career, a question
might arise as to whether a new employee must sell certain stocks related
to his or her agency's mission or whether he or she can continue to participate in a stock-option plan established by a former employer. Similarly,
when one is planning to leave government service, questions on the propriety of certain forms of subsequent employment could become quite
important. The same is true if one marries or receives a substantial
inheritance during one's career. These sorts of issues pertain more to the
milestones of one's personal and professional life than to one's daily routine. When they do arise, they are terribly important, and agency counsellors should be consulted.[11] For educational purposes, however, such
issues do not arise with sufficient regularity to warrant more than an
assurance that the reader is aware of the problem and of the "Caesar's
wife" rationale that underlies conflict-of-interest legislation.[12]

This awareness is far more valuable than a detailed mastery of the
intricacies of conflict-of-interest laws. It will prompt the thoughtful
reader to reflect on why government employees are subject to legal
restrictions—often sanctioned with criminal penalties—that are virtually
unknown in other occupations. Such reflection is conducive to a sound
understanding of professional ethics for it will provide the bureaucrat with
an awareness of what the public expects of those who claim to serve.[13]

It will be helpful if we conclude our discussion of conflict of interest by
placing it in a broader philosophical framework. Traditionally, the study
of ethics has focused on two questions—doing good and avoiding evil. Just
what is meant by "good and evil" is, of course, the very stuff of the history
of ethics. Prohibitions against bribery and conflict of interest are aimed
at avoiding evil. They are necessarily negative in tone and substance.
Ethical considerations that aim at developing a sense of professional commitment in the career civil service must include the more positive aspects
of the opportunities for public service. Hence, if we are to get on with our
work, we must presuppose that future or present bureaucrats reading this
book have every intention of avoiding conflicts of interest and that if at
some time in their careers they are not sure if one exists, they will ask
the appropriate agency counsel for advice.[14]

Watergate

A second "false start" that should be avoided at all costs is to focus on the
sins and follies of Watergate. This is somewhat paradoxical because the
current interest in ethics in government is due in no small part to the
Watergate scandals. We should reject a "what-can-we-learn-from-
Watergate" approach to ethics for bureaucrats for the simple reason that

Watergate was not a problem involving the career civil service.[15] Indeed,
one might argue that the dreadful months of Watergate actually reflected
considerable credit upon the career civil service. The routine business of
government was conducted in a reasonably efficient manner despite a collapse in political leadership that lasted several months. The outcome of a
discussion of Watergate among career bureaucrats is likely to be a justi-
fiable sense of self-righteousness vis-à-vis their politically appointed
superiors. Self-righteousness, even the justified variety, is a dubious
starting point for serious ethical reflection.

Another reason for rejecting Watergate as an entrée to ethics is the
need to avoid the alleged failing of military academies—training new officers to fight old wars. An excessive preoccupation with the concrete
details of Watergate is more likely to attune the reader to the dangers of'
the past rather than the problems of the future. This is not to say that we
have nothing to learn from Watergate. Obviously, we can learn, and
already have learned, a great deal, but the lessons of Watergate point
more in the direction of institutional reform than personal ethical
standards.[16]

Resignation in Protest

A third "false start" is to concentrate upon the concept of "resignation in
protest." This is particularly tempting because there is a growing body of
readily available literature on the phenomenon of resignation in protest that
is often combined with "whistle-blowing."[17] Despite the interesting and,
at times, exciting literature on this topic, it does not provide a suitable
focus for the study of ethics for bureaucrats. There are two reasons for
this. The first is that most bureaucrats will probably never find themselves in such an extremely difficult situation that resignation on grounds
of conscience would be a serious consideration. Resignation in protest is
a marginal problem in government life as a whole, even though it is of
tremendous significance for those individuals for whom the problem does
arise. For most bureaucrats, though, the question is probably of academic
interest only.

The second reason for deemphasizing resignation in protest is a bit
more complicated. A brief quotation from George Bernard Shaw might
shed some light on the problem. Shaw, who was actively involved in the
British Labour party, was annoyed to hear that a Labour candidate named
Joseph Burgess had refused to compromise on an issue and had thereby
lost his seat in Parliament. Shaw had this to say:

> When I think of my own unfortunate character, smirched with compro-
> mise, rotted with opportunism, mildewed by expediency, dragged
> through the mud of borough council and Battersea elections, stretched

out of shape with wire-pulling, putrefied by permeation, worn out by twenty-five years pushing to gain an inch here, or straining to stem a backrush, I do think Joe might have put up with just a speck or two on those white robes of his for the sake of the millions of poor devils who cannot afford any character at all because they have no friend in Parliament. Oh, these moral dandies, these spiritual toffs, these superior persons. Who is Joe, anyhow, that he should not risk his soul occasionally like the rest of us? [18]

There are several points in Shaw's comment that are worthy of our attention. The first is the simple fact that all forms of organizational life demand compromises of values one holds dear. The person who is unwilling to "risk his soul occasionally like the rest of us" cannot contribute constructively to any organization. The significant ethical question is not whether one should compromise but when one should do so—that is, how important are the values at stake? Indeed, compromise is itself one of the most important values of any organization that is effective and enduring. It is the catalyst that makes possible the realization of other values.

The second point involves the relationship between economic class and conscientious resignation. For the most part resignation in protest is an upper-class phenomenon. [19] Those who do this sort of thing often have a profession, business, or prominent family to fall back on after their resignation. This observation is not intended to disparage the motives of those who have resigned from public office on grounds of conscience. It is mentioned only to indicate why it might be unwise to focus on resignation as a central concern in our treatment of ethics. It seems to me that it would be irresponsible to create an "ethos of resignation" among those who intend to seek careers in government. Such an atmosphere could be particularly dangerous for conscientious and impressionable young people who have just begun their careers and are in no position either financially or professionally to take unnecessary risks with their futures. Resignation should be presented as the ultimate weapon rather than as an opening salvo in an intraagency dispute over a value-laden issue. Prospective government employees of modest means and limited experience should be encouraged to "work within the system" as far as basic decency will allow. If we are not willing to offer this advice, we should discourage young people from entering government service in the first place rather than encourage them to resign at the first hint of a moral crisis.

Basic Decency

A final approach that must be rejected is to emphasize what might be called questions of basic human decency. Decency and thoughtfulness are as precious to government employees as they are to anyone else in any walk of life—commercial, industrial, academic, military, religious, and so on. To stress, however, such universal human values as consideration for, and sensitivity to, the needs of others runs the risk of ignoring the distinctive qualities of government employment that must be stressed in meaningful reflections on professional ethics. There is little usefulness in exhorting future bureaucrats to treat their peers, supervisors, and subordinates decently because such an exhortation does not get at the ethical problems peculiar to a career in public administration.

Although one might quarrel with certain self-serving aspects of the codes of ethics developed by the medical and legal professions, there is little doubt that it is the high sense of professional definition among physicians and lawyers that accounts for the relatively clear ethical standards of their professions. They have some understanding of what it is that makes them different from everyone else. Ethical norms of behavior are then deduced from these differences. Government managers might well follow a similar course, and for this reason we should not emphasize the broad human values that we look for in every profession. It is quite possible for a surgeon with impeccable ethical standards in his professional life to be an absolutely irresponsible parent, a compulsive gambler, an incorrigible lecher, and so forth. Unless we are willing to acquiesce in the same possibility for government managers, we shall not make much progress in developing meaningful ethical standards for managers in the career civil service.

Lest the previous two paragraphs seem a bit harsh, it might be helpful to note that humane and thoughtful treatment of one's fellow workers is a salient consideration in a great deal of the literature associated with organizational development (OD) and participative management. The same might be said of the emphasis on "negotiation" in the literature on management by objectives (MBO). Profound ethical issues can surface in areas that are not labeled "ethics." The emphasis on participative management, OD, and MBO in management education today might well be interpreted as a harbinger of humane managerial styles. These developments should certainly be encouraged. Nevertheless, if we are to get on with the task of developing ethical standards (or at least ethical attitudes and values) that are peculiar to government managers, we must in principle reject the emphasis on basic human decency as our starting point. Instead we must try to state as clearly as possible the precise nature of the ethical issue peculiar to career government managers. This we shall do in Chapter 1.

NOTES

1. Some authors use "public" to include more than governmental activities. See Harlan Cleveland, The Future Executive: A Guide for Tomorrow's Managers (New York: Harper & Row, 1972). Although

such "public" managers may find this essay to be of interest, its focus
is nevertheless on governmental employees.

2. For an excellent treatment of the relationship between ethics and the
American regime, see Martin Diamond, "Ethics and Politics: The
American Way" (Paper delivered at the 1976 meeting of the American
Political Science Association). It has appeared in Robert Horowitz,
ed., The Moral Foundations of American Democracy (Charlottesville:
University of Virginia Press, 1977).

3. The results of the survey of the students were reported in the Wall
Street Journal and cited in Susan Wakefield, "Ethics and the Public
Service: A Case for Individual Responsibility," Public Administration
Review 36 (November-December 1976): 663. Wakefield's essay pre-
sents a brief but clear review of the literature on the topic of ethics
and the public service.

4. Thomas Aquinas Summa Theologiae, I-II, q. 57, a. 1-5; and q. 58,
a. 3.

5. Plato Laws, 718, 719; Aristotle Nichomachean Ethics 10.9 (1179B-
1181A); Galatians 3:24-25.

6. Plato Crito, 50A-54B.

7. For classroom purposes, I have found it best to use actual court
opinions and then put questions to the text. Elsewhere I have discussed in essay form the relationship between constitutional law and
substantive regime values. See John A. Rohr, "Privacy: Law and
Values," Thought 49 (December 1974): 353-373; and "Property Rights
and Social Reform," America 133 (July 19, 1975): 27-30.

8. The Federalist Papers, No. 10.

9. Letter to Dr. Walter Jones, March 31, 1801. Cited by Fawn M.
Brodie, Thomas Jefferson: An Intimate History (New York: Bantam,
1974), p. 573.

10. The criminal penalties pertaining to conflict of interest can be
found in 18 USC §§ 201-209. President Johnson's Executive Order
11222 of May 8, 1965 (30 F.R. 6469) specified administrative
penalties for activities not explicitly regulated by statute. The full
text of this executive order appears in 18 USCA § 201. Some minor
changes were added by President Nixon's Executive Order 11590
of April 23, 1971 (36 F.R. 7831). Civil Service regulations on
employee conduct can be found in 5 C.F.R. 735. Although Civil
Service regulations affect all government employees subject to the
commission's jurisdiction, individual agencies, subject to the commission's approval, may promulgate rules of conduct that directly
affect their particular missions. Thus employees of the Securities
and Exchange Commission are forbidden to allow their names "to be
associated in any way with any legal, accounting, or other professional
firm or office" (17 C.F.R. § 200.735-4 [a]). Likewise, employees
of the Federal Reserve System are forbidden from engaging "in

speculative dealings (as distinguished from investments) whether on a
margin or a cash basis, and whether in securities, commodities, real
estate, exchange, or otherwise" (12 C.F.F. 264.735-6 [c] [4] [iii]).

11. Civil Service Commission regulations require every agency head to
"designate a top-ranking employee of his agency who has appropriate
experience, preferably legal, . . . to be the counsellor for the agency
and to serve as the agency's designee to the Commission on matters
concerned by this part [namely, ethics and conduct]" (5 C.F.R.
735.105 [a]). These "ethics counsellors" are to be assisted by deputy
counsellors who must be prepared to give "authoritative advice and
guidance" on ethical questions (5 C.F.R. 735.105 [b]). The agencies
are further mandated to notify their employees of the availability of
these counselling services and "of how and where these services are
available" (5 C.F.R. 735.105 [c]). The counselling system was
severely criticized in Serving Two Masters: A Common Cause Study
of Conflicts of Interest in the Executive Branch (Washington, D.C.:
Common Cause, 1976). Recently the Civil Service Commission has
taken some positive action to vitalize the counselling system. The
General Counsel's Office has appointed David Reich, an attorney with
considerable experience in government and private practice, to serve
as the Commission's "Ethics Counsel." It is Reich's responsibility to
provide information and advice to the ethics counsellors in each
agency. Since his arrival, several conferences of ethics counsellors
have been held in the Washington area and a series of "Ethics in
Action" memoranda have been sent to the ethics counsellors to keep
them apprised of recent developments concerning questions of ethics.

12. Conflict of interest legislation is unusual because of its anticipatory
character. That is, it punishes behavior that might lead to corruption.
The "Caesar's wife" principle is at the heart of conflict of interest
legislation because these laws are concerned with appearances of
impropriety. As one knowledgeable commentator has put it: "The
whole is greater than the sum of the parts: a subjectively innocent
gift combined with a subjectively innocent official performing an innocent act can combine to constitute an offense against conflict of
interest principles." Bayless Manning, Federal Conflict of Interest
Law (Cambridge, Mass.: Harvard University Press, 1964), p. 4.
Manning's study of conflict of interest is a thorough and comprehensive
treatment of the topic. Another excellent analysis is Roswell Perkins,
"The New Federal Conflict of Interest Law," Harvard Law Review 76
(April 1963): 1113-1169. A more recent and quite critical study of
current conflict of interest legislation can be found in the previously
cited Serving Two Masters: A Common Cause Study of Conflicts of
Interest in the Executive Branch. The best study on Congress and
conflict of interest is Robert S. Getz, Congressional Ethics: The
Conflict of Interest Issue (Princeton, N.J.: D. Van Nostrand, 1966).

An analysis of the conflict-of-interest laws in each of the fifty states can be found in Ethics: State Conflict of Interest/Financial Disclosure Legislation, 1972—75 (Lexington, Ky.: Council of State Governments, 1976).

13. This theme appears repeatedly in official statements. For example, see the "Code of Conduct" for government employees adopted by Congress in House Concurrent Resolution 175, 85th Congress, 2nd session, 1958; or President Johnson's Executive Order 11222 (30 F.R. 6469 and 18 USCA § 201). A particularly eloquent statement of this theme can be found in Chief Justice Warren's opinion in U.S. v. Mississippi Valley Generating Company 364 U.S. 520 at 562 (1961).

14. See note 11 above.

15. The accuracy of this statement depends, of course, on how broadly one wishes to interpret the term "Watergate related." I do not consider the shocking disclosures concerning the CIA and FBI to be "Watergate related." Although this point is arguable, there can be no argument over the relatively good record of the career civil service in matters directly related to the break-in at the Watergate Complex and the subsequent cover-up.

16. For example, see Frederick C. Mosher et al., Watergate: Implications for Responsible Government (New York: Basic Books, 1974). For a criticism of this book, see "Watergate in Retrospect: The Forgotten Agenda," Public Administration Review 36 (May-June 1976): 306-310.

17. Edward Weisband and Thomas M. Frank, Resignation in Protest (New York: Grossman, 1975); Ralph Nader, Peter J. Petkas, and Kate Blackwell, eds., Whistle Blowing: The Report of the Conference on Professional Responsibility (New York: Grossman, 1972); Charles Peters and Taylor Branch, eds., Blowing the Whistle: Dissent in the Public Interest (New York: Praeger, 1972).

18. Cited by Stephen K. Bailey, "Second Edition/Ethics and the Politician," The Center Magazine 1 (July 1968): 66.

19. This point is discussed in Weisband and Frank, Resignation in Protest, pp. 158-162.

1

Stating the Problem

*He'll sit here, and he'll say, "Do This! Do
That!" And nothing will happen. Poor Ike -
it won't be a bit like the Army. He'll find it
very frustrating.*

Harry S Truman

The purpose of this chapter is to state as precisely as possible the nature
of the ethical issue peculiar to bureaucrats. The pages that follow will
present the argument that administrative discretion is at the heart of this
issue. Through administrative discretion, bureaucrats participate in the
governing process of our society; but to govern in a democratic society
without being responsible[1] to the electorate raises a serious ethical
question for bureaucrats. Indeed, so to govern defines the ethical issue
peculiar to them.[2]

This argument will be developed in four steps: (1) an examination of
the nineteenth-century debate on civil service reform with particular
emphasis on the argument of the antireformers (the "spoilsmen") that the
proposed merit system was undemocratic; (2) an analysis of Woodrow
Wilson's contribution to the debate with his attempt to answer the spoilsmen by introducing his contemporaries to the distinction between politics
and administration; (3) a review of political science literature and other
sources that have demonstrated the inadequacy of Wilson's distinction and
thereby raised the ghost of the spoilsmen's argument; (4) some concluding remarks.

THE REFORM DEBATE

The Spoils System

Public administration in the United States has not always been based on a
merit system. Every school child has heard of the "spoils system" associated with Jacksonian democracy. Although Andrew Jackson invented
neither the name nor the reality of "spoils," Jacksonian democracy is most
commonly associated with the system, and the system itself is usually
associated with its worst excesses.[3] The spoils system, which was more
commonly referred to by its supporters as "rotation in office," was introduced into the federal government by Jackson as a reform measure.[4] To
be sure, Jackson was not the first president to base his appointments on
partisan grounds. No less a figure than Thomas Jefferson felt justified in
removing from office over one hundred public servants appointed by
Washington and Adams. To justify these partisan removals, Jefferson
appealed to the need to redress the imbalance created by the virtual
monopoly on public office held by Federalists to the detriment of his own
Republican followers.

The difference between Jefferson and Jackson, however, lay in the
explanations they offered for their partisan actions. For Jefferson it was
a necessity created by the excessive partisanship of his predecessor,
John Adams. In principle he accepted Washington's high-toned rule that
"fitness of character" should be the norm for selecting government personnel.[5] What Jefferson justified as a temporary departure from principle
necessitated by unhappy circumstances, Jackson defended as a good in
itself. Appointing one's political supporters to public office would open
public life to the ordinary citizen who had, to a considerable extent, been
excluded from office by the aristocratic norms of personnel selection
employed by Jackson's predecessors. Secondly, partisan removals and
appointments would strengthen the public service by removing superannuated clerks and administrators who, in the absence of a compulsory
retirement age, held on to their positions as long as they could.[6] The dis-
taste of Jackson's predecessors for partisan personnel policies had the
advantage of creating a permanent and relatively stable civil service. This
permanence and stability, however, was purchased at the high price of the
inefficiency inevitably generated by an aging bureaucracy that had staked
out an unofficial but frequently quite effective "claim" to public office.
Further, when death or infirmity created a vacancy, a close relative of the
deceased or infirm public servant would sometimes assume the kinsman's
position.[7] Thus, stability at times degenerated into nepotism. Finally,
there was the argument that democracy requires government to be in the
hands of those selected by the majority of the people, and because parties
were the institutional structure for manifesting the popular will, appointments should be made on a partisan basis.

Armed with these arguments and abetted by his followers' passion for office, Jackson proceeded to remove nearly 1,000 federal employees. His opponents were shocked at this action, but once the Whigs had elected a president of their own in 1840, they outstripped Jackson in their zeal for partisan removal and appointments. Thus, "spoils" became a "system" by receiving the enthusiastic support of both parties. By the eve of the Civil War, the partisan nature of personnel selection had become so pervasive that Jackson's innovation looked quite modest indeed.

The patronage pressures of the spoils system gradually weakened the presidency except during the wartime administrations of James K. Polk and Abraham Lincoln. Although the attempt to remove Andrew Johnson by impeachment failed by one vote, the institution of the presidency was nevertheless profoundly humiliated. The scandal-ridden administration of President Grant, Johnson's successor, accelerated the decline of the office. The administrative problems created by the waning power of the executive branch, combined with an ethical climate that had long acquiesced in making public office a reward for partisan service, made calls for reform inevitable. A modest merit system was begun in 1872 but terminated three years later when Congress refused to appropriate funds for the commission that administered the examinations. By this time, however, the call for reform had ceased to be the cry of isolated voices in the wilderness. Writers, professors, politicians, clergy, newspaper editors, and other community leaders organized a powerful and articulate movement for civil service reform. The assassination of President Garfield by a "disappointed office seeker" in 1881 provided the reformers the impetus they needed to bring their case before a public that was willing to listen. In 1883 Congress passed the Pendleton Act, which started the merit system—albeit on a very limited scale—that has gradually matured into the federal personnel system we have today.

In attempting to replace rotation in office with a merit system, the civil service reform movement supported the need for efficiency in public service, but the major emphasis in its argument was the need for a merit system as a step toward _moral_ reform. George William Curtis, the leading spokesman of the reformers, made it quite clear that "civil service reform is not merely the observance of certain rules of examination. It is the correction of corruption in politics."[8] Rotation in office "perverts public trusts into party spoils, . . . ruins the self-respect of public employees, destroys the function of party in a republic, prostitutes elections into a desperate strife for personal profit, and degrades the national character by lowering the moral tone and standard of the country."[9]

Carl Schurz, who, according to Leonard White, "became a civil service reformer when he stepped off the ship that brought him to America," reinforced Curtis's moralistic arguments. Addressing the United States Senate in 1871, he maintained that the issue of whether government agencies are managed efficiently is "an insignificant question" when it is compared with the more important issue of the "demoralization which the now prevailing mode of distributing office has introduced into the body politic."[10]

There can be no doubt that the reformers were correct in their assessment of the moral tone of public life in the years after the Civil War. The administration of President Grant offered several spectacular examples of corruption in high places. The Credit Mobilier affair was only the most famous of these.[11] It was also during Grant's administration that the House of Representatives impeached Secretary of War William W. Belknap for accepting a bribe for awarding an Indian trading post to a prominent New York contractor. Similar scandals disgraced the office of the Attorney General, the Navy Department, and the Bureau of Internal Revenue.

The case for civil service reform grew stronger with every disclosure of corruption and dishonesty until the reformers finally triumphed with the passage of the Pendleton Act in 1883. The major argument of the reform- ers was that a merit system—even the very modest merit system of the Pendleton Act—would be a vehicle for moral reform. It was difficult to dispute this position because almost any change in the spoils system would have been a vehicle for moral reform.

The Antireform Argument

The defenders of rotation in office did not seriously contest the reformers' shock and outrage at the undeniable evidence of widespread corruption. Instead they based their counterargument on the threat that a merit system presented to the values of a democratic regime. The spoilsmen contended that the abuses of rotation in office should not be corrected by destroying the rotation system. Their argument followed the "baby/bath water" analogy that is so common in contemporary political discourse. It is a classic conservative stance—one must remove the abuses of the existing system without destroying the system itself. The argument in itself, of course, is neither weak nor forceful; its merit depends on circumstances and the nature of the system in question. The spoilsmen maintained that rotation in office was the only personnel system compatible with demo- cratic institutions. To support this argument Andrew Jackson's first annual message to Congress was "the law and the prophets."

In this famous address Jackson articulated the underlying rationale of his personnel system. He felt that only by rotating public office in accord- ance with electoral results could we safeguard against the danger of public servants acquiring "a habit of looking with indifference upon the public interests and of tolerating conduct from which an unpracticed man would revolt."[12] Contrary to present personnel principles, Jackson was not impressed by the need for long-term stability in government careers.

Indeed, he confessed, "I cannot but believe that more is lost by the long continuance of men in office than is generally to be gained by their experience." [13] His skepticism toward the value of experience and continuity in employment was justified by his belief that "the duties of all public officers are, or at least admit of being made, so plain and simple that men of intelligence may readily qualify themselves for their performance."[14]

Jackson's view of the simplicity of government work may seem strange today with the massive presence of government in the areas of space, health, environment, and energy; but in his day it was quite plausible. Most government work then was more often clerical than technical. By the time of the civil service debate of the 1870s, the nature of government work had begun to change. The beginning of the shift from an agrarian to an industrialized society was underway. These nascent changes in the role of government, however, were largely ignored by those opposing the reformers' proposal for a merit system based on entrance examinations. The spoilsmen launched their counterattack from the high ground of Jacksonian orthodoxy.

Thus Representative John A. Logan of Illinois opposed an early effort at removing partisan considerations from federal appointments by arguing that the principles of republican government demanded that the people maintain their superiority "by having their agents constantly before them that their acts may be denounced or confirmed." [15] Referring to the political appointments that would be affected by the proposed bill, Logan maintained that "a share in those appointments and the right to become for a time a portion of the administrative force of the Government is one of the recognized rights of the people of which it is proposed by this bill, utterly and forever, to deprive them."[16]

In 1882, just one year before the adoption of the Pendleton Act, William Martin Dickson, writing in the North American Review, reaffirmed the Jacksonian faith in arguing against the proposed reform:

> With a reasonable rotation every citizen of political aspirations and experience who reaches middle life and conducts himself well may hope to crown his family with the reflected honor which office confers. This prospect is a motive to good work. This is the peerage which the republic offers, not to a particular class, but to every one who serves her. [17]

The examinations that would be a necessary part of the proposed merit system were a particular source of irritation to the spoilsmen. They attacked them on two grounds: (1) examinations are elitist because they will inevitably create a caste system in government; and (2) they are useless because academic skills are unrelated to job skills. On the second point Senator Carpenter observed in a Senate debate:

So, sir, it comes to this at last, that . . . the dunce who has been
crammed up to a diploma at Yale, and comes fresh from his cramming,
will be preferred in all civil appointments to the ablest, most successful, and most upright business man of the country, who either did not
enjoy the benefit of early education, or from whose mind, long
engrossed in practical pursuits, the details and niceties of academic
knowledge have faded away as the headlands disappear when the
mariner bids his native land good night. [18]

In the House of Representatives James B. Beck of Kentucky orches-
trated the same theme:

Take, for instance, the men who are engaged in the life-saving stations along our coast. They are men who have been trained for years
in that service until they have attained the utmost efficiency; they can
man the boats, brave the storms, and save the lives of human beings
in the midst of tempests. If these men are required to go before the
civil-service commission to come into competition with schoolmasters
who may not have the courage to go within a hundred feet of a wave nor
the slightest qualification for that special service, yet because he
knows something about geography and something about spelling the
schoolmaster will get the place. [19]

The argument that the public service would be transformed into a caste
system was articulated in John Logan's attack on an early reform bill proposed in 1869. He felt the examination requirement would inevitably lead
to the creation of two national schools for public service—one for military
officers and one for civilian officials. The major concern of graduates of
these schools, Logan maintained, would be to be sure their children were
enrolled in them as well and thereby confirm the worst Jacksonian fears of
"office as a species of property." [20]

The civil service reform movement was successful in rebutting the
spoilsmen's position on the danger of competitive examinations. The
reformers never tired of insisting that a common school education would be
quite sufficient for a successful performance in the proposed examinations.
They were as good as their word.

The annual report of the Civil Service Commission for 1885-1886
reported that of 7138 participants in the general examination, 6053 had no
more than the ordinary public school education, 327 were from business
schools, while only 758 had been to college. [21]

While the antiexamination argument of the spoilsmen was easily
refuted, their attack on the principle of merit selection proved more
troublesome. This argument, as we have seen, rested on the assumption
that in a democratic society appointed officeholders should be subject to

elected officials who, in turn, are subject to the people. This position was uncomplicated and appealing in its simplicity. The reformers, of course, pointed to the blatant corruption involved in making public office a matter of patronage. To be sure, they were correct, but this argument failed to meet the principled argument of the spoilsmen. Indeed, the reformers' position might prove too much. If they argued that such corruption was inherent in rotation in office without challenging their opponents' position that democratic principles demand such rotation, they were in danger of implying that democracy was inherently corrupt! This simply would not do. Such a position would never win any support in the public forum. Nevertheless, the corruption involved in the spoils system was so exten-sive that it was hard to avoid the conclusion that it was inherent. If this were the case, the reformers would have to meet the principled argument of the spoilsmen directly. They would have to attack the firmly entrenched doctrine that rotation in office is more democratic in principle than merit selection. This would be no easy task for there was something undeniably persuasive in the spoilsmen's position. How can the people maintain their supremacy if their elected representatives cannot control the government's personnel system?[22] Does not the merit system actually provide two gov-ernments—one elected by the people and responsive to popular sentiment and the other appointed under a merit system and entrenched in power regardless of the electorate? It would not suffice to argue that the corrup-tion of the spoils system would undermine democratic institutions if the proposed reform were vulnerable to the charge of being in itself undemocratic.

Although the reformers won a great victory in passing the Pendleton Act in 1883, their victory was by no means secure. As mentioned above, an earlier Civil Service Commission, established by President Grant in 1872, passed out of existence three years later when Congress failed to appropriate funds for its continuation. The question about the democratic character of the merit system was an embarrassment the reformers could ill afford in their continuing efforts to muster popular support for the fledgling Civil Service Commission. Public support was crucial if the reform was to succeed because prosecutions for violations of the Pendleton Act were within the discretionary power of the U.S. district attorneys. These men were themselves frequently beholden to the spoils system and often approached enforcement of the Pendleton Act with something less than enthusiasm. At times the best the Civil Service Commission could do was to investigate and expose violations in the hope that public opinion would force the Justice Department to prosecute. If the misgivings about the democratic propriety of civil service reform could be removed, the reformers' cause would be substantially strengthened and their victory of 1883 rendered more secure.

POLITICS AND ADMINISTRATION

Fortunately for the reformers, an essay by Woodrow Wilson, then a
reform-minded professor of political science, provided the basis for a
defense of the compatibility between civil service reform and democratic
government. The article, which appeared in the Political Science
Quarterly in 1887, was originally delivered as a lecture on "The Study of
Administration" at Cornell University in the previous year.[23] The major
significance of Wilson's essay was the distinction he drew between politics
and administration. Although Wilson's position on the precise nature of
this distinction is not always clear,[24] there is no doubt that the effect of
his work was to popularize the distinction—and eventually the dichotomy—
between politics and administration and thereby provide the reformers with
a response to the spoilsmen's challenge to the merit system as being
undemocratic. It would permit reformers to argue that such a system was
indeed suitable for democratic government. The strength of the response
lay in separating politics and administration and contending that democracy
as a political system pertained to politics but not to administration. The
latter was a "science" with principles that could be taught and applied in
any regime—democratic or otherwise. Hence, the merit system, in
removing the nonelected public servant from politics, was not antidemo-
cratic. It was simply an institutionalized way of acknowledging the true
nature of administration as a science, a profession, a politically neutral
technique. To appoint administrators on political grounds is no exigency
of democracy; it is simply a failure to recognize the true character of
administration.
     Wilson's essay merits our attention in some detail because of its con-
siderable influence on subsequent administrative theory. Because of this
influence, it is more important for us to analyze what Wilson was perceived as saying rather than what he actually meant. The latter is a
matter of considerable dispute among students of administrative history.
At times he seems to take back with one hand what he has just given with
the other. One recent commentator found such hedging "exasperating for
any careful reader."[25] Perhaps the readers of Wilson's day were less
careful than contemporary critics, or, more likely, they saw the practical
value of the major thrust (however well qualified) of his argument—the
distinction between politics and administration. This distinction gained
wide acceptance among political scientists[26] and harmonized nicely with
the scientific management movement that dominated private industry in the
early decades of the twentieth century. Thus, industrial management and
public administration coalesced to form a "science" of administration—a
"businesslike" approach to government based on "principles" common to
any type of organization and designed to promote "economy and efficiency"
in executing policies determined by the administrator's political (that is,

elected) superiors. Max Weber's model of the "ideal type" bureaucracy vigorously reinforced this tendency in such a way that by the late 1930s and 1940s the Wilsonian distinction between politics and administration had matured into a rigid dichotomy that was high doctrine throughout govern- ment circles. Despite incessant criticism of the dichotomy by political scientists for the past thirty years, it remains the dominant ideology of the government's personnel system to this day.[27]

Tracing the causal connections between ideas and social movements is a hazardous enterprise. Wilson's essay alone did not cause the dichotomy between politics and administration to become the bureaucratic orthodoxy of the twentieth century, but it was undeniably significant among the causes of this development. What is curious is why an academic essay by an obscure professor in the 1880s could have had such a tremendous influence on public life, whereas innumerable academic treatises in the past thirty years, which persuasively challenged Wilson's position, have had only marginal success in dislodging the Wilsonian orthodoxy. The most plausi- ble explanation for this phenomenon is that Wilson's essay had the immedi- ate practical effect of answering the troublesome argument of the spoilsmen that a merit system was not democratic. Let us look more closely at how Wilson distinguished politics and administration and thereby provided a theoretical justification for the merit system.[28]

In developing his argument Wilson makes four major points about the nature of administration: (1) it is a science; (2) it is businesslike; (3) it is independent of cultural variables; and (4) it is responsible to elected officials.

The scientific character of administration is asserted in the opening paragraph of the essay. Administration is a "practical" science with a body of principles that can be taught the way other sciences are taught. Once the American people understand this, we can look forward to the establishment of schools that will impart the principles and technical skills demanded of the well-trained administrator. Once such schools have been established, the public will recognize that administration involves profes- sional expertise and will be less likely to become "meddlesome" when administrators are applying the skills they have learned in their formal training. The cardinal principle required to initiate the scientific study of administration is to establish its independence from politics. As long as this distinction is maintained in fact and in principle, Wilson maintains, we can pursue the scientific techniques and principles of administration with- out threatening the supremacy of the people in political questions.

Administration is also "a field of business." As such, it is free from the "hurry and strife of politics." The purpose of the study of administra- tion "is to rescue executive methods from the confusion and costliness of empirical experiment and set them upon foundations laid deep in stable principle." Once civil service reform has succeeded in "clearing the

moral atmosphere of official life," government will be managed on a businesslike basis, and this will eliminate the wastefulness associated with
rotation in office.[29]

The science of administration is independent of cultural variables. A
democratic people need not be alarmed at the prospect of importing an
administrative system created and perfected in autocratic regimes. We
can enjoy Prussia's administrative skill without enduring Prussia's history. Precisely because administration is a science we have no more to
fear from its foreign origins than we do from using any other form of
scientific knowledge regardless of whence it comes.[30]

Finally, although administration involves the use of power, it is
power that will be exercised in a responsible way—that is, the administrative technician will take his or her orders from, and will be accountable to,
political superiors. Wilson's model of public management is clearly
hierarchical. The science of administration deplores divided authority
because it always obscures and occasionally obliterates the lines of
responsibility. As long as power is centralized "in the heads of the
service," there will be no problem. These superiors will be immediately
responsible to elected officials and therefore, ultimately, to the people.
If these lines of power and responsibility are observed, as the science of
administration requires, there will be no threat to democratic government. "Self-government does not consist in having a hand in everything,
any more than housekeeping consists necessarily in cooking dinner with
one's own hands."[31]

Wilson also responded to defenders of the spoils system who feared
that civil service reform would encourage the growth of an irresponsible
ruling class:

> [T]o fear the creation of a domineering, illiberal officialism as a
> result of the studies I am here proposing is to miss altogether the
> principle upon which I wish most to insist. That principle is, that
> administration in the United States must be at all points sensitive to
> public opinion. A body of thoroughly trained officials serving during
> good behavior we must have in any case; that is a plain business
> necessity. But the apprehension that such a body will be anything
> un-American clears away the moment it is asked, What is to consti-
> tute good behavior? For that question obviously carries its own
> answer on its face. Steady, hearty allegiance to the policy of the
> government they serve will constitute good behavior. That policy will
> have no taint of officialism about it. It will not be the creation of
> permanent officials, but of statesmen whose responsibility to public
> opinion will be direct and inevitable. Bureaucracy can exist only
> where the whole service of the state is removed from the common
> political life of the people, its chiefs as well as its rank and file. Its
> motives, its objects, its policy, its standards, must be bureaucratic.

It would be difficult to point out any examples of impudent exclusive-
ness and arbitrariness on the part of officials doing service under a
chief of department who really served the people, as all our chiefs
of departments must be made to do.[32]

In other words, the democrat's fear that a permanent civil service will
become a "domineering, illiberal officialism" is illusory because policy
will remain in the hands of politically responsible officials. Indeed, how
could it be otherwise as long as there is a dichotomy between politics and
administration? This dichotomy was the primary conceptual tool employed
by Wilson in his efforts to promote the scientific study of administration
and it is because of this dichotomy that Wilson's essay became a landmark
in the field of public administration.

Despite Wilson's commitment to the dichotomy between politics and
administration, however, there are some ambiguities in his essay that are
of considerable interest. The most obvious of these is the way he hedges
the independence of administration from cultural variables. He acknowledges that before we import a foreign administrative system, "we must
Americanize it . . . in thought, principle, and aim. . . . It must learn
our constitutions by heart; must get the bureaucratic fever out of its veins;
must inhale much free American air."[33] Elsewhere in speaking of the
imported science of administration, he says we must "filter it through our
constitutions," "put it over a slow fire of criticism and distill away its
foreign gases."[34] The thrust of these images calls into question the precise and clear distinction between political and administrative systems that
is salient in Wilson's essay.

Further, despite the distinction between politics and administration,
Wilson would safeguard the civil service from "arbitrariness and class
spirit" in two ways: "by means of elections and constant public counsel."
It is no surprise that Wilson would rely upon elections to keep bureaucrats
in line. This is simply a corrollary of the dichotomy. Administrators
take their cues from their politically responsible superiors who are either
themselves elected or appointed by an elected official. Wilson's reference
to "constant public counsel" is more interesting. The purpose of taking
this counsel is to keep the bureaucrat from losing touch with popular sentiment. But what if a bureaucrat finds that popular sentiment is at odds with
what his or her politically responsible superior wants accomplished? If
the bureaucrat simply does his or her superior's bidding, there was little
point in consulting the public. If he or she devises stratagems to circum-
vent the will of the superior in order to accommodate popular sentiment,
has the bureaucrat not become an agent in the political process and thereby
overstepped the line dividing politics and administration?

In mentioning these ambiguities in Wilson's essay, one might say that
they are simply an indication of the richness and complexity of his thought.
Less charitably, one might conclude that Wilson's thinking was confused

and muddled. Fortunately, the need to make any such judgment is beyond
the scope of this book. More important for our purposes is to recall that
the ambiguities in Wilson's essay were frequently overlooked. His essay
was interpreted as a defense of the dichotomy between politics and
administration—which undoubtedly it was. The ambiguities (or contra-
dictions?) were ignored. They would do little for the cause of civil service
reform. If the dichotomy between politics and administration could replace
rotation in office as political orthodoxy, the reformers would have a solid
response to the spoilsmen. They could no longer argue that a merit system was undemocratic simply because government jobs remain in the same
hands regardless of how the electorate votes. The dichotomy renders this
objection irrelevant. Government jobs are administrative not political.
The science of administration can serve any party the people choose to
elect. The civil service is politically neutral and stands ready to do the
bidding of whatever political master the sovereign people should choose.

THE DEMISE OF THE DICHOTOMY

The purpose of this section is to demonstrate the inadequacy of the dichotomy between politics and administration. It is with some embarrassment
that I announce this theme because those familiar with public administration literature will recognize that at this late date the task of attacking the
Wilsonian dichotomy is best left to the masters of the obvious. Indeed, so
obvious is the inadequacy of the dichotomy that one recent author was
willing to quip that the political nature of administration is "a proposition
now certainly established in the theology"[35] of public administration.
From the years immediately following World War II, the Wilsonian dichotomy has been attacked so incessantly and so effectively that I do not believe
it is an exaggeration to say that no serious student of public administration
accepts it today.[36]
     Despite the long-standing, academic rejection of the dichotomy
between politics and administration, there are three reasons why it is
necessary to review this familiar question in this essay.
     The first is that the political character of public administration is an
absolutely crucial step in our argument that aims at defining the precise
nature of the ethical problem peculiar to bureaucrats.
     Secondly, despite the persuasive case academics have made to estab-
lish the political character of administration, the old Wilsonian world view
still appears to be the prevailing ideology among practicing bureaucrats.
In the hope that this book might find its way into the hands of practitioners
untutored in the ways of academic public administration, it may be best to
present some old arguments that just might be new to such readers.
     Thirdly, among academics themselves there has been a surprising

reluctance to address the serious normative questions that arise from their own insights that have so impressively demonstrated the political character of public administration.[37] There are a variety of possible explanations for this reluctance. Perhaps the most plausible is that most of the research that demonstrated the political character of administration was carried on at a time when value-free social science was the order of the day and scholars were somewhat uneasy about addressing normative issues. Also, there was the sheer novelty of what they were saying—to discover the political character of administration must have been rather heady wine for a generation of scholars trained in the legacy of the reform tradition. As Herbert Storing has put it, they "discovered that the world is not so reasonable or so simple as they were taught in the 'reform' school; and, like small boys in similar circumstances, they [found] a good deal of naughty pleasure in telling everyone about it."[38] Even when academics did address the normative issues consequent upon the demise of the dichotomy between politics and administration, they did so in terms of institutional reform rather than personal ethics.[39] This, of course, was quite understandable because institutional analysis is what one would expect from political scientists and organizational theorists. Because, however, there are limits to the effectiveness of any institutional reform, there remain substantial problems flowing from the political character of administration that can be handled only in terms of personal ethics. This question has received little attention in the literature.[40]

The demonstration of the inadequacy of the Wilsonian dichotomy will be presented in three steps: (1) defining terms; (2) a review of the literature; and (3) an analysis of some administrative situations.

Defining Terms

The first point in establishing the political character of public administration is to explain what is meant by "politics." For the purpose of this argument any one of several definitions will suffice—for example, David Easton's "authoritative allocation of values" or Harold D. Lasswell's "who gets what, when, how."[41]

Ordinarily, the way one defines politics is very important. Thus Easton's definition is consistent with his "systems" approach to the study of politics. Likewise, Lasswell's definition is suitable for his behavioralist methodology. I prefer to define politics as the process by which a civil society achieves its common good through the agency of the state.[42] Although this definition is more congruent with the normative questions raised in this book, all three definitions (and many others as well) are suitable for the discussion of the relation of politics to administration. In other words, the illustrations offered to support the argument that bureau-

crats are necessarily involved in politics cuts across methodological disputes in the field of political science.[43] These illustrations will show that
bureaucrats authoritatively determine the allocation of values, that they
frequently decide who gets what, and that they pursue the common good of
our society through the agency of the state. A definition that restricts
politics to the electoral process, however, would be unacceptable. Perhaps no one has ever offered such a definition explicitly, but it is implicit
in Wilson's argument, in much of the rhetoric and tradition of the Civil
Service Commission, and, unfortunately, in a great deal of our contemporary political discourse. Indeed, it was this implicit identification of
politics with elections that supported the principle underlying the Hatch
Acts—by restricting the electoral activities of government workers,
Congress can keep them out of politics. To be sure, elections are a very
important part of politics, but they do not exhaust the political process.
To argue that they do would imply that only regimes with elected officials
are truly political. Further, it would suggest that when values are allo-
cated authoritatively, or when the common good is pursued by the state
outside the electoral process, the activity in question is simply not political. This would be a very improverished concept of politics.[44]

Impoverished or not, the word "politics" is so often used exclusively
in its partisan-electoral sense that in this book the term "administrative
discretion" will appear frequently as a synonym for the political activity of
bureaucrats. This avoids the Hatch Acts' overtones of "politics" without
compromising the notion that bureaucrats authoritatively allocate values.
Unfortunately, "administrative discretion" has its own semantic problems—
especially for those trained in administrative law where the term often
refers to the formal decision maker rather than to the entire process by
which a discretionary decision is made. It is this process that concerns
us because it involves the managerial and executive personnel who provide
the focus of this essay. Decisions issued in the name of the secretary of
commerce or the Federal Communications Commission are profoundly
influenced by many "men without faces" who shape the issue that is finally
presented for a formal decision. The process by which the issue is shaped
provides innumerable opportunities to exercise "administrative discretion," though few examples are ever made public or even clearly identified
by the participants in the process itself. Thus by "administrative discretion" I mean the discretionary activity of bureaucrats in which they advise,
report, respond, initiate, inform, question, caution, complain, applaud,
encourage, rebuke, promote, retard, and mediate in a way that has an
impact upon what eventually emerges as "agency policy." All these activities can be highly discretionary even though they might not be recognized
as "administrative discretion" in a treatise on administrative law.

The Literature

A favorite theme of political scientists is the government agency that has
been "captured" by private interests. These analyses are quite helpful in
demonstrating how some agencies—usually of a regulatory character—are
inextricably involved in the political process. For example, a careful
study of the Grazing Service (now part of the Bureau of Land Management)
has shown how its formal structure and personnel selections were designed
to favor the interests of the stockmen who used public land for grazing.[45]
The Federal Extension Service in USDA has been the object of similar
analyses that provide evidence of an agency remarkably responsive to the
interests of the American Farm Bureau Federation.[46] The same can be
said of the manner in which the Interstate Commerce Commission has been
found supporting the railroad industry[47] or of the close, historic ties
between the Army Corps of Engineers and the Rivers and Harbors
Congress.[48]

   Examples of specific political decisions made by mid-level career
bureaucrats can be found in the Inter-University Case Program, a series
of richly detailed studies published over the past quarter century. One
study shows how the State Department relied upon foreign service officers
in Indonesia to determine American policy toward the Dutch colonial
regime and the emerging Indonesian nationalists at the end of World War
II.[49] Another shows the important role of certain naval officers in supporting a powerful senator's efforts to get President Truman to establish
military bases in Spain.[50] A third study explores the process by which a
career bureaucrat during World War II made the difficult decision to
recommend that the Office of Price Administration (OPA) cancel unused
ration stamps despite a public announcement by the OPA that it would never
do this.[51] A fourth study documents the bizarre tale of how officials in the
Agriculture Department decided to burn a publication of the Agricultural
Marketing Service that might have proven embarrassing to Secretary
Ezra Taft Benson.[52]

   The field of administrative law provides further examples of how the
discretionary authority of bureaucrats has a substantial impact on Amercan
life. In his widely read essay, Discretionary Justice, Kenneth C. Davis
lists twelve instances of discretionary judgments made within the administrative process. The first nine of these examples pertain to decisions
made by career bureaucrats. They support directly the argument that the
bureaucracy authoritatively allocates values through its discretionary
power. The last three examples refer to decisions made at least nominally
by political appointees. Hence, they are less directly related to our purposes, but even in these examples it does not take a great deal of imagina-

tion to conjecture on how bureaucratic subordinates of these political appointees might prudently use their discretion to suggest ways of improving the decision-making processes of their agencies. The following are Davis's examples:

1. Through plea bargaining a prosecutor agrees with one defendant to reduce a felony charge to a misdemeanor but refuses to do so with another defendant.
2. The manager of a public housing project, following the customary system, evicts a mother and four children on the ground of "undesirability" without giving any more specific reason.
3. To prevent a riot, city police round up ninety Negro youths and keep them in jail for a month through impossibly high bail and delayed proceedings.
4. A traffic policeman warns a violator instead of writing a ticket, because the violator is a lawyer and the police of the city (Chicago) have a long-standing custom of favoring lawyers.
5. A government procurement officer in negotiating for an item whose cost of production is likely to drop drastically because of rapid technological developments suggests to a corporate executive that he is more likely to win the contract if he reduces his own salary to a specified figure for the duration of the contract.
6. A social worker, who is without training in social work and has serious psychiatric problems of her own, refrains from reporting evidence that a mother who is receiving aid for her dependent children has a man in the house; then the social worker, over the mother's bitter opposition, prescribes policies for controlling the children, using as an effective sanction the threat of discontinuing aid payments because of the man in the house.
7. The intake officer who is helping administer the program of aid to families of dependent children rejects a woman's application on the ground that the woman cannot find her absent husband. The applicable regulation provides that the applicant must "aid" in finding an absent spouse but it does not require that the applicant "find" the spouse.
8. Two students study together in the same department of the same university. The facts about each that are relevant to the draft are identical. One is drafted because his draft board follows one rule. The other is given a student deferment because his draft board, a different one, follows another rule. No administrative, judicial, or legislative authority requires the two boards to decide the same question the same way.
9. The Assistant Attorney General in charge of the Antitrust Division

institutes a prosecution against a corporation. His successor, disagreeing with his prosecution policy, dismisses the prosecution, without stating facts, without stating reasons, without publicly relating the case to policies developed in other similar cases, and without any public statement of the basic policies involved.

10. A student in India wins a scholarship in an American university, studies chemistry, leads his class, receives an offer of an excellent position in a large American corporation, but is ineligible to have his student visa changed to allow him to remain legally in the United States. Responding to the pressures of the corporation, the Immigration Service nevertheless agrees informally not to prosecute. The Indian excels and is rapidly promoted. Then he receives a message that his mother is dying in India. An executive of his corporation asks the Immigration Service to approve his visiting India for two weeks. A top officer of the Service says no. The Indian must choose between keeping his position and visiting his dying mother.

11. The Federal Trade Commission grants a merger clearance to two corporations, without public announcement, without a systematic statement of the facts, without a reasoned opinion, without a comparison of the case to relevant precedents, without supervision or check by any other authority, without the knowledge or participation of the commission's staff, and without opening any of the related papers to public inspection.

12. The United States Parole Board, without stating reasons, denies parole to a prisoner who has waited five years for eligibility. The Administrative Procedure Act requires a statement of reasons, but the board, in a 1964 printed pamphlet entitled "Functions of the United States Parole Board," explains that "the board does not sit as a group" to decide cases, that each member votes separately, and that "it is therefore impossible to state precisely why a particular prisoner was or was not granted parole."[53]

To conclude this brief review of the literature, let us turn to Theodore Lowi's remarkably perceptive account of the historical development of the power of administrators over the past ninety years.[54] In The End of Liberalism, Lowi provides considerable insight into the evolution of the political role of the bureaucrat. The process began with the difficulties that faced Congress in attempting to regulate a modern industrial economy with detailed statutes. The legislative process was too cumbersome for this. An irresistible tendency developed for Congress simply to point out

a problem area and to give administrators discretionary authority to
develop substantive public policies. At first, the discretion of the administrators was carefully circumscribed by law. Thus, the Interstate Commerce Commission, created in 1887, was to regulate maximum rates for
railroads. Railroads and maximum rates are concrete and specific areas
of jurisdiction. So are the trusts that were to be regulated by the Sherman
Act of 1890. Less concrete and specific, however, was the task given to
administrators under the Food and Drug Act of 1906. Under this act,
bureaucrats were directed to regulate substandard food and impure drugs.
Such value-laden concepts broadened the discretion of the administrators
and shifted the political thrust of the lobbyists from congressional committees to administrative agencies. The creation of the Federal Trade
Commission in 1914 was a further step in the same direction. The commission was to stop "unfair" competition. "Unfair" is as difficult a
word to define as "impure" or "substandard," but, prior to the creation of
the FTC, bureaucrats were concerned with regulating concrete things —
drugs, food, and railroads. The FTC was given jurisdiction over an
abstraction—"competition." This considerably increased administrative
discretion because administrators, not Congress, would have to decide the
meaning of "competition" as well as "unfair." Lowi maintains that the
"move from concreteness to abstractness in the definition of public policy
was probably the most important single change in the entire history of
public control in the United States." [55]
       Bureaucratic discretion continued to grow when Congress created the
Securities and Exchange Commission and charged it with the vague
responsibility of maintaining a "fair and orderly market." This meant
that the bureaucracy would regulate not only behavior within the market
but access to the market as well. The power to determine what securities
are marketable authorized administrators to determine who the players
would be, as well as the rules by which they would play. The power
enjoyed by the Federal Communications Commission to grant radio and
television licenses as "the public interest, convenience or necessity"
dictates is another example of almost unfettered bureaucratic discretion to
control access to a competitive market. The same could be said of
administrators' licensing power in such diverse areas as the airlines,
satellite communication, and atomic energy.
       Perhaps the clearest example of the growth of administrative discre-
tion (and therefore power) comes from contrasting what Lowi has called
the "Old Welfare" (Social Security Act of 1935) with the "New Welfare"
(Economic Opportunity Act of 1964). [56] The Social Security Act of 1935 is
best known for its contributory system of old-age insurance, but it also
provided a noncontributory aid program for the aged, the blind, and
dependent children. The statute defined the categories with some precision and specified the minimum grants to be given to persons falling
within the categories. Thus, the Old Welfare limited the discretion of

bureaucrats responsible for the administration of the act. The New Welfare attacked poverty through community action programs rather than by simply giving money to needy people in clearly defined categories. The massive political question, of course, was to determine which community action programs were to be the recipients of federal largess. This decision was made by bureaucrats.

Sargent Shriver, who served as the first director of the Office of Economic Opportunity, gave extremely broad discretion to his bureaucratic subordinates in deciding which programs would be funded. He maintained there was only one basic criterion—the community action program had to be "broadly representative of the interests of the community." The funded programs could be public or private, as long as they enjoyed the support of "the relevant elements of community government." Instead of specifying the kind of behavior required of programs seeking federal funding, Shriver's directive merely stated that "it is likely" that funded agencies would include activities "such as the following." He then went on to enumerate some fifteen activities that one might be "likely" to find in funded community action programs. By using the device of a "such as" clause followed by a nonexclusive list of acceptable activities, Shriver conferred tremendous discretionary power upon the field representatives (that is, bureaucrats) of OEO in determining what community organizations would be funded. This, of course, is the very stuff of politics and illustrates dramatically just how far the government is willing to go in thrusting bureaucrats into the political process by conferring unfettered discretion upon them.[57]

Administrative Situations

The cursory review of the literature in the previous section dealt, for the most part, either with abuses of administrative discretion or with an excessive willingness on the part of agencies to further the goals of special interests. To a considerable extent, political scientists have been interested in examining administrative behavior in the light of some general problem calling for corrective measures. Hence, it is not surprising to find that they emphasize organizational pathologies. For our purposes, however, the abuses and excesses of administrative discretion are less important than its mere existence. For it is through discretion—regardless of how it is exercised—that bureaucrats govern; this is the central point in our rejection of the dichotomy between politics and administration.

This section is intended to balance any excessive emphasis in the literature upon abuses of discretion. It merely provides a series of brief descriptions of significant but basically routine problems in public management that require some degree of discretionary judgment by career managers and those who report to them. Consider the following situations:

1. A civil engineer whose division of the Department of Housing and Urban Development must decide what Congress meant by "maximum practical improvements" when it provided in the Energy Conservation Act of 1976 that HUD was to draw up "performance standards for new residential and commercial buildings which are designed to achieve the maximum practical improvements in energy efficiency and increases in the uses of nondepletable sources of energy": Since the standards recommended by the engineer and his staff will probably be incorporated into building codes throughout the country, their work is the object of intense interest on the part of the housing industry. The New York Times went so far as to state that the decisions this engineer's division makes "may ultimately be more crucial to most people than whether the Senate approves the Panama Canal Treaties or the President dismisses a Federal prosecutor [in Philadelphia]."[58]

2. A statistician with the Bureau of Labor Statistics who believes that the present components of the Consumer Price Index—the statistical aggregates that define the "market basket" and the "typical consumer"—are no longer adequate measures of cost of living: The statistician thinks the components should be changed but knows that organized labor will vigorously resist any moves in this direction.

3. The director of a staff of 11 legal paraprofessionals with G.S. grades ranging from 5 through 9 in the Voting Section of the Civil Rights Division of the Justice Department: It is the director's responsibility to review decisions of these paraprofessionals on whether the Department of Justice should object to proposed changes in voting procedures submitted for approval by those states (mostly southern) required under the Voting Rights Act of 1965 to obtain "preclearance" before any changes in voting laws or regulations can go into effect. The paraprofessionals initiate the decision-making process which determines whether a proposed change has a "discriminatory purpose and effect" and thereby violates the Voting Rights Act.[59]

4. An Internal Revenue Service (IRS) collector who reads in the newspaper the following description of himself and his peers in a report prepared by the Administrative Conference of the U.S.:

   Nearly all IRS officers agreed that a taxpayer's behavior was an important element in determining what collection action would be taken. . . . Thus, a courteous, pleasant taxpayer would more likely receive favorable treatment than one in a similar situation who is discourteous, hostile or generally unpleasant. . . . Without any guidelines to steer employee conduct, it is likely to be whimsical, inconsistent, unpredictable and highly personal. . . . The result is a large body of discretionary authority given to the

IRS to collect taxes forcibly. . . . Inevitably, such discretionary power is not uniformly exercised and is open to administrative abuse. . . . As a result, the exercise of the formidable collection powers at times poses troublesome conflicts between the right of government to exact taxes and the property rights of the individual citizens.[59]

5. An officer in the Department of Housing and Urban Development responsible for investigating and making recommendations on a developer's application for subsidized housing. Department policy is to disperse subsidized housing throughout metropolitan areas and to prevent concentration of minorities in urban ghettoes. The officer is to apply the following guideline in making recommendations on specific proposals:

    It is HUD policy to provide minority families with opportunities for housing in a wide range of locations; to open up non-segregated housing opportunities that will contribute to decreasing the effects of past housing discrimination.[61]

6. A Department of Transportation attorney participating in a 1974 task force charged with recommending possible changes in regulations requiring the governor's approval before a federally financed highway can be built within any state: The recommendation of the task force would affect a bitter dispute between the late Mayor Daley of Chicago who wanted a "Crosstown" Expressway and former Governor Walker of Illinois who opposed it.[62]

7. A HUD officer in the Philadelphia regional office in 1972 whose advice the regional director had sought in the following situation: The Multicon Construction Corporation had entered into a contract with the city of Philadelphia to build low-income housing that would be financed in part by HUD. When white citizens residing near the proposed site of the project learned that many of their new neighbors would be black, a series of heated protests ensued. During the mayoral campaign of 1971, candidate Frank L. Rizzo took a strong stand against continuing the project, and once he was elected, Multicon found it could get no cooperation from the city in its efforts to proceed with the terms of the contract. On the basis of this background the New York Times provided the following brief narrative:

    Lawyers for Multicon went to Washington in May, 1972, to plead for some form of assistance from the Housing Agency, including the possibility that the Agency administer the project. But David Maxwell, then General Counsel of the Department, told them that a take over was against its policy and while the Department was sympathetic it would do nothing to help.

Later in the summer the redevelopment authority of Philadelphia tried to cancel the contract with Multicon. The HUD area
office objected. [63]

The reason "the HUD area office objected" was because
somebody in that office had the courage to take on Mayor Rizzo
even though there was little hope of solid support from
Washington.

8. A caseworker who must make the initial decision in the following
   situation and who knows that her supervisor upholds caseworkers
   in over 95 percent of the decisions that are appealed: A divorcee
   living alone with two children applies for public aid even though
   her income is too high to meet the welfare standards. Her
   available resources, however, are actually below the eligibility
   maximum because she must pay a babysitter to look after her
   children while she attends classes at a nursing college. In the
   absence of rules covering this situation, the caseworker must
   decide whether this is a "legitimate expense" or a "luxury." [64]

9. A personnel specialist attached to the staff of a regional personnel
   office of the Labor Department who is asked to assist the regional
   office in drawing up a "name request" for the brother of a local
   congressman who has applied for a GS-11 position as a work training program specialist: Unfortunately, the congressman's brother
   has no experience in work training. Indeed, his only gainful employment has been as a jeweler. The personnel specialist is asked
   if there is some way the job description can be rewritten to integrate the need for a background as a jeweler into the requirements for a job training specialist. [65]

10. A procurement officer for an R&D agency who is aware of regu-
    lations that assure special considerations for "unsolicited
    proposals"—that is, proposals that are not submitted in response
    to a government initiated "request for proposal" (RFP). He
    wonders how far he can go in discussing with a prospective con-
    tractor a project his agency is considering and still classify an
    incoming proposal resulting from the discussion as "unsolicited."

11. A staff member of the Office of Civil Rights who is serving on a
    committee charged with recommending a response to public school
    officials who have inquired whether a traditional "father-son"
    evening sponsored by the school district is a violation of Title IX
    of the Civil Rights Act. [66]

12. A biochemist with the Food and Drug Administration (FDA) whose
    research on chicken embryos reveals that cyclamates caused
    substantial and grotesque deformities in the embryos: Eighteen
    months after reporting her findings through FDA channels nothing
    had been done. As word of her research circulated throughout the

scientific community, she was asked for an interview by NBC-TV
in which she would have an opportunity to show the ghastly results
of her research on the evening news. Although FDA officials were
unwilling simply to forbid her to grant the interview, she was
under considerable agency pressure to refuse the invitation.[67]

13. A contracting officer for the air force who receives a protest from
a company unsuccessful in bidding for a defense contract: The
armed services procurement regulations confer broad discretionary powers upon such an officer. If the protest is filed in a
timely manner, the "award shall not be made until the matter is
resolved, unless the contracting officer determines that: (i) the
items to be procured are urgently required; or (ii) delivery or
performance will be unduly delayed by failure to make the award
promptly; or (iii) a prompt award will otherwise be advantageous
to the government."[68]

14. An OSHA inspector who must decide whether several safety violations in a small factory are "serious" or "nonserious": The
agency's guidelines are extremely vague but he knows that the
average fine for serious violations is about $600 whereas non-
serious violations average about $25.[69]

15. An office services supervisor, aware of a General Services
Administration rule against duplicating certain forms, is told by
a division chief that critical work of the organization will come to
a halt unless he authorizes the printing.

16. A division chief with two subordinates who are under consideration for a single position, a promotion: One is highly capable,
productive, and aggressively ambitious. Much of the division's
output depends on him. The other's performance is satisfactory
but his loss would not affect the division adversely. On paper
their credentials are the same. If either goes, it will take at
least three months to hire a replacement. The division's work is
critical.

17. A branch chief who has just been told that other branches of the
division need a computer but cannot justify its acquisition:
Though he does not foresee a need for additional computer capa-
bility in his branch, he is asked to help justify the new acquisition
by documenting ways he might be able to use it if it were available
and underutilized.[70]

  The impact of these decisions on government revenue, public policy,
and who gets what in our society should suffice to establish the point that
the men and women who make these decisions must balance a variety of
competing interests in the light of their own perception of the common
good. That is, bureaucrats govern.

CONCLUSION

It has been the purpose of this chapter to state as precisely as possible the
nature of the ethical issue peculiar to bureaucrats. At the outset I
declared my intention of demonstrating that the following statement defines
this issue: "Through administrative discretion, bureaucrats participate in
the governing process of our society; but to govern in a democratic society
without being responsible to the electorate raises a serious ethical question for bureaucrats." I have tried to show that the key ethical issue for
bureaucrats is intimately connected with a personnel system based on
merit. I do not for a moment suggest that we go back to a spoils system
or anything like it. Despite its many warts and wrinkles, our present
personnel system is by no means unworkable. The civil service reformers of the last century rendered signal service to the Republic, but in
solving a moral problem of massive proportions they created a new one
that can only grow more severe as we become increasingly enamored of the
benefits and blandishments of the administrative state. The nature of this
ethical problem was long hidden under a rhetorical cover that dichotomized
politics and administration. For the past thirty years scholars have been
exposing the inadequacy of this dichotomy, but, perhaps out of an excessive deference to the erstwhile dominance of the fact-value distinction in
the social sciences, they frequently failed to address the ethical implications of their findings. This chapter has attempted to make these implications explicit.

   To do this it has been necessary only to highlight the normative
aspects of what organization theory and, indeed, common sense itself have
long known—decision-making processes do not adhere slavishly to the
diagrammatic simplicities of organizational charts. This point was
recognized quite explicitly by Congress in its conflict-of-interest legislation in 1962. Previous congressional attempts to deal with this issue
tended to focus on the formal decision maker, the one who "signs off" on a
decision.[71] The 1962 legislation revealed a more sophisticated understanding of decision making. Criminal penalties were attached to any government employee who "participates personally and substantially through
decision, approval, disapproval, recommendation, the rendering of
advice, investigation, or otherwise in a judicial or other proceeding,
application, request for a ruling or other determination, contract, claim,
controversy, charge, accusation, arrest, or other particular matter in
which, to his knowledge, he . . . has a financial interest."[72]

   This complex model of bureaucratic decision making has been reinforced by a presidential executive order and consequent Civil Service Commission regulations requiring financial disclosures from all employees
classified at GS-13 or above whose work "requires the incumbent to exercise judgment in making a government decision . . . [that has] an
economic impact on the interest of any nonfederal enterprise."[73]

Furthermore, individual agencies may, with Civil Service Commission approval, require disclosure statements from employees well below the GS-13 level. The Food and Drug Administration, for example, requires some inspectors classified at GS-4 and GS-5 to disclose their financial holdings.[74] These formal enactments are eloquent testimony to official recognition of the significance of career bureaucrats in the decision-making processes that govern the United States.[75]

To highlight the role of the bureaucrat in decision making, however, does not imply that persons with formal responsibilities are merely the tools of their less visible underlings. To be influenced by one's subordinates is not tantamount to losing control over them. Certainly, important decisions will ordinarily receive the close attention of a person who is formally in charge. No executive officer aboard a naval vessel will open fire on an unidentified ship without the captain's approval. No judge will declare a legislative act unconstitutional solely on the basis of a memorandum from a clerk. President Kennedy's role in the Cuban missile crisis was more than merely formal and so was the role of Transportation Secretary William Coleman in permitting the SST to land at Dulles International Airport on an experimental basis.

Thus, when organizational theory and formal enactments of government tell us that bureaucratic subordinates influence decisions, they are not saying that the role of formally responsible officials is a charade. For our purposes, however, the problem is not that bureaucrats are excessively involved in policy formation but that they are involved at all. This is a problem for a democratic society because to influence public policy as a public official is to govern. Those who govern in a democracy should be sensitive to the demands of the electorate, but the most fundamental intent and result of the present personnel system is precisely to discourage such sensitivity. The civil service reformers of a century ago succeeded admirably in removing the federal personnel system from partisan politics, but they did not, because they could not, thereby render administration nonpolitical. They brought about a great reform but not a miracle.

In stating the ethical problem for bureaucrats as a direct consequence of the present personnel system, the analysis presented in this chapter necessarily suggests that a new self-image of the bureaucrat is in order. Wilsonian orthodoxy has taught bureaucrats to look upon themselves as feckless pawns of their political masters. As a result, an "office-boy" self-image—powerless and alienated—is salient in many government agencies.[76] Bureaucrats frequently resist the idea that they have an impact on public policy until they see for themselves that they use the word "policy" to describe something that by definition is done by someone else. They succumb to the fallacious reasoning that because others (political appointees, members of Congress, judges, presidents, et al.) have much power, they themselves have none. Not only is this reasoning fallacious, but it is dangerous as well, for it is always dangerous when the

powerful are unaware of their own power. They become vulnerable to
manipulation and fail to play their limited but significant role in our constitutional system.

It is the broad, constitutional principle of limited government that at
times is the cause of the bureaucrats' feeling of powerlessness. The same
principle affects presidents as well as bureaucrats. In the last days of his
presidency, Harry Truman wryly speculated on the surprises that awaited
his successor: "He'll sit here, and he'll say, 'Do this! Do that!' And
nothing will happen. Poor Ike—it won't be a bit like the Army. He'll find
it very frustrating." [77] Nearly every prominent American statesman has
expressed similar sentiments and most have eventually, if not always
graciously, acquiesced in the limitations visited upon them by a Constitution that wisely tolerates frustration as a by-product of freedom.

Bureaucrats seldom link their routine frustrations with the grand
principles of the Republic. This is not because the link is illusory, but
because they have not been educated to look for it. The "political" orientation of their superiors, the "meddling" of the courts, the "harassment"
from congressional committees—these are precisely the ways in which the
constitutional word becomes flesh. If the bureaucracy were looked upon,
not as a neutral instrument of management, but as a mighty institution of
government, the bureaucrat might develop a self-image that is more
directly connected with the public interest that he or she inevitably affects.
This would highlight the relevance for the bureaucrat of the ethical impera-
tives of American constitutional morality—above all the sense of disciplined
restraint in the use of power.

Because a public interest model of bureaucracy rests on the fact that
bureaucrats govern, the ethical training and education of the bureaucrat
should encourage reflections aimed at developing the virtues we look for in
those who govern. Among these virtues—at least in a democracy—is a
keen alertness to the values of those in whose name and for whose benefit
one governs. The contribution that schools of public administration might
make to this effort provides the substance of the next chapter.

NOTES

1. "Responsible" is used here in the sense of "accountable." Thus it
   should be distinguished from "responsive," which describes the attitude of one who stands ready to meet certain needs with or without
   formal accountability. For a thorough discussion of the various mean-
   ings of "responsibility," see Herbert J. Spiro, Responsibility in
   Government: Theory and Practice (New York: Van Nostrand, 1967),
   chap. 2, pp. 14-20.

2. Conflict of interest is not a problem peculiar to bureaucrats; they share it with members of Congress, judges, politically appointed executives, and others.

3. The famous slogan "To the victor belong the spoils" was first uttered by Senator William L. Marcy of New York in 1832. See Leonard D. White, The Jacksonians: A Study in Administrative History (New York: Macmillan, 1954), p. 320.

4. "Rotation in office" was not the only reform associated with the Jackson administration. Matthew Crenson makes a fascinating and persuasive argument that it was during the Jackson years that "bureaucracy" became the dominant mode of organization in the federal government and that this innovation was introduced as a vehicle for moral reform. Matthew A. Crenson, The Federal Machine: Beginnings of Bureaucracy in Jacksonian America (Baltimore: Johns Hopkins University Press, 1975).

5. Even Washington, however, gave some consideration to such political factors as making sure "that every region of the country was represented among the principal officers, and that field stations were staffed almost entirely from the populations of the localities served." Naturally, he sought some assurance that his appointees supported the new system of government. Also, some preference was shown to officers of the Revolutionary army. See Herbert Kaufman, "The Growth of the Federal Personnel System," in The Federal Government Service, 2nd ed., ed. Wallace S. Sayer (Englewood Cliffs, N.J.: Prentice-Hall, 1965), p. 13.

6. The problem of superannuated personnel became especially acute in the War of 1812 when army leadership was dominated by elderly officers, many of whom had distinguished themselves in the Revolutionary War nearly forty years earlier. As a young general in the War of 1812, Jackson would have been quite sensitive to this problem.

7. The Nourse family of Virginia provided the best example of government service on a family basis. Joseph Nourse was appointed Register of the Treasury by Washington in 1789 and continued in that post until Jackson removed him in 1829. One of his sons, Major Charles J. Nourse, became chief clerk of the War Department. Three other members of the family, Joseph, Michael, and John, held positions in the Treasury Department. The omnipresent Nourses prompted Jackson's bon mot that if elected president, he "would clean out the Noursery." Leonard D. White, The Jeffersonians (New York: Macmillan, 1956), pp. 358, 370.

8. Leonard D. White, The Republican Era (New York: Macmillan, 1958). p. 299.

9. Ibid.

10. Ibid.

11. Credit Mobilier was a corporation organized to finance railroad con-
    struction. Shares in the company were sold to prominent members of
    Congress for one-half the market price in an effort to win congression-
    al support for projects favorable to the company's interests.
12. White, The Jacksonians, p. 318.
13. Ibid.
14. Ibid.
15. White, The Republican Era, p. 292.
16. Ibid.
17. Ibid.
18. Ibid., pp. 293-294.
19. Ibid., p. 293.
20. Ibid., pp. 294-295.
21. Ibid., p. 348.
22. For a contemporary version of this position, see the "Malek Manual."
    Fred Malek served as White House personnel officer during the Nixon
    administration. The essay attributed to him is a cookbook approach
    on how to get around the rules of the federal personnel system. It is
    breathtakingly candid in the strategy it announces and distressingly
    perceptive in the tactics it advocates. The essay can be found in The
    Bureaucrat 4 (January 1976): 347-508. A commentary accompanies
    the text.
23. Wilson's lecture and article received considerable attention in the
    1880s and has since become a venerable classic in the study of public
    administration. As Leonard White remarked, "Wilson introduced the
    country to the idea of administration" (The Republican Era, p. 46). A
    recent article in the American Political Science Review (vol. 67,
    June 1973, p. 582), Richard J. Stillman's "Woodrow Wilson and the
    Study of Administration," attests to the abiding interest in Wilson's
    work. The publication of the first twelve volumes of Wilson's papers
    has shed considerable light on the intellectual traditions that influenced
    Wilson's ideas on administration. Stillman's article is especially
    helpful in this regard. Although it is impossible to state precisely
    Wilson's motivation in publishing his essay, there can be little doubt
    that one of his reasons was to assist the reform movement of his
    time. Another reason, closely related to the question of reform, was
    to strengthen the executive branch in its struggle with Congress. The
    excessive power of Congress—especially its committee system—was a
    major theme in Wilson's first book, Congressional Government.
    Wilson's essay, "The Study of Administration," first appeared in
    Political Science Quarterly 2 (June 1887): 197-222.
24. For contrasting interpretations of Wilson's essay, see Frederick C.
    Mosher, Democracy and the Public Service (New York: Oxford
    University Press, 1968), and Fred Riggs, "Relearning Old Lessons,"
    Public Administration Review 25 (March 1971).

25. Stillman, "Woodrow Wilson and the Study of Administration," p. 587.

26. For example, see Frank J. Goodnow, Politics and Administration (New York: Macmillan, 1914).

27. This is not to say that contemporary bureaucrats are aware of the Wilsonian origins of the dichotomy. My point is simply that they live by it. I think this is fairly obvious to anyone who has spent some time working in a government agency or talking with those who do. "Policy" is always made by somebody else. Down here in the agency we simply carry out what someone "up there" has decided. See Herbert J. Storing, "Political Parties and the Bureaucracy" in Political Parties U.S.A. , ed. Robert Goldwyn (Chicago: Rand McNally, 1961), pp. 143-145, and Victor G. Rosenblum, "On Davis on Confining, Structuring, and Checking Administrative Discretion," Law & Contemporary Problems 37 (Winter 1972): 60.

28. Wilson was not the first to distinguish politics and administration. In his essay he acknowledges his dependence upon German and French professors. The distinction was not unknown among civil service reformers prior to Wilson, but Wilson was the first to develop an argument using the distinction to support the compatibility of administrative reform with democratic institutions.

29. Wilson, "The Study of Administration," pp. 209-210.

30. Ibid. , p. 220.

31. Ibid. , p. 214

32. Ibid. , pp. 216-217.

33. Ibid. , p. 202.

34. Ibid. , p. 219.

35. York Willbern, "Is the New Public Administration Still With Us?" Public Administration Review 33 (July-August 1973): 377.

36. Among the early postwar critics of the Wilsonian dichotomy, Nicholas Henry lists the following: John M. Gaus, ed. , Reflections on Public Administration (Tuscaloosa: University of Alabama Press, 1947); Robert H. Dahl, "The Science of Public Administration: Three Problems," Public Administration Review 7 (Winter 1947): 1-11; Fritz von Morstein-Marx, ed. , Elements of Public Administration (Englewood Cliffs, N.J.: Prentice-Hall, 1946); Dwight Waldo, The Administrative State (New York: Ronald, 1948); and Herbert Simon, Administrative Behavior (New York: Macmillan, 1947). See Nicholas Henry, "Bureaucracy, Technology and Knowledge Management," Public Administration Review 35 (November-December 1975): 572-578. In addition to the works cited by Henry, I would also include Norton Long, "Power and Administration," Public Administration Review 9 (Summer 1949): 257-264; and Paul Appleby, Morality and Administration in Democratic Government (Baton Rouge: LSU Press, 1952), especially chap. 8. For a fascinating interpretation of Leonard White's shifting his main interest to history, see Herbert J. Storing,

"Leonard D. White and the Study of Public Administration," Public Administration Review 25 (March 1965): 38-51. Although there is good reason for Henry's including Herbert Simon as one of the early critics of the dichotomy, I would suggest that Simon's own position is ultimately a restatement of the dichotomy he attacks. For a discussion of Charles Merriam's sophisticated manipulation of the dichotomy in the 1920s, see Barry D. Karl, Charles E. Merriam and the Study of Politics (Chicago: University of Chicago Press, 1974), p. 132.

37. There are notable exceptions—particularly Dwight Waldo. See also Francis E. Rourke, Bureaucracy, Politics and Public Policy (Boston: Little, Brown, 1969), and Jack L. Walker, "Brother Can You Spare a Paradigm?" P.S. 5 (Fall 1972): 419-422.

38. Storing, "Political Parties and the Bureaucracy," in Political Parties U.S.A., ed. Goldwyn, p. 145.

39. For example, see Theodore Lowi, The End of Liberalism (New York: Norton, 1969), chap. 10.

40. See O. Glenn Stahl, Public Personnel Administration, 6th ed. (New York: Harper & Row, 1971), chap. 16, "Public Service Ethics in a Democracy." Although Stahl is not interested in attacking the dichotomy between politics and administration, he bases his analysis of ethics on administrative discretion. A similar point is mentioned in George A. Graham, "Ethical Guidelines for Public Administrators: Observations on Rules of the Game," Public Administration Review 34 (January-February 1974): 90-92.

41. David Easton, A Framework for Political Analysis (Englewood Cliffs, N.J.: Prentice-Hall, 1965), p. 50, and Harold D. Lasswell, Politics: Who Gets What, When, How (New York: McGraw-Hill, 1936).

42. See Jacques Maritain, Man and the State (Chicago: University of Chicago Press, 1951), pp. 1-27; and John Courtney Murray, We Hold These Truths (New York: Sheed & Ward, 1960). See also the following articles by Murray in Theological Studies: "Freedom of Religion: The Ethical Problem" 6 (1945): 229-286; "Contemporary Orientations of Catholic Thought on Church and State in the Light of History" 10 (1949): 177-234; "On Religious Freedom" 10 (1949): 409-432.

43. The methodological debates among political scientists during the 1960s—always interesting and at times acrimonious—may have ended in "peace with honor." See the presidential address of David Easton to the American Political Science Association in The American Political Science Review 53 (December 1969): 1051-1061.

44. In this book I shall use "politics" and "policy" interchangeably, but in the interest of precision, it might be useful to point out that the relationship between the two concepts is one of whole to part. That is, all public policy is political but not all politics is policy. Electoral politics is the most obvious example of political activity frequently unrelated to policy. In this book, when I speak of administration as

"political," I refer, of course, to the policy aspects of politics, not to elections.

45. See Grant McConnell, Private Power and American Democracy (New York: Alfred A. Knopf, 1966), pp. 200-211.

46. See Philip Selznick, TVA and the Grass Roots (Berkeley: University of California Press, 1949), chaps. 3 and 4; McConnell, Private Power and American Democracy, pp. 230-243; Grant McConnell, The Decline of Agrarian Democracy (Berkeley: University of California Press, 1953); Gladys Baker, The County Agent (Chicago: University of Chicago Press, 1939).

47. See Samuel P. Huntington, "The Marasmus of the ICC," Yale Law Journal 61 (1952): 467-509.

48. The classic study of the corps is Arthur Maass, Muddy Waters: The Army Engineers and the Nation's Rivers (Cambridge, Mass.: Harvard University Press, 1951). See also Maass, "Congress and Water Resources," American Political Science Review 44 (September 1950): 576-593; and McConnell, Private Power and American Democracy, pp. 211-230. For a contemporary study of the corps, see Daniel A. Mazmanian and Mordecai Lee, "Tradition be Damned! The Army Corps of Engineers Is Changing," Public Administration Review 35 (March-April 1975): 166-172.

49. Charles Wolf, Jr., Indonesian Assignment (Indianapolis: Bobbs-Merrill, 1952).

50. Theodore J. Lowi, Bases in Spain (Indianapolis: Bobbs-Merrill, 1963).

51. Martin Kriesberg, Cancellation of the Ration Stamps (Indianapolis: Bobbs-Merrill, 1952).

52. Walter A. Rosenbaum, The Burning of the Farm Population Estimates (Indianapolis: Bobbs-Merrill, 1965).

53. Kenneth C. Davis, Discretionary Justice: A Preliminary Inquiry (Baton Rouge: LSU Press, 1969), pp. 9-14. Davis's book remains the foremost study of administrative discretion. It stresses techniques courts might employ to "check, confine, and structure" unnecessary administrative discretion. "Unnecessary" is emphasized because Davis never tires of assuring his readers that discretion itself is not the basis of his concern. His point is that there is too much adminis-trative discretion in American government and that it is exercised in a haphazard way. In addressing the problem of discretion, the task of the courts is "to regularize it, to organize it, to produce order in it." His work has received considerable attention from the courts. See Environmental Defense Fund v. Ruckleshaus 439 F2d 584; Greater Boston Television Corporation v. FCC 444 F2d 841; and FTC v. Crowther 430 F2d 510. Symposia on Davis's work can be found in Law and Contemporary Problems 37 (Winter, 1972), and in Admin-istrative Law Review 22. Although Davis does not address the ethical dimensions of administrative discretion, his concern with consistency

in the exercise of discretionary power has strong normative overtones. His emphasis is on how <u>courts</u> can <u>compel</u> administrative
agencies to "structure" their <u>discretion</u>. There is no reason, however, why administrative agencies could not do this voluntarily. A
decision to do so would be of considerable ethical significance. See
the conclusion of this book, pp. 242-248.

54. Lowi, <u>The End of Liberalism,</u> pp. 125-146.

55. Ibid., p. 137.

56. Ibid., p. 217-239.

57. The discretion Shriver conferred on the field representatives was, in
    my judgment, a major cause of OEO's stormy political history. The
    field representatives had to hurt someone in every decision they made.
    Their discretion made them vulnerable. See John A. Rohr, "Ethics
    for Bureaucrats," <u>America</u> 128 (May 26, 1973): 488-491, where my
    summary of Lowi's position first appeared. To grasp the discretion-
    ary significance of the <u>nonexclusive</u> list, consider the following
    example. A young man is told by his parents to buy suitable clothing
    and is given $200 for this purpose. He asks what "suitable" means
    and is told "it is likely" that suitable clothing will have the following
    characteristics: (1) imported from England; (2) made of wool; and
    (3) dark in color. The young man cannot find anything meeting these
    criteria that appeals to him so he buys a pink polyester jacket made in
    Sheboygan. Has he disobeyed his parents? No, for the simple reason
    that he was never given any commands. Despite the parental guide-
    lines, his discretion was virtually unlimited. Similar nonexclusive
    language appears in OSHA regulations and is not unrelated to the
    problems of that unhappy agency [29 C.F.R. § 1910.212(a)].

58. <u>New York Times,</u> March 18, 1978, p. 25.

59. H. Ball, D. Krane, and T. Lauth, "Discretionary Justice at DOJ:
    Administrative Implementation of Section 5 of the Voting Rights Act of
    1965." Paper delivered at the 1978 National Conference of the
    American Society for Public Administration.

60. <u>Washington Post</u>, November 8, 1975, p. A1.

61. <u>New York Times,</u> September 30, 1971, p. 25.

62. <u>Chicago Sun-Times,</u> June 5, 1974, p. 3.

63. <u>New York Times,</u> November 22, 1976, p. 15. Emphasis added.

64. Jeffrey L. Jowell, <u>Law and Bureaucracy: Administrative Discretion
    and the Limits of Legal Action</u> (Port Washington, N.Y.: Dunellen,
    1975), p. 51. The caseworker decided the expense was a luxury and
    that it was not conducive to good child care because it entailed the
    client's prolonged absence from home. The supervisor upheld the
    caseworker's decision.

65. "A Self Inquiry Into Merit Staffing: Report of the Merit Staffing
    Review Team, U.S. Civil Service Commission," House Committee on
    Post Office and Civil Service, 94th Congress, 2nd session (June 8,
    1976), pp. 51-53.

66. *Washington Post*, July 8, 1976, p. A1.
67. Dr. Jacqueline Verrett granted the interview that led to a storm of protest from several embarrassed companies. Dr. Verrett was publicly censured by HEW Secretary Robert Finch for "unethical conduct." See Charles Peters and Taylor Branch, eds., *Blowing the Whistle: Dissent in the Public Interest* (New York: Praeger, 1972), pp. 190-195.
68. Richard E. Speidel, "Judicial and Administrative Review of Government Contract Awards," *Law and Contemporary Problems* 37 (Winter 1972): 71. Emphasis added.
69. OSHA is an agency that may in one sense have too little rather than too much discretion. Once an inspection is underway, citations *must* be issued if violations are discovered. See Philip J. Harter, "In Search of OSHA," *Regulation* 1 (September-October 1977): 33-39.
70. Examples 15, 16, and 17 were called to my attention by E. C. Wakham and Richard Parker of the United States Civil Service Commission. They first appeared in a training manual that was compiled by Wakham, Parker, and myself. It is entitled *Ethics, Values and Administrative Responsibility* and was published by the General Management Training Center, Bureau of Training, United States Civil Service Commission (Washington, D.C., 1977).
71. For a comparison between the 1962 legislation that is currently in force and previous congressional attempts to regulate conflict-of-interest issues, see Bayless Manning, *Federal Conflict of Interest Law* (Cambridge, Mass.: Harvard University Press, 1964).
72. 18 USC § 208.
73. Federal Personnel Manual 735-17; 5 C.F.R. 735.402(6).
74. From correspondence in files of the General Counsel's Office, United States Civil Service Commission, Washington, D.C.
75. In this context it is interesting to note the fate of President Carter's pledge in his first fireside chat that every new regulation would be signed by its author. The president soon discovered that most regulations do not have identifiable authors but "are frequently the product of many hands." Instead of arbitrarily assigning an "author," the *Federal Register* follows the more sensible course of including with each new regulation the name and address of an agency employee who can be contacted for further information. See David R. Gergen, "Will Carter Put Out the Fire," *Regulation* 1 (September-October 1977): 22.
76. Rosenblum, "On Davis," p. 60; Storing "Political Parties and the Bureaucracy," pp. 143-145.
77. Cited in Richard Neustadt, *Presidential Power: The Politics of Leadership* (New York: Wiley, 1960), p. 9.

2

Regime Values

A constitution is a standard, a pillar, and a bond when it is understood, approved, and beloved. But without this intelligence and attachment, it might as well be a kite or balloon flying in the air.

John Adams

The introduction to this book noted that its primary focus is on the education of bureaucrats. The ethical problem as stated in the previous chapter has ramifications far beyond the sphere of education, but now it is time to narrow our theme to meet the specific purposes of this book. If, indeed, the heart of the ethical issue for American bureaucrats is that through their administrative discretion they govern a democratic polity, how does this affect their professional education? That is, what consequences follow for institutions dedicated to public service education when they attempt to integrate the study of ethics into their curricula?

The post-Watergate era is a propitious time to give serious thought to questions about the ethical dimensions of public service education. It would be a pity if educators simply rode the crest of the current enthusiasm for "ethics in government" without looking for ways to integrate ethical reflections and values into the public administration curriculum in a manner that is systematic, principled, and academically defensible. To rely upon a few pious homilies and anecdotes intended to warn prospective bureaucrats away from the excesses of Watergate simply will not do. Very shortly, we shall be teaching young men and women for whom Watergate will be nothing more than a vague childhood recollection.

Fortunately, for the purpose of this book, the popular interest in ethics is supplemented by the serious academic work that has already been done in the "new public administration." Within the field of public administration, there was considerable interest in normative questions before we knew that Watergate was anything more than an elegant apartment

complex.[1] The "new public administration" has provided the theoretical
foundation to support an investigation of methods of integrating the study of
ethics into a public service curriculum; Watergate has provided an
impetus to get on with it.

In keeping with the argument of the previous chapter, administrative
discretion will serve as the starting point for our ethical reflections. In
basing our analysis on discretion, we are following the sound advice of
Paul Appleby, whose classic essay Morality and Administration is perhaps
the most significant book ever written on this topic by an American
author.[2] Appleby's book was published in 1952—at the very height of the
scandals associated with the Truman administration. Although writing at a
time when there was widespread condemnation of the low level of ethical
sensitivity in government service, Appleby maintained sufficient perspective to remark that "crude wrongdoing is not a major, general problem of
our government." He went on to say that "further moral advance turns
upon more complicated and elevated concerns."[3] What Appleby said then
is still true today. It is not the "crude wrongdoing" of Watergate that
should form the basis of our approach to ethics but the "more complicated
and elevated" issue of administrative discretion.

This chapter has three divisions. The first is a critical review of
several earlier efforts to integrate the study of ethics into a public administration curriculum, while the second sets forth my own view on how this
should be done. The third presents some concluding remarks.

SOME APPROACHES TO ETHICS

This section is subdivided into three parts—general comments, the "low
road" that emphasizes adherence to formal rules, and the "high road" that
stresses social equity.

General Comments

In talking with students, practitioners, and professors of public administration, it is clear that a concern with questions of ethics and values is
widespread and serious. This informal impression is unmistakably confirmed by the prominent place given to such questions for the past few
years at the national meetings of the American Society for Public Administration (ASPA) and in the academic guidelines published by the National
Association of Schools of Public Affairs and Administration (NASPAA).[4]
Although the discussions—both formal and informal—of ethics and values
reveal virtual unanimity in the belief that "we must do something" to
improve the moral tone of government, opinion splinters badly over just

what we should do and how we should do it. Among the highlights in
discussions of ethics, one finds an outpouring of righteous indignation
against the villains of Watergate; a verbal thrashing of the CIA and the
FBI; wise sayings of the giants of the past, and sharp condemnations of the
"revolving door" between regulating agencies and regulated industries.

Each of these attitudes has its merits, but none of them is terribly
helpful for curriculum purposes. For one thing, such discussions are
hopelessly negative in tone. Traditionally, ethics as a branch of philosophy
has dealt with questions of doing good as well as avoiding evil. The considerations mentioned above emphasize the latter excessively and provide a
morally impoverished image of public service that students are not likely to
to find very attractive. Secondly, the anecdotal and ad hoc character of
many of these criticisms of integrity in government render them inappropriate for academic investigation. Finally, the criticisms are usually
aimed at persons or offices so high in government as to have little
practical significance for mid-level managers or even career executives.

For these reasons many of the current discussions of ethics and
values, though interesting in themselves, offer little guidance to those
concerned with questions about the management curriculum. This is somewhat distressing because it is hard to put down the uneasy feeling that
unless issues of ethics and values are made part of the curriculum in an
academically satisfying way, contemporary enthusiasts for righteousness
may well be but poor players who strut and fret their hour upon the stage
and then are heard no more.

Unless the current interest in ethics is institutionalized, there is
real danger that the profession as a whole may grow weary of well-
doing as new issues and events present themselves. Ethics and values
will then no longer be topical and current; indeed, they may suffer the
ultimate condemnation—irrelevance. To avoid this, educators should
seize the moment at hand. With the post-Watergate morality still upon
us and with a congenital moralist in the White House, these are the
years of plenty. Like the pharoah advised by Joseph, we would do well
to gather up the present abundance to "be in readiness against the
famine to come." Among our tasks is that of refining, organizing, and
systematizing the myriad issues that currently fall under the rubric of
ethics. Moralistic bombast and pious platitudes must be purged in the hope
of presenting ethics in a way that is appropriate for an academic
inquiry.[5]

The Low Road

The purpose of this section is to present a critical review of one specific
approach to handling the issue of ethics for career civil servants. It is

called the "low road" because it addresses ethical issues almost exclusively
in terms of adherence to agency rules. The approach in question appears
in "Ethics and Conduct"—a workshop training manual designed by a private
corporation for the United States Department of Agriculture (USDA). [6]

The manual is composed of five exercises intended to enhance the
understanding of USDA employees on the sorts of conduct that are permissible or not under departmental regulations. In one exercise the course
participants are confronted with a series of statements with which they are
supposed either to agree or disagree. The "Leader's Guide" provides
school solutions to each situation. Participants are divided into small
groups. Each participant must first indicate whether he agrees or dis-
agrees (circle A or D) with the statement and then after some discussion a
group decision is made. For example:

An employee who willfully uses or authorizes the use of a Government-owned vehicle for other than official purposes may be suspended for one month or removed from office.

PERSONAL CHOICE		GROUP CHOICE	
A	D	A	D

[School Solution]

The answer to this statement is "A" agree. The penalties . . . for will-fully using or authorizing the use of a Government-owned vehicle are suspension for at least one month or removal from position.

Among the topics covered in this exercise are the following:
(1) whether office equipment can be used for personal business; (2) whether
government telephones can be used for personal calls; (3) whether USDA
can take action against employees who fail to pay personal debts; and so
on.

A second exercise provides the participants with three boxes marked
P (permissible), NP (not permissible), and PWA (permissible with
written approval). They are to mark one of these boxes in response to
situations such as the following:

On a Sunday afternoon, on the way to a field location in an official Government vehicle, a USDA employee who was traveling on Sunday to be at his destination for a Monday morning assignment, drove approximately 8 miles off the main route he was taking to visit some relatives whom he had not seen for several years.

PERSONAL CHOICE			GROUP CHOICE		
P	NP	PWA	P	NP	PWA

[School Solution]

This statement is questionable. One could easily make the point that it is permissible, not permissible, or possibly even permissible but only with prior written approval. It is probably safe to say, however, that such a situation should be avoided, if at all possible.

An employee on a two-week field trip was spending a weekend at a motel; during the weekend, he used a Government vehicle to take his laundry into town to a local laundromat. Public transportation was available, but much less convenient than the use of the automobile.

PERSONAL CHOICE			GROUP CHOICE		
P	NP	PWA	P	NP	PWA

[School Solution]

. . .[T]his statement is questionable. There is no single correct answer here, though. It is likely that if the laundry needed dry cleaning because it was soiled from the business trip, it would be permitted; an employee is generally allowed to take such actions while away on business, where such personal services are required.

These examples will suffice to suggest the tone of the manual and its hopelessly negative approach to public service. Ethical behavior is reduced to staying out of trouble. These exercises provide a clear example of the worst aspects of the mentality that continues to dichotomize politics and administration. The manual is innocent of any reference whatsoever to the influence that career civil servants might have on USDA policy. It reinforces the powerless, alienated, "office-boy" image of the bureaucrat that is destructive of the self-respect so necessary for mature moral growth.

Further, the emphasis on meticulous attention to trivial questions— for example, is it permissible for an employee to use a government phone to cancel a dental appointment—runs the risk of developing a dangerous attitude of pharisaism on the part of government employees. USDA personnel exposed to this manual just might get the idea that they are ethically upright employees because, when traveling on government business, they take public transportation to laundromats! The manual offers little encouragement to USDA employees to examine their attitudes toward, and relationship with, such key forces in the private sector as the lumber industry or the American Farm Bureau Federation. "Woe to you, scribes and Pharisees, hypocrites . . . who strain out a gnat and swallow a camel."

One might defend the USDA manual on the grounds that at least it conveys some information on agency rules. This it does but it is not the stated purpose of the exercises. Participants are told to "measure" their success in the exercise "by the number of new ideas you gain and not necessarily by the frequency with which you personally achieve the 'right' solution to a situation." It is perhaps of some significance that the participants are told to measure success by the number of new ideas they gain. Such a directive makes sense only on the very shaky epistemological presupposition that all ideas are equal. Perhaps USDA personnel would do better if they would judge the success of the course by the quality and truth of their ideas rather than by their number and novelty, even though evaluating ideas is harder than counting them. [7]

Our purpose in rehearsing the defects of the USDA manual is not simply to gain a cheap triumph over a man of straw. Rather, the purpose is to establish an important point in our argument—that not all values are equal. The current interest in ethics and values is such that virtually anyone who has anything to say on the topic will have little trouble finding an audience. Management training institutions in both the public and private sectors are quite anxious to go on record that they are "doing something" about ethics and values. Unfortunately, at times a certain frantic scrambling for relevance characterizes these efforts. Surely, it is more important to know what these institutions are doing than simply to know that something is being done. This is the lesson of the USDA manual. Because the manual reinforces a false ("office-boy") image of the career civil service, because it systematically trains the bureaucrat to emphasize the trivial and to ignore the ethically significant dimensions of his or her work, and because it is likely to create a smug, self-righteousness, I think it is quite reasonable to conclude that it would have been far better for USDA to have done absolutely nothing about ethics and values. USDA would do well to heed Frank Marini's word of caution that public administrators must not become "easy marks for every huckster who has fancy equipment and fashionable patter."[8]

The High Road

In this section two approaches to ethics based on the "social equity" literature associated with the "new public administration" are critically examined. One of the approaches is grounded in political philosophy and the other in humanistic psychology. H. George Frederickson's essay "Toward a New Public Administration"[9] suggested that social equity be added to the classical norms of efficient, economical, and coordinated management as criteria for evaluating the performance of public administrators. Although he did not define the term precisely, his examples indicated quite clearly that the equitable administrator is one who actively intervenes to enhance the political power and economic well-being of disadvantaged minorities in order to redress the neglect suffered by such minorities at the hands of the customary procedures of representative democracy. The content of social equity is undoubtedly egalitarian in principle and redistributive in policy.[10]

Early in 1974 Public Administration Review featured a "Symposium on Social Equity and Public Administration" that was edited by Frederickson. In his "Introductory Comments" he repeated some of his earlier observations and added his hope that the essays in the symposium would explain the concept of social equity and show how it might be applied in practice.[11] The first essay in the symposium presented an able theoretical exposition of the meaning and merit of social equity.[12] There followed a series of essays applying the concept in such diverse areas as the internal aspects of organizational life,[13] public personnel policies,[14] measurements of social service productivity,[15] public finance,[16] and research methodologies in policy analysis.[17] These essays showed that "social equity" was more than a pious phrase. An administrator looking for guidance along normative lines would find in the symposium sound advice presented in a careful and persuasive manner.

Although the symposium was the most formal treatment of social equity in the literature, other books and articles have appeared that reflect the same underlying values. For example, Larry Kirkhart's "consociated model"[18] or the "charettes" discussed by Fred Thayer might well be included in the "social equity" literature.[19] The same could be said of

Michael Harmon's work on the "proactive" administrator and the work of
David K. Hart and William G. Scott in political theory.[20] For our purposes it is not terribly important to determine just what is and what is not
"social equity" literature. As far as curriculum issues on ethics are concerned, it is clear that social equity, like the "new public administration,"
bases its moral position to a considerable extent on normative political
theory and humanistic psychology. Although both of these disciplines
would enrich any curriculum, the appropriateness of basing the ethical
aspects of the professional education of bureaucrats on either of them is
questionable.

Political Philosophy

As far as political philosophy is concerned, the reason for questioning
its propriety as the foundation for the study of ethics is that it is too
demanding to be included as part of a course in ethics. If it were possible
to include several courses in political philosophy as a preparation for the
study of ethics, I would withdraw my objection. I fear, however, that
other demands of the curriculum would make this quite unlikely in schools
of public administration and simply unthinkable in management training
centers.

As far as schools are concerned, one might readily sympathize with
David Hart's call for "a new tradition of administrative philosophy" leading
to curriculum revision with new courses that "must reflect the rigor of the
philosophic tradition."[21] Less persuasive, however, is Hart's position
that John Rawls's theory of justice should provide the philosophic foundation of such courses. If we are to follow the "rigor of the philosophic
tradition," we would have to examine carefully the foundations of Rawls's
position. There is, of course, a formidable (and growing) body of literature critical of Rawls.[22] Students would have to be familiarized with this
literature before accepting Rawls as a starting point. One might add that
to understand Rawls, one should first read Kant and that Kant is unintel-
ligible unless one understands Hume's influence upon him.[23]

My point is not to enter a full-scale debate over the merits of Rawls's
position but simply to point out the kinds of questions that are inevitably
triggered when one addresses the issues of political philosophy.[24] The
"rigor of the philosophic tradition" demands that issues of politics be
related to broader issues of linguistics, psychology, metaphysics, and
epistemology. This is both the glory and the frustration of philosophy. If
a public administration curriculum is to maintain its professional focus,
certain valuable intellectual investigations must be sacrificed. We can
hope that graduate students in public administration programs have already
acquired a rich background in the liberal arts and rejoice when our
expectations are fulfilled. But I do not think we can prudently demand
extensive philosophical investigations from public administration students

after they have started their professional studies. To settle for a smatter-
ing of political philosophy as part of a course in ethics would not be fair
either to the students or to philosophy itself. For this reason we must look
elsewhere for the foundation for a course in ethics.[25]

Humanistic Psychology

Humanistic psychology can also provide a normative foundation for
many of the values salient in both social equity and the "new public administration" literature.[26] By humanistic psychology, I mean the writings of
such prominent thinkers as Abraham Maslow, Carl Rogers, and Lawrence
Kohlberg. Peter Berger's work in the sociology of knowledge might also
be included. The writings of these men provide many normative insights
that are extremely useful in organizational life—for example, Berger's
warning against the danger of "reifying" existing structures and institutions.[27] To the extent that public administration deals with organizations,
the contribution of humanistic psychology to organizational theory is a
welcome addition to the literature. Organizational theory, however, is not
coextensive with public administration. The public aspects of public
administration are more amenable to the traditional inquiries of law
and political science than to the methods of organizational theory. Law
and political science[28] take seriously the formal distinction between
public and private that is at the heart of our ethical inquiry. The discretion of the public administrator raises an ethical problem quite different from the discretion conferred upon officers of corporations or
private associations.[29]

Humanistic psychology, like organizational theory, is not concerned
with the distinction between public and private. When Maslow writes about
a person who is "self-actualized," it makes no difference if the person is a
bureaucrat, a carpenter, a dentist, or a novelist. The same is true of the
six stages of moral development in Kohlberg. It is the individual person
that is important in humanistic psychology—not how the person is employed.
Because the starting point of our problem is the discretion consequent upon
a certain type of employment (public), a normative system based upon the
individual person is not suitable for our purposes.

The criticism of a normative system based on the individual must not
be confused with an attempt to dichotomize personal and political morality.
All morality is personal in the sense that only persons are morally
accountable.[30] A person, however, is morally accountable in different
ways for different aspects of his or her life. Familial morality, business
morality, sexual morality, political morality, and so on—are all matters
that concern individual human beings. The same man is father, salesman,
husband, and citizen. He might well believe that beating his children,
cheating his customers, committing adultery, and failing to pay taxes are
all morally reprehensible, but the reasons for condemning each of these

forms of behavior might be quite different. Humanistic psychology could
be quite helpful in assisting individuals to integrate the various roles they
must play, but it is less helpful in raising specific questions pertaining to
one of these values. Because the focus of our inquiry is the ethics of one
very specific role, it seems that the moral foundation we are looking for
must be judged in terms of the demands of that limited role rather than
expanded to consider the broader question of how to be a well-integrated
human being. Obviously, government agencies are no less in need of well-
integrated human beings than any other institutions in our society; but if
specific questions of ethics for governmental administrators must be post-
poned until such persons have first become well-integrated human beings,
we may never get on with our work.

Jacques Maritain once used the term "hypermoralism" to describe a
moral stance that applied ethical norms suitable for interpersonal relations to political situations.[31] Maritain argues persuasively that "hypermoralism" is as dangerous as "amoralism" for they both lead to moral
cynicism. In judging political actions in interpersonal terms, one puts
intolerable strains upon the political system for the simple reason that the
behavior consequent upon a commitment of civic friendship can never
measure up to the rigorous demands of an "I-Thou" relationship.[32] For
Maritain politics is a part of ethics, but unless one distinguishes in
principle the norms for appropriate behavior in governmental relationships
and personal relationships, one will soon be disillusioned with public life
and despair of the relevance of any moral consideration in government. At
times the best is enemy of the good.

In questioning the usefulness of political philosophy and humanistic
psychology for bureaucratic ethics, I do not intend to launch a diatribe
against these disciplines. A public administration curriculum that ignored
them would be impoverished indeed. My point is simply to question the
propriety of either discipline as the foundation for a course in ethics for
bureaucrats.

The propriety of political philosophy is questioned on the practical
grounds that other curriculum demands would preclude the possibility of
the student acquiring the philosophical habitus that is the reward and goal
of philosophical studies. A haphazard perusal of the works of the great
philosophers will yield nothing more than a gentleman's veneer. Although,
unfortunately, this is the case in many institutions of higher education
today, for the most part it is merely unfortunate. For the study of ethics,
it could be disastrous—both for bureaucrats personally and for their
ethical impact on policy. Ethical reflections must be soundly rooted in
principle if they are to yield the moral vigor necessary in public life.
Political philosophy is undoubtedly capable of offering such principles but
in the context of today's educational climate, will "realistic" curriculum

demands allow political philosophy to reveal its treasures? Probably not.
If this is true for universities, it applies with even greater force to centers
for management training.

Opposition to humanistic psychology as the foundation of the study of
bureaucratic ethics is based on principled rather than pragmatic considerations. Humanistic psychology is relevant for ethics in general but not for
ethics for bureaucrats. Certain considerations in humanistic psychology
yield attractive, normative principles for organizational life, but these
principles relate to organizational life in general rather than governmental
organization in particular. As such, they contribute significantly to
normative discussions of internal management problems within an
organization (any organization, government or otherwise), but they have
nothing to say about the output that is distinctive of governmental organization—public policy.

REGIME VALUES

As an alternative to political philosophy and humanistic psychology, I would
suggest "regime values" as the most appropriate method for integrating the
study of ethics into a public administration curriculum. At the outset, let
us clarify the word "regime." As indicated earlier, it is not used here in
the journalistic sense of the "Nixon regime," the "Carter regime," and so
forth. Rather it is proposed as the most appropriate English word to suggest what Aristotle meant by "polity."[33] More specifically, "regime
values" refer to the values of that political entity that was brought into
being by the ratification of the Constitution that created the present
American republic.

The method of regime values rests on three considerations:

1. That ethical norms should be derived from the salient values of the
   regime
2. That these values are normative for bureaucrats because they have
   taken an oath to uphold the regime[34]
3. That these values can be discovered in the public law of the regime[35]

The remainder of this chapter will be devoted to explaining and justifying these statements. The explanation and justification can be presented
most coherently by recalling that the term "regime values" describes a
method that addresses the ethical dimensions of professional education for
bureaucrats. Let us begin by analyzing the implications of the three words
"professional," "bureaucrats," and "education."

Professional Education for Bureaucrats

Professional

If "professional" education means anything at all, it implies a narrower and more focused academic enterprise than education in general.
Schools of law, for example, are not trade schools, but neither are they
liberal arts colleges. The same can be said of schools of medicine,
divinity, architecture, engineering, and so forth. These institutions, in
conferring professional expertise and credentials, necessarily exact a
price. The price is the relative narrowness of the curriculum. The narrowness will be reflected throughout the curriculum—including the treatment of professional ethics if it is taken seriously as part of the professional preparation of the student. In narrowing the curriculum to suit the
goals of a professional school, certain questions that may be of themselves
far more important than anything in the curriculum are nevertheless quite
properly ignored. For example, a course in medical ethics would probably devote very little time to discussing whether life is better than nonlife
or sickness better than health.[36] From an absolute point of view these
questions are undoubtedly more important than the medical ethics of
eugenics or practicing "defensive medicine" to avoid malpractice suits.
However, one could hardly blame medical students who would prefer to
learn more about ethical problems relating directly to their profession
than about questions that in an absolute sense may be more important to
them as human beings. Nor could one blame professors of medical ethics
who conducted their courses on the presupposition that all their students
believed that health is better than sickness and life better than nonlife. In
a word, professional education necessarily involves a canon of selectivity
appropriate to its peculiar goals even at the expense of ignoring questions
that may be inherently more interesting and important.

For Bureaucrats

Because students of public administration either already hold or aspire
to positions of leadership within the bureaucracy of a particular regime,
the values of that regime are the most likely starting point for their ethical
reflections. This is especially true in countries like our own where
bureaucrats are expected to take an oath to uphold the Constitution. An
oath is an important moral event in the personal history of an individual.
This is especially true in a pluralistic society like the United States where
there are myriad philosophical and religious starting points from which
people derive their ethical norms. Pluralism of this nature makes it
almost impossible to hope for an operational understanding of the public
interest derived from some common metaphysical premise. Despite our

pluralism, however, I think it is safe to assume that most of us would
agree that one should adhere steadfastly to the oaths one has taken.[37]
Because the Constitution of the United States is the preeminent symbol of
our political values, an oath to uphold the Constitution is a commitment to
uphold the values of the regime created by that instrument. Thus the oath
of office provides for bureaucrats the basis of a moral community that our
pluralism would otherwise prevent. It is the moral foundation of ethics for
bureaucrats.[38]

In arguing the normative character of the values of the regime, we
are, of course, avoiding the more important question of the fundamental
justice of the regime itself.[39] Before one asks oneself, "How can I reinforce the values of the regime?" one should first ask, "Is the regime
fundamentally just?" That is, "Can I be a good human being and a good
citizen at the same time?" Although this is the more important question,
it cannot be the focus of the course in ethics unless this course is simply
to collapse into political philosophy. To say the justice of the regime cannot be the focus of the ethics course, however, does not mean the question
is simply ignored. An argument might be made that one should not enter
a career in government unless one is first convinced that the regime is
fundamentally just. Once he or she is so convinced, the public servant
can then investigate the full implications of the values of the regime whose
justice he or she acknowledges.

Unfortunately, however, the moral universe is never this tidy. The
very nature of judging the justice of a regime is an ongoing process rooted
in contingency. Such a judgment cannot be made once and for all unless,
of course, one is willing to acquiesce in the moral abdication symbolized
by "my country right or wrong." Any serious consideration by a bureaucrat of how he or she might further the regime's values will continually
invite higher questions of the moral authenticity of these values, and,
therefore, of the justice of the regime itself. Nevertheless, the justice
of the regime cannot be the focus of the course if it is to retain its identity
as a course in ethics for bureaucrats. It must, however, remain the
backdrop against which the course in ethics examines the less majestic
questions of regime values.

The price, then, that the professional study of ethics for bureaucrats
exacts from the curriculum is that questions of political philosophy ("Is
the regime just?"[40]) must yield to less fundamental questions such as,
"How can I promote the values of the regime?" The method of regime
values eschews metaphysics and addresses the students in the existential
situation in which it finds them—persons who have taken or are about to
take an oath to uphold the values of a particular regime. It admonishes
them that taking such an oath presupposes an acceptance of the fundamental
justice of the regime[41] but does not inquire into how the students arrived
at the conclusion that the regime is just.[42]

Education

Certain consequences flow from the fact that the method of regime values deals with education. As indicated earlier, the word "education" is used in this book in such a way as to include most forms of management training as well. It will be helpful, however, to distinguish between inter- and intraagency training. The former is more closely related to what is attempted in schools of public administration. Academic courses in the schools prepare students for careers in a wide variety of agencies. Similarly, interagency training sessions bring together practitioners with remarkably diverse working experiences. Both of these activities can be contrasted with intraagency training where relatively narrow and specific issues can be examined. As far as the study of ethics is concerned, it is only intraagency training that can afford to be specific, concrete, and directly operational in its objectives. Interagency training and the formal teaching of the schools must necessarily emphasize broad and general principles at the expense of concrete directives pertinent to one or only a few agencies. They should stress values rather than behavior and should aim at inviting reflection rather than providing answers.

Because of the broad and general nature of education, we must shift the direction of the argument we have developed up to this point. Hitherto we defended a relatively narrow focus for a course in ethics for bureaucrats as a consequence of the career orientation of education in public administration. This was the reason for rejecting political philosophy and humanistic psychology as the foundation for a course in ethics. Now we must confess to the practitioner of public administration that the method of regime values is not "practical" in any immediate or operational sense. It is offered as an educational device and as such is necessarily somewhat removed from the "real" world of government.

There are several good reasons why the study of ethics for bureaucrats must not become too practical. We have already discussed the obvious consideration that the student population either already is or soon will be employed in many different agencies. The practical problems they will face are so varied that it would be impossible to discuss them seriously in a way that would be pertinent to all the students. Hence, it seems wise to retreat from the concrete problems in the agencies to the higher ground of regime values that cut across the entire administrative process—for example, "equality" as a salient value of the American regime should be of normative interest to any American administrator.

Secondly, an emphasis on practical ethical problems runs the risk of educating tomorrow's leaders with today's answers. Military academies have often been accused of preparing young officers to fight the last war rather than the next one. The same mistake could be made in the area of ethics. For example, if a course in ethics today tried to "solve" the problems associated with affirmative action, its educational value would be quite questionable. The student who completes the course in ethics with a "position" on affirmative action really has little to show for his or her efforts. For one thing, the student may find that this "position" is utterly unworkable and must be drastically revised (or even abandoned) in the light of what he or she learns at the experiential level after graduation. The student may also find that within a few years of graduation affirmative action is no longer a serious issue. By the time he reaches the middle-management level and begins to have a substantial impact on policy, his "practical" position on affirmative action will be hopelessly passé and he will not have developed the skills in ethical reflection that will enable him to address the new problems of the day. Had the student spent his time in school reflecting on affirmative action as an indicator of the meaning of equality as a regime value, he would be far better prepared to meet the short-term problems of affirmative action and the long-term problems of whatever lies ahead.

To conclude this discussion of professional education for bureaucrats, let us consider a brief example of the kind of ethical behavior we might hope the method of regime values would encourage once the student had begun to advance in his career.

Chester A. Newland is a former director of the Federal Executive Institute (FEI) in Charlottesville, Virginia. The purpose of FEI is to provide intensive, high-level training for federal executives (GS-16 through GS-18). On occasion during Newland's tenure, prominent political figures would be invited to FEI to address the executives on matters of administration policy and management. As the details of such visits were being worked out, the prominent guests would sometimes request accommodations outside the institute. Occasionally, they would ask for reservations at a nearby private club that excluded blacks.

Part of the training program at FEI was intended to ensure that the executives were made sensitive to the needs and feelings of minority groups. If FEI were to arrange accommodations for some of the top officials in government at an all-white club, the institute would undercut part of its own mission.

The problem was delicate. The racial exclusionary policy of the club was, of course, quite legal and an appointed official's choice of where he might want to spend the night was, at least ostensibly, a private matter. FEI was acting merely as a conduit of the VIP's personal choice. Those VIPs unfamiliar with the details of the institute's program—particularly its emphasis on human dignity—might have some difficulty seeing just how the choice of a night's lodging could harm FEI's mission.

Newland's solution was simple but effective. Whenever a visiting VIP asked for accommodations at the segregated club, Newland instructed his staff to reply along the following lines: "Oh, I'm sure the assistant secretary [or whoever] is not aware of the club's racial policies. We wouldn't want to cause him any embarrassment by booking him there." This solved the problem. No one ever replied that he knew perfectly well the club was segregated and wanted to stay there anyway.

This simple narrative illustrates several points developed previously in this book. First, Newland's decision was clearly discretionary; he could have ignored the whole problem. Secondly, the situation confronting Newland involved a _regime_ value, equality, rather than values related to purely personal preferences. Thirdly, the ethical dimensions of the problem were positive rather than negative—that is, in classical terms, the decision involved an opportunity to "do good" rather than the necessity of "avoiding evil." Finally, the decision involved a routine matter of no dramatic significance. The fate of the Republic did not turn on Newland's decision but it was the kind of situation that occurs thousands of times every year through government at all levels. The sheer volume of such decisions made in routine situations influences at least the dominant tone, if not the ultimate fate, of the Republic.

A course in ethics for bureaucrats might well aim at developing in the student above all an ability to recognize the sort of problem Newland recognized and, secondly, an ability to evaluate the discretionary options available for solving the problem in a prudent and effective manner.

Law and Values

In describing the method of regime values above, we stated that the values of a regime could be discovered in its public law and that this was particularly true of the United States. In developing this point we shall comment briefly on American values and then show how the study of Supreme Court opinions offers interpretations of values that are useful for our purposes. Before pursuing this matter further, two caveats are in order.

First, it should be recalled that no question can have an answer that is more precise than its subject matter admits. For example, a question asking the product of four and eight requires far more precision than a question calling for an explanation of the difference between jazz and rock, and both these questions require more precision than a question about the meaning of beauty.

In questions of ethics, classical moral doctrine has always recognized that reasoned judgments by the practical intellect become less certain as they become more specific: "Quanto magis ad propria descenditur, tanto magis invenitur defectus" ("The more we descend to particulars, the more defects we discover").[43] In contemporary terms, it is much easier to make the moral case for racial equality than for "forced" busing.

One who ignores the difference in the degree of precision demanded by different questions invites Procrustean solutions to his or her problems. In constructing an ethic for bureaucrats, it is imperative that differences in degree of precision be kept in mind. Our purpose is to enable the bureaucrat to respond to the values of the American people. It is simply in the nature of things that such a response cannot be rigidly programmed into behavioral categories. Bureaucrats must not become discouraged if reflection on the values of the people in whose name they administer public affairs fails to yield the precise directives of a conflict-of-interest statute.

Secondly, bureaucrats should be cautioned against letting their consideration of American values harden into a rigid political orthodoxy. Reflection on salient values must not be used to justify a witch hunt for those who do not share these values. The point developed in the three previous paragraphs should safeguard against a quest for values degenerating into a witch hunt. One need only recall the imprecise nature of the questions involving American values to vanquish the temptation to become an arbiter of political orthodoxy. It should be clear that a bureaucrat's reflection on American values will not and should not lead to a dogmatic assertion that "the following are the values of the American people and this is what they must mean for all bureaucrats." Our concern is not to persuade bureaucrats that they should act in a certain way in the light of certain values. On the contrary, it is to provide them with a method for discovering these values themselves and putting them into practice as they see fit.

The starting point of such a method is the simple assertion that the American people have some values. I include earlier generations as well as our contemporaries within the term "American people." By "values" I mean beliefs, passions, and principles that have been held for several generations by the overwhelming majority of the American people.[44] A good example of what I mean appears in the final paragraph of the concurring opinion of Justice Frankfurter in Cooper v. Aaron. The case involved the painful experience surrounding the racial integration of Little Rock's Central High School in the mid-1950s. The Supreme Court upheld a federal court order that had been defied by Governor Faubus. In closing his concurring opinion, Frankfurter said:

> Lincoln's appeal to "the better angels of our nature" failed to avert a fratricidal war. But the compassionate wisdom of Lincoln's First and Second Inaugurals bequeathed to the Union, cemented with blood, a moral heritage sure to find specific ways and means to surmount difficulties that may appear to be insurmountable.[45]

The "moral heritage" to which Frankfurter refers is an example of what I mean by a value. It is vague and imprecise but by no means meaningless unless one chooses to identify the meaningful with the empirically verifiable. In citing the moral heritage bequeathed by Lincoln's inaugural addresses, Frankfurter offers the nation a standard to which it can rally in a period of unrest.

The method of regime values involves two tasks. The first is to identify American values and the second is to look for meaningful statements about them. The first of these tasks is much easier than the second, provided one is content to identify just some values rather than attempting to provide an exhaustive list. Indications of the values of the American people can be found in a wide variety of sources. Among these are the writings and speeches of outstanding political leaders, major Supreme Court opinions, scholarly interpretations of American history, literary works of all kinds, religious tracts and sermons, and even the rhetoric of standard Fourth of July oratory. For example, it would seem that one could safely assert that freedom, property, and equality are values of the American people.[46] To be sure, these three are not the values of the American people but are simply among our many values. To safeguard their widespread appeal, they must be presented without any gloss on their meaning. The equality affirmed in the Declaration of Independence may be quite different from the equality underlying the equal protection clause of the Fourteenth Amendment, but we shall get ahead of ourselves if we make such distinctions now. For the present it is sufficient to offer freedom, property, and equality as examples of American values. Most Americans would have little trouble in saying they "believe" in such values as long as they were not pressed to say just what these values mean.

Far more difficult than simply naming some values of Americans is the task of infusing them with meaning suitable for ethical reflection. A good starting point might be to dwell on the fact that values like freedom, property, and equality command almost universal allegiance among our people. Perhaps this might be the beginning of a moral consensus. One might object, however, that splendid generalities like freedom, property, and equality are universally accepted only because they mean nothing. I do not think such an objection is sound. There is a difference between a word or a symbol that is vague and one that is meaningless. For example, the three symbols of the French Revolution, liberté, fraternité, égalité, are vague and indeterminate. They have been invoked by French citizens of remarkably diverse political persuasions for nearly two centuries. For many years these symbols appeared on French coins, but during the years of Marshall Pétain's Vichy regime the customary symbols disappeared from the coins and were replaced with travail, famille, patrie. These symbols, like the ones they replaced, were vague but they were not meaningless. They said something about the character of the Vichy regime. To be sure, a French citizen could be quite devoted to work, family, and fatherland without being a Nazi sympathizer. Nevertheless, the change in symbols had some significance. It represented an attempt by the Nazis to signal the arrival of a new order in France with a consequent change in traditional French values.

When Americans invoke symbols such as freedom, property, and equality—both in serious and trivial discourse—there is some minimal content to which these symbols point, and this content embodies some of the values of our society. These values may not be the highest values to which a regime might aspire, but nevertheless they carry some normative weight for American bureaucrats precisely because they are values of the American people. These values are normative because they are regime values, and bureaucrats have taken an oath to uphold the Constitution that brought this regime into being and continues to state symbolically its spirit and meaning.

The search for meaningful statements about our values is a more difficult task than simply naming them. At this point the consensus that would support certain values in a general, abstract way begins to fall apart. For example, some of those who would agree that equality is a fundamental value of the American people might not agree that this value should govern the relationships between the sexes as well as among the races and economic classes. Or, for some, equality might mean no more than equality of opportunity, while others would insist it means equality of income as well. Property might mean "big business" to one person, a modest dwelling to another, and a right to gainful employment to a third. Freedom could mean freedom for a woman to have an abortion on demand or Exxon's freedom from government regulation.

Thus, as the general values of the regime become sufficiently specific to have a practical effect on bureaucratic decision making, bureaucrats will have to decide which of many interpretations they will take seriously in their efforts to respond to the values of the American people. This is a very difficult undertaking. Eminent scholars after years of research reach very different conclusions on the "meaning of America."[47] This would seem to suggest that there is no one interpretation of the American tradition so compelling as to win the assent of all thoughtful persons. Further, we must recall that we are dealing with bureaucrats and not academicians. Bureaucrats are busy men and women whose energy and attention are focused primarily on the practical tasks of daily governmental routine. It would be unrealistic to expect them to interrupt their careers to undertake a profound study of American institutions and values. Students preparing themselves for careers in government could do more along these lines, but even for them other professional considerations will almost surely preclude a solid mastery of the American tradition.[48]

Supreme Court Opinions

In the pages that follow we shall outline a method for encouraging bureaucrats to reflect on American values in a disciplined and systematic manner that will invite them to develop their own understanding of what these values mean. This method does not promise instant wisdom nor is it offered as a substitute for serious scholarly investigation of the American tradition. It is put forth, however, as a practical teaching device to enable busy bureaucrats to be more thoughtfully concerned with the values of the people they serve.

Our method involves the study of major Supreme Court decisions on such salient values as freedom, property, and equality. As a keynote to this approach, let us consider Ralph Lerner's characterization of the Supreme Court as "republican schoolmaster."[49]

In developing this image, Lerner shows how the early Supreme Court justices used their circuit-riding responsibilities to instruct the citizenry on the character of the new Republic. This was done primarily through the charge to the grand jury with which the presiding judge formally opened the proceedings of a circuit court session. These charges covered a wide range of subjects far beyond technical questions of the law and were given substantial press coverage. While at times the charges were extremely partisan and heavy-handed, at other times they represented a serious effort to instruct the public on the meaning of "republican virtue."[50] Of these serious efforts Lerner remarks: "Then, as now, the judges had the option of teaching by cases. By these decisions—and especially through a coherent explanation of the grounds of their decisions—the judges could . . . transfer to the minds of the citizens the modes of thought lying behind legal language and the notions of right fundamental to the regime."[51] It is this function of the judicial process that we shall focus upon—the relationship between the reasons the Court gives for its decisions and "the notions of right fundamental to the regime."[52] We do so in the hope of bringing about what Alexander Bickel has said of the stately language of due process and equal protection—"They breed attitudes, they tend toward a mind-set, they influence future thought and action."[53]

There are four characteristics of Supreme Court decisions that make them particularly suitable for ethical reflection on the values of the American people. Supreme Court decisions are (1) institutional, (2) dialectic, (3) concrete, and (4) pertinent. Let us examine each of these characteristics.

Institutional

In studying the values of the American people, the bureaucrat must distinguish between stable principles and passing whims. A "value" in the life of a person as well as a nation suggests a pattern of attitudes or behavior that recurs with some frequency. An attitude or a passion or a principle must have a history—either personal or societal—before it becomes a "value." It is this need for historical continuity that makes the opinions of Supreme Court justices particularly useful "value indicators"

when compared with the writings and speeches of most prominent political
leaders and philosophers. Every individual is, of course, somewhat
limited by the vision of his or her time in history. This is no less true of
Supreme Court justices than of political leaders and philosophers. But
because the justice is part of an institution, his time-bound reasoning can
be balanced, nuanced, and therefore enriched by the reasoning of other
justices writing at other points in our history. Thus, Chief Justice Taney
did not say all there is to say about racial equality in Dred Scott; nor did
Chief Justice Warren in Brown v. Board of Education. Somewhere
between the opinions of these two men are the majority and dissenting
opinions of the justices who first addressed the problem of separate but
equal facilities for blacks and whites. In recent years the Court has manifested its attitude on equality in decisions dealing with public accommodations, poll taxes, housing, and public employment. This network of
jurisprudence offers the bureaucrat insights into the values of our society
that are always rich and complex, frequently confusing and occasionally
contradictory. It is the bureaucrats themselves who must decide just how
the moral values (and nonvalues) underlying the Court's opinions will affect
their decision making. By looking at what the Court has said at other
points in history, bureaucrats avoid becoming imprisoned by their own
historical circumstances.

Finally, the institutional character of the Court's decisions suggests
a parallel between the development of a society's public morals and an
individual's personal morality that is useful for our purposes. In interpreting such majestic generalities as "due process of law" and "equal
protection," the Court must constantly remain in touch with its past. The
nature of the judicial process requires that the Court must at least consider the original meaning of the phrases as well as its own precedents.
This ensures some kind of continuity with the past. To be sure, the Court
has shown remarkable skill in distinguishing precedents, but this is
because the focus of the Court is on current problems that cannot always
be settled equitably on the basis of precedent alone. The nature of the
judicial process involves tension between past and present. Courts frequently solve current issues with a creative interpretation of a familiar
principle. This enables a political society to address new problems without sacrificing the stability and continuity that come from invoking
familiar principles. In a word, the Court is a contemporary institution in
dialogue with its past.

A similar process often characterizes the moral development of
individuals. The principles learned in childhood from parents, teachers,
and churches may never be abandoned, but they may be constantly reinterpreted to meet changing times and the demands of adulthood. For
example, a child who has been taught to love her country may manifest
fidelity to that principle by approaching the daily salute to the flag
seriously even though her friends may be giggling and playing. As an

adult the same person may show her devotion to the maxim "love your country" by participating in a civil rights march. The familiar principle, "love your country," is now being applied in a more sophisticated manner that an earlier generation might neither understand nor approve. The individual, however, has maintained her personal moral continuity along with her integrity by remaining in dialogue with her past. An individual, of course, can do this only for the limited years of a lifetime, but an institution can do this sort of thing for centuries. This is one of several reasons for urging bureaucrats to look to Supreme Court decisions for meaningful statements of American values.

Dialectic

The presence of concurring and dissenting opinions in Supreme Court decisions makes the work of the Court dialectic. Such opinions offer the bureaucrat the opportunity to follow a public debate in a highly structured and formal context. Because constitutional cases usually turn to the interpretation of such vague phrases as "due process of law," "equal protection," or "commerce among the states," these public debates necessarily point to higher questions on the nature of the common good. When the Court must decide the constitutionality of a minimum wage law, a censorship ordinance, a public accommodations act, or an antimiscegenation statute, the justices nearly always include in their arguments some of their own views on the nature of a just American society. Because many Supreme Court justices have been men of considerable experience and talent, such argumentation can be quite instructive for the bureaucrat seeking enlightenment on the meaning of American values.

Concurring and dissenting opinions offer bureaucrats alternative ways of looking at the same problem and thereby help them avoid the danger of accepting dogmatic assertions uncritically. A vigorous dissent can at times force the majority of the Court to provide better reasons for its decision than it would have offered if there had been no challenge. The reasons may not always be altogether compelling, but public confidence should be increased, not diminished, when serious argument replaces bland assertion.

An interesting illustration of this point can be seen in the concurring opinion of Justice Goldberg in Bell v. Maryland.[54] The case involved a trespass conviction of several black students who had remained in a restaurant after the proprietor had told them to leave because he did not serve blacks. The incident took place in 1962 when neither Maryland nor the United States had a public accommodations act. The case was complicated by the fact that after the trespass conviction and before the appeal to the Supreme Court, Maryland passed a law prohibiting racial discrimination in restaurants. The Supreme Court overturned the conviction with Justice Brennan writing the opinion of the Court. Justices Goldberg and

Douglas wrote separate concurring opinions and Justice Black filed a vigorous dissent. Goldberg's opinion was a clear and quite controversial
argument that the Fourteenth Amendment alone prohibits racial discrimination in public accommodations and that, therefore, the trespass conviction
with or without a Maryland public accommodations act, could not be upheld.
This argument was supplemented by Douglas's opinion, considerably modified by Brennan's, and rejected outright in Black's dissent. Shortly before
Bell v. Maryland was decided, Goldberg had given an address entitled
"Equality and Governmental Action" at the New York University Law
School.[55] Here he had a "bully pulpit" where he could proclaim his controversial views on equality without subjecting himself to the "peer
evaluation" he received when he offered similar views on the bench. In the
law school address, dogmatic assertions on equality passed unchallenged
whereas the same views were closely examined by Goldberg's colleagues
in Bell v. Maryland. The bureaucrat looking for the meaning of American
values would find a much richer learning experience in reading Bell v.
Maryland than in attending the New York University lecture.

Concrete

For our purposes one of the most useful aspects of Supreme Court
decisions is that they are concrete. A justice may soar to the highest
abstractions in discussing such lofty generalities as due process of law,
but eventually he must decide whether the confession was admissible or the
book obscene or the statement libelous. He is disciplined by reality in a
way that the philosopher is not. He must apply immediately to a concrete
situation whatever wisdom he may possess. This aspect of the Court's
work should win warm approval from bureaucrats who are constantly
called upon to perform similar tasks themselves. Not only do the Court's
opinions offer reflection on American values, but they show what these
values mean in practice as well. This model of decision making should be
most helpful to bureaucrats. As practical persons, they might be bored
by discourse that is purely theoretical, but the Court's opinions provide an
excellent illustration of how theory and practice combine to generate public
policy.

Another instructive aspect of the concrete element in the Court's
decisions is that value-oriented questions are usually not legal in a
merely technical sense. That is, the justices seldom decide such
questions by mechanically applying a principle learned long ago in law
school. Value-oriented questions usually involve the use of considerable
discretion by the Court. As Justice Brennan remarked in Wyman v.
James: "This Court has occasionally pushed beyond established contours
to protect the vulnerable and to further basic human values."[56]

Bureaucrats, like judges, enjoy considerable discretion. Take, for
example, the familiar practice of plea-bargaining in which law enforcement

agencies enjoy tremendous power to give or withhold concessions from persons accused of crimes. There are (perhaps unfortunately) few precise rules instructing prosecutors on how they are to conduct themselves in plea bargaining. Here would be an area in which bureaucrats in law enforcement agencies might "occasionally push beyond established contours to protect the vulnerable and to further basic human values." It would be wise, of course, to do this, as Brennan suggests, only "occasionally." Naturally, such a procedure is fraught with danger for all concerned, but a careful reading of Supreme Court decisions might give the bureaucrat some ideas on how to "push beyond established contours" in a responsible manner.

Pertinent

Supreme Court opinions are pertinent in the sense that they raise questions that are useful for reflection on fundamental values. So significant has the role of the Court been in this area that one eminent constitutional historian has commented on the "fact that the study of American constitutional law casts its followers, willy-nilly, in the role of political theorists."[57] De Toqueville remarked long ago on the tendency of Americans to transform major political problems into legal issues. The accuracy of his remark has been generously confirmed by the fact that such crucial issues as slavery in the territories, a federal tax on income, and government regulation of industry have all found their way into the courts. In recent years antiwar activists never tired of initiating litigation in the hope that the courts would find the Vietnam War or the draft unconstitutional. The Watergate scandals offer further confirmation of de Tocqueville's insight. The unflagging fascination with such questions as whether a president must surrender tapes and documents to a Senate Committee and/or a grand jury, whether he can be indicted while still in office, whether he can claim executive privilege against a congressional committee considering his own impeachment, and what is the meaning of high crimes and misdemeanors—all these questions reveal the American tendency de Tocqueville noticed so long ago.

There can be no doubt that the questions raised by the Watergate scandals had a profound relation to the values of the American people. The revelations were literally front-page news for two years. Such sustained interest can be explained only by a widespread awareness that serious questions of public morality were at stake—questions that reflect and affect our values as a political society. The fact that nearly all parties involved in the controversy turned almost instinctively to the courts is eloquent testimony to our confidence in the courts as arbiters of values. The fact that Americans have followed this pattern so often in their history is one reason why Supreme Court opinions are especially, and perhaps even

uniquely, suitable for the bureaucrat seeking enlightenment on the meaning
of American values.

The specific cases the bureaucrat might study for insight into
American values are many and varied. Some cases, however, would
probably appear on anyone's list—for example, Dred Scott[58] and Brown v.
Board of Education[59] on equality, Dartmouth College[60] and Home Building
and Loan Association v. Blaisdell[61] on property, and the two flag salute
cases of the early 1940s on freedom.[62] In addition to studying individual
cases, the bureaucrat might profit from studying "clusters" of cases dealing with the same problems.

For example, in the early 1960s the Court was faced with a series of
cases involving trespass convictions of black demonstrators for "sitting
in" at places of business commonly considered private property. These
convictions put the competing values of equality and property on a collision
course. The Court, aware of its "teaching" role in the regime, could not
uphold the convictions without seeming to give its approval to the racism
that prompted the exclusion of the blacks. However, in its efforts to avoid
the appearance of approving of racism, the Court could not afford to
ignore trespass laws either.

To get out of this dilemma, the Court developed a strategy of looking
for connections between the proprietors' efforts to exclude blacks and the
public policy of the state in which the offense occurred. Once such a connection was established, the case ceased to involve trespass and became
instead a question of state-supported racial segregation, which is, of
course, clearly unconstitutional. The search for state action involved
some very creative jurisprudence on the part of the Court. Thus the discriminatory policies of a Delaware restaurant were found to involve state
action because the establishment rented its quarters in a building owned by
an agency of the state.[63] In another case racial segregation in a restaurant was found to be carried on with such enthusiastic encouragement from
city officials as to amount to state action.[64] Eventually, Congress came
to the Court's rescue by passing the Civil Rights Act of 1964, which forbade racial discrimination in all public accommodations. This act
furthered equality without disturbing the law of trespass. In the years
prior to the act of Congress, however, the Court gave an instructive
example of how to manipulate technical questions in a way that would
encourage movements of high moral purpose without undermining traditional values. As Alexander Bickel once remarked of the Supreme Court:
"It was doing what it does best; it was seeking some procedural accommodation to avoid the clash of ultimates."[65]

Other "clusters" of cases are available to study the Court's position
on changing values in our society. The long list of decisions on church-
state relations handed down by the Court over the past quarter century
offers a fine study of the competing values of contemporary secularization

and the traditional religious heritage of our society. The same might be said of the Court's efforts to interpret the meaning of obscenity. The opinions in this area present some carefully reasoned arguments over the conflict between traditional and contemporary sexual mores. One might add that in both these areas the Court's success in winning popular support for its position has been quite modest. This, however, is irrelevant for our purposes as long as the bureaucrat studies the concurring and dissenting opinions as well as the majority opinions. It is the public argument among the justices rather than the actual holding of the Court that will be most useful for reflecting on values.

Another interesting "cluster" of cases surrounds the idea of the "new property" suggested by Charles Reich.[66] In the past five or six years the Supreme Court has cautiously extended the traditional concept of property into such new areas as welfare benefits,[67] garnisheed wages,[68] contract sales,[69] and public employment.[70] The upshot of this development has been to redeem the reactionary connotations of property by highlighting certain redistributive implications in giving legal protection to the property interests of the poor. In this way the Court is once again making a connection between liberty and property as it has at other times in our history, but this time the thrust is egalitarian and redistributive rather than oligarchic and conservative.[71] These recent cases might be instructively compared with some of the famous cases on the contract clause settled by the Marshall Court. One might argue that both the Marshall Court and the present Supreme Court see property rights as "functional" values within the regime—that is, values that serve higher political ends. For Marshall the higher end was to strengthen the nationalistic tendencies of the new Republic. For the present Court the higher end might be to stabilize existing institutions through a more equitable distribution of wealth.

CONCLUSION

In studying Supreme Court opinions, bureaucrats will be exposed to·many conflicting interpretations of American values. Wherever possible, they will look for some consistency in the values of the American people, and the judicial process with its concern for precedent will be of some help. Frequently, however, mutually exclusive values will arise within the tradition, and bureaucrats will have to choose the position they find most appealing and persuasive. There should be no embarrassment if two bureaucrats choose interpretations of American values that are mutually exclusive. The purpose of regime values is not to make all bureaucrats march in lock-step. There is no one "authoritative" interpretation of the American experience that all bureaucrats must adopt. What is important is that they accept the moral obligation to put themselves in touch with the values of the American people through the values of the American regime.

Just how those values are interpreted is a decision only the bureaucrat can make.

One might object that all this is terribly subjective—that in the final analysis bureaucrats respond to those values to which they choose to respond. [72] This is true, but the subjective character of the method proposed here is intended to respect the radical responsibility of bureaucrats to their God, their conscience, their philosophy, or to whatever forms the basis of their moral life as persons. Bureaucrats, like all other human beings, must be faithful to their deepest beliefs if they are to preserve their moral integrity. Hopefully, regime values will enable bureaucrats to refine the content of their deepest political beliefs. In upholding the duty of bureaucrats to "follow their consciences," we are not suggesting that they simply "do their own thing." It is unfortunate that these two phrases have become confused in popular speech. We can hope that our method might help to provide bureaucrats with informed consciences that would lead them into dialogue with the political society they serve and that they would ponder its values seriously. After submitting themselves to this discipline, they would be free to follow their consciences.

The subjective element of this method means we must—at least to some degree—trust the bureaucrats who govern us. We must trust them to take our values seriously and to try to let these values have some influence upon the decisions they make. We want to be governed by persons responsive to our values, but we also want to be governed by persons who are imaginative, creative, and free. There is an obvious (and healthy) tension between these desires. It would not be wise or desirable to distort the principle of responsibility in government into meaning that we simply present our bureaucrats with a checklist of acceptable American values they must swear to uphold. Indeed, to do so would itself be contrary to our fundamental values. The best we can do—at least in schools of public administration—is to encourage bureaucrats to reflect upon our values, suggest a method for doing so, and then trust them to exercise their discretion along lines compatible with those values.

It is ironic that we should close this discussion with the observation that bureaucrats must be trusted. Trust would seem to be more characteristic of aristocratic politics than of democratic politics. And yet the starting point of our argument was an appeal to democratic politics—that the discretionary power of the bureaucracy in a democratic regime demands some kind of responsibility to the people. Regime values offers a method of encouraging responsibility that supplements our traditional reliance upon elections, appellate procedures, judicial review, and the "representative" character of bureaucracy in a demographic sense. It aims at developing an understanding of responsibility that includes an informed patriotism and sound judgment on the part of public administrators. To call upon aristocratic virtues to reinforce democratic values is paradoxical only if one ignores the rich complexity of the mixed

character of the American regime itself.[73] At its best the American
bureaucracy is, as Herbert Storing has observed, "a kind of democratic
approximation to a hereditary aristocracy whose members are conscious
of representing an institution of government which extends into the past and
into the future beyond the life of any individual member."[74] The method of
regime values aims at informing this historic and futuristic consciousness
of the bureaucracy with an attitude toward American values that will
encourage bureaucrats to address contemporary problems with bold and
creative applications of the traditional values of the people in whose name
they govern.

NOTES

1. Frank Marini, ed., Toward a New Public Administration (Scranton:
   Chandler, 1971); William G. Scott and David K. Hart, "The Moral
   Nature of Man in Organization," Academy of Management Journal 14
   (June 1971): 241-255. The interest in normative questions in public
   administration is not, of course, confined to authors associated with
   the "new public administration." For example, see Wayne A. R. Leys,
   Ethics for Policy Decisions: The Art of Asking Deliberative Questions
   (New York: Prentice-Hall, 1952) and "Ethics in American Business
   and Government," Annals of the American Academy of Political and
   Social Sciences, July 1961, pp. 34-44; Herbert J. Storing, "Political
   Parties and the Bureaucracy," in Political Parties, U.S.A., ed.
   Robert A. Goldwyn (Chicago: Rand-McNally, 1964); Lewis C.
   Mainzer, "Injustice and Bureaucracy," Yale Review 51 (Summer 1962):
   559-573 and "Honor in Bureaucratic Life," Review of Politics 26
   (January 1964); Herbert J. Spiro, Responsibility in Government:
   Theory and Practice (New York: Van Nostrand, 1969); George A.
   Graham, Morality in American Politics (New York: Random House,
   1952); and Stephen K. Bailey, "Ethics and the Public Service," Public
   Administration Review 24 (December 1964): 234-243.
2. Paul H. Appleby, Morality and Administration in Democratic Government (Baton Rouge: Louisiana State University Press, 1952).
3. Ibid., p. 56.
4. Guidelines and Standards for Professional Masters' Degree Programs
   in Public Affairs/Public Administration (Washington, D.C.: National
   Association of Schools of Public Affairs and Administration, 1974).
5. An important issue discussed by educators for the public service is
   whether the curriculum should have a course in ethics or whether
   each course already in the curriculum should have a module on ethics.
   A persuasive argument can be made for the modular approach. If well
   executed, it would be a powerful recognition of the pervasive character
   of ethical issues vis-à-vis public management. Ethics, unlike public

finance or personnel management, is not simply a part of public management. It pervades the entire process because ethical issues necessarily arise in the areas of personnel, finance, project management, planning, and so forth. To have the ethical dimensions of each of these areas highlighted in the pertinent courses would be an attractively symbolic way for a faculty to announce its recognition of the moral nature of its entire enterprise—that is, the connection between the education of the public servant and the common good.

There are practical problems with this approach, however. First, some teachers by training or temperament may feel uncomfortable in discussing these issues. This may be especially true of those deeply committed to empirical methods of inquiry. They may look upon values as being of great human significance but not as appropriate objects of "knowledge." Consequently, they might resent any suggestions that they revise their syllabi to include questions of ethics and values. Or, conversely, they might welcome the opportunity to hold forth on ethical issues but then do so in a heavy-handed, preaching manner that would be quite out of tune with the rest of a course, which might otherwise be quite rigorous in its method and cautious in its conclusions. This could have a disastrous effect on the students. It would seem wise to charge with the responsibility of teaching ethics only those instructors who are convinced on professional grounds that ethics and values are worthy subjects of academic inquiry.

The second practical problem with trying to incorporate ethical issues into all the courses in the curriculum is that responsibility becomes too diffuse. It is almost axiomatic that tasks assigned to everyone are completed by no one.

For these practical reasons it may often be best to sacrifice the symbolic value of the modular approach in favor of clearly designated courses while urging other instructors to address value-laden issues as their subject matter dictates.

6. Ethics and Conduct: A Series of Workshop Exercises (Cranford, N.J.: Didactic Systems, Inc., 1976).

7. For another example of misapplied zeal to quantify, see W.J. Reddin's Effective Management by Objectives (New York: McGraw-Hill, 1970). On p. 60 Reddin discusses the efforts of a physical education director to draw up his "effectiveness areas." On his first attempt one of his effectiveness areas was "character building." Reddin is pleased to report that on his second try the director dropped character building entirely because he had "no practical measuring device" for it. This is a gross example of "the triumph of technique over substance." Reddin's mindless passion to measure and quantify could lead managers into moral disasters. Reddin's approach might be contrasted with Peter Drucker's sensible flexibility to show that nonquantifiable issues of values have a legitimate place in MBO.

8. Marini, Toward a New Public Administration, p. 359.

9. Ibid., pp. 309-331.

10. Further light is shed on the origin of the term in "new public administration" literature in Marini's introductory essay in Toward a New
Public Administration, p. 15.

11. H. George Frederickson, "Introductory Comments," Public Administration Review 34 (January-February 1974): 1.

12. David K. Hart, "Social Equity, Justice, and the Equitable Administrator," pp. 3-11.

13. Michael M. Harmon, "Social Equity and Organizational Man: Motivation and Organizational Democracy," pp. 11-18.

14. Eugene B. McGregor, "Social Equity and the Public Service,"
pp. 18-29.

15. Stephen R. Chitwood, "Social Equity and Social Service Productivity,"
pp. 29-35.

16. David O. Porter and Teddie W. Porter, "Social Equity and Fiscal
Federalism," pp. 36-43.

17. Orion White and Bruce L. Gates, "Statistical Theory and Equity in the
Delivery of Social Services," pp. 43-51

18. Larry Kirkhart, "Toward a Theory of Public Administration" in
Toward a New Public Administration, ed. Marini, pp. 127-164.

19. Frederick C. Thayer, An End to Hierarchy! An End to Competition!
(New York: Franklin Watts, 1973), pp. 28-33.

20. I am very grateful to Michael Harmon for his generosity in letting me
examine his work on the "proactive" administrator in draft form. His
application of Kohlberg's stages of moral growth to public administration will be a significant contribution to the literature. See William G.
Scott and David K. Hart, "The Moral Nature of Man in Organization"
and "Administrative Crisis: The Neglect of Metaphysical Specula-
tion," Public Administration Review 33 (September-October 1973):
415-422.

21. Hart, "Social Equity, Justice and the Equitable Administrator," p. 10.

22. For example, see "Symposium: John Rawls's A Theory of Justice,"
University of Chicago Law Review 40, pp. 486-555. Ronald Dworkin's
contribution to the symposium, "The Original Position," is especially
persuasive. See also, "Justice: A Spectrum of Responses to John
Rawls's Theory," The American Political Science Review 69 (June
1975): 588-674. Allan Bloom's attack on Rawls (pp. 648-662) is particularly pertinent. If, as Bloom argues, Rawls is an apologist for a
liberal democratic regime, his work would be particularly inappropriate as the foundation for a course in ethics for bureaucrats in such
a regime. There would be a real danger that the unsophisticated student would uncritically accept as abiding principle that which is merely
congruent with contemporary moral sentiment. This might be good
indoctrination, but it would be disastrous education.

23. Questions of this nature could, of course, simply be finessed if one were willing to take only the conclusions (help the disadvantaged) of Rawls's argument and either ignore or uncritically accept its foundations. Such a strategy might indoctrinate some administrators with the values of "social equity" but it would not be worthy of the efforts of an educator and would involve a gross betrayal of the "philosophic tradition" to which Hart appeals. Conclusions without supporting arguments are simply slogans. We might as well say "social equity" means "all power to the people" and be done with it.

24. For example, in their article, "The Moral Nature of Man in Organizations," Scott and Hart suggest certain parallels between the anthropologies of Hobbes and Taylor, Locke and Mayo, and McGregor and Rousseau. Although the article is fascinating, I would object that the authors exaggerate the differences between Hobbes and Locke. I would also question their interpretation of Locke's Second Treatise in the relation between liberty and property. I am not sure my criticisms are correct, but I think they would have to be investigated before making applications to current administrative problems.

25. This same criticism applies to Wayne Leys's Ethics for Policy Decisions. Leys's book is an excellent example of an effort to join the worlds of philosophy and praxis, but I wonder if students without a generous background in philosophy have benefited from this book. A more recent effort to apply normative philosophical arguments to public management appears in Michael Harmon's insightful essay "Social Equity and Organizational Man: Motivation and Organizational Democracy" (see notes 11 and 13 above), where the author presents a careful argument based on Rawls for organizational democracy within governmental agencies. In reviewing the literature on participative management and organizational democracy, Harmon finds a dominant utilitarian theme that he challenges on the basis of the absolute principles set forth by Rawls. Harmon has no quarrel with the outcome of the utilitarian argument; he is quite prepared to admit that organizational democracy "works"—that it can be defended on pragmatic grounds. His point, however, is that a principled argument rests on a more solid foundation that is not vulnerable to the vagaries of empirical evidence. As Harmon puts it: "Although most of the evidence reported by Likert and others suggests that democratic (or participative) management and high productivity are positively associated, evidence which consistently demonstrated the reverse could, for the utilitarian, justify authoritarianism as an appropriate managerial style" (p. 15). This could not happen to the principled argument based on Rawls. Again quoting Harmon: "Rawls' position suggests that empirical evidence about the effect of organizational democracy on productivity, whatever it might demonstrate, is beside the point insofar as it is offered in support of one approach to

management or another. Rawls' theory shifts the basis of the argument from empirical to normative grounds and asserts that the
principles of equal liberty and open positions necessarily dictate a
normative commitment to internal organizational democracy and
participative management" (pp. 16-17).

Harmon's argument, though a refreshing departure from the pragmatic tone that dominates most personnel literature, raises serious
questions about the accuracy of his interpretation of Rawls. It is true
that "equal liberty" is an absolute principle in Rawls's analysis but it
is an absolute as an output of a political system—that is, it is an
absolute requirement of public policy. It is not an absolute for intraorganizational structures. The focus of Rawls's analysis is the
constitutive principles of the regime especially as embedded in its
fundamental law. A Theory of Justice is a treatise in political
philosophy not organizational theory. Harmon, of course, is perfectly
justified in applying the spirit of Rawls's analysis to spheres outside
those touched upon by Rawls himself. To this extent, Harmon's
article is a significant and creative contribution to the literature on
participative management and organizational democracy. He errs,
however, in applying the absolute principles Rawls demands of the just
regime to the internal organization of agencies within the regime. For
if Rawls were shown on empirical grounds that a heavy-handed, authoritarian style of management were the only way to secure the
absolutely essential civil liberties of all citizens (including the down-
trodden bureaucrats in their capacity as citizens), his own argument
would compel him to acquiesce. To be sure, it is not very likely that
such an argument would ever be supported on empirical grounds.
Heavy-handed, authoritarian bureaucrats have a poor track record as
champions of civil liberties. The point, however, is that as long as
this remains a possibility, management styles based on Rawls are as
vulnerable to empirical findings as those based on the most unabashed
utilitarians. This is not because Rawls is ultimately a utilitarian.
By no means! Harmon is correct in emphasizing the absolutist character of Rawls's position and contrasting it with the pragmatism of the
utilitarians. His error lies in transferring the locus of Rawls's
absolutism from the character of the regime to intraorganizational
life. As far as the latter is concerned, Rawls must be pragmatic
precisely because of the absolutism he espouses for the just regime.
Without basic civil liberties (equal liberty of speech, assembly, conscience, and so on) the regime, for Rawls, is unjust. All other
considerations must yield to protecting this first principle and if
(albeit unlikely) an authoritarian management style was required to do
this, the logic of Rawls's argument would dictate compliance.

The purpose of this lengthy note is to illustrate the main problem
with applying philosophical principles directly to questions of public

management. The problem is that the interesting issues are joined at the philosophical level rather than at the level of management. I am sure Michael Harmon could offer an able rejoinder to my criticism, but to do so he would have to defend his interpretation of Rawls. This would move the discussion "upward" toward philosophy and away from public management. The application of Rawlsian principles to public management would be rather mechanical and automatic once we had settled our disagreement over just what those principles are. It is the latter that is the more inviting and interesting question, but this does not mean it is necessarily the more appropriate question within the context of an ethics course in a public administration curriculum.

26. Marini, Toward a New Public Administration, p. 350.

27. Peter L. Berger and Thomas Luckmann, The Social Construction of Reality: A Treatise in the Sociology of Knowledge (New York: Doubleday, 1966), chap. 2.

28. This has been true of political science traditionally at least until the "behavioral revolution." There is an obvious tension between a behavioral methodology and an acknowledgment of the significance of the formal distinction of public from private.

29. Two recent books in the public administration field that reject the public-private distinction are Fred Thayer's An End to Hierarchy! An End to Competition! and Harlan Cleveland's The Future Executive (New York: Harper & Row, 1972). The best-known contemporary defense of this distinction is Sheldon Wolin, Politics and Vision (Boston: Little, Brown, 1960), chap. 2. See also Robert Biller's insightful essay, "Adaptation Capacity and Organizational Development," in Toward a New Public Administration, ed. Marini, pp. 93-120. Biller does not reject the distinction of public from private, but he argues that it should not be identified with the distinction between governmental and nongovernmental.

30. I see no need to get into the question of collective guilt here.

31. Jacques Maritain, Man and the State (Chicago: University of Chicago Press, 1951), pp. 61-62.

32. On this point see Harvey Cox, The Secular City (New York: Macmillan, 1965), pp. 41-42.

33. For those who distinguish state and society, "regime," as used in this essay, is closer to society than state. Although the distinction of state and society is a philosophical question of the first order, I do not think it makes any difference for the purposes of this book just where one stands on this great issue. Those who, like Aristotle, do not distinguish state and society may perhaps feel more comfortable with the words "regime" or "polity" than those who make this distinction. The latter may prefer the somewhat ambiguous term "society values." It is important to note, however, that I am not talking about the

values of the "state"—the authoritative and coercive agent of a
political society.

34. I have not investigated just how widespread is the American custom of
requiring an oath to uphold the Constitution. In nations where no such
oath is required, I presume that some sort of adherence to the primary political symbols of the regime is implied in accepting public
office.

35. This point is simply a corollary of the principle that laws reflect the
values of the regime. Obviously, laws are not the only repository of
public values. As political scientists have recognized for centuries,
the study of a regime's laws must be supplemented by empirical findings—see Aristotle's Politics, Book 2. In the case of bureaucrats, it
seems safe to assume they have some empirical awareness of public
values.

36. Yet the issue of the relative importance of life and death is in itself of
profound practical importance to many people. It is not uncommon
to hear persons with serious religious beliefs say of a deceased loved
one that "he is happier now." One can acknowledge the importance of
such questions without dropping all other questions until the most
important ones are solved.

37. Even Hobbes goes this far. See De Cive 3, 3.

38. It is unfortunate that the oath of office is administered in such a per-
functory way in most agencies. While not everyone can be sworn into
office by the chief justice of the United States on the steps of the
Capitol, it does seem a bit more imagination could be shown in
accommodating the profound, human need to surround moral commit-
ments with appropriate symbol and ritual. The failure of government
to provide an appropriate ceremonial milieu may help to explain why
the oath is seldom regarded as a moral commitment. Although
ceremony and ritual can neither confer nor substitute for moral vigor,
they can at least remind us of what it is we are becoming by our
pledged word. Despite the sterility of the atmosphere in which the
oath is administered, it can become meaningful after the fact when one
is reminded of the pledge one has given. This is true of any ceremony
that surrounds a moral commitment. Marriage vows are often given
in a shallow and sentimental way, but after many years of loving
dedication they become in retrospect the symbol of something that is
now abiding and profound.

39. I must beg the readers' indulgence for continually repeating the word
"fundamental." It is very important, however, that we distinguish
between a regime that is fundamentally just and one that is perfectly
just. To attempt to defend a theory of the meaning of fundamental
justice would require nothing less than a recapitulation of the history
of political thought. To give the term some content, let me simply
assert that the following questions might help one decide whether he or

she considers a particular regime fundamentally just: (1) What are the
professed values of the regime? (2) Are the professed values consistent with one's personal values? (3) To what extent does the regime
achieve its professed values? (4) To the extent that it falls short of its
professed values, are there corrective mechanisms that offer some
hope of reform? It should be noted that these questions will lead to no
more than a subjective understanding of justice that falls far short of
the question that philosophers have raised over the centuries.

40. Obviously, there are other questions in political philosophy but few, if
any, are more salient than the character of regimes. The fact that
authors as diverse in time and content as Aristotle and Rawls are concerned primarily with the justice of regimes is a sound indication of
the perennial importance of this issue.

41. If I may be permitted a personal aside, I have found that by simply
announcing that I shall presuppose that the students in my course have
settled to their own satisfaction the question of the fundamental justice
of the regime, many students are sufficiently provoked (and at times
outraged) that they soon find themselves giving serious thought to what
they were told was presupposed.

42. See Abraham Kaplan, American Ethics and Public Policy (New York:
Oxford University Press, 1963), pp. 8-10, for an argument that in
matters of public values a conclusion is more important than the
principles on which it is based. See also Maritain's position on
Christian and secularist support for the Universal Declaration of
Human Rights, Man and the State, p. 77. For a more recent and
somewhat different approach to the same issue, see Albert R. Jonsen
and Lewis H. Butler, "Public Ethics and Policy Making," The Hastings
Center Report 5 (August 1975): 19-31. The authors attempt to rescue
the ethics of policy choices from "metaethical" issues that necessarily spill over into epistemology and semantics.

43. Thomas Aquinas, Summa Theologiae, I-II, 94, 4c.

44. The definition of "values" given in the text is admittedly a bit thin when
one considers the staggering quantity of literature available on this
topic. A discussion of value theory, clarification of values, and so
forth, is beyond the scope of this book. For a brief but lucid discussion of values, see Irving Kristol, "Can Values Do the Job Morals
Used to Do? Namely: Keep People Moral," Dividend, Spring 1976.
Dividend is the magazine of the Graduate School of Business Administration of the University of Michigan. The article consists of
excerpts and summaries from an address given by Kristol at the
business school's "Values Week" program. Kristol maintains the
reason we speak of "values" rather than "morals" today is because the
modern understanding of morality is divorced from religion. The
word "morals" is just "too objective" for most moderns. "Values" is
more subjective and creative. Instead of having his morality handed to

him authoritatively, modern man prefers to "invent his own, individual, unique, appropriate morality." Kristol does not think this can be
done. For him the urgent, practical question is given in the lengthy
title of the article.

45. 358 U.S. 1 (1958).
46. I do not believe that anyone would contest the presence of freedom and
    property among American values. Equality might be somewhat con-
    troversial. See Willmore Kendall and George W. Carey, The Basic
    Symbols of the American Political Tradition (Baton Rouge: LSU
    Press, 1970).
47. Take, for example, the differences among scholars like Turner,
    Beard, Parrington, and Boorstin. On February 22, 1976, the
    Washington Post's "Book World" section featured an article in which
    six leading American historians were asked the following two ques-
    tions: (1) What books have had the greatest impact on the course of
    American history? (2) What books in American history would be most
    valuable for the general reader? The historians were Henry Steel
    Commager, Eugene D. Genovese, Samuel Eliot Morrison, J. H.
    Plumb, Arthur Schlesinger, Jr., and C. Vann Woodward. The
    responses were breathtakingly diverse.
48. The importance of the study of American history for high-ranking
    government personnel was underscored in William V. Shannon's
    editorial on "The Sad Young Men"—the White House officials who
    appeared before the Senate Watergate Committee in the summer of
    1973. Shannon noted that "none of them seems to have ever studied
    any American history." New York Times, July 25, 1973, p. 39.
49. Ralph Lerner, Supreme Court Review, 1967 (Chicago: University of
    Chicago Press, 1967), pp. 127-180.
50. Justice Chase was the worst offender. His charges were at times
    outrageously partisan. The charges of Chief Justice Jay and
    Justice Wilson were usually quite moderate.
51. Lerner, Supreme Court Review, 1967, p. 180.
52. For further discussion on the influence of law on public values, see
    Gordon S. Wood, The Creation of the American Republic, 1776-1787
    (Chapel Hill: University of North Carolina Press, 1969), pp. 118-124.
53. Alexander M. Bickel, The Morality of Consent (New Haven, Conn.:
    Yale University Press, 1975), p. 6.
54. 378 U.S. 226 (1964).
55. New York University Law Review 39 (1964), p. 209.
56. 400 U.S. 309 (1971).
57. Thomas Reed Powell, "The Logic and Rhetoric of Constitutional Law,"
    Journal of Philosophy, Psychology, and Scientific Method 15 (1918):
    654.
58. Dred Scott v. Sandford 19 Howard 393 (1857).
59. Brown v. Board of Education 347 U.S. 483 (1954).

60. Dartmouth College v. Woodward 4 Wheat 518 (1819).
61. Home Building and Loan Association v. Blaisdell 290 U.S. 398 (1934).
62. Minersville School District v. Gobitis 310 U.S. 586 (1940) and West
    Virginia State Board of Education v. Barnette 319 U.S. 624 (1943).
63. Burton v. Wilmington Parking Authority 365 U.S. 715 (1960).
64. Peterson v. Greenville 373 U.S. 244 (1963). See also Lombard v.
    Louisiana 373 U.S. 244 (1963) and Boynton v. Virginia 364 U.S. 454
    (1960).
65. Bickel, The Morality of Consent, p. 10.
66. Charles Reich, "The New Property," Yale Law Journal 73 (April 1964):
    733.
67. Goldberg v. Kelly 397 U.S. 254 (1970).
68. Sniadach v. Family Finance Corporation 395 U.S. 337 (1969).
69. Fuentes v. Shevin 407 U.S. 67 (1972).
70. Perry v. Sinderman 408 U.S. 593 (1972).
71. See Francis S. Philbrick, "Changing Concepts of Property in Law,"
    University of Pennsylvania Law Review 86 (May 1938).
72. The subjective character of the method of regime values is no more
    subjective than other widely accepted ways of articulating a com-
    munity's values. This is true even of the New Testament. In the
    Sermon on the Mount, the poor, the weak, and the merciful are
    declared "blessed," but I do not believe that Christians are expected to
    deduce from these words general rules of behavior that can be applied
    to specific situations. They are expected, however, to read the text
    attentively, ponder its meaning, and develop a sensitivity and aware-
    ness to the values proclaimed therein. It is hoped that the believer
    will translate this awareness into action when the appropriate occasion
    arises.
        When we speak of "Judeo-Christian ethics," there is some mini-
    mal content in these terms that describes a view of man in which the
    importance and dignity of the individual are paramount. Yet the Bible
    itself is at times quite vague and even contradictory on this point.
    One part of the Old Testament tells us that all flesh is grass, while
    another passage says the Lord has made man a little less than the
    angels. In the New Testament Jesus tells his followers to turn the
    other cheek, yet he himself brings "not peace but a sword." Great
    value-creating instruments, like the Bible, are rich, complex, and
    confusing but nevertheless can produce a Judeo-Christian ethic that is
    not merely a subjective term. Indeed, the Judeo-Christian ethic is
    sufficiently objective to have formed the basis of a well-known moral
    analysis of organizational life. See Robert Golembiewski, Man,
    Management and Morality: Toward a New Organizational Ethic (New
    York: McGraw-Hill, 1965).
73. See Paul Eidelberg, The Philosophy of the American Constitution
    (New York: Free Press, 1968).

74. Storing, "Political Parties and the Bureaucracy," in Political Parties
U.S.A., ed. Goldwyn, p. 155.

3

Equality

*The destinies of the two races, in this country,
are indissolubly linked together, and the
interests of both require that the common
government of all shall not permit the seeds
of race hate to be planted under the sanction
of law.*

Justice Harlan,
dissenting in *Plessy v. Ferguson*

As the analysis in the previous chapter has indicated, our concern with equality is restricted to the American understanding of that word, and, indeed, within the American tradition our focus is limited to Supreme Court opinions. In so limiting our focus, we are, of course, sacrificing some fascinating inquiries. [1]

In the ancient world, for example, equality was usually an ideal suitable only for other times (the Romans' golden age of Saturn, the king who had no slaves) or other places (Plato's Laws where the Athenian Stranger's views on equality are clearly utopian). In medieval times, equality continued to be looked upon in otherworldly terms. All men are equal in origin and destiny in that all are children of God and destined for everlasting life with Him at the eschaton.

Modernity has yielded a richly diverse understanding of equality. Calvin based his understanding of equality on man's universal depravity. For Hobbes, men are equal in that they are driven by the same fears and passions. Freud traces the belief in equality to the primal crime of patricide in which a democratic union of brothers, united by sexual envy, band together to kill their father. De Tocqueville saw the rise of equality as at least in part a form of retribution against a decadent aristocracy that failed to measure up to the responsibilities concomitant with its privileges. Nineteenth-century liberals argued for equality in terms of equal rights and equal immunities from state intervention. Marx denounced this bourgeois equality as a fraudulent ideoolgy intended to

justify the advantages of the powerful: true equality will come about only
with the advent of the classless society.

In concentrating on Supreme Court opinions, we must put aside a direct
examination of the grand thoughts of the great philosophers, but in doing so
we shall find many of these profound speculations reappearing in humbler
garb and speaking with a decidedly American accent in the concrete "cases
and controversies" addressed by the Supreme Court. In listening to that
American accent one seldom hears paeans to equality as such. Unlike the
early Bolsheviks, we are not likely to jump at the bait of arguing over
whether the principle of equality is violated by the presence of a conductor
in a symphony orchestra. Somewhat characteristically, we structure our
discussion of equality in terms of equal protection of the law.[2]

The scope of the questions examined by the Court under the rubric of
equal protection is something marvelous to behold. It ranges from the
trivial to the sublime. For example: Is the equal protection clause violated when a state orders the owners of cedar trees to destroy their
property in order to save apple orchards from cedar rust? Can Wisconsin
tax oleomargarine at a higher rate than butter? Can Virginia forbid marriages between blacks and whites on the grounds that the prohibition falls
equally on both races? Can Louisiana preclude the illegitimate children of
a deceased mother from bringing a tort action because of her wrongful
death when her legitimate children could bring such an action? Can
California outlaw billiard halls for hire but make an exception for hotels
with twenty-five or more rooms? Can an Idaho probate statute prefer
males to females when both are equally entitled to administer an estate?
Can Kentucky require the forfeiture of land for nonpayment of taxes under
conditions that exist only in part of the state? Can the right to vote for the
local school board be limited to persons who either own property or have
children in school? Does California's inheritance tax violate the due
process clause by taxing the transmission of property to a brother or sister
while exempting a similar transmission to a son-in-law or daughter-in-
law? Can a state tax foreign and domestic corporations at different rates?
Can the punishment Massachusetts imposes upon persons convicted twice of
the same type of offense be more severe than the punishment inflicted upon
first offenders?[3]

Each of these cases offers interesting observations on what equal protection of the laws means in the concrete, but for our purposes of examining fundamental regime values it will suffice to examine in detail only two
areas of equal protection—race and sex.

RACE

It is perhaps no exaggeration to say that questions of race, in one form or
another, have been the most important issues in American politics. They

have certainly been the most abiding—from the troubling compromises in
the Constitution itself,[4] through the great debate over slavery in the territories, the Civil War, the postwar amendments, the segregated South of
the first half of the present century, the civil rights movement of the past
decade, and right on up to the "forced" busing we can read about in this
morning's paper. These are issues that quite literally tried men's souls
and at times found them sadly wanting but at other times found them mag-
nificently equal to the most severe moral challenges a society can face.

Before the Civil War, questions of race were inextricably linked with
the slavery issue. Although not all blacks were enslaved, for all practical
purposes it was only blacks who were enslaved. Thus the United States
not only practiced slavery but housed an enslaved race. Emancipated
blacks escaped the legal status of slavery, but they could never escape the
humiliation that relentlessly tracked them because of their race. The
notorious "Black Codes" of the pre-Civil War era restricted the rights of
free blacks to own property, specified certain crimes that pertained only
to them, and severely limited their access to the courts. Because of the
legal disabilities that followed freedmen, it was quite obvious that the
Thirteenth Amendment's prohibition of slavery was only the first step
toward true racial equality. The Fourteenth Amendment addressed the
sort of discrimination that was likely to be visited upon blacks in their new
status as freedmen. The first section of this amendment declared all
persons born in the United States to be citizens of the United States and of
the state wherein they reside. More significantly for our purposes, it
also prohibited the states from denying to any person the equal protection
of the laws. The most significant cases concerning the relationship
between blacks and whites have turned on the Supreme Court's interpretation of the meaning of equal protection.[5]

It would be a pleasant task if an examination of Supreme Court opinions on racial equality could be restricted to those exhilarating moments
when the Court was roundly condemning segregation and similar abomina-
tions. Happy indeed is the raconteur who need only tell that part of the
story; he is the bearer of glad tidings. The sad truth, of course, is that
the Court, like the people whose Constitution it interprets, has at times
been unable to exorcise the demon of racism. Even the cursory examination of equality presented in this chapter would be irresponsibly incomplete
if Dred Scott and Plessy v. Ferguson[6] were quietly set aside in embarrassed silence. In these cases the Court announced principles that have
long since been discredited as good constitutional law. The residue of
these principles, however, still lingers and at times surfaces but thinly
veiled in public and private discourse. To know these cases is to know a
part of ourselves as a people in history. Even as we wince at the harsh
words that are a part of our heritage, we draw comfort from the vigorous
dissents of Justice Curtis in Scott and Justice Harlan in Plessy. In their
own times, theirs may have been voices crying in the wilderness, but

eventually the good news they sent forth reached their fellow citizens and their voices prevailed. It is perhaps worthy of some reflection on our part that when the Supreme Court finally came around to prohibiting racial segregation in the public schools, there was no dissenting opinion.

Dred Scott v. Sandford

Dred Scott v. Sandford[7] is perhaps the most unfortunate decision the Supreme Court has ever rendered. The tone and substance of Chief Justice Taney's opinion inflamed abolitionist and moderate opinion in the North and, in the judgment of some historians, made the Civil War all but inevitable. Leaders of the newly formed Republican party charged that the decision was part of a proslavery conspiracy involving the Supreme Court and the newly elected Democratic president, James Buchanan. While the political background of the case is of considerable historical significance, it is the legal argument developed by the Court that is instructive for our purposes.

The facts of the case were that Dred Scott, a slave born in Missouri, was brought by his master, Dr. Emerson, an army surgeon, to the state of Illinois where slavery was forbidden. Subsequently, he was taken to Fort Snelling, an outpost located in the section of the Louisiana Territory in which slavery had been forbidden by the Missouri Compromise of 1820. Later he returned to Missouri with his master. After his return to Missouri, he was sold to Sandford, a citizen of New York. Thereupon, Scott brought suit for his freedom in a federal court in Missouri. He brought the suit in a federal court because Article III of the Constitution extends "the judicial power of the United States to cases and controversies arising between citizens of different states." Scott maintained that his sojourn in free territory had made him a free man and that because he had been born in Missouri, he was now a citizen of that state.

In this case, all nine justices of the Supreme Court gave opinions. This fact in itself is eloquent testimony to the complexity and importance of the issues presented. For our purposes, the most important aspect of the case was Chief Justice Taney's handling of Scott's claim to be a citizen, for this was the basis of the federal jurisdiction of his suit. Taney put the issue as follows:

> The question is simply this: Can a negro, whose ancestors were imported into this country, and sold as slaves, become a member of the political community formed and brought into existence by the constitution of the United States, and as such become entitled to all the rights, and privileges, and immunities, guaranteed by that instrument to the citizen? One of which rights is the privilege of suing in a court of the United States in the cases specified in the constitution.

It will be observed, that the plea applies to that class of persons only whose ancestors were negroes of the African race, and imported into this country, and sold and held as slaves. The only matter in issue before the court, therefore, is, whether the descendants of such slaves, when they shall be emancipated, or who are born of parents who had become free before their birth, are citizens of a state, in the sense in which the word citizen is used in the constitution of the United States. And this being the only matter in dispute on the pleadings, the court must be understood as speaking in this opinion of that class only, that is, of those persons who are the descendants of Africans who were imported into this country, and sold as slaves.

The way Taney puts the question is important. He is not asking whether a slave can be a citizen but whether a Negro can be a citizen. No one—not even Dred Scott himself—claimed that a person could be a slave and a citizen at the same time. The two roles are mutually exclusive. Scott's contention was that his residence in free territory made him a free man and that once he was free, his race was no barrier to citizenship. Taney structures the question in such a way that the issue is whether any Negro can ever become a citizen of a state and, therefore, qualify for the privileges consequent upon state citizenship as outlined in the Constitution. Taney, of course, was aware that some states had conferred citizenship upon freed slaves and the descendants of slaves. The question he asks, however, is whether such citizens are citizens of a state "in the sense in which the word citizen is used in the constitution of the United States."
Taney answers this question in the negative and in so doing utters the most blatantly racist statements ever issued in an opinion of the Supreme Court. His point was that at the time of the framing of the Constitution, Negroes, whether enslaved or emancipated, were not considered part of the "people of the United States" and were therefore excluded—along with their progeny—from the political community created by the new Constitution. To explain why they were excluded, Taney offered the following account:

> They had for more than a century before been regarded as beings of an inferior order, and altogether unfit to associate with the white race, either in social or political relations; and so far inferior, that they had no rights which the white man was bound to respect; and that the negro might justly and lawfully be reduced to slavery for his benefit. He was bought and sold, and treated as an ordinary article of merchandise and traffic, whenever a profit could be made by it. This opinion was at that time fixed and universal in the civilized portion of the white race. It was regarded as an axiom in morals as well as in politics, which no one thought of disputing, or supposed to be open to dispute; and men in every grade and position in society daily and

habitually acted upon it in their private pursuits, as well as in matters of public concern, without doubting for a moment the correctness of this opinion.

Taney's interpretation of history was vigorously challenged by the dissenters in the Dred Scott case and his outrageous statement that at the time of the founding of the Republic "they [Negroes] had no rights which white men were bound to respect" ignited a firestorm of abolitionist invective.

In attempting to justify his reading of history, Taney was considerably embarrassed by the unequivocal statement in the Declaration of Independence that "all men are created equal." The Declaration, of course, is not part of the Constitution, but Taney was not about to maintain that in the "critical period" between the two documents American political leaders had been transformed from egalitarians to racists. As a result, he offered the following interpretation of the clause in the Declaration affirming that all men are created equal:

The general words above quoted [All men are created equal] would seem to embrace the whole human family, and if they were used in a similar instrument at this day would be so understood. But it is too clear for dispute, that the enslaved African race were not intended to be included, and formed no part of the people who framed and adopted the declaration; for if the language, as understood in that day, would embrace them, the conduct of the distinguished men who framed the Declaration of Independence would have been utterly and flagrantly inconsistent with the principles they asserted; and instead of the sympathy of mankind, to which they so confidently appealed, they would have deserved and received universal rebuke and reprobation.

Yet the men who framed this declaration were great men—high in literary acquirements—high in their sense of honor, and incapable of asserting principles inconsistent with those on which they were acting. They perfectly understood the meaning of the language they used, and how it would be understood by others; and they knew that it would not in any part of the civilized world be supposed to embrace the negro race, which, by common consent, had been excluded from civilized Governments and the family of nations, and doomed to slavery. They spoke and acted according to the then established doctrines and principles, and in the ordinary language of the day, and no one misunderstood them. The unhappy black race were separated from the white by indelible marks, and laws long before established, and were never thought of or spoken of except as property, and when the claims of the owner or the profit of the trader were supposed to need protection.

Taney's reading of the Declaration did not pass unchallenged. In his dissenting opinion, Justice Curtis had this to say:

> I shall not enter into an examination of the existing opinions of that period respecting the African race, nor into any discussion concerning the meaning of those who asserted, in the Declaration of Independence, that all men are created equal; that they are endowed by their Creator with certain inalienable rights; that among these are life, liberty, and the pursuit of happiness. My own opinion is, that a calm comparison of these assertions of universal abstract truths, and of their own individual opinions and acts, would not leave these men under any reproach of inconsistency; that the great truths they asserted on that solemn occasion, they were ready and anxious to make effectual, wherever a necessary regard to circumstances, which no statesman can disregard without producing more evil than good, would allow; and that it would not be just to them, nor true in itself, to allege that they intended to say that the Creator of all men had endowed the white race, exclusively, with the great natural rights which the Declaration of Independence asserts. But this is not the place to vindicate their memory. As I conceive, we should deal here, not with such disputes, if there can be a dispute concerning this subject, but with those substantial facts evinced by the written Constitutions of States, and by the notorious practice under them. And they show, in a manner which no argument can obscure, that in some of the original thirteen States, free colored persons, before and at the time of the formation of the Constitution, were citizens of those States.

Let us look more closely at the interpretations of the Declaration of Independence offered by Taney and Curtis. Both men share a common basis in fact and value. The fact is the indisputable historical truth that some of those who proclaimed the equality of all men condoned the institution of slavery and were themselves slaveholders. The value Taney and Curtis had in common was to avoid dishonoring the memory of the signers of the Declaration. Thus neither was about to say the men of 1776 were shameless hypocrites. Taney defends them by appealing to their consistency. He looks at their behavior and deduces what their beliefs must have been on the grounds that men of such integrity would never be inconsistent no matter how outrageous their beliefs. Curtis maintains they believed what they said even though they tacitly recognized that their beliefs could be only partially fulfilled because of the need to adapt, at least temporarily, to certain unfortunate historical circumstances. Which argument more effectively honors the memory of the signers of the Declaration and thereby promotes the value Taney and Curtis held in common? Which is more accurate historically?

    The Declaration of Independence could have been worded differently.
Jefferson might have written words to the effect that even though all men
are created equal, it is not always possible to give concrete embodiment in
political institutions to the noblest of principles, but that Americans were
pledged to strive vigorously to bring about a social order in which such
principles could eventually be realized. Such a statement would have been
more "consistent" than the unqualified language of the Declaration, but
would it have been morally superior? Looking back on the Declaration
from our vantage point today, do you think we would be more committed to
equality as a value if Jefferson had tempered his language to describe more
accurately the actual practices of the day? Is it honest to take certain
liberties with language in value-creating statements like the Declaration of
Independence? If so, it then becomes important to determine what sort of
statements are "value creating." What about campaign platforms and
speeches? Inaugural addresses? In an administrative context, what about
a new agency's mission statement? Is its primary purpose to inform or to
inspire? What about a press release announcing an agency's new program?
Or a speech by a senior agency official to a group interested in the work of
the agency?

Plessy v. Ferguson

Shortly after the end of the Civil War, Congress passed and the states ratified the Thirteenth Amendment, which abolished slavery. This action,
however, did not avoid the damage brought by the Dred Scott opinion.
Taney's argument was that blacks—whether free or slave—were excluded
from membership in the American political community. This argument
was answered by the Fourteenth Amendment, which provided that all persons born or naturalized in the United States "are citizens of the United
States and of the state wherein they reside." The same amendment went on
to provide that no state shall "deny to any person within its jurisdiction the
equal protection of the laws" and conferred upon Congress the power to
enforce this provision by appropriate legislation.
    Armed with these powers, Congress passed the Civil Rights Act of
1875, which forbade racial discrimination in "inns, public conveyances on
land or water, theatres, and other places of public amusement." In 1883,
however, the Supreme Court found this law unconstitutional on a very
questionable interpretation of the Fourteenth Amendment. The Court held
that the powers enjoyed by Congress under this amendment were limited to
correcting discriminatory actions by state governments. That is, the
Fourteenth Amendment was concerned with state action alone. It had
nothing to do with the discrimination practiced by private persons whose
public accommodations excluded blacks. The failure of the state to

prohibit such discrimination was not state action and hence could not be corrected by Congress. [8]

This decision was obviously a stunning setback to the advancement of blacks to the full equality implied in their newly acquired citizenship. In 1896 the case of Plessy v. Ferguson[9] came before the Court. This time there could be no doubt that state action was involved. The Louisiana legislature had passed a statute in 1890 requiring railroads operating in that state "to provide equal, but separate, accommodations for the white and colored races by providing two or more passenger coaches for each passenger train or by dividing the passenger coaches by a partition so as to secure separate accommodations." Plessy, a black citizen of the United States residing in Louisiana, was ordered by a conductor of the East Louisiana Railroad Company to vacate the seat he had occupied in the coach reserved for whites and "take a seat in another coach assigned to persons of the colored race." This Plessy refused to do and because of this refusal was fined and imprisoned by Judge Ferguson of the criminal district court for the parish of Orleans.

The Supreme Court upheld Judge Ferguson's action in a lengthy opinion written by Justice Brown. A central point in Brown's argument was that the Fourteenth Amendment was intended

> to enforce the absolute equality of the two races before the law, but in the nature of things it could not have been intended to abolish distinctions based upon color, or to enforce social, as distinguished from political equality, or a commingling of the two races upon terms unsatisfactory to either. Laws permitting, and even requiring, their separation in places where they are liable to be brought into contact do not necessarily imply the inferiority of either race to the other, and have been generally, if not universally, recognized as within the competency of the state legislatures in the exercise of their police power.

A careful examination of Brown's argument may enable us to discover something about our own understanding of equality. Brown makes a distinction between social and political equality and contends that the Fourteenth Amendment was intended to protect the latter but not former. The same distinction had been made by Booker T. Washington in his famous address at the Atlanta exposition of 1895—just one year before Plessy. What do you think of this distinction of political and social equality? Is it simply unsound in principle? Is it sound in principle but applied unwisely to public transportation in Plessy?

In the paragraph quoted above, Justice Brown seems to indulge in a bit of verbal legerdemain when he says it is not the intent of the equal protection clause "to enforce social, as distinguished from political equality, or a commingling of the two races upon terms unsatisfactory to either." Even if the distinction of social and political equality is sound in principle, he surely distorts it when he equates social with "a commingling of the two races upon terms unsatisfactory to either." This would imply that the Fourteenth Amendment was not intended to reach any situation in which the races might "commingle" and someone might happen to complain! In his dissenting opinion in this case, Justice Harlan ridicules the absurdity of this contention by spelling out its implication for jury service from which no one may be constitutionally excluded on racial grounds but which necessarily involves some "commingling."

> May it not now be reasonably expected that astute men of the dominant race, who affect to be disturbed at the possibility that the integrity of the white race may be corrupted, or that its supremacy will be imperilled, by contact on public highways with black people, will endeavor to procure statutes requiring white and black jurors to be separated in the jury box by a "partition," and that, upon retiring from the court room to consult as to their verdict, such partition, if it be a moveable one, shall be taken to their consultation room, and set up in such way as to prevent black jurors from coming too close to their brother jurors of the white race. If the "partition" used in the court room happens to be stationary, provision could be made for screens with openings through which jurors of the two races could confer as to their verdict without coming into personal contact with each other.

Harlan is also critical of Brown's contention that riding in a railroad car involves a social situation and therefore is beyond the reach of the Fourteenth Amendment:

> That a railroad is a public highway, and that the corporation which owns or operates it is in the exercise of public functions, is not, at this day, to be disputed. Mr. Justice Nelson, speaking for this court . . . said that a common carrier was in the exercise "of a sort of public office, and has public duties to perform, from which he should not be permitted to exonerate himself without the assent of the parties concerned." Mr. Justice Strong, delivering the judgment of this court in Olcott v. The Supervisors, said: "That railroads, though constructed by private corporations and owned by them, are public highways, has been the doctrine of nearly all the courts ever since such conveniences for passage and transportation have had any existence. Very early the question arose whether a State's right of eminent domain could be exercised by a private corporation created for the purpose of constructing a railroad. Clearly it could not, unless taking land for such a purpose by such an agency is taking land for public use. The right of eminent domain nowhere justifies taking

property for private use. Yet it is a doctrine universally accepted that a state legislature may authorize a private corporation to take land for the construction of such a road, making compensation to the owner. What else does this doctrine mean if not that building a railroad, though it be built by a private corporation, is an act done for a public use?"

How would you analyze this dispute between Brown and Harlan? Is the heart of the problem Brown's willingness to distinguish the social and political spheres in the context of the Fourteenth Amendment? After all, a decade before Plessy, the Supreme Court had decided that the amendment referred only to state action. Does it make any sense to distinguish political and social spheres where state action is concerned? Prescinding from the context of the Fourteenth Amendment, the distinction between social and political equality seems quite sound. Indeed, without it we would have a totally politicized or "totalitarian" society. It is the distinction between social and political that explains why we would be outraged to hear of an election judge who denied a ballot to a duly registered voter on grounds of race, but we would not be particularly disturbed to hear that the same judge refused to invite into her home members of a race other than her own. While the distinction of political and social is undoubtedly sound in principle, can it be applied to a situation in which state action is involved? Doesn't the fact that the state has taken some action mean the situation in question is necessarily political and therefore render the distinction meaningless?

Legislating Morality

The closing paragraph of Brown's opinion is instructive for our purposes:

The argument [against segregation in railroad cars] also assumes that social prejudices may be overcome by legislation, and that equal rights cannot be secured to the negro except by an enforced commingling of the two races. We cannot accept this proposition. If the two races are to meet upon terms of social equality, it must be the result of natural affinities, a mutual appreciation of each other's merits and a voluntary consent of individuals. As was said by the Court of Appeals of New York . . . "this end can neither be accomplished nor promoted by laws which conflict with the general sentiment of the community upon whom they are designed to operate. When the government, therefore, has secured to each of its citizens equal rights before the law and equal opportunities for improvement and progress, it has accomplished the end for which it was organized and performed all of

the functions respecting social advantages with which it is
endowed." Legislation is powerless to eradicate racial instincts or
to abolish distinctions based upon physical differences, and the
attempt to do so can only result in accentuating the difficulties of
the present situation.

In this paragraph the Court is articulating the familiar argument that
the state cannot "legislate morality." Is this true? Do you agree with
Brown's statement that "legislation is powerless to eradicate racial
instincts"? Has the Supreme Court's attack upon racial segregation for
the past twenty years changed public morals in this matter? Did the
Court's approval of racial segregation on legal grounds in Plessy contain a
tacit approval of the underlying moral issues that supported the institutional arrangements of segregation? What connection is there between
"legislating morality" in race relations and in other areas of human behavior such as abortion, pornography, sexism, and the use of alcoholic
beverages and marijuana?

Color-Blind Constitution

Harlan's dissenting opinion contains the following statement:

[In the] view of the Consititution, in the eye of the law, there is in the
country no superior, dominant, ruling class of citizens. There is no
caste here. Our Constitution is color-blind, and neither knows nor
tolerates classes among citizens. In respect to civil rights, all
citizens are equal before the law. The humblest is the peer of the
most powerful. The law regards man as man, and takes no account of
his surroundings or of his color when his civil rights as guaranteed
by the supreme law of the land are involved. It is, therefore, to be
regretted that this high tribunal, the final expositor of the fundamental
law of the land, has reached the conclusion that it is competent for a
State to regulate the enjoyment of citizens of their civil rights solely
upon the basis of race.

Harlan's statement that the Constitution is "color-blind" is justly
famous. Although it certainly was not true in 1896, is it true today?
If not, should it be? If so, what happens to affirmative action? Is
affirmative action a violation of the principle that the Constitution is
color-blind; or is it simply a temporary accommodation of the principle
to an unusual set of circumstances; or is it perfectly consistent with a
color-blind constitution? Is there any parallel between the position of
today's proponents of affirmative action and Justice Curtis's interpretation
of the motives of the signers of the Declaration of Independence? (See
discussion of the Dred Scott case above.) Why is the choice of language a
particularly delicate matter for bureaucrats administering affirmative

action programs? Is affirmative action simply a euphemism for "reverse racism"? If not, why not?

The Destinies of the Races

Mr. Justice Harlan went on to say in dissent:

> [It] seems that we have yet, in some of the States, a dominant race—a superior class of citizens, which assumes to regulate the enjoyment of civil rights, common to all citizens, upon the basis of race. The present decision, it may well be apprehended, will not only stimulate aggressions, more or less brutal and irritating, upon the admitted rights of colored citizens, but will encourage the belief that it is possible, by means of state enactments, to defeat the beneficient purposes which the people of the United States had in view when they adopted the recent amendments of the Constitution, by one of which the blacks of this country were made citizens of the United States and of the States in which they respectively reside, and whose privileges and immunities, as citizens, the States are forbidden to abridge. Sixty millions of whites are in no danger from the presence here of eight millions of blacks. The destinies of the two races, in this country, are indissolubly linked together, and the interests of both require that the common government of all shall not permit the seeds of race hate to be planted under the sanction of law. What can more certainly arouse race hate, what more certainly create and perpetuate a feeling of distrust between these races, than state enactments, which, in fact, proceed on the ground that colored citizens are so inferior and degraded that they cannot be allowed to sit in public coaches occupied by white citizens? That, as all will admit, is the real meaning of such legislation as was enacted in Louisiana.

Was Harlan's prophecy accurate? Note the political character of Harlan's argument. He does not condemn racial segregation out of sense of compassion for blacks but on grounds of the mutual interests of both races. That is, whites will suffer from segregation as much as blacks because the "destinies of the two races in this country are indissolubly linked together." Is this a persuasive argument? Is it realistic? Does the appeal to mutual self-interest involve a "higher" or "lower" motivation than an appeal made exclusively to whites that they should be compassionate and sensitive to the needs of blacks? Which appeal takes the dignity of blacks more seriously?

Chinese Exclusion

In his dissent Harlan compared the treatment of blacks under the Plessy doctrine with the treatment afforded Chinese:

There is a race so different from our own that we do not permit those belonging to it to become citizens of the United States. Persons belonging to it are, with few exceptions, absolutely excluded from our country. I allude to the Chinese race. But by the statute in question, a Chinaman can ride in the same passenger coach with white citizens of the United States, while citizens of the black race in Louisiana, many of whom, perhaps, risked their lives for the preservation of the Union, who are entitled, by law, to participate in the political control of the State and nation, who are not excluded, by law or by reason of their race, from public stations of any kind, and who have all the legal rights that belong to white citizens, are yet declared to be criminals, liable to imprisonment, if they ride in a public coach occupied by citizens of the white race. It is scarcely just to say that a colored citizen should not object to occupying a public coach assigned to his own race. He does not object, nor perhaps, would he object to separate coaches for his race, if his rights under the law were recognized. But he objects, and ought never to cease objecting to the proposition, that citizens of the white and black races can be adjudged criminals because they sit, or claim the right to sit, in the same public coach on a public highway.

Harlan's allusion to the Chinese is interesting. He does not deplore the discrimination practiced against Chinese but he finds it intolerable that black citizens should be subjected to mistreatment from which Chinese, who are ineligible for citizenship, are exempt. Thus the basis of his argument for equal treatment is citizenship, not humanity. This may be quite consistent with the fact that before the Civil War Harlan had been a slaveholder but after the passage of the Fourteenth Amendment he became the Court's most eloquent defender of the rights of blacks. Harlan's attack on racial segregation is grounded in the citizenship enjoyed by blacks. For Harlan, it is all citizens but not necessarily all men who must be treated equally. Would Harlan's argument carry much weight today? Are we more impressed by appeals to our common humanity than to citizenship? Which line of argument do you find more persuasive? Why? Which line of argument is more likely to lead to concrete, institutional expressions of equality?

Yick Wo v. Hopkins

Although the most celebrated cases involving equal protection have concerned the black community, other groups have been affected by the clause as well. The problems encountered on the west coast by Chinese in the late nineteenth century were addressed by the Court in Yick Wo v.

Hopkins. [10] Yick Wo is remembered today not only because of the benefits
it brought to a harassed minority but because of the careful analysis it gave
to the meaning of "equal protection." The term is somewhat disturbing
because most legislation necessarily makes distinctions among various
types of persons and thereby treats them unequally. Consider, for
example, how accustomed we are to dividing persons into citizens and
aliens; and aliens into those eligible for citizenship and those not eligible.
Many legal consequences follow upon the distinction between those over
eighteen or twenty-one and those under these ages. The Internal Revenue
System is based on an elaborate series of distinctions based on income.
Likewise, welfare benefits are similarly structured. Senior citizens enjoy
certain benefits denied to their juniors. Corporations fall under different
regulatory schemes depending on their volume of business, the number of
employees, the place of incorporation, and so on. It is perhaps only a
slight exaggeration to say that there can be no legislation without creating
some kind of unequal treatment.

The equal protection clause, then, brings small comfort to the
doctrinaire egalitarian. It is a term that is not self-explanatory. It
demands qualification and compromise if it is to be an effective guideline
rather than empty rhetoric. The opinion of Justice Matthews in Yick Wo is
an excellent example of one of the earliest efforts to analyze the meaning
of equal protection.

This case involved a San Francisco ordinance of 1880 that forbade anyone to operate a laundry in a wooden building without the consent of the
board of supervisors. Laundries operated in brick buildings were exempt
from the ordinance. Thus, the ordinance involved two distinctions:
(1) the distinction between laundries in brick buildings and those in wooden
buildings; and (2) among the laundries in wooden buildings, the distinction
between those whose owners obtained the consent of the supervisors and
those whose owners did not. The second distinction, of course, was the
more important of the two because those who failed to obtain the board's
consent were subject to imprisonment for continuing to operate their
businesses. At the time the ordinance was passed, there were about 320
laundries in San Francisco. All but ten of these were in wooden buildings.
Nearly 240 of the 320 laundries were operated by Chinese. In practice,
then, the ordinance meant that nearly every laundry operator had to get the
consent of the board of supervisors if he wished to stay in business. The
ordinance did not provide any guidelines by which the Board was to determine which laundries were to be permitted to stay open. De facto the
Board was using its unlimited discretion to put Chinese merchants out of
business. Yick Wo continued to operate his laundry without the Board's
consent, and was consequently arrested, tried, convicted, and sentenced
to six months in prison. After an unsuccessful appeal to the Supreme
Court of California, he appealed to the Supreme Court of the United States.

Justice Matthews delivered the opinion of the Court, which overturned
the conviction of Yick Wo. In so doing, the Justice analyzed the
San Francisco ordinance as follows:

> We are . . . constrained at the outset, to differ from the Supreme
> Court of California upon the real meaning of the ordinances in ques-
> tion. That court considered these ordinances as vesting in the board
> of supervisors a not unusual discretion in granting or withholding their
> assent to the use of wooden buildings as laundries, to be exercised in
> reference to the circumstances of each case, with a view to the pro-
> tection of the public against the dangers of fire. We are not able to
> concur in that interpretation of the power conferred upon the super-
> visors. There is nothing in the ordinances which points to such a
> regulation of the business of keeping and conducting laundries. They
> seem intended to confer, and actually do confer, not a discretion to be
> exercised upon a consideration of the circumstances of each case, but
> a naked and arbitrary power to give or withhold consent, not only as to
> places, but as to persons. So that, if an applicant for such consent,
> being in every way a competent and qualified person, and having com-
> plied with every reasonable condition demanded by any public interest,
> should, failing to obtain the requisite consent of the supervisors to
> the prosecution of his business, apply for redress by the judicial
> process of mandamus, to require the supervisors to consider and act
> upon his case, it would be a sufficient answer for them to say that the
> law had conferred upon them authority to withhold their assent, without
> reason and without responsibility. The power given to them is not
> confined to their discretion in the legal sense of that term, but is
> granted to their mere will. It is purely arbitrary, and acknowledges
> neither guidance nor restraint.

Note that Matthews distinguishes "discretion in the legal sense of that
term" from "mere will." Black's Law Dictionary offers the following
definition of "discretion":

> When applied to public functionaries, discretion means a power of
> right conferred upon them by law of acting officially in certain circum-
> stances, according to the dictates of their own judgment and con-
> science, uncontrolled by the judgment or conscience of others. This
> discretion undoubtedly is to some extent regulated by usage, or, if the
> term is preferred, by fixed principles. But by this is to be under-
> stood nothing more than that the same court cannot, consistently with
> its own dignity, and with its character and duty of administering
> impartial justice, decide in different ways two cases in every respect
> exactly alike. The question of fact whether the two cases are alike in

every color, circumstance, and feature is of necessity to be submitted
to the judgment of some tribunal.

Think of some discretionary power enjoyed by an administrative
agency with which you are familiar. Does it possess discretion "in the
legal sense of that term" or "mere will"? Do you know of any agency that
in reality exercises "mere will" masquerading as discretion?

Citing two previous Supreme Court decisions, Justice Matthews maintained that the equal protection clause of the Fourteenth Amendment
requires

> that no impediment should be interposed to the pursuits of any one,
> except as applied to the same pursuits by others under like circum-
> stances; that no greater burdens should be laid upon one than are laid
> upon others in the same calling and condition; and that in the adminis-
> tration of criminal justice no different or higher punishment should be
> imposed upon one than such as is prescribed to all for like offenses.
> Class legislation, discriminating against some and favoring others, is
> prohibited, but legislation which, in carrying out a public purpose, is
> limited in its application, if within the sphere of its operation it affects
> alike all persons similarly situated, is not within the amendment [sic].

By "not within the amendment," Matthews means, of course, not prohibited by the Fourteenth Amendment. The requirement that legislation
affect "alike all persons similarly situated" has become a consecrated
phrase in American constitutional law. It does not forbid distinctions and
classifications among persons but demands that those persons who fall
within the classification be treated alike.

Matthews continued:

> The ordinance drawn in question in the present case is of a very dif-
> ferent character. It does not prescribe a rule and conditions for the
> regulation of the use of property for laundry purposes, to which all
> similarly situated may conform. It allows without restriction the use
> for such purposes of buildings of brick or stone; but, as to wooden
> buildings, constituting nearly all those in previous use, it divides the
> owners or occupiers into two classes, not having respect to their
> personal character and qualifications for the business, nor the situa-
> tion and nature and adaptation of the buildings themselves, but merely
> by an arbitrary line, on one side of which are those who are permitted
> to pursue their industry by the mere will and consent of the super-
> visors, and on the other those from whom that consent is withheld,
> at their mere will and pleasure. And both classes are alike only in
> this, that they are tenants at will, under the supervisors, of their
> means of living. The ordinance, therefore, also differs from the not

unusual case, where discretion is lodged by law in public officers or bodies to grant or withhold licenses to keep taverns, or places for the sale of spirituous liquors, and the like, when one of the conditions is that the applicant shall be a fit person for the exercise of the privilege, because in such cases the fact of fitness is submitted to the judgment of the officer, and calls for the exercise of a discretion of a judicial nature.

Justice Matthews's position here deserves careful attention. He mentions the two distinctions spelled out in the ordinance. The first involves the distinction between buildings of brick and stone, on the one hand, and wooden buildings on the other. This distinction does not trouble the Justice presumably because of the relationship between this distinction and fire prevention. It is the distinction involving owners of laundries in wooden buildings that concerns Matthews. These owners are divided into two classes—those who may continue to operate their businesses and those who may not. The basis of the distinction is the success of the laundry owners in getting the approval of the board of supervisors mentioned in the ordinances. Because the ordinance gives no guidance to the board, Justice Matthews finds the distinction purely arbitrary and, therefore, a denial of equal protection. The first section of the ordinance reads as follows: "It shall be unlawful, from and after the passage of this order, for any person or persons to establish, maintain, or carry on a laundry within the corporate limits of the city and county of San Francisco without having first obtained the consent of the board of supervisors, except the same be located in a building constructed either of brick or stone." How would you rewrite this ordinance to remove its arbitrary character?

The "similarly situated" rule was sufficient to overturn Yick Wo's conviction and thereby thwart San Francisco's efforts to discriminate against Chinese laundry operators. This rule, of course, is procedural rather than substantive. It does not in itself forbid any kind of classification of citizens; it merely requires that no matter what classification is made, those persons falling within the classification must be treated alike. While sound procedures usually suffice to achieve substantive justice, they may occasionally fall short of this goal. Suppose, for example, that after Yick Wo, the Board of Supervisors in San Francisco had rewritten the ordinance in such a way that Chinese were explicitly forbidden from operating laundries. Would the "similarly situated" rule help the Chinese launderers? Couldn't the board argue that their new rule treated alike those "similarly situated"—that is, all Chinese are explicitly forbidden from operating laundries? Fortunately, the San Francisco Board never took such a step, but the possibility that they could have points out one of the limitations of relying exclusively on procedures to achieve substantive

justice. Can you identify substantive and procedural regulations in an
agency with which you are familiar? Are procedural regulations usually
sufficient for furthering the goals and values of the agency?

Had San Francisco actually attempted a brazen and overt discrimination against the Chinese by explicitly excluding them from the laundry
industry, the courts would surely have voided this effort on the substantive
grounds that the classification was "unreasonable." In his Yick Wo opinion,
Justice Matthews foreclosed any possibility that the "similarly situated"
rule might be distorted to justify overt and blatant discrimination:

> It appears that the petitioners have complied with every requisite,
> deemed by the law or by the public officers charged with its adminis-
> tration, necessary for the protection of neighboring property from
> fire, or as a precaution against injury to the public health. No reason
> whatever, except the will of the supervisors, is assigned why they
> should not be permitted to carry on, in the accustomed manner, their
> harmless and useful occupation, on which they depend for a livelihood.
> And while this consent of the supervisors is withheld from them and
> from two hundred others who have also petitioned, all of whom happen
> to be Chinese subjects, eighty others, not Chinese subjects, are per-
> mitted to carry on the same business under similar conditions. The
> fact of this discrimination is admitted. No reason for it is shown,
> and the conclusion cannot be resisted, that no reason for it exists
> except hostility to the race and nationality to which the petitioners
> belong, and which in the eye of the law is not justified. The discrimin-
> ation is, therefore, illegal, and the public administration which
> enforces it is a denial of the equal protection of the laws and a viola-
> tion of the Fourteenth Amendment of the Constitution. The imprison-
> ment of the petitioners is, therefore, illegal, and they must be
> discharged. . . .

Matthews's opinion in Yick Wo, then, highlights two important aspects
of equal protection—the procedural rule that those "similarly situated"
must be treated alike and the substantive rule that the Court will not abide
classifications made on the basis of racial hostility. Is the substantive
aspect of Yick Wo the same as Harlan's view in Plessy that the Constitution
is "color-blind"? Does a color-blind constitution forbid only those classifications of persons that are based on racial hostility or does it forbid
every form of racial classification regardless of whether its motive is
benign or hostile? Is there such a thing as a benign racial classification?
Can you give an example? Do you think the equal protection clause should
be interpreted to permit such classifications?

Brown v. Board of Education

The "separate but equal" formula associated with Plessy v. Ferguson provided the constitutional foundation for segregation in many areas of
American life other than public transportation, which had been the point at
issue in Plessy. Segregation in theaters, beaches, golf courses, and other
places frequented by the public was defended on the grounds of the separate
but equal doctrine. The most significant application of the Plessy principle, however, arose in the area of public education. Long before Plessy,
many schools in all parts of America had been segregated, but efforts after
Plessy (1896) to challenge this practice on constitutional grounds were
doomed by the doctrine announced in that case. By the beginning of the
twentieth century most northern states had forbidden racial segregation in
their own school systems, but the practice flourished in the South, in the
border states, and in the District of Columbia.

Although the separation called for by the separate but equal formula
was strictly enforced, the equality promised by the same formula proved
illusory. With few exceptions, the buildings designated for the education
of black children were miserably inferior in all physical appointments from
heating to toilet facilities. Black teachers were paid less than their white
counterparts; bus transportation to black schools was frequently irregular
and at times nonexistent; the compulsory attendance laws were enforced
against black children in a most relaxed manner. In a word, public education in nearly every segregated school district was rigidly separate and
grossly unequal.

During the 1930s, attorneys for the National Association for the
Advancement of Colored People (NAACP) adopted the prudent strategy of
attacking the separate but equal doctrine where it was most vulnerable—the
manifest inequality that characterized segregated schooling. A further
refinement of this strategy was to concentrate on professional and graduate
schools in segregated state universities where comparatively few black
students would be involved. In such instances, it was assumed, the courts
might be more willing either to order integration or to fashion some other
suitable remedy than they would be in cases involving the large numbers of
black students enrolled in primary and secondary schools. The overall
objective of this cautious plan was, first, to enlist the courts in the cause
of forcing the states to provide truly equal educational facilities for blacks
and then, if (or more likely when) this proved impossible on financial
grounds, to get the courts simply to prohibit racial segregation in schools
that could not provide equal services.

This strategy proved most effective. In 1938 the NAACP successfully
challenged Missouri's practice of providing "equal" treatment to prospective black law students by sending them to out-of-state law schools and
defraying whatever additional tuition expenses the students might incur
because of their out-of-state status. The Supreme Court found this

practice denied equal protection of the laws. [11] Missouri responded by
establishing a separate law school for blacks, and several other segregated states did likewise. This arrangement was declared unconstitutional
in 1950 when the Supreme Court, in Sweatt v. Painter, [12] found there was
no equality between the prestigious white law school at the University of
Texas and the patently inferior law school for blacks that was graced with
only five professors and a woefully inadequate library.

On the same day that the Court rejected the constitutionality of the
separate law schools, it also voided another form of postgraduate segregation. Oklahoma had provided for the admission of blacks to the previously all-white university at Norman whenever a black student could not
find the courses he needed in the black schools. On this basis George
McLaurin, a sixty-eight year old black man with a master's degree, was
admitted to the University of Oklahoma as a full-fledged graduate student
pursuing a Ph.D. in education. [13] There was a catch, however; in fact
there were several. McLaurin was directed to a classroom seat sur-
rounded by a railing marked "Reserved for Negroes." A similar arrangement was provided for him in the library where he was assigned to a
mezzanine desk behind a carload of newspapers and in the cafeteria where
he ate at a separate table at an hour when no whites were present.
McLaurin contested the constitutionality of this treatment and his challenge
was upheld. The Court found that such segregation within the all-white
institution impaired McLaurin's "ability to study, to engage in discussions
and exchange views with other students, and, in general, to learn his
profession." [14]

The 1950 decisions of Sweatt and McLaurin were significant milestones in the epic of the blacks' quest for equality. In Sweatt the Supreme
Court had ordered a hitherto all-white school to admit a black student and
in McLaurin it had held that once admitted, the black student could not be
segregated from his white peers. More fundamental, however, and therefore more distressing was the Court's reluctance to disturb the Plessy
ruling. Segregation was still the law of the land. The Court was careful
to point out the narrow basis of its decisions. It was the failure of Texas
and Oklahoma to provide truly equal education that enabled the Court to
order integration. Then, too, there was the fact that Sweatt and McLaurin
involved postgraduate education, which affected only a handful of blacks.
There was no indication that the Court was willing to apply its reasoning to
the more politically volatile issue of the elementary and secondary schools
where millions of black youngsters would be involved.

The NAACP strategists, however, took comfort in some unusual
language that appeared in the graduate school cases of 1950. Chief
Justice Vinson, for example, had spoken of "those qualities which are
incapable of objective measurement but which make for greatness in a law
school. Such qualities, to name but a few, include reputation of the
faculty, experience of the administration, position and influence of the

alumni, standing in the community, traditions and prestige." Why should
this kind of reasoning be applied only to law schools? Perhaps there are
certain intangible factors in any school at any level that might keep it from
fulfilling its purpose and perhaps among these intangible factors is the
stigma of racial segregation.

The McLaurin case went even further. The only basis for saying
McLaurin's education was unequal was the simple fact of segregation. The
prestige of the University of Oklahoma was as much his as that of any white
student. He could attend the same classes and use the same books. The
Court's argument clearly implied that there was something inherently
unequal in segregating a student within an educational institution. Couldn't
this same line of reasoning be applied to segregated institutions
themselves?

This precise point was raised in Brown v. Board of Education of
Topeka[15] and four companion cases that came up from South Carolina,
Virginia, Delaware, and the District of Columbia. These cases were first
argued in December 1952 and reargued in October of the following year.
On May 17, 1954, Chief Justice Warren delivered the unanimous opinion of
the Court:

> These cases come to us from the States of Kansas, South Carolina,
> Virginia, and Delaware. They are premised on different facts and
> different local conditions, but a common legal question justifies their
> consideration together in this consolidated opinion.
>
> In each of the cases, minors of the Negro race, through their
> legal representatives, seek the aid of the courts in obtaining admis-
> sion to the public schools of their community on a nonsegregated basis.
> In each instance, they have been denied admission to schools attended
> by white children under laws requiring or permitting segregation
> according to race. This segregation was alleged to deprive the
> plaintiffs of the equal protection of the laws under the Fourteenth
> Amendment. In each of the cases other than the Delaware case, a
> three-judge federal district court denied relief to the plaintiffs on the
> so-called "separate but equal" doctrine announced by this Court in
> Plessy v. Ferguson. Under that doctrine, equality of treatment is
> accorded when the races are provided substantially equal facilities,
> even though these facilities be separate. In the Delaware case, the
> Supreme Court of Delaware adhered to that doctrine, but ordered that
> the plaintiffs be admitted to the white schools because of their
> superiority to the Negro schools.
>
> The plaintiffs contend that segregated public schools are not
> "equal" and cannot be made "equal," and that hence they are deprived
> of the equal protection of the laws. Because of the obvious importance
> of the question presented, the Court took jurisdiction. . . .

Reargument was largely devoted to the circumstances surrounding the adoption of the Fourteenth Amendment in 1868. It covered exhaustively consideration of the Amendment in Congress, ratification by the states, then existing practices in racial segregation, and the views of proponents and opponents of the Amendment. This discussion and our own investigation convince us that, although these sources cast some light, it is not enough to resolve the problem with which we are faced. At best, they are inconclusive. The most avid proponents of the post-War Amendments undoubtedly intended them to remove all legal distinctions among "all persons born or naturalized in the United States." Their opponents, just as certainly, were antagonistic to both the letter and the spirit of the Amendments and wished them to have the most limited effect. What others in Congress and the state legislatures had in mind cannot be determined with any degree of certainty.

An additional reason for the inclusive nature of the Amendment's history, with respect to segregated schools, is the status of public education at that time. In the South, the movement toward free common schools, supported by general taxation, had not yet taken hold. Education of white children was largely in the hands of private groups. Education of Negroes was almost nonexistent, and practically all of the race were illiterate. In fact, any education of Negroes was forbidden by law in some states. Today, in contrast, many Negroes have achieved outstanding success in the arts and sciences as well as in the business and professional world. It is true that public school education at the time of the Amendment had advanced further in the North, but the effect of the Amendment on Northern States was generally ignored in the congressional debates. Even in the North, the conditions of public education did not approximate those existing today. The curriculum was usually rudimentary; ungraded schools were common in rural areas; the school term was but three months a year in many states; and compulsory school attendance was virtually unknown. As a consequence, it is not surprising that there should be so little in the history of the Fourteenth Amendment relating to its intended effect on public education.

In the first cases in this Court construing the Fourteenth Amendment, decided shortly after its adoption, the Court interpreted it as proscribing all state-imposed discriminations against the Negro race. The doctrine of "separate but equal" did not make its appearance in this Court until 1896 in the case of Plessy v. Ferguson, involving not education but transportation. American courts have since labored with the doctrine for over half a century. In this Court, there have been six cases involving the "separate but equal" doctrine in the field of public education. In Cumming v. County Board of Education and Gong Lum v. Rice, the validity of the doctrine itself was not challenged. In more recent cases, all on the graduate school level, inequality was found in that specific benefits enjoyed by white students were denied to Negro students of the same educational qualifications. . . . In none of these cases was it necessary to re-examine the doctrine to grant relief to the Negro plaintiff. And in Sweatt v. Painter, the Court expressly reserved decision on the question whether Plessy v. Ferguson should be held inapplicable to public education.

In the instant cases, that question is directly presented. Here, unlike Sweatt v. Painter, there are findings below that the Negro and white schools involved have been equalized, or are being equalized, with respect to buildings, curricula, qualifications and salaries of teachers, and other "tangible" factors. Our decision, therefore, cannot turn on merely a comparison of these tangible factors in the Negro and white schools involved in each of the cases. We must look instead to the effect of segregation itself on public education.

In approaching this problem, we cannot turn the clock back to 1868 when the Amendment was adopted, or even to 1896 when Plessy v. Ferguson was written. We must consider public education in the light of its full development and its present place in American life throughout the Nation. Only in this way can it be determined if segregation in public schools deprives these plaintiffs of the equal protection of the laws.

Today, education is perhaps the most important function of state and local governments. Compulsory school attendance laws and the great expenditures for education both demonstrate our recognition of the importance of education to our democratic society. It is required in the performance of our most basic public responsibilities, even service in the armed forces. It is the very foundation of good citizenship. Today it is a principal instrument in awakening the child to cultural values, in preparing him for later professional training, and in helping him to adjust normally to his environment. In these days, is it doubtful that any child may reasonably be expected to succeed in life if he is denied the opportunity of an education. Such an opportunity, where the state has undertaken to provide it, is a right which must be made available to all on equal terms.

We come then to the question presented: Does segregation of children in public schools solely on the basis of race, even though the physical facilities and other "tangible" factors may be equal, deprive the children of the minority group of equal education opportunities? We believe that it does.

In Sweatt v. Painter, in finding that a segregated law school for Negroes could not provide them equal educational opportunities, this Court relied in large part on "those qualities which are incapable of objective measurement but which make for greatness in a law school."

In McLaurin v. Oklahoma State Regents, . . . the Court, in requiring
that a Negro admitted to a white graduate school be treated like all
other students, again resorted to intangible considerations: " . . .
his ability to study, to engage in discussions and exchange views with
other students, and, in general, to learn his profession." Such considerations apply with added force to children in grade and high
schools. To separate them from others of similar age and qualifications solely because of their race generates a feeling of inferiority as
to their status in the community that may affect their hearts and minds
in a way unlikely ever to be undone. The effect of this separation on
their educational opportunities was well stated by a finding in the
Kansas case by a court which nevertheless felt compelled to rule
against the Negro plaintiffs:

> Segregation of white and colored children in public schools has a
> detrimental effect upon the colored children. The impact is greater
> when it has the sanction of the law; for the policy of separating the
> races is usually interpreted as denoting the inferiority of the negro
> group. A sense of inferiority affects the motivation of the child to
> learn. Segregation with the sanction of law, therefore, has a
> tendency to [retard] the educational and mental development of
> negro children and to deprive them of some of the benefits they
> would receive in a racial[ly] integrated school system.

Whatever may have been the extent of psychological knowledge at the
time of Plessy v. Ferguson, this finding is amply supported by modern
authority. Any language in Plessy v. Ferguson contrary to this finding is rejected.

We conclude that in the field of public education the doctrine of
"separate but equal" has no place. Separate educational facilities are
inherently unequal. Therefore, we hold that the plaintiffs and others
similarly situated for whom the actions have been brought are, by
reason of the segregation complained of, deprived of the equal protection of the laws guaranteed by the Fourteenth Amendment. This disposition makes unnecessary any discussion whether such segregation also
violates the Due Process Clause of the Fourteenth Amendment.

Because these are class actions, because of the wide applicability
of this decision, and because of the great variety of local conditions,
the formulation of decrees in these cases presents problems of considerable complexity. On reargument, the consideration of appropriate relief was necessarily subordinate to the primary question—the
constitutionality of segregation in public education. We have now
announced that such segregation is a denial of the equal protection of
the laws. In order that we may have the full assistance of the parties
in formulating decrees, the cases will be restored to the docket, and
the parties are requested to present further argument on Questions 4

and 5 previously propounded by the Court for the reargument this
Term. The Attorney General of the United States is again invited to
participate. The Attorneys General of the states requiring or permitting segregation in public education will also be permitted to
appear as amici curiae upon request to do so by September 15, 1954,
and submission of briefs by October 1, 1954.

For our purposes it will be helpful to compare Warren's opinion in
Brown with the excerpts we have already examined from Harlan's dissent
in Plessy. Both opinions, of course, reject the separate but equal
doctrine of the Plessy Court but they do so on very different grounds.
Before reading any further, stop for a moment and ask yourself which of
the two approaches you found more persuasive. Do not reread Brown and
the excerpts from Harlan's dissent but simply reflect on your general
reaction.
        Now let us examine the two approaches a bit more closely. In the
seventh paragraph of Warren's opinion (beginning "In the instant cases")
the Chief Justice says that the Court must focus its attention on "the effect
of segregation" on public education (emphasis added). Compare this with
Harlan's attack on segregation as being incompatible with the nature of
citizenship. Which argument provides a more fundamental attack on
segregation by race?
        Toward the end of his opinion, Warren maintains that modern psy-
chological and sociological research is at odds with the Court's position in
Plessy that segregation does not create feelings of inferiority on the part
of minority groups. To support this criticism of Plessy, the Chief
Justice adds the following footnote:

K.B. Clark, Effect of Prejudice and Discrimination on Personality
Development (Midcentury White House Conference on Children and
Youth, 1950); Witmer and Kotinsky, Personality in the Making (1952),
c. VI; Deutscher and Chein, The Psychological Effects of Enforced
Segregation: A Survey of Social Science Opinion, 26 J. Psychol. 259
(1948); Chein, What Are the Psychological Effects of Segregation
Under Conditions of Equal Facilities? 3 Int. J. Opinion and Attitude
Res. 229 (1949); Brameld, Educational Costs, in Discrimination and
National Welfare (MacIver, ed. , 1949), 44-48; Frazier, The Negro in
the United States (1949), 674-681. And see generally Myrdal, An
American Dilemma (1944).

This footnote led to severe criticism of Warren's opinion, especially
among lawyers. The reason for the criticism was that the Court supported
a crucial point in its argument not with the customary legal citations but
with the findings of psychologists and sociologists. The first authority
cited, K.B. Clark, had conducted a series of tests in which black children

were told to make choices between pink dolls and brown dolls. The children were told to select "the nice doll," the "doll that looks bad," and so on. On the basis of these and similar tests, Clark maintained that racial segregation had a harmful effect on the psyche of black children. [16]

What do you think of the place of such evidence in a Supreme Court opinion? Was the lawyers' complaint an example of a narrow and self-serving professional pique or was there some merit to it? How reliable is the evidence of social science for influencing constitutional as opposed to legislative or administrative issues? What would happen if new psychological studies showed that integrated education retarded a black child's ability to develop a sense of black identity and thereby adversely affected his or her ability to learn? Should the moral question of racial segregation be decided on empirical grounds, that is, on the effects it produces? Or should it be decided deductively from the nature of citizenship as Harlan would have it?

Which argument—Warren's or Harlan's—is broader in its impact? To answer this question, take the hypothetical case of a thirty-year-old black man arrested for playing golf on a public course for "whites only" one year after Brown. Would Warren's opinion be sufficient to overturn this conviction? Would Harlan's dissent, had it become the law of the land?

In fairness to Warren, we should acknowledge that the previous paragraphs may have been a bit too hard on him. One reason Harlan's opinion—despite its somewhat antiquated language—may appear more attractive is that Harlan was writing a dissenting opinion in which no other justice joined whereas Warren was writing an opinion for a unanimous Court. Thus Harlan had the advantage of being able to express his ideas because they were his ideas alone. Administrators who have had to submit task force or committee reports will readily sympathize with Chief Justice Warren. He knew the Court's decision would be extremely unpopular in the South. The governor of South Carolina had openly threatened to close the public schools of his state before he would let black and white children go to the same school. In such a political climate it was crucial that the Supreme Court present a united front. A five-to-four or six-to-three decision would have given the segregationists the hope that, like Plessy itself, Brown might someday be overturned. This would have made enforcement of Brown even more difficult than it turned out to be. To get unanimous backing, Warren had to accommodate some very divergent viewpoints among the nine justices. [17] As a result, his opinion should be read as an act of judicial statesmanship with high moral purpose and not as an essay on moral philosophy.

One of the companion cases to Brown was Bolling v. Sharpe, [18] a case originating in the District of Columbia. The companion cases involving other states were settled on the same basis as Brown—that is, racial segregation in public schools violates the provision of the Fourteenth Amendment that "no state shall . . . deny to any person within its

jurisdiction the equal protection of the laws." Because the District of
Columbia is not a state, its actions are not governed by the equal protection clause. Hence, there was the possibility—albeit remote—that the
Court would find that state legislatures could not segregate students in the
schools under their jurisdiction but that Congress could!

Chief Justice Warren held that the due process clause of the Fifth
Amendment, which does apply to Congress, provided sufficient legal
grounds to forbid racial segregation in the schools of the District of
Columbia. He closed his opinion with a sentence that is quite significant
for our purposes: "In view of our decision that the Constitution prohibits
the states from maintaining racially segregated public schools, it would be
unthinkable that the same Constitution would impose a lesser duty on the
Federal Government."

Warren was undoubtedly correct that it would be unthinkable—regardless of constitutional fine points—for the federal government to impose
upon the state a higher standard of racial justice than it imposes upon
itself. Why is this so? What are the value implications of Warren's
observation? Has this always been true in American history? If not,
when did this become the case? Does it apply only to moral issues involving race or to other issues of public morality as well?

After handing down its decision declaring segregation in public
schools unconstitutional, the Supreme Court was faced with the problem of
enforcement. Justice Frankfurter, in particular, was deeply concerned
about this issue. He felt there would be nothing worse the Court could do
than to announce boldly the lofty principles of racial justice and then reveal
itself impotent to effect any practical results consequent upon its announcement. The concern of Frankfurter and the other justices may well
have been motivated by two closely related considerations. The first, and
most obvious, consideration would be to save the Court from looking ridiculous. The second consideration would be that institutions that appear
ridiculous by overreaching themselves are thereby rendered incapable of
achieving reforms that they might otherwise have been able to bring about.
Thus there is at times a connection between an organization's image and its
ability to promote moral values. This proposition is, of course, quite
obvious for the simple reason that there is a connection between an organization's image and its ability to do anything at all—moral, immoral, or
amoral. The proposition is highlighted here to serve as a reminder that
an organization's concern with its self-image—at least to the extent of not
appearing absurd—can be freighted with moral values. Concerns about
"saving face" are not necessarily motivated by narrow self-interest alone.
Can you apply this principle in a concrete way to government organizations
with which you are familiar?

In the aftermath of Brown, the Court rejected two extreme alternatives in formulating an enforcement policy. For the reasons discussed in
the previous paragraph, it did not order the immediate desegregation of all

school districts forthwith. Nor did it fashion an order granting relief only
to the litigants of Brown and its companion cases. The Court could have
taken this very cautious approach but this would have forced black children
in segregated states to undertake the time and expense of initiating law-
suits to secure what the Court had already announced as their constitutional
rights.

Instead, the Court called for further argument on the enforcement
issue and diplomatically invited the attorneys general of the states requiring or permitting segregation to submit briefs representing their viewpoints. Oral argument was heard in April 1955, and at the end of the
following month the Court issued its decree. After rehearsing the history
of the case, Chief Justice Warren gave the following directives:

> Full implementation of these constitutional principles may require
> solution of varied local school problems. School authorities have the
> primary responsibility for elucidating, assessing, and solving these
> problems; courts will have to consider whether the action of school
> authorities constitutes good faith implementation of the governing
> constitutional principles. Because of their proximity to local condi-
> tions and the possible need for further hearings, the courts which
> originally heard these cases can best perform this judicial appraisal.
> Accordingly, we believe it appropriate to remand the cases to those
> courts.
>
> In fashioning and effectuating the decrees, the courts will be
> guided by equitable principles. Traditionally, equity has been charac-
> terized by a practical flexibility in shaping its remedies and by a
> facility for adjusting and reconciling public and private needs. These
> cases call for the exercise of these traditional attributes of equity
> power. At stake is the personal interest of the plaintiffs in admission
> to public schools as soon as practicable on a nondiscriminatory basis.
> To effectuate this interest may call for elimination of a variety of
> obstacles in making the transition to school systems operated in
> accordance with the constitutional principles set forth in our May 17,
> 1954, decision. Courts of equity may properly take into account the
> public interest in the elimination of such obstacles in a systematic and
> effective manner. But it should go without saying that the vitality of
> these constitutional principles cannot be allowed to yield simply
> because of disagreement with them.
>
> While giving weight to these public and private considerations, the
> courts will require that the defendants make a prompt and reasonable
> start toward full compliance with our May 17, 1954, ruling. Once
> such a start has been made, the courts may find that additional time is
> necessary to carry out the ruling in an effective manner. The burden
> rests upon the defendants to establish that such time is necessary in
> the public interest and is consistent with good faith compliance at the

earliest practicable date. To that end, the courts may consider problems related to administration, arising from the physical condition of
the school plant, the school transportation system, personnel,
revision of school districts and attendance areas into compact units to
achieve a system of determining admission to the public schools on a
nonracial basis, and revision of local laws and regulations which may
be necessary in solving the foregoing problems. They will also consider the adequacy of any plans the defendants may propose to meet
these problems and to effectuate a transition to a racially nondiscriminatory school system. During this period of transition, the
courts will retain jurisdiction of these cases.

The judgments below are accordingly reversed and the cases are
remanded to the District Courts to take such proceedings and enter
such orders and decrees consistent with this opinion as are necessary
and proper to admit to public schools on a racially nondiscriminatory
basis with all deliberate speed the parties to these cases. . . . [19]

To put the Court's decision in management terms, it opted for a
strategy of decentralization and then delegated broad, discretionary authority to the district courts. It provided no timetable; neither the fixed date
for ending segregation requested by NAACP counsel Thurgood Marshall
nor the ninety-day deadline for school boards to file a desegregation plan
suggested by the Justice Department. The only temporal admonition the
Court offered was that the school districts get on with the work of desegregation "with all deliberate speed." The phrase was borrowed from Francis
Thompson's poem "The Hound of Heaven." The selection was an apt one
for subsequent events revealed that the black children seeking admission
to previously all-white schools would need patience approaching the divine.
Ten years after Brown less than 2 percent of the black children residing in
the eleven states of the Confederacy were going to schools with white
youngsters.

It would be unfair to blame the Court alone for this dismal record.
The other two branches of government indulged in unconscionable foot-
dragging for many years after Brown. Eventually Congress passed
important legislation in the areas of civil rights and education. Pursuant
to this legislation, HEW in the late 1960s threatened to suspend federal
education aid to segregated school districts. This broke the logjam, and
the school boards of the South started to implement Brown in a serious
way. By 1973 over 46 percent of the black children in the states of the
Confederacy were attending predominantly white schools. No other section
of the nation could boast of such an impressive record of integration.

What lessons might be drawn from all this for our purposes? The
comforting thought that time heals all? The critical position that the
Court was excessively concerned with not overreaching itself and conse-

quently fashioned too lenient a decree? The constitutional reflection that causes of high moral purpose need the cooperation of all three branches of government? The economic observation that money talks—southern school boards stalled until threatened with monetary reprisals? The prudential consideration that one must be "sensitive" to varying moral climates in different parts of the country and that this "sensitivity" is, after all, a concomitant of federalism? The unbending stance that it is simply indefensible to delay the enforcement of constitutional rights in certain parts of the country because of the likelihood of resistance?

Loving v. Virginia

If in 1954 the Court was willing to extirpate racial segregation in public schools only "with all deliberate speed," by the late 1960s the mood of both Court and nation was such that a broader condemnation of racism was in order. A Virginia antimiscegenation statute provided an opportunity for the Supreme Court, in Loving v. Virginia,[20] to issue one of its most unequivocal statements on racial discrimination.

In 1958, two residents of Virginia, Mildred Jeter, a black woman, and Richard Loving, a white man, were married in the District of Columbia and returned to Virginia to establish their home in Caroline County. The following year they were convicted of violating a Virginia statute forbidding "any white person [to] intermarry with a colored person or any colored person [to] intermarry with a white person." The same statute forbade such persons to leave the state for the purpose of being married with the intention of returning to Virginia and cohabiting therein. At their trial the Lovings pleaded guility and were sentenced to one year in jail. The trial judge suspended the sentence on the condition that the Lovings leave Virginia and not return for twenty-five years. For the edification of all concerned, the judge felt obliged to explain the wisdom of Virginia's prohibition on racially mixed marriages. To this end, he added to the following gloss on the Book of Genesis:

> Almighty God created the races white, black, yellow, malay, and red, and he placed them on separate continents. And but for the interference with his arrangement there would be no cause for such marriages. The fact that he separated the races shows that he did not intend for the races to mix.[21]

The Lovings moved to the District of Columbia and in 1963 filed a motion with the trial court to set aside their sentence on the ground that the statutes they had violated were unconstitutional. The motion was denied, and, upon appeal, Virginia's Supreme Court of Appeals upheld the

constitutionality of the antimiscegenation statute. The Lovings then
appealed to the Supreme Court of the United States. Chief Justice Warren
delivered the opinion of the Court:

> [T]he State argues that the meaning of the Equal Protection Clause, as
> illuminated by the statements of the Framers, is only that state penal
> laws containing an interracial element as part of the definition of the
> offense must apply equally to whites and Negroes in the sense that
> members of each race are punished to the same degree. Thus, the
> State contends that, because its miscegenation statutes punish equally
> both the white and the Negro participants in an interracial marriage,
> these statutes, despite their reliance on racial classifications, do not
> constitute an invidious discrimination based upon race. The second
> argument advanced by the State assumes the validity of its equal
> application theory. The argument is that, if the Equal Protection
> Clause does not outlaw miscegenation statutes because of their
> reliance on racial classifications, the question of constitutionality
> would thus become whether there was any rational basis for a State to
> treat interracial marriages differently from other marriages. On this
> question, the State argues, the scientific evidence is substantially in
> doubt and, consequently, this Court should defer to the wisdom of the
> state legislature in adopting its policy of discouraging interracial
> marriages.
>
> Because we reject the notion that the mere "equal application" of
> a statute containing racial classifications is enough to remove the
> classifications from the Fourteenth Amendment's proscription of all
> invidious racial discriminations, we do not accept the State's conten-
> tion that these statutes should be upheld if there is any possible basis
> for concluding that they serve a rational purpose. The mere fact of
> equal application does not mean that our analysis of these statutes
> should follow the approach we have taken in cases involving no racial
> discrimination where the Equal Protection Clause has been arrayed
> against a statute discriminating between the kinds of advertising which
> may be displayed on trucks in New York City, . . . or an exemption in
> Ohio's ad valorem tax for merchandise owned by a nonresident in a
> storage warehouse. . . . In these cases, involving distinctions not
> drawn according to race, the Court has merely asked whether there is
> any rational foundation for the discriminations, and has deferred to the
> wisdom of the state legislatures. In the case at bar, however, we deal
> with statutes containing racial classifications, and the fact of equal
> application does not immunize the statute from the very heavy burden
> of justification which the Fourteenth Amendment has traditionally
> required of state statutes drawn according to race. . . .
>
> The State finds support for its "equal application" theory in the
> decision of the Court in Pace v. Alabama, 106 U.S. 583 (1883). In

that case, the Court upheld a conviction under an Alabama statute forbidding adultery or fornication between a white person and a Negro which imposed a greater penalty than that of a statute proscribing similar conduct by members of the same race. The Court reasoned that the statute could not be said to discriminate against Negroes because the punishment for each participant in the offense was the same. However, as recently as the 1964 Term, in rejecting the reasoning of that case, we stated "Pace represents a limited view of the Equal Protection Clause which has not withstood analysis in the subsequent decisions of this Court." . . . As we there demonstrated, the Equal Protection Clause requires the consideration of whether the classifications drawn by any statute constitute an arbitrary and invidious discrimination. The clear and central purpose of the Fourteenth Amendment was to eliminate all official state sources of invidious racial discrimination in the States. . . .

There can be no question but that Virginia's miscegenation statutes rest solely upon distinctions drawn according to race. The statutes proscribe generally accepted conduct if engaged in by members of different races. Over the years, this Court has consistently repudiated "[d]istinctions between citizens solely because of their ancestry" as being "odious to a free people whose institutions are founded upon the doctrine of equality." . . . At the very least, the Equal Protection Clause demands that racial classifications, especially suspect in criminal statutes, be subjected to the "most rigid scrutiny," . . . and, if they are ever to be upheld, they must be shown to be necessary to the accomplishment of some permissible state objective, independent of the racial discrimination which it was the object of the Fourteenth Amendment to eliminate. Indeed, two members of this Court have already stated that they "cannot conceive of a valid legislative purpose . . . which makes the color of a person's skin the test of whether his conduct is a criminal offense." . . .

There is patently no legitimate overriding purpose independent of invidious racial discrimination which justifies this classification. The fact that Virginia prohibits only interracial marriages involving white persons demonstrates that the racial classifications must stand on their own justification, as measures designed to maintain White Supremacy. We have consistently denied the constitutionality of measures which restrict the rights of citizens on account of race. There can be no doubt that restricting the freedom to marry solely because of racial classifications violates the central meaning of the Equal Protection Clause.

Although this case involved criminal penalties, the Court has applied the same standard in recent civil matters as well—that "the clear and central purpose of the Fourteenth Amendment was to eliminate all official state sources of invidious racial discrimination in the States."

Do you find this statement adequately reflects your own views? Do you find the use of the word "invidious" redundant? That is, can there be racial discrimination that is not invidious? This raises the same issue we saw in Yick Wo v. Hopkins: Is "benign" racial discrimination possible?

Do you think the Court used the word "invidious" to leave open the possibility of some sort of benign racial discrimination? If this was the Court's intention, the use of "invidious" is not altogether appropriate. In terms of formal logic, the obverse of invidious is "noninvidious." "Noninvidious" is not synonomous with "benign." The former is a broader term than the latter because logically it included "neutral" as well as "benign." Despite the niceties of formal logic, does it make any sense to speak of discrimination that is neutral? Is "neutral discrimination" a contradiction in terms? Is all discrimination necessarily either invidious or benign? Indeed, is it appropriate to speak of benign discrimination at all? If we treat people differently on the basis of race out of a benign motivation, is it best to avoid the word "discrimination" altogether? If so, what should we call such treatment?

A careful self-examination of just how we use words can be a useful value-clarification exercise. Judges are frequently constrained in their use of language because their decisions usually follow established precedents and at times create new ones. Professional proprieties demand adherence to certain terms of art. While this adherence has the wholesome effect of conferring stability on our legal institutions, it can also have the less happy effect of stultifying ideas. Words are symbols and, as such, point to, but do not exhaust, the richness of our thoughts. For professional reasons, judges must at times rest content with repeating consecrated phrases from the past that do not precisely convey their personal beliefs. As individuals, however, we are not so constrained. We can and should express our thoughts as clearly as language will allow. How would you state your own views on when, if ever, and under what circumstances, if any, an American government (national, state, or local) could be morally justified in treating people differently on the basis of race alone?[22]

SEX

From a constitutional point of view, there are some similarities between discrimination based on race and discrimination based on sex. Certain aspects of Chief Justice Warren's opinion in Loving anticipate important arguments that appear in the cases on sex discrimination examined below. In Loving, Warren draws a distinction between classifications based on race and other types of classification—for example, "a statute discriminating between the kinds of advertising which may be displayed on trucks in New York City, Railway Express Agency, Inc. v. New York, . . . or an exemption in Ohio's ad valorem tax for merchandise owned by a non-resident in a storage warehouse, Allied Stores of Ohio Inc. v. Bowers." Warren is suggesting here what some commentators once called a "two-tier theory" of equal protection. What this means is that the Court applies two different types of "tests" to state action challenged on equal protection grounds. The appropriate test is selected on the basis of the type of classification created by the state. For example, New York City forbade the operation in its streets of motor vehicles displaying advertisements of any business other than the products of the owner of the vehicle. Railway Express Agency contested this ordinance on the grounds that the equal protection clause prohibits discrimination in favor of vehicles carrying advertising of their owners' products as opposed to vehicles, like those of Railway Express, that advertise the products of other companies. The Supreme Court "tested" the New York City ordinance by finding a "reasonable relation" between the challenged classification and the city's interest in promoting public safety in its thoroughfares. Thus, the test of reasonableness is a relatively easy one for the states to pass; it is the standard by which the courts judge and usually approve state regulations of business and economic interests. Classifications based on race, however, must pass a far more severe test than mere reasonableness. As Chief Justice Warren stated in Loving, where racial classifications are involved, "we do not accept the State's contention that these statutes should be upheld if there is any possible basis for concluding that they serve a rational purpose. . . . In the case at bar . . . we deal with statutes containing racial classifications, and the fact of equal application does not immunize the statute from the very heavy burden of justification which the Fourteenth Amendment has traditionally required of state statutes drawn according to race." Race is a suspect classification and, hence, is subject to "strict judicial scrutiny," which requires that the state show some "compelling state interest" to justify the classification.

One of the most important issues in the area of sex discrimination has been whether the Court would declare sex to be a suspect classification. If it should do so, then it would be extremely difficult for government at any level to justify different treatment of its citizens on the basis of sex. When "strict judicial scrutiny" is applied, the Court seldom finds "a compelling state interest."

Long before the Court was interested in questions of suspect classifications and compelling interests, the issue of sexual discrimination was presented for its considered judgment in Bradwell v. Illinois,[23] an 1873 case dealing with the constitutionality of the refusal of the state of Illinois to license women to practice law. The Court rejected the challenge and added a few gratutitous reflections that might allow us to call Bradwell the Dred Scott of women's liberation:

The civil law, as well as nature itself, has always recognized a wide difference in the respective spheres and destinies of man and woman. Man is, or should be, woman's protection and defender. The natural and proper timidity and delicacy which belongs to the female sex evidently unfits it for many of the occupations of civil life. The constitution of the family organization, which is founded in the divine ordinance, as well as in the nature of things, indicates the domestic sphere as that which properly belongs to the domain and functions of womanhood.[24]

Frontiero v. Richardson

Decisions rendered by the Supreme Court in recent years have retired Bradwell to the status of a quaint relic of the distant past. In Reed v. Reed,[25] the Court struck down an Idaho probate law that gave males preference over females when both were equally entitled to administer an estate. More important than the outcome of Reed, however, was the rationale of the decision. This proved somewhat problematic, as the Court was to discover two years later, when four justices interpreted Reed as having defined sex as a suspect classification while three others— including Chief Justice Burger who had written the Reed opinion—denied the Court had said any such thing. The case that occasioned this split, Frontiero v. Richardson,[26] involved a female lieutenant in the United States Air Force, Sharron A. Frontiero, whose civilian husband was denied dependency status for the purpose of obtaining increased quarters allowances as well as certain medical and dental benefits. Under the statute challenged by Frontiero, a serviceman could claim his wife as a dependent "without regard to whether she is dependent upon him for any part of her support." A servicewoman, however, could not claim her husband as a dependent unless he is in fact dependent upon her for over one-half his support. Joseph Frontiero was a full-time student with monthly expenses of $354. Because he received $205 per month in veterans' benefits from his own previous military service, he did not qualify as his wife's dependent. Had the roles been reversed, that is, if Joseph had been on active duty and his wife had been a full-time student, she would have automatically qualified as his dependent regardless of whatever other income she might have had. The Supreme Court agreed unanimously that this arrangement was unconstitutional. Four of the Justices (Brennan, Douglas, Marshall and White) found in Reed "at least implicit support" for declaring sex a suspect category. In the light of this finding, the air force's contention that the discriminatory treatment was instituted for administrative convenience was easily defeated. In a concurring opinion, Justice Powell, joined by Justice Blackmun and Chief Justice Burger, upheld Frontiero's position but disagreed that sex was a suspect category.

I agree that the challenged statutes constitute an unconstitutional discrimination against service women in violation of the Due Process
Clause of the Fifth Amendment, but I cannot join the opinion of Mr.
Justice Brennan, which would hold that all classifications based upon
sex, "like classifications based upon race, alienage, and national
origin," are "inherently suspect and must therefore be subjected to
close judicial scrutiny." It is unnecessary for the Court in this case
to characterize sex as a suspect classification with all of the far-
reaching implications of such a holding. Reed v. Reed, which
abundantly supports our decision today, did not add sex to the narrowly
limited group of classifications which are inherently suspect. In my
view, we can and should decide this case on the authority of Reed and
reserve for the future any expansion of its rationale.

Although Powell was unwilling to classify sex as a suspect category,
he did not say that gender-based distinctions could be justified by the
relaxed rule of mere reasonableness alone. Instead, he found in Reed sufficient authority to strike down the air force regulation without telling us
exactly how he interpreted Reed. Whatever it was the Court had said in
Reed, it was enough to uphold Frontiero's claim. By refusing, on the one
hand, to find sex a suspect classification and by refusing, on the other, to
declare the air force's policy unreasonable, Justice Powell upset the tidy
scheme of the two-tier approach to equal protection. He seemed to be saying that classifications based on sex were somewhere between the two
tiers—more suspect than classification by type of motor vehicle and less
suspect than classification by race. Justice Powell justified his adherence
to this muddled middle as follows:

There is another, and I find compelling reason for deferring a general
categorizing of sex classifications as invoking the strictest test of
judicial scrutiny. The Equal Rights Amendment, which, if accepted,
will resolve the substance of our precise question, has been approved
by the Congress and submitted for ratification by the States. If this
Amendment is duly adopted, it will represent the will of the people
accomplished in the manner prescribed by the Constitution. By acting
prematurely and unnecessarily as I view it, the Court has assumed a
decisional responsibility at the very time when state legislatures,
functioning within the traditional democratic process, are debating the
proposed Amendment. It seems to me that this reaching out to pre-
empt by judicial action a major political decision which is currently in
process of resolution does not reflect appropriate respect for duly
prescribed legislative processes.

Justice Powell's point here is that if the Court should consider sex a
suspect classification, it would be extremely difficult for the states or the

United States to justify any form of discrimination based on sex. Hence, the Court would settle by judicial interpretation a very substantial part of the precise point that is at issue in the state legislatures that are debating the Equal Rights Amendment. Does Powell's restraint have any parallel in the administrative process? Are there times when it is wise to avoid settling certain issues under consideration by other agencies or institutions even though one's own agency could take definitive action? What about times of presidential (or gubernatorial) transitions? Can you think of any agency with which you are familiar that deliberately left an important policy unsettled until President Carter had replaced President Ford, or President Nixon had replaced President Johnson, or President Kennedy had replaced President Eisenhower? Conversely, can you think of any policies that agency personnel rushed to "lock in" before a new president (or governor) took over? Is there any principled rule you could formulate on the propriety of not using an agency's power in a value-laden issue out of a sense of deference to the outcome of the electoral process?

Kahn v. Shevin

Kahn v. Shevin[27] centered on a Florida statute that provided for widows an annual property tax exemption of $500. Mel Kahn, a widower, applied for this exemption to the Dade County Tax Assessor's Office. When his request was denied, he sought a declaratory judgment in the circuit court for Dade County that the statute violated the equal protection clause of the Fourteenth Amendment. Kahn's position was upheld in the circuit court but this decision was reversed by the Florida Supreme Court. The court found "the classification valid because it has a 'fair and substantial relation to the object of the legislation,' that object being the reduction of 'the disparity between the economic capabilities of a man and a woman.'" Kahn appealed to the Supreme Court of the United States.

The opinion of the Court was delivered by Justice Douglas.

There can be no dispute that the financial difficulties confronting the lone woman in Florida or in any other State exceed those facing the man. Whether from overt discrimination or from the socialization process of a male dominated culture, the job market is inhospitable to the woman seeking any but the lowest paid jobs. . . . The disparity is likely to be exacerbated for the widow. While the widower can usually continue in the occupation which preceded his spouse's death, in many cases the widow will find herself suddenly forced into a job market with which she is unfamiliar, and in which, because of her former economic dependency, she will have fewer skills to offer. . . .

This is not a case like Frontiero v. Richardson, where the Government denied its female employees both substantive and procedural

benefits granted males "solely for administrative convenience." . . .
(emphasis in original). We deal here with a state tax law reasonably
designed to further the state policy of cushioning the financial impact
of spousal loss upon the sex for whom that loss imposes a disproportionately heavy burden. We have long held that "[w]here taxation is
concerned and no specific federal right, apart from equal protection,
is imperilled, the States have large leeway in making classifications
and drawing lines which in their judgment produce reasonable systems
of taxation." . . . A state tax law is not arbitrary although it "discriminate[s] in favor of a certain class . . . if the discrimination is
founded upon a reasonable distinction, or difference in state policy,"
not in conflict with the Federal Constitution. . . . This principle has
weathered nearly a century of Supreme Court adjudication, and it
applies here as well. The statute before us is well within those limits.

In a footnote to his opinion, Justice Douglas pointed out, quite correctly, that "gender has never been rejected as an impermissible classification in all instances." What he failed to explain, however, is why he had
joined Justice Brennan's opinion in Frontiero, which found sex to be an
inherently suspect classification. He distinguished the present case from
Frontiero on the ground that the latter dealt "solely" with questions of
administrative convenience. Although this is true, it does not explain why
Douglas found sex a suspect classification in Frontiero but not in Kahn.
    Following the logic of their position in Frontiero, Justices Brennan,
Marshall, and White dissented in Kahn. They did so, however, on somewhat different grounds. First let us consider Brennan's dissent in which
he was joined by Marshall:

In my view . . . a legislative classification that distinguishes potential beneficiaries solely by reference to their gender-based status as
widows or widowers, like classifications based on race, alienage, and
national origin, must be subjected to close judicial scrutiny, because
it focuses upon generally immutable characteristics over which
individuals have little or no control, and also because gender-based
classifications too often have been inexcusably utilized to stereotype
and stigmatize politically powerless segments of society. . . . The
Court is not therefore free to sustain the statute on the ground that it
rationally promotes legitimate governmental interests; rather, such
suspect classifications can be sustained only when the State bears the
burden of demonstrating that the challenged legislation serves overriding or compelling interests that cannot be achieved either by a
more carefully tailored legislative classification or by the use of
feasible less drastic means. While, in my view, the statute serves a
compelling governmental interest by "cushioning the financial impact
of spousal loss upon the sex for whom that loss imposes a

disproportionately heavy burden," I think that the statute is invalid
because the State's interest can be served equally well by a more narrowly drafted statute.

Gender-based classifications cannot be sustained merely because
they promote legitimate governmental interests, such as efficacious
administration of government. . . . But Florida's justification of
§ 196.191 (7) is not that it serves administrative convenience or helps
to preserve the public fisc. Rather, the asserted justification is that
§ 196.191 (7) is an affirmative step toward alleviating the effects of
past economic discrimination against women.

I agree that, in providing special benefits for a needy segment of
society long the victim of purposeful discrimination and neglect, the
statute serves the compelling state interest of achieving equality for
such groups. No one familiar with this country's history of pervasive
sex discrimination against women can doubt the need for remedial
measures to correct the resulting economic imbalances. . . . By
providing a property tax exemption for widows, [the statute] assists
in reducing the economic disparity for a class of women particularly
disadvantaged by the legacy of economic discrimination. In that circumstance, the purpose and effect of the suspect classification is
ameliorative: the statute neither stigmatizes nor denigrates widowers
not also benefited by the legislation. Moreover, inclusion of needy
widowers within the class of beneficiaries would not further the State's
overriding interest in remedying the economic effects of past sex discrimination for needy victims of that discrimination. While doubtless
some widowers are in financial need, no one suggests that such need
results from sex discrimination as in the case of widows.

The statute nevertheless fails to satisfy the requirements of equal
protection, since the State has not borne its burden of proving that its
compelling interest could not be achieved by a more precisely tailored
statute or by use of feasible less drastic means. Section 196.191 (7)
is plainly overinclusive, for the $500 property tax exemption may be
obtained by a financially independent heiress as well as by an unemployed widow with dependent children. The State has offered nothing
to explain why inclusion of widows of substantial economic means was
necessary to advance the State's interest in ameliorating the effects of
past economic discrimination against women.

Moreover, alternative means of classification, narrowing the
class of widow beneficiaries, appear readily available. The exemption is granted only to widows who complete and file with the tax
assessor a form application establishing their status as widows. By
merely redrafting that form to exclude widows who earn annual
incomes, or possess assets, in excess of specified amounts, the State
could readily narrow the class of beneficiaries to those widows for

whom the effects of past economic discrimination against women have been a practical reality.

Thus for Brennan the Florida statute is unconstitutional not because it discriminates against widowers but because its gender-based classification is "overinclusive" in its effort to redress the effects of economic discrimination against women. It is overinclusive because it comes to the aid of rich widows as well as poor ones. Brennan does not fault the statute for excluding poor widowers because no matter how genuine their poverty may be, it cannot be the result of gender-based discrimination.

Justice White dissented on different grounds:

The Florida tax exemption at issue here is available to all widows but not to widowers. The presumption is that all widows are financially more needy and less trained or less ready for the job market than men. It may be that most widows have been occupied as housewife, mother and homemaker and are not immediately prepared for employment. But there are many rich widows who need no largess from the State; many others are highly trained and have held lucrative positions long before the death of their husbands. At the same time, there are many widowers who are needy and who are in more desperate financial straits and have less access to the job market than many widows. Yet none of them qualifies for the exemption.

I find the discrimination invidious and violative of the Equal Protection Clause. There is merit in giving poor widows a tax break, but gender-based classifications are suspect and require more justification than the State has offered.

I perceive no purpose served by the exemption other than to alleviate current economic necessity, but the State extends the exemption to widows who do not need the help and denies it to widowers who do. It may be administratively inconvenient to make individual determinations of entitlement and to extend the exemption to needy men as well as needy women, but administrative efficiency is not an adequate justification for discriminations based purely on sex.

It may be suggested that the State is entitled to prefer widows over widowers because their assumed need is rooted in past and present economic discrimination against women. But this is not a credible explanation of Florida's tax exemption; for if the State's purpose was to compensate for past discrimination against females, surely it would not have limited the exemption to women who are widows. Moreover, even if past discrimination is considered to be the criterion for current tax exemption, the State nevertheless ignores all those widowers who have felt the effects of economic discrimination, whether as a member of a racial group or as one of the many who cannot escape the cycle of poverty. It seems to me that the State in this case is merely conferring an economic benefit in the form of a tax exemption and has not adequately explained why women should be treated differently than men.

    I dissent.

Weinberger v. Wiesenfeld

Weinberger v. Wiesenfeld,[28] like Kahn, involved benefits available to widows but denied to widowers and, like Frontiero, involved men whose wives provided the principal source of family income. Stephen Wiesenfeld's wife, Paula, died in childbirth in June 1972. She had been a teacher before and after her marriage. Her salary was considerably more than that of her husband. Stephen Wiesenfeld, left with the sole responsibility for caring for his infant son, applied to his local Social Security office for suvivors' benefits for himself and his child. He had no trouble obtaining the benefits for his son but was denied any benefits for himself. Under 24 USC § 402, only female survivors are eligible for benefits. Had he been a woman, he would have received $248.30 per month as long as he was not working and, if working, that amount would have been reduced by $1.00 for every $2.00 earned annually above $2,400. Wiesenfeld challenged the constitutionality of this arrangement. Because a federal program was involved, he based his challenge on the due process clause of the Fifth Amendment.

    The Court upheld Wiesenfeld's challenge. In a lengthy opinion, Justice Brennan held that "the gender-based distinction made by § 402 is indistinguishable from that involved in Frontiero." He maintained that an "archaic and overbroad generalization, not . . . tolerated by the Constitution, underlies the distinction drawn by § 402, namely that male workers' earnings are vital to the support of their families, while earnings of female wage-earners do not significantly contribute to their families' support." The government had attempted to justify the discriminatory legislative scheme on the basis of Kahn v. Shevin—that female survivors received preferential treatment as a compensation for the traditional discrimination against women in the job market. Thus the government construed the statute as favoring women on a remedial basis. The way in which Justice Brennan handled this argument is a particularly illuminating example of the interaction between law and values.

> The Government seeks to characterize the classification here as one reasonably designed to compensate women beneficiaries as a group for the economic difficulties which still confront women who seek to support themselves and their families. The Court held in Kahn v. Shevin . . . that a statute "reasonably designed to further the state policy of cushioning the financial impact of spousal loss upon that sex

for whom that loss imposes a disproportionately heavy burden" can survive an equal protection attack. . . . But the mere recitation of a benign, compensatory purpose is not an automatic shield which protects against any inquiry into the actual purposes underlying a statutory scheme. Here, it is apparent both from the statutory scheme itself and from the legislative history of § 402 (g) that Congress' purpose in providing benefits to young widows with children was not to provide an income to women who were, because of economic discrimination, unable to provide for themselves. Rather, § 402 (g) linked as it is directly to responsibility for minor children, was intended to permit women to elect not to work and to devote themselves to the care of children. Since this purpose in no way is premised upon any special disadvantages of women, it cannot serve to justify a gender-based distinction which diminishes the protection afforded to women who do work.

That the purpose behind § 402 (g) is to provide children deprived of one parent with the opportunity for the personal attention of the other could not be more clear in the legislative history. The Advisory Council on Social Security, which developed the 1939 amendments, said explicitly that "[s] uch benefits [§ 402 (g)] are intended as supplements to the orphans' benefits with the purpose of enabling the widow to remain at home and care for the children. . . . In the Council's judgment, it is desirable to allow a woman who is left with the children the choice of whether to stay at home to care for the children or to work." . . .

Indeed, consideration was given in 1939 to extending benefits to all widows regardless of whether or not there were children. The proposal was rejected, apparently because it was felt that young widows without children can be expected to work, while middle-aged widows "are likely to have more savings than young widows, and many of them have children who are grown and able to help them. . . ." Thus, Congress decided not to provide benefits to all widows even though it was recognized that some of them would have serious problems in the job market. Instead, it provided benefits only to those women who had responsibility for minor children, because it believed that they should not be required to work.

The whole structure of survivors' benefits conforms to this articulated purpose. Widows without children obtain no benefits on the basis of their husband's earnings until they reach age 60 or, in certain instances of disability, age 50. Further, benefits under § 402 (g) cease when all children of a beneficiary are no longer eligible for children's benefits. If Congress were concerned with providing women with benefits because of economic discrimination, it would be entirely irrational to except those women who had spent many years at home rearing children, since those women are most likely to be without the

skills required to succeed in the job market. . . . Similarly, the Act
now provides benefits to a surviving divorced wife who is the parent of
a covered employee's child, regardless of how long she was married
to the deceased or of whether she or the child was dependent upon the
employee for support. . . . Yet, a divorced wife who is not the
mother of a child entitled to children's benefits is eligible for benefits
only if she meets other eligibility requirements and was married to
the covered employee for 20 years.[29] . . . Once again, this distinction among women is explicable only because Congress was not concerned in § 402 (g) with the employment problems of women generally
but with the principle that children of covered employees are entitled
to the personal attention of the surviving parent if that parent chooses
not to work.

Given the purpose of enabling the surviving parent to remain at
home to care for a child, the gender-based distinction of § 402 (g) is
entirely irrational. The classification discriminates among surviving
children solely on the basis of the sex of the surviving parent. Even in
the typical family hypothesized by the Act, in which the husband is
supporting the family and the mother is caring for the children, this
result makes no sense. The fact that a man is working while there is
a wife at home does not mean that he would, or should be required to,
continue to work if his wife dies. It is no less important for a child to
be cared for by its sole surviving parent when that parent is male
rather than female. And a father, no less than a mother, has a constitutionally protected right to the "companionship, care, custody, and
management" of "the children he has sired and raised, [which] undeniably warrants deference and, absent a powerful countervailing
interest, protection." Further, to the extent that women who work
when they have sole responsibility for children encounter special problems, it would seem that men with sole responsibility for children will
encounter the same child-care related problems. Stephen Wiesenfeld,
for example, found that providing adequate care for his infant son
impeded his ability to work.

Brennan's argument is interesting for several reasons. First, the
entire issue of sex as a suspect classification was ignored because the
statute was voided on the more fundamental grounds of being unreasonable —
that is, there was no reasonable relation between the classification (sex)
and the purpose of the statute (protection of surviving children).

Secondly, the way in which Brennan distinguishes this case from Kahn
is particularly instructive for our purposes.[30] In Kahn the different treatment afforded widows and widowers was approved by the Court because of
the remedial character of the benefit given to widows alone. There was a
clear connection between making a distinction based on sex and conferring
a gender-based monetary benefit upon the sex that had suffered economic

deprivation in the past.[31] In Wiesenfeld, however, the purpose of the
statute was not remedial via-à-vis past injustices suffered by women, but
rather it was intended to aid children who had suffered the loss of a wage-
earning parent. To single out women for this benefit is not only unfair to
male survivors and their children, but, more importantly, such discrimination reinforces the stereotype of a woman's work as trivial compared to
that of her husband. The clear implication of the Social Security provision
was that the loss of the mother's income would pose a relatively insignificant burden upon the family in comparison with the loss of the father's
income. Although, at present, this may frequently be the case, it is constitutionally offensive for the government to presume this is the case.
Such a presumption reinforces sexist stereotypes about the work of women.

The distinction between remedial and stereotypical gender-based discrimination seems to be the best way to reconcile the results of Kahn and
Wiesenfeld. The same distinction can be found in at least one other
Supreme Court case. In Ballard v. Schlessinger,[32] the Court upheld a
navy regulation that applied different "up or out" standards to male and
female officers. Female lieutenants were allowed thirteen years in grade
whereas male lieutenants were given only nine. Ballard, a male lieutenant,
challenged this arrangement, but the Court rejected his argument on the
grounds that other navy regulations so limited the activities of female
officers that they needed more time in grade than their male counterparts
to build a satisfactory record for promotion. In upholding this gender-
based classification, the Court seemed to be giving its approval to a form
of favoritism that is remedial in character.

On the surface, it would seem that Ballard could not be reconciled
with Frontiero in which the Court struck down a gender-based classification in air force regulations. In Frontiero, however, the intent of the
discrimination was not remedial. Wives were not automatically declared
dependents in order to correct some injustice in the past. The air force
based its case on "administrative convenience." It was a stereotyped
image of women that prompted the presumption of what would constitute
administrative convenience.

The Supreme Court has not articulated a clear doctrine that distinguishes sexual classifications along remedial and stereotypical lines.[33]
This is rather the work of commentators who try to impose some order
upon the judicial chaos in the area of sex discrimination. Do you find the
remedy-stereotype distinction persuasive? Is there some way in which
you might apply it in your own agency or other agencies with which you are
familiar? Does it provide a response to those who maintain that affirmative action for women is simply a form of "reverse discrimination"?
Would it be a useful back-up position for the women's movement should the
Equal Rights Amendment fail to pass? Might it do more for women's
rights than ERA if the stark language of ERA is interpreted to forbid all
(including remedial) forms of gender-based distinctions by government?

Or is the severe simplicity of ERA a more eloquent statement of women's dignity: "Equality of rights under the law shall not be denied or abridged by the United States or by any State on account of sex."[34] See additional comments on page 278.

NOTES

1. A good survey of equality as a philosophical concept can be found in Sanford A. Lakoff, Equality in Political Philosophy (Cambridge, Mass.: Harvard University Press, 1964).
2. The "protective" aspect of the equal protection clause has received little attention from the Court over the years. For all practical purposes, the clause is usually construed as though it dealt with equality before the law. For a discussion of the significance of protection, see Robert J. Harris, The Quest for Equality (Baton Rouge: LSU Press, 1960).
3. In recent years, the equal protection clause has assumed a position of tremendous significance in areas other than its traditional association with racial discrimination. Justice Holmes's disdain for the equal protection clause as the "usual last resort of constitutional arguments," Buck v. Bell 274 U.S. 200 (1927), is clearly out of date.
4. The Constitution avoids the use of the word slavery but Article I, Section 3, makes the following provision: "Representatives and direct taxes shall be apportioned among the several states which may be included within this Union, according to their respective Numbers, which shall be determined by adding to the whole Number of Free Persons, including those bound to service for a term of years, and excluding Indians not taxed, three-fifths of all other persons." The use of the euphemism "all other persons" for slaves is an excellent example of the Framers' sensitivity to the powerful symbolism of law. They were not about to abolish slavery but neither would they enshrine the word in the Constitution. See also Article I, Section 9, and Article IV, Section 2.
5. Because the equal protection clause refers only to the states, the Court has found it necessary to apply the due process clause of the Fifth Amendment against the federal government. The due process clause is the legal basis of four of the cases mentioned in this chapter: Bolling v. Sharpe, Frontiero v. Richardson, Ballard v. Schlessinger, and Weinberger v. Wiesenfeld.
6. Plessy v. Ferguson was the case that interpreted the equal protection clause as permitting the states to order "equal but separate" facilities in public vehicles.
7. 19 Howard 393 (1857).

8. C. Herman Pritchett says of the Civil Rights Cases of 1883 that "[T]here is scarcely a more striking instance in American constitutional history of outright judicial disregard of congressional intent." The American Constitution, 2nd ed. (New York: McGraw-Hill, 1968), p. 712. These cases are also discussed and roundly condemned in Harris, The Quest for Equality, pp. 87 ff.

9. 163 U.S. 537 (1896).

10. 118 U.S. 356 (1886).

11. Missouri ex rel. Gaines v. Canada 305 U.S. 337 (1938).

12. 339 U.S. 629 (1950).

13. Thurgood Marshall explains why the NAACP took the case of George McLaurin as follows: "The Dixiecrats and the others said it was horrible. The only thing Negroes were trying to do, they said, was to get social equality. As a matter of fact, there would be intermarriage, they said. The latter theory was the reason we deliberately chose Professor McLaurin. We had eight people who had applied and were eligible to be plaintiffs, but we deliberately picked Professor McLaurin because he was sixty-eight years old and we didn't think he was going to marry or intermarry. . . . They could not bring that one up on us, anyhow." Richard Kluger, Simple Justice (New York: Knopf, 1976), p. 266.

14. McLaurin v. Oklahoma State Regents 339 U.S. 637 (1950).

15. 347 U.S. 483 (1954); 349 U.S. 294 (1955).

16. For a detailed discussion of Clark's test, see Kluger, Simple Justice, pp. 315-345.

17. Ibid., pp. 582-616, 657-747.

18. 347 U.S. 497 (1954).

19. 349 U.S. 294 at 299-301 (1955).

20. 388 U.S. 1 (1967).

21. Quoted by Chief Justice Warren, ibid. at 3.

22. For a good analysis of charges of "reverse" discrimination in government personnel hiring practices, see David H. Rosenbloom and Carole Cassler Obuchowski, "Public Personnel Examinations and the Constitution: Emergent Trends," Public Administration Review 37 (January-February 1977): 9-18.

23. 16 Wall. 130 (1873).

24. Ibid., at 141.

25. 404 U.S. 71 (1971).

26. 411 U.S. 677 (1973). Because this case involved the federal government it focused on the due process clause of the Fifth Amendment rather than the equal protection clause. See discussion of Bolling v. Sharpe above, pp. 113-114.

27. 416 U.S. 351 (1974).

28. 420 U.S. 636 (1975).
29. The position of divorced wives of men eligible for Social Security
    benefits for retirement or disability was addressed by the Court in
    Matthews v. DeCastro 97 S. Ct. 431 (1976); discussed in New York
    Times, December 14, 1976, p. 1.
30. Recall that Brennan dissented in Kahn, but now that Kahn is the "law
    of the land," it was incumbent upon Brennan to show that its rationale
    did not control Wiesenfeld.
31. In his dissent in Kahn, Brennan found this benefit "overinclusive" in
    that it would assist rich as well as poor widows.
32. 419 U.S. 498 (1975).
33. Brennan's dissent in Kahn comes closest to developing this distinction.
34. The debate continued in Califano v. Goldfarb; decided March 1, 1977.
    U.S. Law Week 45, pp. 4237-4249. In this case, the Court declared
    unconstitutional a provision of the Social Security Act that provided
    survivors' benefits automatically to widows of deceased wage earners
    but required widowers to prove actual dependence at the time of the
    death of their wives.

4

Freedom

If there be any among us who would wish to dissolve this Union or to change its Republican Form, let them stand undisturbed as monuments of the safety with which error of opinion may be tolerated where reason is left free to combat it.

Thomas Jefferson

Writing in 1949, two prominent political scientists were able to state that "nothing in the annals of our law better reflects the primacy of American concern with liberty over equality than the comparative careers of the due process and equal protection clauses of the Fourteenth Amendment."[1] From what we have seen in the previous chapter, contemporary commentators might use more cautious language today because of the explosion of equal protection issues in the past quarter century. The gap between American concern with freedom and equality is closing, but freedom (or liberty) is still well in the lead.

The due process clause of the Fourteenth Amendment prohibits the states from depriving any person of life, liberty, or property without due process of law. The Fifth Amendment posts an identical prohibition against the federal government. The Bill of Rights lists certain substantive liberties—for example, speech, press, religion, trial by jury, no double jeopardy—applicable against the federal government literally and against state governments by judicial interpretation.

Weighty tomes have been written on each of these constitutional liberties. Our modest effort here is simply to reflect on some aspects of American freedom as a value that might be of ethical significance to career bureaucrats. The first two sections of this chapter deal with First Amendment liberties of speech, press, and religion. The third section examines the famous Japanese relocation case, Korematsu v. U.S.[2] in the hope of finding some enlightenment on what freedom means when it is most severely tested in times of war. The final section deals with freedom in a context unrelated to the Bill of Rights. It seemed best not to restrict our analysis of American freedom to the Bill of Rights because one of the explicit purposes of the unamended Constitution is to "preserve the blessings of liberty for ourselves and our posterity." An exclusive focus on the Bill of Rights would ignore the intention of the framers of the pristine Constitution to structure a regime that would safeguard freedom. Consequently, the fourth section of this chapter deals with freedom as a value whose protection was intended by the elaborate separation of powers designed by the framers of the Constitution. U.S. v. Nixon,[3] the Watergate tapes case, provides a dramatic and pointed illustration of how freedom asserts itself within the complex institutional arrangements of American government.

SPEECH AND PRESS

Gitlow v. New York

Gitlow v. New York[4] involved the conviction of Benjamin Gitlow for violating New York's criminal anarchy statute shortly after the end of World War I. The statute subjected to criminal penalties any person who "by word of mouth or writing advocates, advises, or teaches the duty, necessity or propriety of overthrowing or overturning organized government by force or violence." The statute also covered persons who printed, published, or knowingly circulated printed materials "advocating, advising, or teaching the doctrine that organized government should be overthrown by force, violence or any unlawful means."

The case was of tremendous significance in the history of constitutional law because for the first time the Supreme Court acknowledged that certain provisions of the Bill of Rights—in this case freedom of speech and of the press—applied to the states as well as the federal government. The First Amendment says that "Congress shall make no law . . . abridging the freedom of speech, or of the press" (emphasis added). Because the amendment dealt only with limitations on congressional power, it had not been considered effective against the states; but in Gitlow the Supreme Court parlayed the First Amendment guarantees of freedom of speech and press with the Fourteenth Amendment's prohibition against the states' depriving any person of "life, liberty, or property without due process of law." In Gitlow the Court held that the word "liberty" in the Fourteenth Amendment included both freedom of speech and press. Thus Gitlow was entitled to challenge his New York conviction in a federal court. It would be hard to exaggerate the importance of Gitlow for the subsequent development of civil liberties in the United States. By a gradual process extending over several decades, nearly all the provisions of the Bill of Rights have been "absorbed" by, or "incorporated" into, the Fourteenth

Amendment and have thereby been applied against the states. This development has enabled the Supreme Court to go a long way in establishing national standards in the areas of civil liberties and criminal procedure.

Despite the paramount historical significance of Gitlow v. New York, the case did little for Benjamin Gitlow himself. Although the Court was willing to test New York's criminal anarchy statute by the constitutional freedoms of press and speech, Gitlow's pamphlets were found sufficiently offensive to warrant conviction. The case is of interest for our purposes because it provides two sharply contrasting viewpoints on what freedom of speech and press should mean.

Historically, governments have attempted to suppress certain words and ideas because of a fear that they would eventually find expression in officially disapproved action. Ideas have consequences; words are "not only the keys of persuasion but the triggers of action."[5] Justice Holmes has provided the classic example for justifying legitimate concern on the part of government for what words are spoken in what circumstances. "The most stringent protection of free speech," he once said, "would not protect a man in falsely shouting fire in a theatre and causing a panic."[6] Thus the Supreme Court has never recognized an absolute prohibition against invoking the power of government to punish speech. Once this is admitted, however, the operative question then becomes not if government can punish speech but when and under what circumstances. The history of freedom of speech and press in the United States chronicles a wide variety of efforts to answer this question. A common thread linking these efforts is the almost universal tendency to make some connection between prohibited speech and illegal behavior. Gitlow v. New York provides two good examples of this tendency.

In upholding Gitlow's conviction, Justice Sutherland was careful to point out what the statute did not forbid:

> [A] mere statement or analysis of social and economic facts and historical incidents, in the nature of an essay, accompanied by prophecy as to the future course of events, but with no teaching, advice or advocacy of action, would not constitute the advocacy, advice or teaching of a doctrine for the overthrow of government within the meaning of the statute; . . . a mere statement that unlawful acts might accomplish such a purpose would be insufficient, unless there was a teaching, advising and advocacy of employing such unlawful acts for the purpose of overthrowing government; and . . . if the jury had a reasonable doubt that the Manifesto did teach, advocate or advise the duty, necessity or propriety of using unlawful means for the overthrowing of organized government, the defendant was entitled to an acquittal.

Thus mere discussion of unpopular political views would not be enough to warrant a conviction under the New York law. Unfortunately for Gitlow,

however, his pamphlet, "The Left Wing Manifesto," went beyond mere discussion; so at least it seemed to Justice Sutherland:

> Coupled with a review of the rise of Socialism, it [Gitlow's Manifesto]
> condemned the dominant "moderate Socialism" for its recognition of
> the necessity of the democratic parliamentary state; repudiated its
> policy of introducing Socialism by legislative measures; and advo-
> cated, in plain and unequivocal language, the necessity of accomplish-
> ing the "Communist Revolution" by a militant and "revolutionary
> Socialism," based on "the class struggle" and mobilizing the "power of
> the proletariat in action," through mass industrial revolts developing
> into mass political strikes and "revolutionary mass action," for the
> purpose of conquering and destroying the parliamentary state and
> establishing in its place, through a "revolutionary dictatorship of the
> proletariat," the system of Communist Socialism. The then recent
> strikes in Seattle and Winnipeg were cited as instances of a develop-
> ment already verging on revolutionary action and suggestive of pro-
> letarian dictatorship, in which the strike-workers were "trying to
> usurp the functions of municipal government"; and revolutionary
> Socialism, it was urged, must use these mass industrial revolts to
> broaden the strike, make it general and militant, and develop it into
> mass political strikes and revolutionary mass action for the annihila-
> tion of the parliamentary state.

Gitlow's pamphlet, then, was no detached, academic essay on the
likely merits of scientific socialism. It was a call to action—illegal action.
Given this determination, the crucial question for Sutherland was whether
the constitutional guarantees of freedom of speech and press would prevent
New York from punishing Gitlow for circulating this pamphlet:

> The precise question presented, and the only question which we can
> consider under this writ of error, then is, whether the statute, as
> construed and applied in this case by the state courts, deprived the
> defendant of his liberty of expression in violation of the due process
> clause of the Fourteenth Amendment. . . .
> For present purposes we may and do assume that freedom of
> speech and of the press—which are protected by the the First Amend-
> ment from abridgment by Congress—are among the fundamental per-
> sonal rights and "liberties" protected by the due process clause of the
> Fourteenth Amendment from impairment by the States. . . .
> It is a fundamental principle, long established, that the freedom
> of speech and of the press which is secured by the Constitution, does
> not confer an absolute right to speak or publish, without responsibility,
> whatever one may choose, or an unrestricted and unbridled license

that gives immunity for every possible use of language and prevents the punishment of those who abuse this freedom. . . .

That a State in the exercise of its police power may punish those who abuse this freedom by utterances inimical to the public welfare, tending to corrupt public morals, incite to crime, or disturb the public peace, is not open to question. . . .

By enacting the present statute the State has determined, through its legislative body, that utterances advocating the overthrow of organized government by force, violence and unlawful means, are so inimical to the general welfare and involve such danger of substantive evil that they may be penalized in the exercise of its police power. That determination must be given great weight. Every presumption is to be indulged in favor of the validity of the statute. . . . And the case is to be considered "in the light of the principle that the State is primarily the judge of regulations required in the interest of public safety and welfare"; and that its police "statutes may only be declared unconstitutional where they are arbitrary or unreasonable attempts to exercise authority vested in the State in the public interest." . . . That utterances inciting to the overthrow of organized government by unlawful means present a sufficient danger of substantive evil to bring their punishment within the range of legislative discretion is clear. Such utterances, by their very nature, involve danger to the public peace and to the security of the State. They threaten breaches of the peace and ultimate revolution. And the immediate danger is none the less real and substantial, because the effect of a given utterance cannot be accurately foreseen. The State cannot reasonably be required to measure the danger from every such utterance in the nice balance of a jeweler's scale. A single revolutionary spark may kindle a fire that, smouldering for a time, may burst into a sweeping and destructive conflagration. It cannot be said that the State is acting arbitrarily or unreasonably when in the exercise of its judgment as to the measures necessary to protect the public peace and safety, it seeks to extinguish the spark without waiting until it has enkindled the flame or blazed into the conflagration. It cannot reasonably be required to defer the adoption of measures for its own peace and safety until the revolutionary utterances lead to actual disturbances of the public peace or imminent and immediate danger of its own destruction; but it may, in the exercise of its judgment, suppress the threatened danger in its incipiency. In People v. Lloyd, it was aptly said: "Manifestly, the legislature has authority to forbid the advocacy of a doctrine designed and intended to overthrow the government without waiting until there is a present and imminent danger of the success of the plan advocated. If the State were compelled to wait until the apprehended danger became certain, then its right to protect itself would come into being simultaneously with the overthrow of the government, when there would be neither prosecuting officers nor courts for the enforcement of the law."

We cannot hold that the present statute is an arbitrary or unreasonable exercise of the police power of the State unwarrantably infringing the freedom of speech or press; and we must and do sustain its constitutionality.

This being so it may be applied to every utterance—not too trivial to be beneath the notice of the law—which is of such a character and used with such intent and purpose as to bring it within the prohibition of the statute. . . . In other words, when the legislative body has determined generally, in the constitutional exercise of its discretion, that utterances of a certain kind involve such danger of substantive evil that they may be punished, the question whether any specific utterance coming within the prohibited class is likely, in and of itself, to bring about the substantive evil, is not open to consideration. It is sufficient that the statute itself be constitutional and that the use of the language comes within its prohibition.

Justice Sutherland's position relies on what is generally called the "bad tendency" test. That is, while constitutional guarantees prevent government from arbitrarily and indiscriminately suppressing speech, they do not prevent official enactments from classifying as criminal those types of speech that <u>could</u> or are <u>likely</u> to bring about a situation the government has a legitimate interest in preventing—such as its own destruction. Hence, the legitimacy of governmental suppression of speech is determined by whether the proscribed speech has a "bad tendency."

There is a certain persuasiveness to this line of reasoning. If a government can prevent its own destruction, why can it not prevent words and actions that <u>might</u> bring about this destruction? This seems to be what Justice Sutherland is getting at when he says that "statutes may only be declared unconstitutional where they are arbitrary or unreasonable attempts to exercise authority vested in the State in the public interest." It would be arbitrary and unreasonable for government to forbid discussion of hopscotch, the World Series, or the merits of bidding six no trump with only two aces; such topics are unrelated to the preservation of the government and the furtherance of its policies. The advocacy of the violent overthrow of the government, however, can reasonably be suppressed because of its bad tendency. To do so might be unwise, unenlightened, and illiberal, but it certainly would not be unreasonable and therefore not unconstitutional; so argues Justice Sutherland.

There are some problems with Sutherland's position. First, there is the question of just what the First Amendment adds to the Constitution. If it does nothing more than prevent the government from acting unreasonably, does this suggest that in its absence the government could act unreasonably? If so, this does not reflect very favorably on the framers of the original, unamended Constitution. If not, what is the point of having a First Amendment if the original Constitution would have authorized only the reasonable exercise of power?

Secondly, there is the problem of suppressing speech on the grounds of what it might or could lead to. In terms of logic, it is, of course, very difficult to prove a negative. One would be hard pressed indeed to prove that a certain pamphlet might not be that single revolutionary spark that will ignite the great conflagration that engulfs us all. For the same reason, however, it would be difficult to prove that there is no tooth fairy.

Finally, there is the ends-means form of reasoning in Sutherland's position that is a bit disconcerting for those familiar with moral analyses. He seems to be arguing that because the government has a legitimate interest in its own survival, it can make use of any means reasonably related to that end—including suppression of speech with a "bad tendency." This is not the place for a full dress review of all the philosophical nuances of the moral relationship of ends and means. The issue, however, is never far from us, whether it is warfare, abortion, capital punishment, or wiretapping that we are discussing. For our purposes, it will suffice to note that any type of reasoning that predestines significant human values to collapse in the face of whatever is expedient for survival must be regarded as morally questionable. This is precisely the point that Sutherland ignores. He argues that constitutional guarantees must not prevent the government from suppressing speech that might reasonably be considered as a potential threat to national survival. This position ignores the likelihood that the First Amendment embodies values that are not to be discarded simply because they might inhibit the government from taking any action reasonably connected with its own survival.

Let us see if Justice Holmes's dissenting opinion in Gitlow improves on Sutherland's position. Like Sutherland, Holmes, too, is interested in making a connection between prohibited speech and illegal action:

> Mr. Justice Brandeis and I are of opinion that this judgment should be reversed. The general principle of free speech, it seems to me, must be taken to be included in the Fourteenth Amendment, in view of the scope that has been given to the word "liberty" as there used, although perhaps it may be accepted with a somewhat larger latitude of interpretation than is allowed to Congress by the sweeping language that governs or ought to govern the laws of the United States. If I am right, then I think that the criterion sanctioned by the full Court in Schenk v. United States . . . applies. "The question in every case is whether the words used are used in such circumstances and are of such a nature as to create a clear and present danger that they will bring about the substantive evils that [the State] has a right to prevent." It is true that in my opinion this criterion was departed from in Abrams

v. <u>United States</u> . . . but the convictions that I expressed in that case
are too deep for it to be possible for me as yet to believe that it and
<u>Schaefer</u> v. <u>United States</u> have settled the law. If what I think
the correct test is applied, it is manifest that there was no present
danger of an attempt to overthrow the government by force on the part
of the admittedly small minority who shared the defendant's views. It
is said that this manifesto was more than a theory, that it was an
incitement. Every idea is an incitement. It offers itself for belief
and if believed it is acted on unless some other benefit outweighs it or
some failure of energy stifles the movement at its birth. The only
difference between the expression of an opinion and an incitement in
the narrower sense is the speaker's enthusiasm for the result. Elo-
quence may set fire to reason. But whatever may be thought of the
redundant discourse before us it had no chance of starting a present
conflagration. If in the long run the beliefs expressed in proletarian
dictatorship are destined to be accepted by the dominant forces of the
community, the only meaning of free speech is that they should be
given their chance and have their way.

If the publication of this document had been laid as an attempt to
induce an uprising against government at once and not at some indef-
inite time in the future it would have presented a different question.
The object would have been one with which the law might deal, subject
to the doubt whether there was any danger that the publication could
produce any result, or in other words, whether it was not futile and
too remote from possible consequences. But the indictment alleges
the publication and nothing more.

In his dissent, Holmes refers to the "clear and present danger test"
which he himself had formulated in <u>Schenck</u> v. <u>U.S.</u> Although courts today
seldom use this test, the term has become part of our daily idiom and
appears in contexts far removed from the cases originally addressed by
Holmes. The clear and present danger test differs from the bad tendency
test in that it will not countenance governmental suppression of speech
merely on speculative grounds of what might possibly happen at some
remote time in the future. It requires a connection between the spoken
word and the illegal action in the here and now. Unlike the bad tendency
test, it does not allow the government to do all that might reasonably be
done to ensure the survival of existing institutions. Indeed, no matter how
reasonably government officials might deplore certain types of speech,
they cannot suppress them unless the danger of substantive evil is both
clear and present.

The clear and present danger test may not be the most satisfactory
formula for articulating the proper relationship between offensive words
and illegal action. One constitutional commentary has complained that the
test has "incited more questions than it answers."[7] One of these questions

is whether before we can say a danger is "present" we must "wait until the putsch is about to be executed, the plans have been laid and the signal awaited."[8] The words "clear and present" are not self-explanatory; they involve the use of considerable discretion on the part of judges.

Whatever limitations the clear and present danger test may have, it has served the purpose of safeguarding unpopular speech from suppression merely on speculative grounds.[9] This is the main point for the purposes of our analysis. Although most government managers never face the strictly constitutional question of when to suppress speech, the "spirit" of the First Amendment can certainly affect one's style of management. To what extent do you or your agency encourage free circulation of ideas— including unorthodox and unpopular ideas? Such encouragement, of course, can often be justified on pragmatic principles of management alone. The more interesting question, however, is one of principle: Should govern-ment managers be particularly alert to foster an environment of free and open communication within their organizations? In other words, should government managers, precisely because they are government managers, give more support and encouragement to those willing to think the unthink-able thought than their counterparts in private industry? To put the same question in more personal terms, let us take the example of a successful manager in private industry who assumes a managerial position in govern-ment. Does his oath to uphold the Constitution oblige him to be more tolerant of internal dissent than he would have been in industry? Should his tolerance of dissent be merely prudential? That is, should he allow it only insofar as it proves helpful in terms of agency goals? Or should he go beyond this "reasonable" approach? Should he tolerate and even encourage dissent on the grounds that government agencies should be suffused with constitutional values and among these values is freedom of speech? To put the same question somewhat differently: Is governmental management dif-ferent in style from industrial management and, if so, is that difference owing at least in part to a constitutional climate that should pervade gov-ernment agencies? Is it possible that the interests of the public might be served more faithfully by sacrificing some efficiency and economy in order to preserve an atmosphere of open inquiry and discussion within a govern-ment agency?

Branzburg v. Hayes

Branzburg v. Hayes[10] was one of three cases decided simultaneously by the Supreme Court. All three cases raised the same constitutional issue— does the First Amendment protect a reporter from being compelled by a grand jury to reveal the identity of confidential sources of information?

The first case involved a reporter for the Louisville Courier-Journal, Paul Branzburg, who had written articles on processing hashish from marijuana. He refused to comply with an order to answer questions of the grand jury concerning the identity of the individuals he had observed making the hashish and brought proceedings to restrain Judge John Hayes from imposing a contempt ruling. He argued that the guarantees of a free press contained in the First Amendment and applied to the states by the Fourteenth Amendment created an immunity against compulsory testimony that would interfere with the free flow of news. The Kentucky Court of Appeals rejected his position.

In the other two cases, Paul Pappas, a New England television newsman, and Earl Caldwell, a New York Times reporter, refused to answer grand jury questions concerning possible criminal actions by the Black Panthers. In both cases the newsmen would have had to have violated assurances of confidentiality given to the Panthers. Like Branzburg, they argued that such a betrayal would destroy their rapport with militant groups and thereby curtail the flow of news.

The cases raised an interesting conflict of values between freedom and equality. The strength of the argument of the reporters lay in their contention that if freedom of the press is to be meaningful, the source of information as well as its uninhibited dissemination must be protected. The weakness of their position was the implication that somehow the press was a privileged group above the ordinary legal requirement that grand juries are entitled to every person's evidence. This point became acutely embarrassing during the Watergate scandal when President Nixon's refusal to surrender his tapes to the grand jury rested on a position not altogether dissimilar from that of the reporters in Branzburg.

In a five-to-four decision, the Supreme Court rejected the reporters' argument. In denying the existence of a constitutional privilege to protect a reporter's sources from grand jury inquiries, the Court was quite careful to point out that this did not give grand juries a license to harass the press. Justice Powell's concurring opinion was particularly emphatic on this point. In a dissenting opinion, Justice Douglas found an "absolute" privilege for reporters to conceal their sources and roundly scolded the New York Times for not making a similar claim for its own employees. Justice Stewart, whose dissenting opinion was joined by Justices Brennan and Marshall, found what might best be called a qualified privilege not to reveal confidential sources. According to Stewart, such information can be demanded by a grand jury only if the government can "(1) show that there is probable cause to believe that the newsman has information which is clearly relevant to a specific probable violation of law; (2) demonstrate that the information sought cannot be obtained by alternative means less destructive of First Amendment rights; and (3) demonstrate a compelling and overriding interest in the information."

The following excerpts from the Court's opinion will give the flavor of the clash of values that surfaced in this case.

Justice White wrote the opinion of the Court, which was delivered by Chief Justice Burger:

> We do not question the significance of free speech, press or assembly to the country's welfare. Nor is it suggested that news gathering does not qualify for First Amendment protection; without some protection for seeking out the news, freedom of the press could be eviscerated. But this case involves no intrusions upon speech or assembly, no prior restraint or restriction on what the press may publish, and no express or implied command that the press publish what it prefers to withhold. No exaction of tax for the privilege of publishing, and no penalty, civil or criminal, related to the content of published material is at issue here. The use of confidential sources by the press is not forbidden or restricted; reporters remain free to seek news from any source by means within the law. No attempt is made to require the press to publish its sources of information or indiscriminately to disclose them on request.
>
> The sole issue before us is the obligation of reporters to respond to grand jury subpoenas as other citizens do and to answer questions relevant to an investigation into the commission of crime. Citizens generally are not constitutionally immune from grand jury subpoenas; and neither the First Amendment nor other constitutional provision protects the average citizen from disclosing to a grand jury information that he has received in confidence. The claim is, however, that reporters are exempt from these obligations because if forced to respond to subpoenas and identify their sources or disclose other confidences, their informants will refuse or be reluctant to furnish newsworthy information in the future. This asserted burden on news gathering is said to make compelled testimony from newsmen constitutionally suspect and to require a privileged position for them. . . .
>
> [To reject the reporters' argument] involves no restraint on what newspapers may publish or on the type or quality of information reporters may seek to acquire, nor does it threaten the vast bulk of confidential relationships between reporters and their sources. Grand juries address themselves to the issues of whether crimes have been committed and who committed them. Only where news sources themselves are implicated in crime or possess information relevant to the grand jury's task need they or the reporter be concerned about grand jury subpoenas. Nothing before us indicates that a large number or percentage of all confidential news sources fall into either category and would in any way be deterred by our holding that the Constitution does not, as it never has, exempt the newsman from performing the citizen's normal duty of appearing and furnishing information relevant to the grand jury's task.

The preference for anonymity of those confidential informants involved in actual criminal conduct is presumably a product of their desire to escape criminal prosecution, and this preference, while understandable, is hardly deserving of constitutional protection. It would be frivolous to assert—and no one does in these cases—that the First Amendment, in the interest of securing news or otherwise, confers a license on either the reporter or his news sources to violate otherwise valid criminal laws. Although stealing documents or private wiretapping could provide newsworthy information, neither reporter nor source is immune from conviction for such conduct, whatever the impact on the flow of news. Neither is immune, on First Amendment grounds, from testifying against the other, before the grand jury or at a criminal trial. The Amendment does not reach so far as to override the interest of the public in ensuring that neither reporter nor source is invading the rights of other citizens through reprehensible conduct forbidden to all other persons. . . .

. . . The administration of a constitutional newsman's privilege would present practical and conceptual difficulties of a high order. Sooner or later, it would be necessary to define those categories of newsmen who qualified for the privilege, a questionable procedure in light of the traditional doctrine that liberty of the press is the right of the lonely pamphleteer who uses carbon paper or a mimeograph just as much as of the large metropolitan publisher who utilizes the latest photocomposition methods. . . . Freedom of the press is a "fundamental personal right" which "is not confined to newspapers and periodicals. It necessarily embraces pamphlets and leaflets. . . . The press in its historic connotation comprehends every sort of publication which affords a vehicle of information and opinion." . . . The informative function asserted by representatives of the organized press in the present cases is also performed by lecturers, political pollsters, novelists, academic researchers, and dramatists. Almost any author may quite accurately assert that he is contributing to the flow of information to the public, that he relies on confidential sources of information, and that these sources will be silenced if he is forced to make disclosures before a grand jury. . . .

In addition, there is much force in the pragmatic view that the press has at its disposal powerful mechanisms of communication and is far from helpless to protect itself from harassment or substantial harm. Furthermore, if what the newsmen urged in these cases is true—that law enforcement cannot hope to gain and may suffer from subpoenaing newsmen before grand juries—prosecutors will be loath to risk so much for so little. Thus, at the federal level the Attorney General has already fashioned a set of rules for federal officials in connection with subpoenaing members of the press to testify before

grand juries or at criminal trials. These rules are a major step in
the direction petitioners desire to move. They may prove wholly sufficient to resolve the bulk of disagreements and controversies between
press and federal officials.

In his dissenting opinion, Justice Douglas offered the following
considerations:

> The starting point for decision pretty well marks the range within
> which the end result lies. The New York Times, whose reporting
> functions are at issue here, takes the amazing position that First
> Amendment rights are to be balanced against other needs or conven-
> iences of government. My belief is that all of the "balancing" was
> done by those who wrote the Bill of Rights. By casting the First
> Amendment in absolute terms, they repudiated the timid, watered-
> down, emasculated versions of the First Amendment which both the
> Government and the New York Times advances in the case. . . .
>   Today's decision will impede the wide open and robust dissemina-
> tion of ideas and counterthought which a free press both fosters and
> protects and which is essential to the success of intelligent self-
> government. Forcing a reporter before a grand jury will have two
> retarding effects upon the ear and the pen of the press. Fear of expo-
> sure will cause dissidents to communicate less openly to trusted
> reporters. And, fear of accountability will cause editors and critics
> to write with more restrained pens.
>   I see no way of making mandatory the disclosure of a reporter's
> confidential source of the information on which he bases his news
> story.
>   The press has a preferred position in our constitutional scheme
> not to enable it to make money, not to set newsmen apart as a favored
> class, but to bring fulfillment to the public's right to know. The right
> to know is crucial to the governing powers of the people. . . . Knowl-
> edge is essential to informed decisions. . . .
>   Today's decision is more than a clog upon news gathering. It is a
> signal to publishers and editors that they should exercise caution in
> how they use whatever information they can obtain. Without immunity
> they may be summoned to account for their criticism. Entrenched
> officers have been quick to crash their powers down upon unfriendly
> commentators. . . .
>   The intrusion of government into this domain is symptomatic of
> the disease of this society. As the years pass the power of govern-
> ment becomes more and more pervasive. It is a power to suffocate
> both people and causes. Those in power, whatever their politics,
> want only to perpetuate it. Now that the fences of the law and the

tradition that has protected the press are broken down, the people are
the victims. The First Amendment, as I read it, was designed precisely to prevent that tragedy.

Justice Stewart was joined in his dissent by Justices Brennan and
Marshall:

The Court's crabbed view of the First Amendment reflects a disturbing insensitivity to the critical role of an independent press in our
society. The question whether a reporter has a constitutional right to
a confidential relationship with his source is of first impression here,
but the principles which should guide our decision are as basic as any
to be found in the Constitution. . . . [T]he Court in these cases holds
that a newsman has no First Amendment right to protect his sources
when called before a grand jury. The Court thus invites state and
federal authorities to undermine the historic independence of the press
by attempting to annex the journalistic profession as an investigative
arm of government. Not only will this decision impair performance
of the press' constitutionally protected functions, but it will, I am
convinced, in the long run, harm rather than help the administration
of justice. . . .
    The right to gather news implies, in turn, a right to a confidential
relationship between a reporter and his source. This proposition follows as a matter of simple logic once three factual predicates are
recognized: (1) newsmen require informants to gather news;
(2) confidentiality—the promise or understanding that names or certain
aspects of communications will be kept off-the-record—is essential to
the creation and maintenance of a news-gathering relationship with
informants; and (3) the existence of an unbridled subpoena power—the
absence of a constitutional right protecting, in any way, a confidential
relationship from compulsory process—will either deter sources from
divulging information or deter reporters from gathering and publish-
ing information.
    It is obvious that informants are necessary to the news-gathering
process as we know it today. If it is to perform its constitutional
mission, the press must do far more than merely print public statements or publish prepared handouts. Familiarity with the people and
circumstances involved in the myriad background activities that result
in the final product called "news" is vital to complete and responsible
journalism, unless the press is to be a captive mouthpiece of
"newsmakers."
    It is equally obvious that the promise of confidentiality may be a
necessary prerequisite to a productive relationship between a newsman and his informants. An officeholder may fear his superior; a
member of the bureaucracy, his associates; a dissident, the scorn of

majority opinion. All may have information valuable to the public discourse, yet each may be willing to relate that information only in
confidence to a reporter whom he trusts, either because of excessive
caution or because of a reasonable fear of reprisals or censure for
unorthodox views. The First Amendment concern must not be with the
motives of any particular news source, but rather with the conditions
in which informants of all shades of the spectrum may make information available through the press to the public. . . .

   After today's decision, the potential informant can never be sure
that his identity or off-the-record communications will not subsequently be revealed through the compelled testimony of a newsman. A
public spirited person inside government, who is not implicated in any
crime, will now be fearful of revealing corruption or other governmental wrong-doing, because he will now know he can subsequently be
identified by use of compulsory process. The potential source must,
therefore, choose between risking exposure by giving information or
avoiding the risk by remaining silent.

   In his dissent, Justice Stewart predicts the likely effects this decision
will have on the behavior of "a member of the bureaucracy" and a "public
spirited person inside government." Do you agree with him?

RELIGION

Cases involving religion have been among the most intractable the Court
has faced. This is not terribly surprising because religion and politics
have always provided a volatile mix throughout Western history. In the
United States the problem has focused primarily on the twofold guarantee
in the First Amendment that prohibits Congress and the states[11] both from
establishing religion and from limiting its free exercise. The opening
sentence of the Bill of Rights reads: "Congress shall make no law
respecting an establishment of religion or prohibiting the free exercise
thereof." Few Americans indeed would quarrel with either of these provisions. It has been a long time since a serious argument has been heard
in this country in favor of an established church and even longer since
there has been serious discussion over whether Catholics should be permitted to attend Mass or Jews to worship at the synagogue.

   Unfortunately, however, not all issues involving religion have been
quite so simple. In the late 1940s the Supreme Court held that the prohibition against religious establishment went beyond merely preventing a
state or the United States from singling out a particular domination for
favored treatment.[12] The ban on religious establishment mandated
neutrality on the part of the state between religion and nonreligion. Government must neither favor religion nor be hostile to its interests.

Although this doctrine might be quite acceptable in principle, its application became somewhat confused when it was combined with the clause guaranteeing the free exercise of religion. It was the question of bible reading in public schools that made the confusion apparent, for it seemed that the two religion clauses of the First Amendment were on a collision course. The establishment clause cannot allow bible reading because this practice clearly favors religion over nonreligion and therefore violates the neutrality principle; but how can a state forbid prayer or bible reading in the schools without making dreadfully severe inroads on the free exercise of religion? In Abington Township v. Schempp[13] the Supreme Court tried to reconcile these conflicting principles, but many observers of the Court remained unconvinced.

Adding to the confusion was a 1960 Supreme Court decision that interpreted the free exercise clause as protecting not only conventional theistic religion but "those religions founded on different beliefs" as well. [14] Among the nontheistic beliefs considered to be religious, the Court named "Buddhism, Taoism, Ethical Culture, Secular Humanism, and others." [15]

The extension of First Amendment protection to nontheistic beliefs seemed, like the principle of state neutrality between religion and nonreligion, to be quite fair and sensible. Once again, however, the difficult issue of religion in public schools caused the Court some embarrassment. If the recital of the Lord's Prayer favors religion over nonreligion, could one not argue that a universal ban on prayer in public schools favored the "religion" of secular humanism and ethical culture over traditional theistic religion?

Prayer in public schools is, of course, but one of many difficult issues that Courts have faced in trying to reconcile the demands of public order with the prohibition against the establishment of religion and the guarantee of its free exercise. Among the more interesting cases, one finds the following questions: Can Massachusetts require compulsory vaccinations of those whose religious beliefs are offended by such practices?[16] Can the United States prosecute Mormons for bigamy without violating the free exercise of religion?[17] Can Maryland pass a Sunday Closing Law without both establishing Christianity and limiting the free exercise of religion of Orthodox Jews who are conscience-bound to close their businesses on Saturday as well?[18] Does Arkansas violate the establishment clause when it forbids any instructor in a public school to "teach the theory or doctrine that mankind ascended or descended from a lower order of animals"?[19] Is there a constitutional difference between state aid to students in parochial elementary and secondary schools on the one hand and to students in religiously affiliated colleges and universities on the other?[20] What role can the states play in resolving property disputes that arise within a religious denomination?[21] Can Tennessee forbid the handling of poisonous snakes when members of the Holiness Church believe that Chapter 16 of Mark's Gospel assures them that true believers in Christ will not be harmed by such beasts?[22] Can Jehovah's Witnesses refuse blood transfusions that are necessary to save their own lives or the lives of their children?[23] Can Dr. Timothy Leary use illegal drugs as part of a religious rite?[24]

These examples will suffice to outline the broad range of questions in which courts have found themselves entangled when religious issues are litigated. For our purposes, it will be enough to restrict our attention to cases involving religiously based claims for exemption from general legal obligations. These cases will give some insight into the role of religion in our society, but, more important for the purposes of this book, they will offer the reader illustrations of how the Court handles pleas for exemptions from the routine enforcement of policy. This should be useful for managers in bureaucratic organizations because routine is such an important aspect of bureaucratic life. For the most part, exemptions from standard procedure are abhorred because they can create at least an appearance of favoritism and partiality. Yet there are times when even the most Weberian bureaucrat will make exceptions. The cases that follow show how the Court attempts to reconcile the demands for an impersonal application of law with requests for exceptions based on the important constitutional consideration of the free exercise of religion. Requests for special treatment arising from one's religious beliefs are particularly instructive because the Court must avoid the Scylla of an insensitive reluctance to accommodate religious belief and the Charybdis of being so accommodating as to "establish" a particular religious belief. Although most bureaucrats do not deal directly with religious claims, nearly all bureaucrats must at times decide whether to bend or even ignore ordinary rules and procedure because of some serious claim for special treatment. The cases that follow are submitted in the hope that they may provide some helpful reflections that the reader might apply to situations he or she faces in public service employment.

Flag Salute Cases

These cases involved efforts by school boards in Pennsylvania and West Virginia to require a compulsory flag salute from children in the public schools. The cases are remarkable because the Court reversed itself within a three-year period. In 1940 it upheld the power of the state to compel the salute but in 1943—at the height of World War II—the Court overturned its earlier decision. The reversal was due to a change of mind by Justices Black, Douglas, and Murphy and to the accession to the Supreme Court of Justices Jackson and Rutledge.

Minersville School District v. Gobitis[25]

Justice Frankfurter delivered the Court's opinion:

> A grave responsibility confronts this Court whenever in course of litigation it must reconcile the conflicting claims of liberty and authority. But when the liberty invoked is liberty of conscience, and the authority is authority to safeguard the nation's fellowship, judicial conscience is put to its severest test. Of such a nature is the present controversey.

> Lillian Gobitis, aged twelve, and her brother William, aged ten, were expelled from the public schools of Minersville, Pennsylvania, for refusing to salute the national flag as part of a daily school exercise. . . .

> The Gobitis children were of an age for which Pennsylvania makes school attendance compulsory. Thus they were denied a free education, and their parents had to put them into private schools. To be relieved of the financial burden thereby entailed, their father, on behalf of the children and in his own behalf, brought this suit. He sought to enjoin the authorities from continuing to exact participation in the flag-salute ceremony as a condition of his children's attendance at the Minersville school. . . .

> We must decide whether the requirement of participation in such a ceremony, exacted from a child who refuses upon sincere religious grounds, infringes without due process of law the liberty guaranteed by the Fourteenth Amendment. . . .

> Certainly the affirmative pursuit of one's convictions about the ultimate mystery of the universe and man's relation to it is placed beyond the reach of law. Government may not interfere with organized or individual expression of belief or disbelief. Propagation of belief—or even of disbelief in the supernatural—is protected, whether in church or chapel, mosque or synagogue, tabernacle or meetinghouse. . . .

> But the manifold character of man's relations may bring his conception of religious duty into conflict with the secular interests of his fellow men. When does the constitutional guarantee compel exemption from doing what society thinks necessary for the promotion of some great common end, or from a penalty for conduct which appears dangerous to the general good? To state the problem is to recall the truth that no single principle can answer all of life's complexities. The right to freedom of religious belief, however dissident and however obnoxious to the cherished beliefs of others—even of a majority— is itself the denial of an absolute. But to affirm that the freedom to follow conscience has itself no limits in the life of a society would deny that very plurality of principles which, as a matter of history,

underlies protection of religious toleration. . . . Our present task
then, as so often the case with courts, is to reconcile two rights in
order to prevent either from destroying the other. But, because in
safeguarding conscience we are dealing with interests so subtle and so
dear, every possible leeway should be given to the claims of religious
faith. . . . The religious liberty which the Constitution protects has
never excluded legislation of general scope not directed against
doctrinal loyalties of particular sects. Judicial nullification of legislation cannot be justified by attributing to the framers of the Bill of
Rights views for which there is no historic warrant. Conscientious
scruples have not, in the course of the long struggle for religious
toleration, relieved the individual from obedience to a general law not
aimed at the promotion or restriction of religious beliefs. The mere
possession of religious convictions which contradict the relevant concerns of a political society does not relieve the citizen from the discharge of political responsibilities. The necessity for this adjustment
has again and again been recognized. In a number of situations the
exertion of political authority has been sustained, while basic considerations of religious freedom have been left inviolate. . . . [T]he
question remains whether school children, like the Gobitis children,
must be excused from conduct required of all the other children in the
promotion of national cohesion. We are dealing with an interest
inferior to none in the hierarchy of legal values. National unity is the
basis of national security. . . .

Situations like the present are phases of the profoundest problems
confronting a democracy—the problem which Lincoln cast in memorable dilemma: "Must a government of necessity be too strong for the
liberties of its people, or too weak to maintain its own existence?"
No mere textual reading or logical talisman can solve the dilemma.
And when the issue demands judicial determination, it is not the
personal notion of judges of what wise adjustment requires which must
prevail.

Unlike the instances we have cited, the case before us is not concerned with an exertion of legislative power for the promotion of some
specific need or interest of secular society—the protection of the
family, the promotion of health, the common defense, the raising of
public revenues to defray the cost of government. But all these
specific activities of government presuppose the existence of an
organized political society. The ultimate foundation of a free society
is the binding ties of a cohesive sentiment. Such a sentiment is
fostered by all those agencies of the mind and spirit which may serve
to gather up the traditions of a people, transmit them from generation
to generation, and thereby create that continuity of a treasured common life which constitutes a civilization. "We live by symbols." The

flag is the symbol of our national unity, transcending all internal differences, however large, within the framework of the Constitution. . . .
The precise issue, then, for us to decide is whether the legislatures of the various states and the authorities in a thousand
counties and school districts of this country are barred from determining the appropriateness of various means to evoke that unifying
sentiment without which there can ultimately be no liberties, civil or
religious.

Given this formulation of the "precise issue," it will come as no surprise to discover that Justice Frankfurter went on to uphold the school
board's power to require the compulsory salute. The way in which a
judge—or any decision maker—formulates the "precise issue" frequently
presages the outcome of the decision. For Frankfurter this case involves
an "exemption from doing what society thinks necessary for the promotion
of some great common end." Three years later the Court was to define
the issue quite differently.

Frankfurter stresses the point that the legislation is of "general
scope" and is "not directed against doctrinal loyalties of particular sects."
Suppose a state were to prohibit the sale and consumption of all alcoholic
beverages within its boundaries without making any exception for the use of
wine for sacramental purposes. The Greek Orthodox, Roman Catholics,
and Episcopalians would surely invoke the free exercise clause. Would
Frankfurter's argument support them if the state could show no discriminatory intentions against "high church" religions? Suppose Congress
reenacted conscription laws without providing an exemption for conscientious objectors. Would Frankfurter's position support a free exercise
argument raised by Quakers and Mennonites?

The lone dissenting opinion in Gobitis came from Justice Stone:

The guaranties of civil liberty are but guaranties of freedom of the
human mind and spirit and of reasonable freedom and opportunity to
express them. They presuppose the right of the individual to hold
such opinions as he will and to give them reasonably free expression,
and his freedom, and that of the state as well, to teach and persuade
others by the communication of ideas. The very essence of the liberty
which they guarantee is the freedom of the individual from compulsion
as to what he shall think and what he shall say, at least where the
compulsion is to bear false witness to his religion. If these guaranties
are to have any meaning they must, I think, be deemed to withhold
from the state any authority to compel belief or the expression of it
where that expression violates religious convictions, whatever may be
the legislative view of the desirability of such compulsion.

Note that Stone does not define the point at issue in terms of an exemption from an otherwise sound public policy. He sees the issue more in terms of what powers the state possesses. This point was developed skillfully by Justice Jackson three years later when the Court reversed Gobitis.

Does Stone overstate the compulsory character of the school board's policy? Strictly speaking, there was no compulsion to salute the flag. The flag salute was merely a condition for remaining in the public school. As Justice Frankfurter's opinion notes at the outset, the parents of the Gobitis children put them into private schools. It was in order "to be relieved of the financial burden thereby entailed" that the Gobitis family initiated litigation. Would it be fair, then, to say that this case involved not so much a question of the state forcing children to violate their conscience but of the state forcing the children's parents to choose between their religion and their pocketbook? Are the Jehovah's Witnesses in a position any different in principle from that of the Jewish merchant who is forced by law to close on Sunday and by his conscience to close on Saturday? The state does not make him close on Saturday, although it does make him choose between his religious belief and the economic advantage of closing his store only one day a week instead of two. Or what about Lutheran and Catholic children attending parochial schools? The Supreme Court has upheld a constitutional right to attend nonpublic schools but has insisted that those who exercise this right must pay for it. How would you distinguish the situations of the Jehovah's Witnesses, the Jewish merchants, and the parochial school students?

Would it be helpful to distinguish between moral choices imposed by the state that involve legal commands to do something forbidden by conscience and legal prohibitions against doing something mandated by conscience? That is, does the state impose a more severe moral dilemma upon those who must choose between their pocketbooks and "sins of commission" than upon those who must choose between their pocketbooks and "sins of omission"? The Jehovah's Witnesses and the Jewish merchant must choose between their financial interests and doing something they find offensive—saluting the flag, opening the store on the Sabbath. The Catholic and Lutheran parents must choose between their financial interests and not doing something they find morally desirable—providing their children with a religious education.

One could further distinguish the situations confronting the Jehovah's Witnesses and the Jewish merchant on the grounds that the morally offensive command is directly related to the religious scruples of the Witnesses but only indirectly related to Jewish beliefs. That is, for the Witness the direct command is to salute the flag whereas for the Jew it is to close on Sunday. It is not the direct command that troubles the Jewish merchant, but it is the derivative situation in which he finds himself because of his own beliefs against remaining open on Saturday.

What is your reaction to this line of reasoning? If we take a practical look at the "bottom line," all four religious groups—Jehovah's Witnesses, Jews, Lutherans, and Catholics—are in the same position of having to choose between their pocketbooks and their religious beliefs. If we make a distinction between "sins of commission" and "sins of omission" and a further distinction between direct and indirect commands, we can begin to formulate a scheme for ranking relative conscientious burdens imposed by the state. Should such considerations play a part in formulating exemptions to policies that are likely to compromise the religious beliefs of some citizens? [26]

West Virginia School Board of Education v. Barnette[27]

Despite its decision in favor of the compulsory flag salute, the Court, just three years later, found itself facing the same issue once again. This time the majority opinion was delivered by Justice Jackson:

> This case calls upon us to reconsider a precedent decision, as the Court throughout its history often has been required to do. Before turning to the Gobitis case, however, it is desirable to notice certain characteristics by which this controversy is distinguished.
>
> The freedom asserted by these appellees does not bring them into collision with rights asserted by any other individual. It is such conflicts which most frequently require intervention of the State to determine where the rights of one end and those of another begin. But the refusal of these persons to participate in the ceremony does not interfere with or deny rights of others to do so. Nor is there any question in this case that their behavior is peaceable and orderly. The sole conflict is between authority and rights of the individual. The State asserts power to condition access to public education on making a prescribed sign and profession and at the same time to coerce attendance by punishing both parent and child. The latter stand on a right of self-determination in matters that touch individual opinion and personal attitude. . . .
>
> There is no doubt that, in connection with the pledges, the flag salute is a form of utterance. Symbolism is a primitive but effective way of communicating ideas. The use of an emblem or flag to symbolize some system, idea, institution, or personality, is a short cut from mind to mind. Causes and nations, political parties, lodges and ecclesiastical groups seek to knit the loyalty of their followings to a flag or banner, a color or design. The State announces rank, function, and authority through crowns and maces, uniforms and black robes; the church speaks through the Cross, the Crucifix, the altar

and shrine, and clerical raiment. Symbols of State often convey
political ideas just as religious symbols come to convey theological
ones. Associated with many of these symbols are appropriate
gestures of acceptance or respect: a salute, a bowed or bared head, a
bended knee. A person gets from a symbol the meaning he puts into it,
and what is one man's comfort and inspiration is another's jest and
scorn. . . .

It is also to be noted that the compulsory flag salute and pledge
requires affirmation of a belief and an attitude of mind. It is not clear
whether the regulation contemplates that pupils forego any contrary
convictions of their own and become unwilling converts to the prescribed ceremony or whether it will be acceptable if they simulate
assent by words without belief and by a gesture barren of meaning. It
is now a commonplace that censorship or suppression of expression of
opinion is tolerated by our Constitution only when the expression
presents a clear and present danger of action of a kind the State is
empowered to prevent and punish. It would seem that involuntary
affirmation could be commanded only on even more immediate and
urgent grounds than silence. But here the power of compulsion is
invoked without any allegation that remaining passive during a flag
salute ritual creates a clear and present danger that would justify an
effort even to muffle expression. To sustain the compulsory flag
salute we are required to say that a Bill of Rights which guard the
individual's right to speak his own mind, left it open to public authorities to compel him to utter what is not in his mind.

Note how Justice Jackson's argument uses the distinction between the
state's power to command and forbid. If the government is severely
restricted in its power to forbid speech, it should be even more restricted
in its power to command speech. This distinction recalls the earlier discussion of sins of commission and omission. If it is bad for the state to
silence its citizens, it is even worse to make them speak.

Justice Jackson's opinion continues:

Nor does the issue as we see it turn on one's possession of particular
religious views or the sincerity with which they are held. While
religion supplies appellees' motive for enduring the discomforts of
making the issue in this case, many citizens who do not share these
religious views hold such a compulsory rite to infringe constitutional
liberty of the individual. It is not necessary to inquire whether non-
conformist beliefs will exempt from the duty to salute unless we first
find power to make the salute a legal duty.

The Gobitis decision, however, assumed, as did the argument in
that case and in this, that power exists in the State to impose the flag

salute discipline upon school children in general. The Court only
examined and rejected a claim based on religious beliefs of immunity
from an unquestioned general rule. The question which underlies the
flag salute controversy is whether such a ceremony so touching
matters of opinion and political attitude may be imposed upon the
individual by official authority under powers committed to any political
organization under our Constitution. We examine rather than assume
existence of this power and, against this broader definition of issues
in this case, re-examine specific grounds assigned for the Gobitis
decision.

These two paragraphs are the heart of Jackson's opinion. Unlike
Frankfurter, Jackson does not define the point at issue in terms of whether
the Jehovah's Witnesses can rightfully claim an exemption on religious
grounds from an otherwise legitimate exercise of state power. Instead,
for Jackson the issue is whether the state has the power to compel the flag
salute in the first place. This is a very important difference. It shifts the
entire discussion away from whether the Witnesses are deserving of
special treatment to whether the state can legitimately compel anyone to
proclaim belief in anything. Thus, for Jackson, the case no longer turns
on what the free exercise of religion might mean but upon the nature and
extent of state power in American government.

Jackson's efforts to redefine the issue should be of considerable
interest to government managers who are not infrequently faced with
requests from subordinates or citizens for special treatment. Managers,
like anyone in a position of authority—parents, policemen, schoolteachers,
foremen, and others—are usually made uncomfortable by such requests.
To make exceptions for certain groups or individuals often gives the
appearance of playing favorites. Before getting himself or herself into the
difficult position of having either to grant or deny a request for special
treatment, a wise manager might first examine the entire situation to
make sure that the person requesting special treatment has not been placed
in a situation in which the agency has no business interfering in the first
place.

Justice Jackson concludes his opinion as follows:

It is said that the flag-salute controversy confronted the Court with
"the problem which Lincoln cast in memorable dilemma: 'Must a
government of necessity be too strong for the liberties of its people,
or too weak to maintain its own existence?' " and that the answer
must be in favor of strength. . . .

We think these issues may be examined free of pressure or
restraint growing out of such considerations.

It may be doubted whether Mr. Lincoln would have thought that
the strength of government to maintain itself would be impressively

vindicated by our confirming power of the state to expel a handful of
children from school. Such oversimplification, so handy in political
debate, often lacks the precision necessary to postulates of judicial
reasoning. If validly applied to this problem, the utterance cited
would resolve every issue of power in favor of those in authority and
would require us to override every liberty thought to weaken or delay
execution of their policies. . . .

The very purpose of a Bill of Rights was to withdraw certain subjects from the vicissitudes of political controversy, to place them
beyond the reach of majorities and officials and to establish them as
legal principles to be applied by the courts. One's right to life,
liberty, and property, to free speech, a free press, freedom of worship and assembly, and other fundamental rights may not be submitted
to vote; they depend on the outcome of no elections. . . .

The case is made difficult not because the principles of its decision are obscure but because the flag involved is our own. Nevertheless, we apply the limitations of the Constitution with no fear that
freedom to be intellectually and spiritually diverse or even contrary
will disintegrate the social organization. To believe that patriotism
will not flourish if patriotic ceremonies are voluntary and spontaneous
instead of a compulsory routine is to make an unflattering estimate of
the appeal of our institutions to free minds. We can have intellectual
individualism and the rich cultural diversities that we owe to excep-
tional minds only at the price of occasional eccentricity and abnormal
attitudes. When they are so harmless to others or to the State as
those we deal with here, the price is not too great. But freedom to
differ is not limited to things that do not matter much. That would be
a mere shadow of freedom. The test of its substance is the right to
differ as to things that touch the heart of the existing order.

If there is any fixed star in our constitutional constellation, it is
that no official, high or petty, can prescribe what shall be orthodox in
politics, nationalism, religion, or other matters of opinion or force
citizens to confess by word or act their faith therein. If there are any
circumstances which permit an exception, they do not now occur to us.

We think the action of the local authorities in compelling the flag
salute and pledge transcends constitutional limitations on their power
and invades the sphere of intellect and spirit which it is the purpose of
the First Amendment to our Constitution to reserve from all official
control.

Sherbert v. Verner

Unfortunately, not all claims for exemptions from general laws on
religious grounds can be handled as adroitly as Justice Jackson solved the

problem of the compulsory flag salute. Although the state may not have
the power to compel the affirmation of any particular belief, it is surely
competent to act in many other areas in which claims for the free exercise
of religion are likely to arise. Among these areas is that of a state's
policy on unemployment compensation. In Sherbert v. Verner,[28] the
Supreme Court faced the following situation. The appellant, Sherbert, was
a member of the Seventh-day Adventist Church. She had been discharged
by her employer in South Carolina because she would not work on Saturday,
the day of rest and worship for Seventh-day Adventists. She filed a claim
for unemployment compensation benefits under the South Carolina Unemployment Compensation Act, which provides that a claimant is ineligible
for benefits if he or she has failed, without good cause, to accept available,
suitable work when offered. The State Commission denied Sherbert's
application on the grounds that she would not accept suitable work when
offered and that she therefore failed to meet the statutory requirement of
"availability" for work as a condition of receiving unemployment benefits.
The Supreme Court of South Carolina upheld the State Commission but the
Supreme Court of the United States reversed this decision and found that
South Carolina's failure to accommodate Sherbert's religious scruples was
a denial of the free exercise of her religion. The Supreme Court's decision came as something of a surprise because shortly before Sherbert the
Court had upheld a Maryland Sunday Closing Law over the objection of
Jewish merchants whose Sabbatarian arguments seemed quite similar to
those of Sherbert. Excerpts are given below from the majority opinion of
Justice Brennan, a concurring opinion of Justice Stewart, and the dissenting opinion of Justice Harlan. Which position do you find most persuasive?
     The opinion of the Court was delivered by Justice Brennan:

> The door of the Free Exercise Clause stands tightly closed against any
> government regulation of religious beliefs as such. . . . Government
> may neither compel affirmation of a repugnant belief . . . nor penal-
> ize or discriminate against individuals or groups because they hold
> religious views abhorrent to the authorities . . . nor employ the taxing
> power to inhibit the dissemination of particular religious views. . . .
> On the other hand, the Court has rejected challenges under the Free
> Exercise Clause to governmental regulation of certain overt acts
> prompted by religious beliefs or principles, for "even when the action
> is in accord with one's religious convictions, [it] is not totally free
> from legislative restrictions." . . . The conduct or actions so regu-
> lated have invariably posed some substantial threat to public safety,
> peace or order. . . .
>   Plainly enough, appellant's conscientious objection to Saturday
> work constitutes no conduct prompted by religious principles of a kind
> within the reach of state legislation. If, therefore, the decision of the
> South Carolina Supreme Court is to withstand appellant's constitutional

challenge, it must be either because her disqualification as a beneficiary represents no infringement by the State of her constitutional rights of free exercise, or because any incidental burden on the free exercise of appellant's religion may be justified by a "compelling state interest in the regulation of a subject within the State's constitutional power to regulate." . . .

We turn first to the question whether the disqualification for benefits imposes any burden on the free exercise of appellant's religion. We think it is clear that it does. . . . Here not only is it apparent that appellant's declared ineligibility for benefits derives solely from the practice of her religion, but the pressure upon her to forego that practice is unmistakable. The ruling forces her to choose between following the precepts of her religion and forfeiting benefits, on the one hand, and abandoning one of the precepts of her religion in order to accept work, on the other hand. Governmental imposition of such a choice puts the same kind of burden upon the free exercise of religion as would a fine imposed against appellant for her Saturday worship.

Nor may the South Carolina court's construction of the statute be saved from constitutional infirmity on the ground that unemployment compensation benefits are not appellant's "right" but merely a "privilege." It is too late in the day to doubt that the liberties of religion and expression may be infringed by the denial of or placing of conditions upon a benefit or privilege. . . . [To] condition the availability of benefits upon this appellant's willingness to violate a cardinal principle of her religious faith effectively penalizes the free exercise of her constitutional liberties.

Significantly South Carolina expressly saves the Sunday worshiper from having to make the kind of choice which we here hold infringes the Sabbatarian's religious liberty. When in times of "national emergency" the textile plants are authorized by the State Commissioner of Labor to operate on Sunday, "no employee shall be required to work on Sunday . . . who is conscientiously opposed to Sunday work; and if any employee should refuse to work on Sunday on account of conscientious . . . objections he or she shall not jeopardize his or her seniority by such refusal or be discriminated against in any other manner." . . . No question of the disqualification of a Sunday worshiper for benefits is likely to arise, since we cannot suppose that an employer will discharge him in violation of this statute. The unconstitutionality of the disqualification of the Sabbatarian is thus compounded by the religious discrimination which South Carolina's general statutory scheme necessarily effects.

We must next consider whether some compelling state interest enforced in the eligibility provisions of the South Carolina statute justifies the substantial infringement of appellant's First Amendment right. It is basic that no showing merely of a rational relationship to some colorable state interest would suffice; in this highly sensitive constitutional area, "only the gravest abuses, endangering paramount interests, give occasion for permissible limitation." . . . No such abuse or danger has been advanced in the present case. The appellees suggest no more than a possibility that the filing of fraudulent claims by unscrupulous claimants feigning religious objections to Saturday work might not only dilute the unemployment compensation fund but also hinder the scheduling by employers of necessary Saturday work. But that possibility is not apposite here because no such objection appears to have been made before the South Carolina Supreme Court, and we are unwilling to assess the importance of an asserted state interest without the views of the state court. Nor, if the contention had been made below, would the record appear to sustain it; there is no proof whatever to warrant such fears of malingering or deceit as those which the respondents now advance. . . . [Even] if the possibility of spurious claims did threaten to dilute the fund and disrupt the scheduling of work, it would plainly be incumbent upon the appellees to demonstrate that no alternative forms of regulation would combat such abuses without infringing First Amendment rights. . . .

In these respects, then, the state interest asserted in the present case is wholly dissimilar to the interests which were found to justify the less direct burden upon religious practices in Braunfeld v. Brown. . . . The Court recognized that the Sunday closing law which that decision sustained undoubtedly served "to make the practice of [the Orthodox Jewish merchants'] . . . religious beliefs more expensive." . . . But the statute was nevertheless saved by a countervailing factor which finds no equivalent in the instant case—a strong state interest in providing one uniform day of rest for all workers. That secular objective could be achieved, the Court found, only by declaring Sunday to be that day of rest. Requiring exemptions for Sabbatarians, while theoretically possible, appeared to present an administrative problem of such magnitude, or to afford the exempted class so great a competitive advantage, that such a requirement would have rendered the entire statutory scheme unworkable. In the present case no such justifications underlie the determination of the state court that appellant's religion makes her ineligible to receive benefits.

In holding as we do, plainly we are not fostering the "establishment" of the Seventh-day Adventist religion in South Carolina, for the extension of unemployment benefits to Sabbatarians in common with Sunday worshipers reflects nothing more than the governmental obligation of neutrality in the face of religious differences, and does not represent that involvement of religious with secular institutions which it is the object of the Establishment Clause to forestall. . . .

Justice Stewart concurred in the result but was quite critical of the Court's reasoning. (Note: To grasp the point of Stewart's argument, it will be helpful to recall that on the same day the Court decided the present case, it also decided Schempp v. Abington Township—the case mentioned earlier in this chapter in which the Court declared bible reading in public schools to be unconstitutional.)

Although fully agreeing with the result which the Court reaches in this case, I cannot join the Court's opinion. This case presents a double-barreled dilemma, which in all candor I think the Court's opinion has not succeeded in papering over. The dilemma ought to be resolved. . . .

I am convinced that no liberty is more essential to the continued vitality of the free society which our Constitution guarantees than is the religious liberty protected by the Free Exercise Clause explicit in the First Amendment and imbedded in the Fourteenth. And I regret that on occasion, and specifically in Braunfeld v. Brown (the Sunday Closing Case) the Court has shown what has seemed to me a distressing insensitivity to the appropriate demands of this constitutional guarantee. By contrast I think that the Court's approach to the Establishment Clause has on occasion, and specifically in Engel, Schempp and Murray, [the prayer and bible reading in public school cases] been not only insensitive, but positively wooden, and that the Court has accorded to the Establishment Clause a meaning which neither the words, the history, nor the intention of the authors of that specific constitutional provision even remotely suggests.

But my views as to the correctness of the Court's decisions in these cases are beside the point here. The point is that the decisions are on the books. And the result is that there are many situations where legitimate claims under the Free Exercise Clause will run into head-on collision with the Court's insensitive and sterile construction of the Establishment Clause. The controversy now before us is clearly such a case.

Because the appellant refuses to accept available jobs which would require her to work on Saturdays, South Carolina has declined to pay unemployment compensation benefits to her. Her refusal to work on Saturdays is based on the tenets of her religious faith. The Court says that South Carolina cannot under these circumstances declare her to be not "available for work" within the meaning of its statute because to do so would violate her constitutional right to the free exercise of her religion.

Yet what this Court has said about the Establishment Clause must inevitably lead to a diametrically opposite result. If the appellant's

refusal to work on Saturdays were based on indolence, or on a compulsive desire to watch the Saturday television programs, no one would
say that South Carolina could not hold that she was not "available for
work" within the meaning of its statute. That being so, the Establishment Clause as construed by this Court not only permits but affirmatively requires South Carolina equally to deny the appellant's claim for
unemployment compensation when her refusal to work on Saturdays is
based upon her religious creed. For, as said in Everson v. Board of
Education, the Establishment Clause bespeaks "a government . . .
stripped of all power . . . to support, or otherwise to assist any or
all religions . . . , " and no State "can pass laws which aid one
religion. . . ." In Mr. Justice Rutledge's words, adopted by the
Court today in Schempp, . . . the Establishment Clause forbids
"every form of public aid or support for religion." . . . In the words
of the Court in Engel v. Vitale, reaffirmed today in the Schempp
case, . . . the Establishment Clause forbids the "financial support of
government" to be "placed behind a particular religious belief."

To require South Carolina to so administer its laws as to pay
public money to the appellant under the circumstances of this case is
thus clearly to require the State to violate the Establishment Clause as
construed by this Court. This poses no problem for me, because I
think the Court's mechanistic concept of the Establishment Clause is
historically unsound and constitutionally wrong. I think the process of
constitutional decision in the area of the relationships between government and religion demands considerably more than the invocation of
broad-brushed rhetoric of the kind I have quoted. And I think that the
guarantee of religious liberty embodied in the Free Exercise Clause
affirmatively requires government to create an atmosphere of hospital-
ity and accommodation to individual belief or disbelief. In short, I
think our Constitution commands the positive protection by government
of religious freedom—not only for a minority, however small—not only
for the majority, however large—but for each of us.

South Carolina would deny unemployment benefits to a mother
unavailable for work on Saturdays because she was unable to get a
babysitter. Thus, we do not have before us a situation where a State
provides unemployment compensation generally, and singles out for
disqualification only those persons who are unavailable for work on
religious grounds. This is not, in short, a scheme which operates so
as to discriminate against religion as such. But the Court nevertheless holds that the State must prefer a religious over a secular
ground for being unavailable for work—that state financial support
of the appellant's religion is constiutionally required to carry out
"the governmental obligation of neutrality in the face of religious
differences. . . ."

Yet in cases decided under the Establishment Clause the Court has decreed otherwise. It has decreed that government must blind itself to the differing religious beliefs and traditions of the people. With all respect, I think it is the Court's duty to face up to the dilemma posed by the conflict between the Free Exercise Clause of the Constitution and the Establishment Clause as interpreted by the Court. It is a duty, I submit, which we owe to the people, the States, and the Nation, and a duty which we owe to ourselves. For so long as the resounding but fallacious fundamentalist rhetoric of some of our Establishment Clause opinions remains on our books, to be disregarded at will as in the present case, or to be undiscriminatingly invoked as in the Schempp case, . . . so long will the possibility of consistent and perceptive decision in this most difficult and delicate area of constitutional law be impeded and impaired. And so long, I fear, will the guarantee of true religious freedom in our pluralistic society be uncertain and insecure.

Justice Harlan dissented as follows:

Today's decision is disturbing both in its rejection of existing precedent and in its implications for the future. The significance of the decision can best be understood after an examination of the state law applied in this case.

South Carolina's Unemployment Compensation Law was enacted in 1936 in response to the grave social and economic problems that arose during the depression of that period. As stated in the statute itself:

Economic insecurity due to unemployment is a serious menace to health, morals and welfare of the people of this State; involuntary unemployment is therefore a subject of general interest and concern . . . ; the achievement of social security requires protection against this greatest hazard of our economic life; this can be provided by encouraging the employers to provide more stable employment and by the systematic accumulation of funds during periods of unemployment, thus maintaining purchasing power and limiting the serious social consequences of poor relief assistance. § 68-38 (Emphasis added.)

Thus the purpose of the legislature was to tide people over, and to avoid social and economic chaos, during periods when work was unavailable. But at the same time, there was clearly no intent to provide relief for those who for purely personal reasons were or became unavailable for work. In accordance with this design, the legislature provided, in § 68-113, that "[a]n unemployed insured worker shall be eligible to receive benefits with respect to any week only if the

Commission finds that . . . [h]e is able to work and is available for work. . . ." (Emphasis added.)

The South Carolina Supreme Court has uniformly applied this law in conformity with its clearly expressed purpose. It has consistently held that one is not "available for work" if his unemployment has resulted not from the inability of industry to provide a job but rather from personal circumstances, no matter how compelling. The reference to "involuntary unemployment" in the legislative statement of policy, whatever a sociologist, philosopher, or theologian might say, has been interpreted not to embrace such personal circumstances. See, e.g., Judson Mills v. South Carolina Unemployment Compensation Comm'n (claimant was "unavailable for work" when she became unable to work the third shift, and limited her availability to the other two, because of the need to care for her four children); . . .

In the present case all that the state court has done is to apply these accepted principles. Since virtually all of the mills in the Spartanburg area were operating on a six-day week, the appellant was "unavailable for work," and thus ineligible for benefits, when personal considerations prevented her from accepting employment on a full-time basis in the industry and locality in which she had worked. The fact that these personal considerations sprang from her religious convictions was wholly without relevance to the state court's application of the law. Thus in no proper sense can it be said that the State discriminated against the appellant on the basis of her religious beliefs or that she was denied benefits because she was a Seventh-day Adventist. She was denied benefits just as any other claimant would be denied benefits who was not "available for work" for personal reasons.

With this background, this Court's decision comes into clearer focus. What the Court is holding is that if the State chooses to condition unemployment compensation on the applicant's availability for work, it is constitutionally compelled to carve out an exception—and to provide benefits—for those whose unavailability is due to their religious convictions. Such a holding has particular significance in two respects.

First, despite the Court's protestations to the contrary, the decision necessarily overrules Braunfeld v. Brown, which held that it did not offend the "Free Exercise" Clause of the Constitution for a State to forbid a Sabbatarian to do business on Sunday. The secular purpose of the statute before us today is even clearer than that involved in Braunfeld. And just as in Braunfeld—where exceptions to the Sunday closing laws for Sabbatarians would have been inconsistent with the purpose to achieve a uniform day of rest and would have required case-by-case inquiry into religious benefits—so here, an exception to the rules of eligibility based on religious convictions would necessitate judicial examination of those convictions and would

be at odds with the limited purpose of the statute to smooth out the
economy during periods of industrial instability. Finally, the indirect
financial burden of the present law is far less than that involved in
Braunfeld. Forcing a store owner to close his business on Sunday
may well have the effect of depriving him of a satisfactory livelihood if
his religious convictions require him to close on Saturday as well.
Here we are dealing only with temporary benefits, amounting to a
fraction of regular weekly wages and running for not more than
22 weeks. . . . Clearly, any differences between this case and
Braunfeld cut against the present appellant.

Applying Principles

You will find described in the following paragraphs a hypothetical situation
intended to encourage you to analyze more closely the arguments advanced
in the Flag Statute Cases and Sherbert v. Verner. Are there any principles developed in these cases that might help you approach the problem
given below in a principled manner? Obviously, you will not be able to
apply the principles debated by the Court in a mechanical way that will give
a definitive solution to a difficult human situation. The moral universe is
never this tidy. However, the conflicting arguments raised by the Court
should provide you with at least a sound starting point for reaching a
principled stance.

> Time: Summer 1969.
>
> Place: A midwestern city with a population of 300,000.
>
> Persons: Clara Johnson, a GS-11 employed by the Office of Economic
>   Opportunity (OEO) as a Community Action Program (CAP)
>   agent.
>   Pastor Smith of St. Paul's Lutheran Church—a thoroughly
>   dedicated but somewhat abrasive clergyman with a city-wide
>   reputation for being extremely effective in working with
>   underprivileged youths.

Clara is in the process of working out the details of a grant from OEO
to fund a summer enrichment program sponsored by St. Paul's Church.
The proposal submitted by Pastor Smith was simply outstanding and was
enthusiastically received by Clara's local OEO office as well as by the
regional office in Chicago. To minimize constitutional problems that
might arise from the close interaction between government and religious
organizations serving the poor, OEO policy provides that the following
special conditions be met by any church-related institution applying for a
grant:

1. None of the grant funds shall be used for the teaching of religion, for religious proselytization, or religious worship.
2. There shall be no religious instruction, proselytization, or worship in connection with any program supported in whole or in part by this grant.
3. Admission to any of the programs supported by this grant shall not be based directly or indirectly on religious affiliation or on attendance at a church, church-related school, or other church-related institution or organization. Affirmative steps shall be taken to make known the general availability of such programs in the area served.
4. Participation in programs supported in whole or in part by this grant shall not be used as a means of inducing participation in sectarian or religious activities or of recruitment for sectarian or religious institutions.
5. All materials, such as reading materials, used in programs supported in whole or in part by this grant shall be devoid of sectarian or religious content.
6. Facilities renovated or rented for programs financed in whole or in part by this grant shall be devoid of sectarian or religious symbols, decoration, or other sectarian identification. Other facilities used primarily for such programs shall, to the maximum feasible extent, be devoid of sectarian or religious symbols, decoration, or other sectarian identification.
7. Grant funds shall not be used in any manner to release funds regularly expended by the church or church-related institution or organization. For example, grant funds shall not be used to pay in any part costs which would otherwise be incurred by the church or church-related institution or organization in its regular operation.[29]

These conditions had been routinely accepted by every clergyman Clara had dealt with in the past, and so she was somewhat surprised at Pastor Smith's reaction to the second sentence of condition 6—"Other facilities used primarily for such programs shall, to the maximum feasible extent, be devoid of sectarian or religious symbols, decoration, or other sectarian identification." He asked her just what this meant. She replied that in monitoring grants elsewhere in the city she had asked the clergy to remove religious symbols from the walls of the rooms used for the funded program. She added that there had been no problem with this with the sole exception of a nearby Catholic parish in which a gymnasium wall had been transformed into a "people's mural" emphasizing religious themes. Clara did not feel it would be appropriate to demand that this art work be destroyed as a condition of the grant.

Pastor Smith listened attentively to what Clara had to say and then replied that he might have to withdraw his proposal. The room that would serve as the focal point for the summer enrichment program was located in the basement of the church. Over the years it had acquired a large number of religious symbols—crosses, paintings, posters, and so forth, — that had been donated by devout parishioners. The symbols were of no monetary value and of little artistic merit, but Pastor Smith felt they were important to his parishioners and that they simply would not understand why they should be removed even temporarily. Furthermore, he confided in Clara that his effectiveness in dealing with the young was due in no small part to his reputation as a man who stood firm for principle even when the principle in question displeased those in authority. The youngsters were not particularly impressed with the religious bric-a-brac in the church basement, but the more sophisticated among them would surely see the issue as involving an important principle and would be quite critical of him if he appeared to cave in. Finally, he added, "Regardless of what the parishioners and the kids may think, I feel I ought to let you know that I just don't like the idea of the federal government coming in here and telling me to remove religious symbols. I think I understand the position you're in, Ms. Johnson, but I just feel I ought to let you know I don't like it. If I can't keep these crosses and paintings on the wall, you had better count me out."

Clara told Pastor Smith she would give careful thought to the objections he had raised and that she would let him know within a week if she could accommodate his position.

As she went home that evening, Clara weighed several alternatives. One was to "buck" the problem up through channels, but she felt this would almost certainly result in Pastor Smith's losing the grant. Just three weeks ago a memo had come from the regional office directing all CAP agents to adhere closely to the "special conditions" attached to grants involving church-related institutions. Rumor had it that the Chicago office of ACLU had complained to the regional director about some abuses. Although the regional office shared Clara's enthusiasm for Smith's proposal, she presumed that the director would be quite wary of giving an official recommendation to meet the pastor's demands.

She also considered using her own discretionary authority to accept what Pastor Smith wanted. After all, condition 6 said that the facilities should be devoid of religious symbols "to the maximum feasible extent." Previously, she had interpreted this to mean that churches need not remove their crosses from their steeples just because there was a Head Start program going on in the church basement! At least this was the explanation she had given—somewhat in jest—to the clergymen who had taken the trouble to inquire what "maximum feasible extent" might mean. Actually, Clara had never been forced to give the term much serious thought. Six other churches with which she had dealt had willingly complied with her request to remove crucifixes and pictures from auxiliary rooms. Would it be fair, she wondered, to comply with Pastor Smith's request after having told the more compliant clergy that they had to remove the symbols?

If you were Clara Johnson, what would you do? Would you follow the
reasoning of Justice Jackson in <u>Barnette</u>? Is the government's policy of
conditioning a grant upon the willingness of the recipient to remove religious symbols somewhat analogous to West Virginia's policy of conditioning
the benefit of free public education upon the recipients' willingness to
salute the flag? Is the power to make such demands simply outside the
scope of governmental power? If so, Clara might simply give in to
Pastor Smith and, if questioned about her decision, point to her discretionary authority as a justification.

Or would Justice Brennan's reasoning in <u>Sherbert</u> be more helpful?
While the government can legitimately set conditions that grantees must
meet, shouldn't it be particularly flexible in situations in which unusual
hardship, neither foreseen nor intended by the government, might arise'?
Certainly, Smith's position, like that of Sherbert, poses no "substantial
threat to public safety, peace, or order."' This position might leave Clara
vulnerable to the charge of playing favorites—just as Justice Brennan was
accused by Justice Stewart of "establishing" the religion of the Seventh-day
Adventists. A rejoinder to this criticism might be that both Brennan and
Clara modify public policy only when it imposes particular hardships upon
specific individuals. Because Pastor Smith was the only clergyman to
complain, it can be safely assumed that the others did not find the policy
offensive. That is, she is not playing favorites; she would accommodate
anyone who took the trouble to complain.

Or would it be best for Clara to follow Justice Harlan's reluctance to
carve out exemptions from otherwise sound policy simply because of some
citizen's religious scruples. In following this course, Clara could be
assured of upholding some of the constitutional values associated with the
prohibitions against an establishment of religion. Of course, she would
also be sealing the doom of Pastor Smith's excellent proposal and thereby
weakening the effectiveness of her agency.[30]

NATIONAL SECURITY

One of the saddest chapters in the story of World War II was the Supreme
Court's approval in <u>Korematsu</u> v. <u>U.S.</u>[31] of the evacuation and relocation
of persons of Japanese ancestry residing on the west coast. This policy
affected over 100,000 persons among whom were some 70,000 American
citizens. The long-standing prejudice against Orientals on the west coast
joined forces with a combination of wartime hysteria and some legitimate
concerns for national security in demanding that special provisions be made
for persons of Japanese ancestry. In February 1942, President Roosevelt
issued an executive order enabling the secretary of war to designate
military areas from which any or all persons might be excluded in order to
prevent espionage and sabotage. The states of Washington, Oregon, and

California, along with parts of Arizona, were designated military areas, and all persons of Japanese ancestry were ordered to leave these areas. The precise connection between the order to leave the designated areas and the order to report to relocation centers is discussed at length in the opinions that follow.

The major precedent that the Court relied upon was the 1943 case of Hirabayashi v. U.S. in which a military order forbidding persons of Japanese ancestry to leave their homes after 8:00 P.M. had been upheld. Actually, Hirabayashi had been convicted on two counts—failure to obey the curfew and failure to register for evacuation. The sentences for the two offenses were made to run concurrently. In reviewing Hirabayashi's conviction, the Supreme Court addressed the curfew conviction alone. In upholding this conviction, there was no need to review the evacuation conviction because the sentences ran concurrently. This maneuver enabled the Court to confine its approval to the curfew, which was a far less drastic intereference with traditional civil liberties than the exclusion order. In Korematsu, however, the Court could no longer avoid the painful issues presented by the evacuation order. The opinions that follow are an instructive, though quite unfortunate, example of a judicial debate over the competing issues of national security and personal liberty.

The most interesting contrast in the case centers on the sharply divergent ways in which Justice Black, who gave the majority opinion upholding the government's action, and Justice Roberts, who dissented, define the key issues in the case. For Black the issue is whether the government can convict Korematsu of failing to leave his home, which was in an area from which persons of Japanese ancestry were excluded by military orders. Black insists that the issues of where Korematsu would have gone had he complied with the evacuation order and left the area is irrelevant to the disposition of the case at hand. Justice Roberts maintains that Black has closed his eyes to what the case is really about. For Roberts the key point is that the government not only ordered Korematsu to leave his home in California but decided as well that he must go to a "relocation center" established for uprooted Japanese Americans. Thus for Roberts the case involved not only exclusion but detention as well.

Black states his perception of the point at issue in the case as follows:

The petitioner, an American citizen of Japanese descent, was convicted in a federal district court for remaining in San Leandro, California, a "Military Area," contrary to Civilian Exclusion Order No. 34 of the Commanding General of the Western Command, U.S. Army, which directed that after May 9, 1942, all persons of Japanese ancestry should be excluded from that area. . . .

In the light of the principles we announced in the Hirabayashi case, we are unable to conclude that it was beyond the war power of Congress and the Executive to exclude those of Japanese ancestry from the

West Coast war area at the time they did. True, exclusion from the
area in which one's home is located is a far greater deprivation than
constant confinement to the home from 8 P. M. to 6 A. M. Nothing
short of apprehension by the proper military authorities of the gravest
imminent danger to the public safety can constitutionally justify either.
But exclusion from a threatened area, no less than curfew, has a
definite and close relationship to the prevention of espionage and
sabotage.

Roberts opens his dissent with a very different view of what was at
stake in Korematsu:

This is not a case of keeping people off the streets at night as was
Hirabayashi v. United States, nor a case of temporary exclusion of a
citizen from an area for his own safety or that of the community, nor
a case of offering him an opportunity to go temporarily out of an area
where his presence might cause danger to himself or to his fellows.
On the contrary, it is the case of convicting a citizen as a punishment
for not submitting to imprisonment in a concentration camp, based on
his ancestry, without evidence or inquiry concerning his loyalty and
good disposition towards the United States. . . .
    The Government's argument, and the opinion of the court, in my
judgment, erroneously divide that which is single and indivisible and
thus make the case appear as if the petitioner violated a Military
Order, sanctioned by Act of Congress, which excluded him from his
home, by refusing voluntarily to leave and, so, knowingly and inten-
tionally, defying the order and the Act of Congress.

Justice Roberts went on to trace the chronology of wartime measures
taken against persons of Japanese ancestry on the west coast. An area
that included Alameda County, wherein Korematsu resided, was designated as Military Area No. 1. By Public Proclamation No. 4 of March 27,
1942, Lieutenant General DeWitt, Military Commander of the Western
Defense Command, forbade "all alien Japanese and persons of Japanese
ancestry" to leave Area No. 1 "for any purpose until and to the extent that
a future proclamation or order of this headquarters shall so permit or
direct." On May 3, 1942, the General modified the previous order in such
a way that persons of Japanese ancestry were prohibited from remaining in
Military Area No. 1 except for a location designated as an Assembly
Center for Japanese about to be deported to relocation centers in some
remote area of an inland western state. The May 3 order, however, did
not repeal the order of March 27. Thus persons of Japanese ancestry
were permitted neither to leave Area No. 1 nor to remain in it unless they
betook themselves to the designated Assembly Center. Justice Roberts
continued:

The obvious purpose of the orders made, taken together, was to drive all citizens of Japanese ancestry into Assembly Centers within the zones of their residence, under pain of criminal prosecution.

The predicament in which the petitioner thus found himself was this: He was forbidden, by Military Order, to leave the zone in which he lived; he was forbidden, by Military Order, after a date fixed, to be found within that zone unless he were in an Assembly Center located in that zone. General DeWitt's report to the Secretary of War concerning the programme of evacuation and relocation of Japanese makes it entirely clear, if it were necessary to refer to that document—and, in the light of the above recitation, I think it is not—that an Assembly Center was a euphemism for a prison. No person within such a center was permitted to leave except by Military Order.

In the dilemma that he dare not remain in his home, or voluntarily leave the area, without incurring criminal penalties, and that the only way he could avoid punishment was to go to an Assembly Center and submit himself to military imprisonment, the petitioner did nothing. . . .

The Government has argued this case as if the only order outstanding at the time the petitioner was arrested and informed against was Exclusion Order No. 34 ordering him to leave the area in which he resided, which was the basis of the information against him. That argument has evidently been effective. The opinion refers to the Hirabayashi case, . . . , to show that this court has sustained the validity of a curfew order in an emergency. The argument then is that exclusion from a given area of danger, while somewhat more sweeping than a curfew regulation, is of the same nature—a temporary expedient made necessary by a sudden emergency. This, I think, is a substitution of a hypothetical case for the case actually before the court. I might agree with the court's disposition of the hypothetical case. The liberty of every American citizen freely to come and to go must frequently, in the face of sudden danger, be temporarily limited or suspended. The civil authorities must often resort to the expedient of excluding citizens temporarily from a locality. The drawing of fire lines in the case of a conflagration, the removal of persons from the area where a pestilence has broken out, are familiar examples. If the . . . Exclusion Order . . . were of that nature the Hirabayashi case would be authority for sustaining it. But the facts above recited . . . show that the exclusion was but a part of an over-all plan for forceable detention. This case cannot, therefore, be decided on any such narrow ground as the possible validity of a Temporary Exclusion Order under which the residents of an area are given an opportunity to leave and go elsewhere in their native land outside the boundaries of a military area. To make the case turn on any such assumption is to shut our eyes to reality. . . .

We cannot shut our eyes to the fact that had the petitioner attempted to violate Proclamation No. 4 and leave the military area in which
he lived he would have been arrested and tried and convicted for violation of Proclamation No. 4. The two conflicting orders, one which
commanded him to stay and the other which commanded him to go,
were nothing but a cleverly devised trap to accomplish the real purpose
of the military authority, which was to lock him up in a concentration
camp. The only course by which the petitioner could avoid arrest and
prosecution was to go to that camp according to instructions to be
given him when he reported at a Civil Control Center. We know that
is the fact. Why should we set up a figmentary and artificial situation
instead of addressing ourselves to the actualities of the case?

In the majority opinion Justice Black maintained that the Court should
address itself only to the constitutionality of the military order under which
Korematsu was arrested—the exclusion order that forbade him to remain in
Area No. 1 unless he was at the Assembly Center. Black closed his
opinion as follows:

It is said that we are dealing here with the case of imprisonment of a
citizen in a concentration camp solely because of his ancestry, without
evidence or inquiry concerning his loyalty and good disposition towards
the United States. Our task would be simple, our duty clear, were
this a case involving the imprisonment of a loyal citizen in a concentration camp because of racial prejudice. Regardless of the true
nature of the assembly and relocation centers—and we deem it unjusti-
fiable to call them concentration camps with all the ugly connotations
that term implies—we are dealing specifically with nothing but an
exclusion order. To cast this case into outlines of racial prejudice,
without reference to the real military dangers which were presented,
merely confuses the issue. Korematsu was not excluded from the
Military Area because of hostility to him or his race. He was excluded because we are at war with the Japanese Empire, because the
properly constituted military authorities feared an invasion of our
West Coast and felt constrained to take proper security measures,
because they decided that the military urgency of the situation
demanded that all citizens of Japanese ancestry be segregated from
the West Coast temporarily, and finally, because Congress, reposing
its confidence in this time of war in our military leaders—as inevitably it must—determined that they should have the power to do just this.
There was evidence of disloyalty on the part of some, the military
authorities considered that the need for action was great, and time
was short. We cannot—by availing ourselves of the calm perspective
of hindsight—now say that at the time these actions were unjustified.

What do you think of this debate between Black and Roberts? History
has certainly vindicated Roberts's position both in his analysis of what was
really at issue and how it should have been resolved. Black's effort to
distinguish the exclusion question from the detention question appears now,
as it did then, to be nothing more than an elaborate (and not very persuasive) rationalization. Nevertheless, for purposes of analysis, Black's
position may be more interesting than the straightforward and more admi-
rable opinion of Roberts. Put yourself in Black's position and suppose you
had reached the decision that the War Department's relocation program
should be upheld. For the sake of argument, let us prescind from the
question of how you reached this decision other than to say that it was not
racially motivated. That is, you sincerely deplore singling out a racial
minority for adverse treatment and would do so only under extreme provo-
cation, which you find present in this case. Having made this decision,
would you then follow Black's example and try to redefine the issue in such
a way that you minimize the adverse impact of your decision for the future?
Black seemed to be genuinely concerned about not creating as a precedent
the principle that the Constitution permits detention of persons on grounds
of race or national origin. To avoid creating this precedent, he seems to
have deliberately thrown up a smoke screen around the real issue. Once
you had decided to support the government's position, would you consider
it morally better to meet Robert's argument directly or to create a pseudo-
issue, as Black seems to have done, in the hope of mitigating the severity
of the precedential nature of your decision?

Justice Frankfurter wrote a concurring opinion that made the following
significant addition to Black's opinion:

The provisions of the Constitution which confer on the Congress and
the President powers to enable this country to wage war are as much
part of the Constitution as provisions looking to a nation at peace. And
we have had recent occasion to quote approvingly the statement of
former Chief Justice Hughes that the war power of the Government is
"the power to wage war successfully." . . . Therefore, the validity
of action under the war power must be judged wholly in the context of
war. That action is not to be stigmatized as lawless because like
action in times of peace would be lawless. To talk about a military
order that expresses an allowable judgment of war needs by those
entrusted with the duty of conducting war as "an unconstitutional
order" is to suffuse a part of the Constitution with an atmosphere of
unconstitutionality. The respective spheres of action of military
authorities and of judges are of course very different. But within
their sphere, military authorities are no more outside the bounds of
obedience to the Constitution than are judges within theirs. "The war
power of the United States, like its other powers . . . is subject to

applicable constitutional limitations." . . . To recognize that military orders are "reasonably expedient military precautions" in time of war and yet to deny them constitutional legitimacy makes of the Constitution an instrument for dialectic subtleties not reasonably to be attributed to the hard-headed Framers, of whom a majority had had actual participation in war. If a military order such as that under review does not transcend the means appropriate for conducting war, such action by the military is as constitutional as would be any authorized action by the Interstate Commerce Commission within the limits of the constitutional power to regulate commerce. And being an exercise of the war power explicitly granted by the Constitution for safeguarding the national life by prosecuting war effectively, I find nothing in the Constitution which denies to Congress the power to enforce such a valid military order by making its violation an offense triable in the civil courts. . . . To find that the Constitution does not forbid the military measures now complained of does not carry with it approval of that which Congress and the Executive did. That is their business, not ours.

Does Frankfurter seem to be worried about Korematsu creating an unwholesome precedent? Is there anything in Frankfurter's opinion that would prevent the government from detaining persons of Japanese ancestry as well as excluding them from a militarily sensitive area?

The last two sentences of Frankfurter's opinion are an example of "judicial restraint." Elementary constitutional theory tells us that the judiciary should not concern itself with the wisdom or usefulness of a particular law or policy but only with its constitutionality. Frankfurter does not seem terribly impressed with the wisdom of the government's relocation program but, because he does not find it unconstitutional, he can do nothing to stop it. Although it is easy in principle to make distinctions between wisdom and constitutionality on the respective roles of courts and legislatures, it is far more difficult to apply them in practice. Are there parallels to judicial restraint within the administrative process— times when administrators charged with carrying out an unjust law can say of Congress or their political superiors in the executive branch: "That is their business, not ours"? Are there times when it would be morally wrong merely to say "that is their business" and be done with it? Does such a statement absolve administrators (or judges) from moral culpability for what the government does? If you say yes, aren't you condoning a somewhat sophisticated version of the Eichmann argument? If you say no, what alternatives do you suggest?

Frankfurter relies heavily on the argument of former Chief Justice Hughes that the constitutional power of the government to wage war carries with it "the power to wage war successfully." What are the implications of this remark? Does this mean that if military necessity so dictates, all values must be subordinated to national survival? Elsewhere in his opinion, Frankfurter says that military orders that do not "transcend the means appropriate for conducting war" are constitutional. If there are "appropriate" means for conducting war, there must be inappropriate means as well which, presumably, would be unconstitutional. Does this argument qualify the apparent intransigence of the statement that the power to wage war is "the power to wage war successfully"? Or would the distinction between means that are appropriate and inappropriate collapse under the stern demands of military necessity? That is, does the logic of Frankfurter's position lead to the conclusion that in wartime the ultimate test of propriety (and therefore, for Frankfurter, of constitutionality) is a military judgment?[32]

Certain aspects of Frankfurter's concurring opinion are aimed at the dissent of Justice Jackson. Let us now examine an extensive excerpt from Jackson's opinion and then return to Frankfurter's criticism.

A citizen's presence in Military Area No. 1 was made a crime only if his parents were of Japanese birth. Had Korematsu been one of four—the others being, say, a German alien enemy, an Italian alien enemy, and a citizen of American-born ancestors, convicted of treason but out on parole—only Korematsu's presence would have violated the order. The difference between their innocence and his crime would result, not from anything he did, said, or thought, different than they, but only in that he was born of different racial stock.

Now, if any fundamental assumption underlies our system, it is that guilt is personal and not inheritable. Even if all of one's antecedents had been convicted of treason, the Constitution forbids its penalties to be visited upon him, for it provides that "no attainder of treason shall work corruption of blood, or forefeiture except during the life of the person attainted." But here is an attempt to make an otherwise innocent act a crime merely because this prisoner is the son of parents as to whom he had no choice, and belongs to a race from which there is no way to resign. If Congress in peace-time legislation should enact such a criminal law, I should suppose this Court would refuse to enforce it.

But the "law" which this prisoner is convicted of disregarding is not found in an act of Congress, but in a military order. Neither the Act of Congress nor the Executive Order of the President, nor both together, would afford a basis for this conviction. It rests on the orders of General DeWitt. And it is said that if the military commander had reasonable military grounds for promulgating the orders, they are constitutional and become law, and the Court is required to enforce them. There are several reasons why I cannot subscribe to this doctrine.

It would be impracticable and dangerous idealism to expect or insist that each specific military command in an area of probable operations will conform to conventional tests of constitutionality. When an area is so beset that it must be put under military control at all, the paramount consideration is that its measures be successful, rather than legal. The armed services must protect a society, not merely its Constitution. The very essence of the military job is to marshal physical force, to remove every obstacle to its effectiveness, to give it every strategic advantage. Defense measures will not, and often should not, be held within the limits that bind civil authority in peace. No court can require such a commander in such circumstances to act as a reasonable man; he may be unreasonably cautious and exacting. Perhaps he should be. But a commander in temporarily focusing the life of a community on defense is carrying out a military program; he is not making law in the sense the courts know the term. He issues orders, and they may have a certain authority as military commands, although they may be very bad as constitutional law.

But if we cannot confine military expedients by the Constitution, neither would I distort the Constitution to approve all that the military may deem expedient. That is what the Court appears to be doing, whether consciously or not. I cannot say, from any evidence before me, that the orders of General DeWitt were not reasonably expedient military precautions, nor could I say that they were. But even if they were permissible military procedures, I deny that it follows that they are constitutional. If, as the Court holds, it does follow, then we may as well say that any military order will be constitutional and have done with it. . . .

Much is said of the danger to liberty from the Army program for deporting and detaining these citizens of Japanese extraction. But a judicial construction of the due process clause that will sustain this order is a far more subtle blow to liberty than the promulgation of the order itself. A military order, however unconstitutional, is not apt to last longer than the military emergency. Even during that period a succeeding commander may revoke it all. But once a judicial opinion rationalizes such an order to show that it conforms to the Constitution, or rather rationalizes the Constitution to show that the Constitution sanctions such an order, the Court for all time has validated the principle of racial discimination in criminal procedure and of trans-planting American citizens. The principle then lies about like a loaded weapon ready for the hand of any authority that can bring forward a plausible claim of an urgent need. Every repetition imbeds that principle more deeply in our law and thinking and expands it to new purposes. All who observe the work of courts are familiar with what Judge Cardozo described as "the tendency of a principle to expand itself to the limit of its logic." A military commander may overstep

the bounds of constitutionality, and it is an incident. But if we review
and approve, that passing incident becomes the doctrine of the Constitution. There it has a generative power of its own, and all that it
creates will be in its own image. . . .

I should hold that a civil court cannot be made to enforce an order
which violates constitutional limitations even if it is a reasonable
exercise of military authority. The courts can exercise only the
judicial power, can apply only law, and must abide by the Constitution,
or they cease to be civil courts and become instruments of military
policy.

It is Jackson's dissent that Frankfurter had in mind when he said:

To talk about a military order that expresses an allowable judgment of
war needs by those entrusted with the duty of conducting war as "an
unconstitutional order" is to suffuse a part of the Constitution with an
atmosphere of unconstitutionality. . . . To recognize that military
orders are "reasonably expedient military precautions" in time of war
and yet to deny them constitutional legitimacy makes of the Constitution an instrument for dialectic subtleties not reasonably to be attributed to the hard-headed Framers, of whom a majority had had actual
participation in war.

Frankfurter is saying that everything done in the name of the United
States government either is or is not constitutional. Jackson would allow
a constitutional limbo for certain military acts in time of war. This is
more than an argument over the proper role of the courts in our constitutional system. It goes to the heart of the meaning of constitutional government. Which position do you find more compelling?

Although there is greater conceptual clarity in Frankfurter's position,
his argument forces him to make the hard choice of either (1) bestowing
the Court's blessing on what the army has done or (2) challenging the
military judgment that the evacuation-detention order was a military necessity or (3) saying that even if it were militarily necessary it still cannot
be done—ruat caelum, fiat justitia.* Jackson's limbo avoids these
unpleasant alternatives but in so doing his argument is vulnerable to the
objection that the Constitution is useless when we need it most.

Do you agree with Jackson that the Court in upholding the government's
relocation program has compromised liberty more severely than the army
did in ordering the program in the first place? Does the Court's approval
make it likely that high-handed military arrogance will compromise civil
liberties in wartime more extensively than if the Court had followed
Jackson's advice and simply looked the other way?[33]

---

*Though the heavens fall, let justice be done.

SEPARATION OF POWERS

Questions concerning freedom are not restricted to the provisions of the
Bill of Rights. In the preamble to the Constitution, before any amendments
were proposed or adopted, it was stated that among the purposes for which
these United States were ordained and established was the preservation of
"the blessings of liberty for ourselves and our posterity." One of the
means relied upon by the framers of the Constitution to preserve liberty
was the principle of separation of powers, and one of the most spectacular
Supreme Court opinions to expound this principle came in the Watergate
tapes case, U.S. v. Nixon.[34]

The Watergate events that provide the background of this case are sufficiently well known to preclude the need for an extensive introduction—at
least "at this point in time." For our purposes, U.S. v. Nixon is important, not because of its effect on the House Judiciary Committee's historic
decision to recommend the impeachment of Richard Nixon, but because of
certain freedom-oriented questions it raised concerning the relationship
between the constitutional principle of separation of powers and the ultimate constitutional value of limited government. These questions are
particularly relevant to those employed in the executive branch of
government.

It will be recalled that in April 1974, Judge John Sirica of the United
States District Court in Washington, D.C., issued a subpoena to
President Nixon ordering him to produce tapes of certain conversations
requested by Special Prosecutor Leon Jaworski in connection with the
upcoming trial of John Mitchell, H. R. Haldeman, John Ehrlichman, and
four other former high-ranking presidential advisers. The president's
counsel, James St. Clair, filed a motion to quash the subpoena on the
grounds of executive privilege. That is, the subpoenaed tapes were alleged
to have involved confidential discussions between the president and his
advisers and, hence, were "privileged" from disclosure even when needed
as evidence in a criminal trial. Judge Sirica denied St. Clair's motion
and ordered the tapes produced. The president appealed this denial to the
United States Court of Appeals for the District of Columbia. The Special
Prosecutor, fearing an inordinate delay from a series of appeals, asked
and received from the Supreme Court "a writ of certiorari before judgment," which enabled the case to go directly from the district court to the
Supreme Court of the United States. Oral argument was heard on July 8,
1974; a unanimous decision ordering the president to produce the tapes was
handed down on July 24.

A major issue in the case involved the question of the Court's jurisdiction. St. Clair argued that the Special Prosecutor's demand for the
tapes involved "an intra-branch dispute between a subordinate and a
superior officer of the executive branch." Indeed, all parties agreed that
the Special Prosecutor was a member of the executive branch of

government, but Jaworski argued that certain unusual circumstances surrounding the creation of his office conferred an independent status upon him
that enabled the courts to review disputes between the president and himself. The unusual circumstances refer, of course, to the "Saturday night
massacre" of October 20, 1973, in which Jaworski's predecessor,
Archibald Cox, was fired and Attorney General Elliott Richardson and
Deputy Attorney General William Ruckelshaus were forced to resign. The
howls of outrage that greeted this unhappy event forced President Nixon to
agree to reestablish the office of the Special Prosecutor. This was done
on November 2, 1973, by a Justice Department regulation issued by Acting
Attorney General Robert H. Bork. Among the powers granted to the new
Special Prosecutor was the provision that he "shall have full authority for
determining whether or not to contest the assertion of 'executive privilege'
or any other testimonial privilege." It was on the basis of this explicit
grant of power that Jaworski based his right to challenge in the courts the
president's claim of executive privilege over the subpoenaed tapes.

St. Clair maintained that Jaworski's position as a member of the
executive branch was dispositive of the issue regardless of what agreements presidential subordinates, such as an acting attorney general, might
make. He cited several Supreme Court cases to support his position:
(1) that the president as chief executive officer of the Republic has the
ultimate authority to determine questions of an executive nature and
(2) that evidence the government would introduce in a criminal case is
clearly an executive matter. Among the cases St. Clair cited were
Mississippi v. Johnson[35] in which the Supreme Court had somewhat
exuberantly announced that "the President is the Executive Department"
and Marbury v. Madison[36] in which Chief Justice Marshall, in referring
to presidential subordinates, had said that "their acts are his [the president's] acts." The agreement between Bork and Jaworski, St. Clair maintained, did not waive any presidential power to claim presidential
privileges. It merely gave the Special Prosecutor the right to decide
"whether or not to contest the assertion of executive privilege," but the
practical effectiveness of this agreement is no business of the judiciary.
It remains an "intra-branch dispute" and is therefore purely an executive
matter. The Supreme Court replied:

> The mere assertion of a claim of an "intra-branch dispute," without
> more, has never operated to defeat federal jurisdiction; justiciability
> does not depend on such a surface inquiry. In United States v.
> ICC, the Court observed, "courts must look behind names that
> symbolize the parties to determine whether a justiciable case or con-
> troversy is presented. . . ."
>   Our starting point is the nature of the proceeding for which the
> evidence is sought—here a pending criminal prosecution. It is a
> judicial proceeding in the federal court alledging violation of federal

laws and is brought in the name of the United States as sovereign.
Under the authority of Art. II § 2, Congress has vested in the
Attorney General the power to conduct the criminal litigation of the
United States Government. 28 U. S. C. § 516. It has also vested
in him the power to appoint subordinate officers to assist him in the
discharge of his duties. 28 U. S. C. §§ 5.09, 510, 515, 533. Acting
pursuant to those statutes, the Attorney General has delegated particular matters to a Special Prosecutor with unique authority and
tenure. The regulation gives the Special Prosecutor explicit power to
contest the invocation of executive privilege in the process of seeking
evidence deemed relevant to the performance of these specially delegated duties. 38 Fed. Reg. 30739.

So long as this regulation is extant it has the force of law.
Accardi v. Shaughnessy, regulations of the Attorney General delegated
certain of his discretionary powers to the Board of Immigration
Appeals and required that Board to exercise its own discretion on
appeals in deportation cases. The Court held that so long as the
Attorney General's regulations remained operative, he denied himself
the authority to exercise the discretion delegated to the Board even
though the original authority was his and he could reassert it by
amending the regulations. . . .

Here, as in Accardi, it is theoretically possible for the Attorney
General to amend or revoke the regulation defining the Special Prosecutor's authority. But he has not done so. So long as this regulation
remains in force the Executive Branch is bound by it, and indeed the
United States as the sovereign composed of the three branches is bound
to respect and to enforce it. Moreover, the delegation of authority to
the Special Prosecutor in this case is not an ordinary delegation by the
Attorney General to a subordinate officer: with the authorization of
the President, the Acting Attorney General provided in the regulation
that the Special Prosecutor was not to be removed without the "consensus" of eight designated leaders of Congress.

The demands of and the resistance to the subpoena present an
obvious controversy in the ordinary sense, but that alone is not sufficient to meet constitutional standards. In the constitutional sense,
controversy means more than disagreement and conflict; rather it
means the kind of controversy courts traditionally resolve. Here at
issue is the production or non-production of specified evidence deemed
by the Special Prosecutor to be relevant and admissible in a pending
criminal case. It is sought by one official of the Government within
the scope of his express authority; it is resisted by the Chief Executive on the ground of his duty to preserve the confidentiality of the
communications of the President. Whatever the correct answer on the
merits, these issues are "of a type which are traditionally justiciable."
The independent Special Prosecutor with his asserted need for the subpoenaed material in the underlying criminal prosecution is opposed

by the President with his steadfast assertion of privilege against disclosure of the material. This setting assures there is "that concrete
adverseness which sharpens the presentation of issues upon which the
court so largely depends for illumination of difficult constitutional
questions." . . . Moreover, since the matter is one arising in the
regular course of a federal criminal prosecution, it is within the
traditional scope of Art. III power.

 In light of the uniqueness of the setting in which the conflict
arises, the fact that both parties are officers of the Executive Branch
cannot be viewed as a barrier to justiciability. It would be inconsistent with the applicable law and regulation, and the unique facts of this
case, to conclude other than that the Special Prosecutor has standing
to bring this action and that a justiciable controversy is presented for
decision.

Do you find the Court's explanation satisfactory? At the beginning of
the passage just quoted the Court promises us more than merely a "surface
inquiry" but the reliance in the concluding paragraph on the "unique facts
of this case" suggests the Court never did get beneath the surface. To be
sure, the facts of the case were unique and, one might add, zany and
bizarre, for the case involved tape-recorded conversations between the
president and his highest advisers who were defendants in a criminal trial
in which the president himself had been named as an unindicted co-
conspirator. The facts of the case were so outrageous that the Court
could hardly have done other than it did. The short-term result of the
case was to force the president to release the subpoenaed tapes, and that
was all to the good. For our purposes, however, the Court's argument
raises some rather interesting questions on the constitutional place of
employees of the executive branch.

The Court stresses the fact that Congress gives the attorney general
the power to conduct criminal litigation and it was the (acting) attorney
general who delegated the authority to the Special Prosecutor to contest
claims of executive privilege. This is undoubtedly true just as it is true,
as the Court points out, that the Special Prosecutor cannot be removed
from office without the "consensus" of eight designated leaders of
Congress. It would be a mistake, however, to confuse the conferral of the
power of final executive decision-making authority with the power to create
an office or to be consulted on the removal of a particular officeholder
from a particular office. Article II of the Constitution provides that
Congress "may by law vest the appointment of such inferior officers as
they think proper in the President alone, in the courts of law, or in the
heads of departments." The operative word here is "inferior." Regardless of who appoints them or what they do, executive officers are inferior
to the president. If "inferior" means anything at all, it must mean that
subordinates cannot have the final decision-making power over and against
the president on an executive matter. This is the part of St. Clair's

argument that the Court never really addressed. It is a significant question for employees of the executive branch because it raises questions of where their ultimate loyalties lie: to the president, who is clearly their executive superior, or to Congress, by whose authority their agency is established and given specific statutory responsibilities.

If you are a federal employee in the executive branch, where do you place your ultimate loyalty? If you are an employee of the executive branch of a state government, look at your state constitution to see if it creates the same ambiguity as the federal Constitution. Is there a danger of our contemporaries being so overwhelmed by the obvious excesses of the Nixon presidency that we might become insensitive to the value of unified executive leadership? Or, on the other hand, are we more likely to be insensitive to the legitimate interference of the legislature with the executive's perennial demand for unity of command? How do you react to legislative "interference" with a program you are managing? Do you ever think of such "interference" in broader terms of separation of powers, limited government, and freedom itself?

Although the Court downplayed St. Clair's argument based on the executive supremacy of the president, it gave considerable attention to his position supporting executive privilege as a means of ensuring free and uninhibited communication between the president and his advisers. This is the sort of argument that should be quite meaningful to managers involved in the decision-making process.

In support of his claim of absolute privilege, the President's counsel urges two grounds one of which is common to all governments and one of which is peculiar to our system of separation of powers. The first ground is the valid need for protection of communications between high government officials and those who advise and assist them in the performance of their manifold duties; the importance of this confidentiality is too plain to require further discussion. Human experience teaches that those who expect public dissemination of their remarks may well temper candor with a concern for appearances and for their own interests to the detriment of the decision-making process. Whatever the nature of the privilege of confidentiality of presidential communications in the exercise of Art. II powers the privilege can be said to derive from the supremacy of each branch within its own assigned area of constitutional duties. Certain powers and privileges flow from the nature of enumerated powers; the protection of the confidentiality of presidential communications has similar constitutional underpinnings. . . .

However, neither the doctrine of separation of powers, nor the need for confidentiality of high level communications, without more, can sustain an absolute, unqualified presidential privilege of immunity from judicial process under all circumstances. The President's need

for complete candor and objectivity from advisers calls for great
deference from the courts. However, when the privilege depends
solely on the broad, undifferentiated claim of public interest in the
confidentiality of such conversations, a confrontation with other values
arises. Absent a claim of need to protect military, diplomatic or
sensitive national security secrets, we find it difficult to accept the
argument that even the very important interest in confidentiality of
presidential communications is significantly diminished by production
of such material for in camera inspection with all the protection that a
district court will be obliged to provide.

   . . . To read the Art. II powers of the President as providing an
absolute privilege as against a subpoena essential to enforcement of
criminal statutes on no more than a generalized claim of the public
interest in confidentiality of nonmilitary and nondiplomatic discussions
would upset the constitutional balance of "a workable government" and
gravely impair the role of the courts under Art. III.

Do you agree with the Court's analysis of the problem? Is it true that
sound decision making requires that the confidentiality of the advice
rendered by subordinates be respected? Do you have any personal experience along this line?

The Court makes it quite clear that a sharp distinction must be made
between military and diplomatic affairs on the one hand and other governmental matters on the other. The passage just quoted and other sections
of the Court's opinion as well would seem to support an absolute claim of
executive privilege in foreign affairs whereas in domestic matters such a
claim would be balanced against competing values such as the need for
evidence in a criminal trial. Do you think the distinction between domestic
and foreign affairs is important as far as the confidentiality of advice is
concerned? Is the distinction self-explanatory? That is, is it always
obvious which issues are foreign and which are domestic? Was the sur-
reptitious invasion of the office of Daniel Ellsberg's psychiatrist a
domestic or a foreign matter?

The day after U.S. v. Nixon was decided, the Washington Post
reported the following statement from the president: "I was gratified,
therefore, to note that the Court reaffirmed both the validity and the
importance of the principle of executive privilege. . . . [T]his [case] will
prove to be not the precedent that destroyed the principle but the action
that preserved it." There is considerable irony in the former president's
statement. Throughout the Watergate affair one of Nixon's recurrent
arguments was the need to protect the strength of the presidency. He
continually reminded those of us who would "wallow in Watergate" that we
should pay more attention to the adverse affects that compulsory disclosure
would have on the office of the president "in the long run." In U.S. v.
Nixon, the president lost his case; he was forced to release information he

wanted to withhold. However, he quite correctly maintained that the case "reaffirmed both the validity and the importance of the principle of executive privilege." This was indeed ironic because, despite Nixon's somber warnings, the veil of executive secrecy had been partially lifted without degrading the presidency into a hapless pawn of Congress and the courts. One of the main criticisms of the Court's opinion was that it all too clearly established the constitutional legitimacy of executive privilege. Before U.S. v. Nixon, the law surrounding executive privilege was quite ambiguous. Analogies were drawn between executive privilege and the traditional privileges concerning communications between husband and wife, priest and penitent, lawyer and client, and so on. Historical references were made to President Jefferson's handling of a subpoena from Chief Justice Marshall in the Aaron Burr cases and to opinions of attorneys general advising presidents of the meaning of executive privilege. Case law on the subject was scanty and unclear. All this changed however with U.S. v. Nixon. We now know that as a matter of constitutional law the president has a claim to executive privilege that is limited in domestic affairs and virtually absolute in foreign affairs.

It is the absolute character of the presidential claim of executive privilege that has occasioned some criticism of the Court's opinion. Some commentators see in U.S. v. Nixon another example of the wisdom of Justice Holmes's famous aphorism—"hard cases make bad law."

Without trying to decide whether or not U.S. v. Nixon made "bad law," we can use the case to reflect on aspects of decision making that apply to administrators as well as judges. One reason that "hard cases make bad law" is that the "hard" case, almost by definition, implies that regardless of what decision is made certain difficulties and embarrassments cannot be avoided. This is especially true in legal matters because of the precedential nature of judicial decisions. Managerial practice is not as rigid as law, but good managers are usually concerned with avoiding both the appearance and reality of arbitrariness and caprice. Ordinarily, consistency is a desirable trait in management personnel and for this reason "hard" management cases can at times prove as frustrating for managers as hard court cases can be for judges. Over the years the judiciary has developed an impressive array of techniques to avoid hard cases when it seems wise to do so. This aspect of the judicial process is little understood and, when understood, seldom appreciated. Justice Frankfurter once had this to say about popular reaction to judicial efforts to sidestep hard decisions:

> Rigorous adherence to the narrow scope of the judicial function is especially demanded in controversies that arouse appeals to the Constitution. The attitude with which this Court must approach its duty when confronted with such issues is precisely the opposite of that normally manifested by the general public. So-called constitutional questions seem to exercise a mesmeric influence over the popular

mind. This eagerness to settle—preferably forever—a specific problem on the basis of the broadest possible constitutional pronounce-
ments may not unfairly be called one of our minor national traits. An
English observer of our scene has acutely described it: "At the first
sound of a new argument over the United States Constitution and its
interpretation the hearts of Americans leap with a fearful joy. The
blood stirs powerfully in their veins and a new lustre brightens their
eyes. Like King Harry's men before Harfluer, they stand like grey-
houds in the slips, straining upon the start." The Economist, May 10,
1952, p. 370.

The path of duty for this Court, it bears repitition, lies in the opposite direction. [37]

Although the judicial process is not always an appropriate model for
managerial decision making, there are some parallels that might be
instructive. Managers, like judges, frequently feel the hot breath of those
consumed with a passion for action. A good manager is supposed to be an
aggressive "take-charge guy" who is not afraid to run risks in the name
of decisive action. Are there times, however, when sound public management dictates a strategy of postponing and sidestepping important decisions? Is Frankfurter's observation of some relevance to managers?

The circumstances of U.S. v. Nixon were such that it would have been
impossible for the Court to have heeded Frankfurter's counsels of
restraint. Perhaps the case could have been resolved short of recognizing
an absolute claim of executive privilege in foreign affairs. In so doing,
however, the Court might have created different and perhaps even more
severe problems for the delicate balance of power in our Constitution. In
agreeing to hear U.S. v. Nixon, the Court committed itself to clarifying
certain ultimate constitutional questions. It would probably be impossible
for any court to do this without inflicting some damage on our system of
government. One of the strengths of American government is that ultimate
questions trail off into a benign ambiguity. There are blank spaces on the
constitutional canvas that are wisely left untouched in order that the Constitution may continue to fulfill its creative and innovative capacity. Part
of the bitter Nixon legacy is that the Court was forced into transforming
benevolent uncertainty into dangerous dogma. The Supreme Court played
a crucial, perhaps decisive, role in resolving the "long national nightmare" of Watergate, but it did so at a price.

NOTES

1. Joseph Tussman and Jacobus Tenbroek, "The Equal Protection of The
   Laws," California Law Review 37 (September 1949): 341.
2. 323 U.S. 214 (1944).
3. 418 U.S. 683 (1974).

4. 268 U.S. 652 (1925).
5. The quotation is from Judge Learned Hand, cited by C. Herman Pritchett, The American Constitution, 2nd ed. (New York: McGraw-Hill, 1968), p. 415.
6. Schenck v. U.S. 249 U.S. 47.
7. Alpheus T. Mason and William M. Beaney, American Constitutional Law, 5th ed. (Englewood Cliffs: Prentice-Hall, 1972), p. 531.
8. Dennis v. U.S. 341 U.S. 494 (1951).
9. The clear and present danger test never rebounded from its nadir in Dennis v. U.S. where it was used to convict members of the Communist party of violating the Smith Act even though there was no evidence that the accused took any steps to overthrow the government. Following Judge Learned Hand, Chief Justice Vinson reinterpreted the test as follows: "In each case [courts] must ask whether the gravity of the 'evil,' discounted by its improbability, justifies such invasion of free speech as is necessary to avoid the danger." 183 F2d at 212; 341 U.S. at 510. For a subsequent effort to rehabilitate the clear and present danger test, see Martin Shapiro, Freedom of Speech: The Supreme Court and Judicial Review (Englewood Cliffs, N.J.: Prentice-Hall, 1966).
10. 408 U.S. 665 (1972).
11. The First Amendment provisions on religion are applied to the states via the Fourteenth Amendment. See above p. 136.
12. Everson v. Board of Education 330 U.S. 1 (1947), and McCollum v. Board of Education 333 U.S. 203 (1948).
13. 374 U.S. 203 (1963).
14. 367 U.S. 488 (1961) at 495.
15. Ibid.
16. Jacobson v. Mass. 197 U.S. 11 (1905).
17. Reynolds v. U.S. 98 U.S. 145 (1878).
18. Braunfeld v. Brown 366 U.S. 599 (1961).
19. Epperson v. Arkansas 393 U.S. 97 (1968). I regret that it is beyond the scope of this essay to investigate just what the good legislators of Arkansas had in mind when they forbade teaching that mankind had "descended" from a lower order of animals. Perhaps both Moses and Darwin should take careful note.
20. Lemon v. Kurtzman 403 U.S. 602 (1971); Tilton v. Richardson 403 U.S. 672 (1971).
21. Kedroff v. St. Nicholas Cathedral 344 U.S. 94 (1952).
22. Harden v. State 188 Tenn. 17; 216 S.W. 2d 708 (1948).
23. In re Brooks' Estates 32 Ill., 2d 316; 205 N.E. 2d 435 (1965); U.S. v. Georgia 239 F. Supp. 752 (1965); Application of President and Directors of Georgetown College, Inc. 331 F2d 1000 (1963).
24. Leary v. U.S. 383 F2d 851 (1967); 395 U.S. 6 (1969).
25. 310 U.S. 586 (1940).

26. An excellent study of the question of "ranking" burdens on conscience can be found in Richard J. Regan, Public Law and Private Conscience (New York: Fordham University Press, 1972), pp. 1-20.
27. 319 U.S. 624 (1943).
28. 374 U.S. 398 (1963).
29. CAPFORM 29a, March 1966.
30. In going back over the flag salute cases and Sherbert, remember that you are not looking for the one principle that will given an unequivocal solution to Clara Johnson's problem. The purpose of the exercise is to enable you to sort out what you consider to be the most important values at stake and to order them in some principled way. Extensive classroom discussion will probably lead you to modify your views.
31. 323 U.S. 214 (1944).
32. In his deposition before the Senate Select Committee to study Governmental Operations with respect to Intelligence Activities ("Church Committee") former President Nixon responded to the following "Interrogation": "The Committee has received evidence as to a number of illegalities and improprieties committed by, or on behalf of, various components of the United States Intelligence Community. What controls within the Executive, Legislative or Judicial Branches of government could, in your view, best assure that abuses will not occur in the future?" In response, Nixon said:

> I assume the reference to "actions otherwise 'illegal,'" in this interrogatory means actions which if undertaken by private persons would violate criminal laws. It is quite obvious that there are certain inherently governmental actions which if undertaken by the sovereign in protection of the interest of the nation's security are lawful but which if undertaken by private persons are not. In the most extreme case, for example, forceable removal of persons from their homes for the purpose of sequestering them in confined areas, if done by a person—or even by government employees under normal circumstances—would be considered kidnapping and unlawful imprisonment. Yet under the exigencies of war, President Roosevelt, acting pursuant to a broad war-powers delegation from Congress, ordered such action be taken against Americans of Japanese ancestry because he believed it to be in the interest of national security. Similarly under extreme conditions but not at that point constituting a declared war, President Lincoln confiscated vessels violating a naval blockade, seized rail and telegraph lines leading to Washington, and paid troops from Treasury funds without the required congressional appropriation. In 1969, during my Administration, warrantless wiretapping, even by the government, was unlawful, but if undertaken because of a presidential determination that it was in the

interest of national security was lawful. Support for the legality
of such action is found, for example, in the concurring opinion of
Justice White in <u>Katz</u> v. <u>United States.</u>

This is not to say, of course, that any action a president
might authorize in the interest of national security would be lawful.
The Supreme Court's disapproval of President Truman's seizure
of the steel mills is an example. But it is naive to attempt to
categorize activities a president might authorize as "legal" or
"illegal" without reference to the circumstances under which he
concludes that the activity is necessary. Assassination of a
foreign leader—an act I never had cause to consider and which
under most circumstances would be abhorrent to any president—
might have been less abhorrent and, in fact, justified during World
War II as a means of preventing further Nazi atrocities and ending
the slaughter. Additionally, the opening of mail sent to selected
priority targets of foreign intelligence, although impinging upon
individual freedom, may nevertheless serve a salutary purpose
when—as it has in the past—it results in preventing the disclosure
of sensitive military and state secrets to the enemies of this
country.

In short, there have been—and will be in the future—circumstances in which presidents may lawfully authorize actions in the
interests of the security of this country, which if undertaken by
other persons, or even by the president under different circumstances, would be illegal.

33. Justice Murphy also dissented in this case. The implication of his
    position was that if the military situation was as desperate as the army
    claimed, the proper course would have been to have declared martial
    law. In this way the burdens of war could have been shared more
    equitably without disproportionate disabilities being placed upon
    Japanese Americans.
34. 418 U.S. 683 (1974).
35. 4 Wall. 475 (1867).
36. 1 Cr. 137 (1803).
37. <u>Youngstown Sheet and Tube Company</u> v. <u>Sawyer</u> 343 U.S. 579 at 593-4
    (1952).

5
Property

If the United States mean to obtain or deserve the
full praise due to wise and just governments, they
will equally respect the rights of property and the
property in rights.

James Madison

It is only fitting in a book on constitutional values that the chapter on freedom (or liberty) should be followed by one on property. The close connection between these two values was widely recognized at the time of the
adoption of the Constitution and the Bill of Rights. Indeed, so closely
were they related that in the due process clause they stand next to one
another and right behind life itself as the three great values to be protected from arbitrary governmental action. Today, of course, we tend to
draw a distinction between property rights and human rights, but such a
distinction would have made little sense in the early years of the
Republic.[1] Throughout this chapter we shall return several times to this
question of the distinction between human rights and property rights as
well as to the question of the relation between property and freedom.

    To understand property as a regime value, two questions should be
kept in mind: (1) What is the function of property and (2) what sorts of
things are property? That is, what higher, political goals are promoted
by property and what sorts of things might be considered as property for
the purpose of promoting these goals? The two major divisions of this
chapter—"Old Property" and "New Property"—correspond to these two
questions.

OLD PROPERTY

During the early years of the Republic, constitutional issues concerning property usually focused on the contracts clause of Article I, which prohibits the states from "impairing the obligation of contracts." Prior to the adoption of the Fourteenth Amendment in 1868, the Constitution had no explicit due process limitation on state power over life, liberty, or property. Hence, it was the contracts clause that served as the main legal instrument by which the Supreme Court protected property interests from hostile state legislation.

The contracts clause is always associated with the name of Chief Justice John Marshall whose early interpretations of that clause had incalculable effects upon commercial life in America throughout the nineteenth century. Marshall's opinions were politically significant because in deciding just when a state had impaired a contractual obligation, he was defining the limits of state power. Thus his opinions not only developed the law of contracts but, more significantly, developed the constitutional law of federalism.

To understand Marshall's approach to the protection of property through the contractual relationship, one must recall the philosophical milieu of his time, which was permeated with the belief in natural rights antecedent to the formation of civil society. As Marshall put it in one of his rare dissenting opinions:

> If, on tracing the right to contract, and the obligations created by contract, to their source, we find them to exist anterior to, and independent of society, we may reasonably conclude that those original and pre-existing principles are, like many other natural rights, brought with man into society; and although they may be controlled, are not given by human legislation. . . .
>
> [T]he rational inference seems to be . . . that individuals do not derive from government their right to contract, but bring that right with them into society; that obligation is not conferred on contracts by positive law, but is intrinsic, and is conferred by the act of the parties. This results from the right which every man retains to acquire property, to dispose of that property according to his own judgment, and to pledge himself for a future act. These rights are not given by society, but are brought into it. . . .[2]

Marshall's philosophical position was confirmed by the profound displeasure he and other conservatives felt at the prospect of unstable property relationships. The economic difficulties following our own Revolution were distressing enough for patriots of a conservative persuasion, but Marshall's experiences abroad in trying to negotiate with the French

during the period of the Directory gave him an abiding conviction of the
relationship between secure property arrangements and authentic human
freedom. Upon his return from France, he delivered an address in
Richmond in which he roundly condemned the excesses of the French Revolution. He scorned the "despotism, which borrowing the garb and
usurping the name of freedom, tyrannizes over so large and so fair a portion of the earth." From the sorrows of Jacobin France, said Marshall,
"a citizen of the United States, so familiarly habituated to the actual possession of liberty, that he almost considers it as the inseparable companion of man," might well reflect on "the value which he ought to place on
the solid safety and real security he enjoys at home."[3]

The constitutional world of Marshall, then, turned on the bedrock
principle of a natural right to contract and the prudential calculation that
one enters the road to genuine liberty and prosperity by the sure but low
path of "solid safety and real security."[4]

Dartmouth College v. Woodward

Marshall's most famous interpretation of the contracts clause came in
Dartmouth College v. Woodward (1819).[5] The case involved an effort by
the New Hampshire legislature to wrest control of Dartmouth College by
altering the terms of a 1769 charter granted by King George III to the
trustees of the college. The charter conferred upon the trustees the right
to govern the college in perpetuity and to fill vacancies within their own
membership. In 1816, New Hampshire tried to bring Dartmouth College
under state control by replacing the trustees with a board of overseers
appointed by the governor. The trustees turned to the courts for relief.
When the New Hampshire courts upheld the state's action, the trustees
appealed to the Supreme Court of the United States.

The most important question in the case was whether the royal charter was a "contract" protected by the Constitution. It was generally
acknowledged that the contracts clause was intended to protect contracts
between private parties. In earlier cases, however, Marshall had held
that a land grant by a state legislature[6] and a grant of tax immunity[7] were
contracts under the federal Constitution and could not be rescinded by the
states. Thus there was some precedent for finding the acts of state legislatures to be within the scope of the contracts clause. These precedents
and the Dartmouth College case itself raised critical issues of federalism
because the contracts clause was perceived—not altogether incorrectly—
by many of Marshall's critics as a vehicle for undermining the power of
the states to regulate their own internal affairs.

In Dartmouth College Marshall found that the charter was a contract
within the meaning of the federal Constitution:

This is plainly a contract to which the donors, the trustees, and the crown (to whose rights and obligations New Hampshire succeeds) were the original parties. It is a contract made on a valuable considera-tion. It is a contract on the faith of which real and personal estate has been conveyed to the corporation. It is then a contract within the letter of the Constitution, and within its spirit also, unless the fact that the property is invested by the donors in trustees, for the promo-tion of religion and education, for the benefit of persons who are per-petually changing, though the objects remain the same, shall create a particular exception, taking this case out of the prohibition contained in the Constitution.

It is more than possible that the preservation of rights of this description was not particularly in the view of the framers of the Constitution, when the clause under consideration was introduced into that instrument. It is probable that interferences of more frequent recurrence, to which the temptation was stronger, and of which the mischief was more extensive, constituted the great motive for impos-ing this restriction on the State legislatures. But although a particu-lar and a rare case may not, in itself, be of sufficient magnitude to induce a rule, yet it must be governed by that rule, when established, unless some plain and strong reason for excluding it can be given. It is not enough to say, that this particular case was not in the mind of the Convention when the article was framed, nor of the American peo-ple when it was adopted. It is necessary to go further, and to say that, had this particular case been suggested, the language would have been so varied as to exclude it, or it would have been made a special exception. The case being within the words of the rule, must be within its operation likewise, unless there be something in the literal construction so obviously absurd or mischievous, or repug-nant to the general spirit of the instrument, as to justify those who expound the Constitution in making it an exception. . . .

The opinion of the Court, after mature deliberation, is, that this is a contract, the obligation of which cannot be impaired, without violating the constitution of the United States. This opinion appears to us to be equally supported by reason, and by the former decisions of this Court. . . .

As this passage indicates, Marshall's problem in Dartmouth College was whether or not the royal charter was a contract. Although he found it was, candor compelled him to acknowledge that it was quite unlikely that the framers of the Constitution had eleemosynary institutions in mind when they forbade the states to impair the obligation of contracts. In the light of this acknowledgment, he announced as a rule of interpretation that one cannot rest with the mere assertion that a "particular case was not in the mind of the Convention when the article was framed." Instead one must go further and ask whether the Constitution would have been written differently if the case in question had been considered by the framers. This hermeneutic principle expands the scope of the contracts clause and correspondingly reduces the power of the states to regulate their affairs. Given the political context of early nineteenth-century America, this reduction was not only a defense of contractual obligations, but it was an effort in nation building as well.

Home Building and Loan Association v. Blaisdell

A very different method of interpreting the contracts clause surfaced in Chief Justice Hughes's opinion in the 1934 case of Home Building and Loan Association v. Blaisdell.[8] This case involved the Minnesota Mortgage Moratorium Law of 1933, which provided that under certain circumstances state courts could authorize a limited moratorium on mortgage payments during a declared emergency period, which was not to be extended beyond May 1, 1935. The purpose of the law was to assist farmers and home-owners who, because of the dire economic circumstances of the Depression years, faced foreclosure of their mortgages. The constitutionality of this act was challenged on the grounds that in temporarily suspending the need to meet mortgage payments, Minnesota impaired the obligations of contracts. In a five-to-four decision, Chief Justice Hughes rejected this challenge and upheld Minnesota's power to suspend mortgage payments temporarily despite the effects such suspensions would have on contractual obligations. The following sections of his opinion pertain to our investigation:

> In determining whether the provision for this temporary and conditional relief exceeds the power of the State by reason of the clause in the Federal Constitution prohibiting impairment of the obligations of contracts, we must consider the relation of emergency to constitutional power, the historical setting of the contract clause, the development of the jurisprudence of this Court in the construction of that clause, and the principles of construction which we may consider to be established.
>
> Emergency does not create power. Emergency does not increase granted power or remove or diminish the restrictions imposed upon power granted or reserved. The Constitution was adopted in a period of grave emergency. Its grants of power to the Federal Government and its limitations of the power of the States were determined in the light of emergency and they are not altered by emergency. What power was thus granted and what limitations were thus imposed are questions which have always been, and always will be, the subject of close examination under our constitutional system.

   While emergency does not create power, emergency may furnish
the occasion for the exercise of power. "Although an emergency may
not call into life a power which has never lived, nevertheless emergency may afford a reason for the exertion of a living power already
enjoyed." . . . The constitutional question presented in the light of
an emergency is whether the power possessed embraces the particular conditions. Thus, the war power of the Federal Government is
not created by the emergency of war, but it is a power given to meet
that emergency. It is a power to wage war successfully, and thus it
permits the harnessing of the entire energies of the people in a
supreme cooperative effort to preserve the nation. But even the war
power does not remove constitutional limitations safeguarding essential liberties. When the provisions of the Constitution, in grant or
restriction, are specific, so particularized as not to admit of construction, no question is presented. Thus, emergency would not permit a State to have more than two Senators in the Congress, or permit
the election of a President by a general popular vote without regard to
the number of electors to which the States are respectively entitled,
or permit the States to "coin money" or to "make anything but gold
and silver coin a tender in payment of debts." But where constitutional grants and limitations of power are set forth in general clauses,
which afford a broad outline, the process of construction is essential
to fill in the details. That is true of the contract clause. . . .

A well-known commentary on the Constitution maintains that
"Hughes's opinion skirted close to the proposition that an emergency might
empower government to do things which in ordinary times would be unconstitutional."[9] Do you agree with this commentary? Does the opinion
merely "skirt close" to this proposition or does it, in fact, simply affirm
it? What do you think Hughes would say of Marshall's belief that the right
of contract is antecedent to the formation of society? Is your own opinion
closer to that of Hughes or Marshall?
   What is the operational meaning of Hughes's statement that an emergency does not create power, but it may furnish the occasion for the
exercise of power? Does the following selection from Hughes's opinion
shed any light on this question?

   Not only is the constitutional provision [the contracts clause] qualified
   by the measure of control which the State retains over remedial processes, but the State also continues to possess authority to safeguard
   the vital interests of its people. It does not matter that legislation
   appropriate to that end "has the result of modifying or abrogating contracts already in effect." . . . Not only are existing laws read into
   contracts in order to fix obligations as between the parties, but the
   reservation of essential attributes of soverign power is also read into

contracts as a postulate of the legal order. The policy of protecting
contracts against impairment presupposes the maintenance of a government by virtue of which contractual relations are worth while—a
government which retains adequate authority to secure the peace and
good order of society. This principle of harmonizing the constitutional prohibition with the necessary residuum of state power has had
progressive recognition in the decisions of this Court.

Counsel for the Home Building and Loan Association argued that
because the contract involved in this case was between two private parties,
it was precisely the sort of contractual obligation that the framers of the
Constitution intended to safeguard from state interference. Whatever
criticism one might have of Marshall's far-reaching effort to expand the
notion of contract to include agreements to which states are parties, such
objections were clearly irrelevant here. Blaisdell presented a garden-
variety contractual situation between two private parties—a homeowner
and a bank. Hughes's answer to this argument contrasts sharply with
Marshall's understanding of how to interpret the contracts clause when
situations unforeseen by the framers arise. Marshall addressed the issue
of how to interpret the clause in a case involving an eleemosynary institution. Hughes addresses the issue of whether the meaning of the clause
might be affected by the drastic economic changes taking place in the
1930s. His position follows:

> It is no answer to say that this public need was not apprehended a cen-
> tury ago, or to insist that what the provision of the Constitution meant
> to the vision of that day it must mean to the vision of our time. If by
> the statement that what the Constitution meant at the time of its adop-
> tion it means to-day, it is intended to say that the great clauses of the
> Constitution must be confined to the interpretation which the framers,
> with the conditions and outlook of their time, would have placed upon
> them, the statement carries its own refutation. It was to guard
> against such a narrow conception that Chief Justice Marshall uttered
> the memorable warning—"We must never forget that it is a constitu-
> tion we are expounding" (McCulloch v. Maryland) . . . "a constitution
> intended to endure for ages to come, and consequently, to be adapted
> to the various crises of human affairs." . . . When we are dealing
> with the words of the Constitution, said this Court in Missouri v.
> Holland, "we must realize that they have called into life a being the
> development of which could not have been foreseen completely by the
> most gifted of its begetters. . . . The case before us must be con-
> sidered in the light of our whole experience and not merely in that of
> what was said a hundred years ago."
>   Nor is it helpful to attempt to draw a fine distinction between the
> intended meaning of the words of the Constitution and their intended

application. When we consider the contract clause and the decisions which have expounded it in harmony with the essential reserved power of the States to protect the security of their peoples, we find no warrant for the conclusion that the clause has been warped by these decisions from its proper significance or that the founders of our Government would have interpreted the clause differently had they had occasion to assume that responsibility in the conditions of the later day. The vast body of law which has been developed was unknown to the fathers, but it is believed to have preserved the essential content and the spirit of the Constitution. With a growing recognition of public needs and the relation of individual right to public security, the court has sought to prevent the perversion of the clause through its use as an instrument to throttle the capacity of the States to protect their fundamental interests. This development is a growth from the seeds which the fathers planted. . . . The principle of this development is, as we have seen, that the reservation of the reasonable exercise of the protective power of the State is read into all contracts and there is no . . . reason for refusing to apply this principle to Minnesota mortgages. . . .

It is interesting to note that in offering a method of interpreting the Constitution quite different from Marshall's, Hughes cites Marshall himself! He ignores Marshall's opinions dealing with the contracts clause because these opinions invariably tended to restrict state power. Instead he cites Marshall's opinion in McCulloch v. Maryland, a case that involved a broad, expansive interpretation of governmental power at the national level. This was a clever twist in Hughes's argument and of some interest for our purposes. Later in this chapter we shall see that Marshall's commitment to upholding contractual rights against state regulation was not based exclusively upon a doctrinaire hostility to all government power. Rather his defense of property interests might well be seen as an effort in nation building—strengthening the national government at the expense of the states.

Just as Supreme Court justices differ over the meaning of the Constitution, bureaucrats can differ over the meaning of statutes, executive orders, and statements of agency policy. Both Marshall and Hughes infused the contracts clause with a meaning they thought was appropriate for their times. They justified their interpretations with appeals to widely accepted principles of political philosophy. Can you give examples of value-creating situations that arise in government agencies where the outcome of a decision depends on how bureaucrats interpret authoritative statements? If you have ever done this yourself, did you have any broad principle to justify the interpretation you arrived at? Is your attitude on how authoritative documents should be interpreted closer to that of Hughes or Marshall?

Ramifications of Blaisdell

Hughes's argument in Blaisdell has some interesting ramifications that
warrant further examination. Eleven years after Blaisdell, the Supreme
Court found the same issue on its agenda once again in East New York
Savings Bank v. Hahn.[10] In 1933, New York had passed mortgage moratorium legislation similar to that of Minnesota. Each year thereafter it
had been renewed with the result that by the mid-1940s New York banks
still could not foreclose for default on payments of principal. While few
people indeed, then or now, could become terribly exercised over the
problems bankers have in foreclosing on homeowners, the annual reenact-
ment of the mortgage moratorium law does tell us something about what
governments do with powers originally justified because of a temporary
emergency. For our purposes, however, the most interesting point is the
argument the Court adopted in unanimously upholding the New York law
against the bank's challenge to the suitability of emergency legislation long
after World War II had brought a new set of problems to replace the economic tribulations of the Depression years. Gone are the scholastic
niceties of Hughes's delicate distinction between powers created by emergencies and powers whose exercise is occasioned by an emergency. Gone,
too, is the soul-searching of how to reconcile the moratorium legislation
with either the language of the contracts clause or the intent of the framers. In its place is the following blunderbuss from Justice Frankfurter:

> Since Home Bldg. & L. Assn. v. Blaisdell, there are left hardly any
> open spaces of controversy concerning the constitutional restrictions
> of the Contract Clause upon moratory legislation referable to the
> depression. The comprehensive opinion of Mr. Chief Justice Hughes
> in that case cut beneath the skin of words to the core of meaning. . . .
> The Blaisdell case and decisions rendered since . . . yield this gov-
> erning constitutional principle: when a widely diffused public interest
> has become enmeshed in a network of multitudinous private arrange-
> ments, the authority of the State "to safeguard the vital interests of
> its people," . . . is not to be gainsaid by abstracting one such
> arrangement from its public context and treating it as though it
> were an isolated private contract constitutionally immune from
> impairment.
>
> The formal mode of reasoning by means of which this "protective
> power of the State," . . . is acknowledged is of little moment. It may
> be treated as an implied condition of every contract and, as such, as
> much part of the contract as though it were written into it, whereby
> the State's exercise of its power enforces, and does not impair, a
> contract. A more candid statement is to recognize, as was said in
> Manigault v. Springs, that the power "which in its various ramifica-
> tions is known as the police power, is an exercise of the sovereign

right of the Government to protect the . . . general welfare of the people, and is paramount to any rights under contracts between individuals." . . . Once we are in this domain of the reserve power of a State
we must respect the "wide discretion on the part of the legislature in
determining what is and what is not necessary." . . . So far as the
constitutional issue is concerned "the power of the State when otherwise justified," . . . is not diminished because a private contract may
be affected.

In ancient Rome, a popular legal maxim was "salus populi, lex
suprema"—"the welfare of the people is the supreme law." Would it be
fair to characterize the excerpt from Frankfurter's opinion as an echo of
that ancient principle? If not, why not? If so, what happens to the government of limited powers created by the Constitution?

These questions raise the same kinds of problems we saw in the preceding chapter on freedom. Indeed, it is particularly interesting to note
that in upholding the New York law, Frankfurter cited a report to the New
York legislature warning that "the sudden termination of the legislation
which has dammed up normal liquidation of these mortgages for more than
eight years might well result in an emergency more acute than that which
the original legislation was intended to alleviate."

The parallel between Frankfurter's fears of an emergency that might
happen and Justice Sutherland's fears in Gitlow[11] of a revolution that
might be brought about by a frantic socialist tract is suggestive. If you
were critical of Sutherland's opinion in the previous chapter, do you react
the same way to Frankfurter's position here? Would you consider formulating a broad rule that governments should never legislate merely on the
basis of what might happen? Hardly; if we did this there could be no
intelligent planning. What would become of national defense, environmental law, or the elusive national energy policy? Clearly there are
times when governments must act on fears or suspicions of what might
happen.

Can we distinguish between the two opinions? Is there some legitimate reason for protecting speech more than contractual obligations?
Could we stand Marshall's natural rights argument on its head and agree
with him that there are natural rights antecedent to the formation of civil
society but that the right to contract is not among them? Could we then
say that the right of free speech is included in these natural rights? Was
this the argument that Justice Jackson used in West Virginia School Board
of Education v. Barnette? [12] Did he imply that there is a natural right to
be free from coercion against one's religious beliefs or did he say that
there are certain kinds of behavior that government is simply incompetent
to mandate?

Several Supreme Court justices have spoken of First Amendment
liberties of religion, speech, press, and assembly as "preferred

freedoms."[13] The term raises a series of technical questions that need
not concern us here. For our purposes the relevant point is that some
justices have been willing to acknowledge that certain constitutional rights
are more important than others—that freedom of speech is to be preferred
to the right to have one's contractual relationships unimpaired by state
action. Do you agree with this? If so, can you say why? Is it because—
as we hear so often—"human rights are more important than property
rights"?

Another interesting ramification of Hughes's opinion in Blaisdell is the
fact that it was once cited in a context quite different from that of the
Minnesota Mortgage Moratorium Act. Once again, it was Justice Frankfurter who cited Blaisdell. The case is one we have already seen in the
previous chapter—Korematsu v. U.S. wherein Frankfurter wrote a concurring opinion upholding the army's power to relocate American citizens of Japanese extraction. Turn back to that opinion in Chapter 4
and look for the similarities between Hughes's attitude toward governmental power in Blaisdell and Frankfurter's attitude on the same issue
in Korematsu.

At the heart of Frankfurter's opinion is the principle borrowed
from Hughes in Blaisdell—the power to wage war is the power to wage
war successfully. Hughes had used the war power simply as an
example to support the distinction he urged in Blaisdell between
powers created by emergencies and powers whose exercise is occasioned by emergency. Hughes's attention was on the contracts clause,
not the war powers. The reference to the war powers was merely by
way of illustration. It remained for Frankfurter to apply the war
power illustration to a wartime situation to justify the suppression,
not of property rights, but of the most fundamental human rights.
Does the relative ease with which Frankfurter moves from property
rights to personal rights suggest that the distinction between the two
types of rights is not really very helpful in the face of an argument
that the power to do something (wage war, regulate commerce, protect public health, safety, and morals, and so on) implies the power
to do it successfully? Such an argument seems to treat all rights as
of a piece—governments may do whatever must be done to discharge
their responsibilities.

At times certain rights must be temporarily suspended or their exercise curtailed for the duration of an emergency. In the light of such an
argument, it makes little difference in principle whether it is a property
right or a human right that is compromised. The principle underlying the
Hughes-Frankfurter line of reasoning is the political exigency of the
moment rather than the nature of any particular right. What does this
kind of reasoning do to the principles of limited government? If you reject
this kind of reasoning, what alternatives would you suggest when real
emergencies arise—as they will?

Nation Building

Earlier in this chapter, it was noted in passing that there were certain
nation-building aspects in Chief Justice Marshall's defense of property
rights. This consideration will be developed more fully now. The point
here is that Marshall and many of his contemporaries at times proposed a
view of property that was instrumental. That is, property rights,
especially those created by contract, were capable of serving social and
political ends. This idea had been developed most elaborately, of course,
by Adam Smith. As Arnold Toynbee has noted, "Two conceptions are
woven into every argument of the Wealth of Nations—the belief in the
supreme value of individual liberty and the conviction that Man's self-love.
is God's providence, that in pursuing his own interest he is promoting the
welfare of all."[14] Smith, of course, was not alone in making the connection between the pursuit of self-interest and the common good. Blackstone
had earlier praised the law of inheritance because "it sets the passions on
the side of duty."[15] And The Federalist Papers have long been recognized
as championing the wisdom of channeling man's acquisitive passions along
socially constructive lines.

The constitutional expression of this principle can be seen in
Marshall's eagerness to free commercial enterprises from state regulation in the hope of making real the constitutional promise of a national
market that would bring prosperity to the new nation. This was certainly
the thrust of his argument in Gibbons v. Ogden[16] where he joined the commerce clause[17] and an Act of Congress licensing ships engaged in the
coastal trade to declare unconstitutional a New York statute that had conferred a monopoly on a steamboat company. The effect of this decision
was to open the nation's navigable streams to all who wished to compete in
the shipping industry.

In overturning the New York steamboat monopoly, Marshall was, of
course, simply preferring one kind of property over another—the property
of those shippers not favored by the monopoly at the expense of those who
had enjoyed a privileged position. The significant point, however, is that
it was competitive and dynamic property that was favored at the expense of
property that was privileged and static. In so doing, Marshall was contributing to a widespread tendency among American jurists at all levels of
government to interpret property rights in a way that would enhance
economic development.

This tendency can be seen most readily by following the development
of the law of land use and water rights during the first half of the nineteenth century. Legal historians have shown that at the end of the eighteenth century a conservative, static, and gentlemanly view of landed
property was dominant in the courts.[18] That is, land was looked upon as
a private estate to be enjoyed by its owner rather than as a productive
asset. As one commentator observes: "The great English gentry, who

had played a central role in shaping the common law conception of land, regarded the right to quiet enjoyment as the basic attribute of dominion over property." [19] A common legal maxim invoked frequently in eighteenth-century America articulated this conservative viewpoint: "sic utere tuo ut alienum non laedas," "use what is yours in such a way as not to harm what belongs to another." What this meant in practice was that one landowner could not develop his property in a way that would diminish the value of another's property. Thus an upper riparian owner could not dam a river or build a mill that would significantly divert water from lower riparian estates. As a New Jersey Court put it in 1795:

> In general it may be observed, when a man purchases a piece of land through which a natural water-course flows, he has a right to make use of it in its natural state, but not to stop or divert it to the prejudice of another. Aqua currit, et debet currere* is the language of the law. The water flows in its natural channel, and ought always to be permitted to run there, so that all through whose land it pursues its natural course, may continue to enjoy the privilege of using it for their own purposes. It cannot legally be diverted from its course without the consent of all who have an interest in it. . . . I should think a jury right in giving almost any valuation which the party thus injured should think proper to afix to it. [20]

The antidevelopment thrust of the law is clearly seen in the way conflicts between riparian owners were settled. The established principle was that the litigant claiming the more "natural" use of the water was to be preferred. "Natural" meant agrarian, and so preference was given to owners who appropriated water for agriculture or husbandry over those with some commercial enterprise in mind.

In the nineteenth century all this began to change. In what James Williard Hurst has called "The Release of Energy," the law began to find ways to encourage the commercial spirit of the acquisitive entrepreneur at the expense of the landed gentry. The federal Bankruptcy Act of 1841 had the developmental effect of relieving debtors more easily and thereby enabling them to reenter the market. This encouraged men who were willing to take financial risks. In torts, the emphasis upon the "reasonable man" test rather than on the intent of a particular party in litigation provided a more objective standard for liability and, hence, made the precise nature of one's risks more orderly and predictable. This, too, encouraged the commercial spirit. Even the doctrine of "vested rights," which sounds so stuffy and reactionary today, had the effect of releasing creative commercial energy by protecting venture capital.

---

*Water flows and should be allowed to flow.

   Perhaps the most dramatic example of the legal changes that reflected the changes in broad, societal values came in the refashioning of the
law of water rights by mid-century. It will be recalled that in 1795 a New
Jersey court could wax eloquent on the principle that the natural flow of
rivers and streams must not be disturbed. This doctrine came under
severe pressure from the remarkable growth of the textile industry in the
1820s and the 1830s. The need for mills to supply this growing demand
rendered the common-law principles of the natural flow of water hopelessly obsolete. An entirely new question arose with the advent of the
large integrated cotton mills whose voracious appetite for water power
frequently made it impossible for more than one proprietor to develop a
stream without destroying the usefulness of the other mills on the same
stream. When litigation arose between proprietors over who should be
allowed to develop a stream at the expense of his competitor, interested
parties wondered anxiously how the courts would decide.

   In 1844, a Massachusetts court addressed this issue in a remarkable
opinion that shows how dramatically legal thinking had changed since 1795.
Chief Justice Shaw maintained that "one of the beneficial uses of a water-
course, and in this country one of the most important, is its application
to the working of mills and machinery; a use profitable to the owner and
beneficial to the public."[21] Morton Horwitz calls this statement the "new
utilitarian orthodoxy"[22] that differs strikingly from the gentlemanly use
of property that had prevailed just fifty years earlier. For our purposes,
it is particularly important to underscore the connection made between
what is profitable to the owner and what is beneficial to the public. One
of the major factors relied on by the judge in deciding which mill owner
should be favored was the public interest consideration of which one could
better respond to the "usages and wants of the community" and promote
"the progress of improvement in hydraulic works."[23]

   With this background on nineteenth-century law in mind, one may be
able to see more clearly what is meant by the nation-building aspects of
Marshall's jurisprudence. Take, for example, the opinion in which he
sets forth the most extreme defense of the rights of contract ever stated
by any Supreme Court Justice. So extreme was Marshall's opinion in this
case—Ogden v. Saunders[24]—that it was the only time in his thirty-four
years as Chief Justice that he was in the minority on a constitutional
issue. The case involved a New York Bankruptcy Act passed at a time
when there was no federal bankruptcy law in force that would have pre-
empted state action in this area. In an earlier case, Marshall had per-
suaded his colleagues to strike down a New York Bankruptcy Act that
would have affected debts made prior to its passage. The Court found that
the retrospective aspect of the act impaired the obligations of contracts.[25]
In Ogden v. Saunders, however, a second New York statute had only a
prospective effect—that is, it would be operative only upon debts incurred
after the passage of the act. The Court upheld this act and rejected the

argument that it impaired contractual obligations. It reasoned that the new
Bankruptcy Act could be considered as part of every contract entered into
after the act had been passed. Thus no contractual obligations are
impaired by the relief the act affords a bankrupt debtor because when the
creditor entered into the contract he knew the debtor would be protected by
the bankruptcy provisions.

Marshall acknowledged the plausibility of this line of reasoning:

> That there is an essential difference in principle between laws which
> act on past, and those which act on future contracts; that those of the
> first description can seldom be justified, while those of the last are
> proper subjects of ordinary legislative discretion, must be admitted.
> A constitutional restriction, therefore, on the power to pass laws of
> the one class, may very well consist with entire legislative freedom
> respecting those of the other.

Despite this concession, he still maintained the New York Bankruptcy
Act violated the contracts clause. He justified his position by appealing to
the nationalistic and commercial objectives of the Constitution as a whole:

> Yet, when we consider the nature of our Union—that it is intended to
> make us, in a great measure, one people, as to commercial objects;
> that, so far as respects the intercommunication of individuals, the
> lines of separation between states are, in many respects, obliterated—
> it would not be a matter of surprise if, on the delicate subject of con-
> tracts once formed, the interference of state legislation should be
> greatly abridged, or entirely forbidden. In the nature of the provision,
> then, there seems to be nothing which ought to influence our construc-
> tion of the words; and, in making that construction, the whole clause,
> which consists of a single sentence, is to be taken together, and the
> intention is to be collected from the whole.

Thus it is the vision of a great commercial republic that undergirds
the extremes to which Marshall was willing to go in upholding the inviola-
bility of contractual obligations. Interestingly, the policy argument for
bankruptcy laws turned on their effectiveness in promoting economic
development because they mitigated the penalties visited upon those who
take financial risks. Marshall ignores this consideration, however.
Apparently, in the absence of a congressional Bankruptcy Act, Marshall
would prefer no bankruptcy act at all. For our purposes, however, the
important point is that those on both sides of the bankruptcy argument
justified their positions in terms of national economic development. This
underscores the instrumental notion of property.

Marshall's successor as chief justice, Roger B. Taney, differed considerably from his predecessor in temperament and political outlook. The

fact that Marshall had been appointed by John Adams whereas Taney was
an appointee of Andrew Jackson suffices to establish their differences.
Nevertheless, they were quite similar in accepting an instrumentalist view
of property which they related to grand national purposes of economic
development.

This can be seen in the famous case of Charles River Bridge v.
Warren Bridge.[26] In 1785, Massachusetts empowered the Charles River
Bridge Company to build a toll bridge between Charlestown and Boston. An
earlier grant in 1650 had given Harvard College exclusive ferry rights over
this "line of travel," but in the grant of 1785 the college yielded its rights
in return for annual payments from the bridge company. In 1828, the
legislature authorized the Warren Bridge Company to build another bridge
just a few dozen yards from the Charles River Bridge. The Warren Bridge
would charge tolls only until the bridge was paid for; thereafter it would be
free. This, of course, would put the Charles River Bridge out of business,
and so the company brought an action to stop the construction of Warren
Bridge. The company argued that in the grant of 1785 it had acquired
Harvard College's exclusive rights over the "line of travel" between Boston
and Charlestown. Since the grant of 1785 said nothing about an exclusive
right to build a bridge, the point at issue in the case was whether such an
inference could be read into an agreement between a state and a private
party. Taney held it could not. Citing an English precedent on this issue,
he said "that any ambiguity in the terms of the contract must operate
against the adventurers and in favor of the public." Further, "in charters
of this description, no rights are taken from the public, or given to the
corporation, beyond those which the words of the charter, in their natural
power and construction, purport to convey." Finally, he added, "While the
rights of private property are sacredly guarded, we must not foget that the
community also have rights, and that the happiness and well being of every
citizen depends on their faithful preservation."

Such language is quite different from the tone of Marshall's opinions
on the contracts clause. The emphasis on the needs of the community over
and against the rights of the owners of private property heralds an important gloss on the traditional American doctrine on property and considerably qualifies Marshall's concern for vested rights. This qualification
stresses the need to limit such rights when the public interest so requires.
This aspect of the tradition was eclipsed during the laissez-faire era in
American history (1890-1937),[27] but it was salient in the Taney Court and
has certainly been salient once again since the mid-1930s. Despite the
marked difference between Taney's reading of the contracts clause and that
of Marshall, it would be a mistake to contrast the two jurists as simply
antithetical. Taney's opinion in Charles River Bridge was similar to
Marshall's decision in the New York steamboat monopoly case—Gibbons v.
Ogden—at least in the sense that in both cases one form of property was
preferred to another. More significant, however, is the fact that in both

cases it was the same type of property that was preferred.   Property that
is new, dynamic, and competitive gets the nod over that which is old,
static, and privileged.

In justifying his decision in favor of the new bridge, Taney announced
a strong defense of the need to encourage economic development:

> Indeed, the practice and usage of almost every state in the Union, old
> enough to have commenced the work of internal improvement, is
> opposed to the doctrine contended for on the part of the plaintiffs in
> error (Charles River Bridge).   Turnpike roads have been made in
> succession, on the same line of travel; the later ones interfering
> materially with the profits of the first.   These corporations have, in
> some instances, been utterly ruined by the introduction of newer and
> better modes of transportation and travelling.   In some cases, rail-
> roads have rendered the turnpike roads on the same line of travel so
> entirely useless, that the franchise of the turnpike corporation is not
> worth preserving.   Yet in none of these cases have the corporations
> supposed that their privileges were invaded, or any contract violated
> on the part of the state. . . .
>
> And what would be the fruits of this doctrine of implied contracts,
> on the part of the states, and of property in a line of travel by a cor-
> poration, if it should now be sanctioned by this court?   To what
> results would it lead us?   If it is to be found in the charter to this
> bridge, the same process of reasoning must discover it, in the
> various acts which have been passed, within the last forty years, for
> turnpike companies.   And what is to be the extent of the privileges of
> exclusion on the different sides of the road?   The counsel who have
> so ably argued this case, have not attempted to define it by any
> certain boundaries.   How far must the new improvement be distant
> from the old one?   How near may you approach, without invading its
> rights in the privileged line?   If this court should establish the prin-
> ciples now contended for, what is to become of the numerous rail-
> roads established on the same line of travel with turnpike companies;
> and which have rendered the franchise of the turnpike corporations of
> no value?   Let it once be understood, that such charters carry with
> them these implied contracts, and give this unknown and undefined
> property in a line of travelling; and you will soon find the old turnpike
> corporations awakening from their sleep and calling upon this court to
> put down the improvements which have taken their place.   The mil-
> lions of property which have been invested in railroads and canals,
> upon lines of travel which had been before occupied by turnpike cor-
> porations, will be put in jeopardy.   We shall be thrown back to the
> improvements of the last century, and obliged to stand still, until the
> claims of the old turnpike corporations shall be satisfied; and they
> shall consent to permit these states to avail themselves of the lights

of modern science, and to partake of the benefit of those improvements
which are now adding to the wealth and prosperity, and the convenience
and comfort, of every other part of the civilized world. Nor is this
all. This court will find itself compelled to fix, by some arbitrary
rule, the width of this new kind of property in a line of travel; for if
such a right of property exists, we have no lights to guide us in mark-
ing out its extent, unless, indeed, we resort to the old feudal grants,
and to the exclusive rights of ferries, by prescription, between towns;
and are prepared to decide that when a turnpike road from one town to
another, had been made, no railroad or canal, between these two
points, could afterwards be established. This court is not prepared to
sanction principles which must lead to such results.

Taney's opinion in Charles River Bridge did not sway all his colleagues. A lengthy dissent was filed by Justice Story, a distinguished legal
scholar whose jurisprudence had been profoundly influenced by many years
of close personal association with Chief Justice Marshall. Faithful to the
spirit of Marshall, Story predictably condemned Taney's innovative treatment of the contracts clause. The most interesting part of his dissent
occurs, however, when he takes up Taney's developmental argument:

> But it has been argued, and the argument has been pressed in every
> form which ingenuity could suggest, that if grants of this nature are to
> be construed liberally, as conferring any exclusive rights on the
> grantees (Charles River Bridge), it will interpose an effectual barrier
> against all general improvements of the country. . . . For my own
> part, I can conceive of no surer plan to arrest all public improve-
> ments, founded on private capital and enterprise, than to make the out-
> lay of that capital uncertain, and questionable both as to security, and
> as to productiveness. No man will hazard his capital in any enter-
> prise, in which, if there be a loss, it must be borne exclusively by
> himself; and if there be success, he has not the slightest security of
> enjoying the rewards of that success for a single moment. . . .

This dictum in Story's dissent addresses an issue of policy rather than
legal interpretation. The policy in question, however, is which choice of
the judges is more likely to enhance economic development. Taney chooses
the competitive principle that will give us two bridges where we had one and
railroads where we had turnpikes. Story opts for security of venture
capital that hitherto the contracts clause had cherished so warmly. For
our purposes, the significant point is that the entire argument is structured
in utilitarian terms of what property can do to promote the public interest.
This, I suggest, is a salient value in the American regime.

Some Reflections

The purpose of the foregoing discussion of the relationship between property and nation building has been to redeem the concept of property from
the reactionary overtones it inevitably suggests. The same redemptive
purpose is at the heart of the remainder of this chapter, which investigates
the meaning of the "new property." Of the three regime values examined
in this book, only property is in need of redemption. The reasons for this
are many and complex but surely among them is the embarrassment most
thoughtful Americans feel at the shocking excess that our society in general and our courts in particular manifested in defending property rights
during the laissez-faire era. The arguments brought forth ostensibly to
defend property rights were vulgar caricatures of the more serious arguments of an earlier day. These shallow incantations defended the abuses
of property rather than property itself and in so doing lost sight of the
vital link between property and the public interest. This is certainly one
reason why today we may become a bit uneasy at the thought that bureaucrats are sworn to uphold property as a regime value. Just what are they
going to uphold ?
        A deeper reason for our discomfort at the thought of property as a
salient value is that it is not terribly flattering. John Marshall was probably right when he told the citizens of Richmond to pursue "solid safety
and real security," but he was not very complimentary in saying it. Freedom and equality are much more attractive and reassuring values. It is
not very exhilarating to think that one lives and may even be called upon to
die for the low but solid values conferred by the institution of private property. The reason this prospect lacks appeal is that we know that at times
we are capable of responding to higher motives and when we do so the
brighter angels of our nature rejoice. Thus we welcome in sober spirit
Lincoln's stern but uplifting reminder that the new nation was conceived
in, and dedicated to, the higher values of liberty and equality. Regimes,
however, cannot be constructed exclusively on principles that apply only
to their finest hours. Democratic regimes in particular must look hard at
ordinary people acting in very ordinary ways. When one does this, it
becomes clear that political wisdom demands a lowering of one's vision
from the grand and the noble to the safe, the secure, and the solid. And
all this must be done without trailing off into the crass, the base, and the
tawdry. It is no easy task. Property renders yeoman's service in this
effort, and for this reason it has been and remains an important regime
value.
        For an exercise in attempting to apply property as a regime value for
bureaucrats, consider critically the following statement on the role of
bureaucrats in regulatory agencies. If you find it has some merit, try to

apply it to a regulatory agency with which you are familiar. If you find the statement without merit, indicate as clearly as you can just where it is incorrect or offensive.

A Statement on Values

The connection between property rights and the public interest has some bearing upon the discretionary judgments made by contemporary bureaucrats in regulatory agencies. For one thing, it underscores the futility of railing against "corporate greed." Perhaps the problem is not so much that corporations are greedy but that at times the wrong corporations with the wrong kinds of greed have been rewarded by public policy. For bureaucrats in regulatory agencies it might be wise not to fret over how to transform business executives into "industrial statesmen" whose "social awareness" will make them "sensitive" and "responsive" to the needs of the public. Rather, the proper course might be to regard corporate greed as a great national resource and to point this mighty engine in directions that are socially useful. There was a time when we were told that invisible hands and free markets would do this for us. In some instances this may still be true today, but the nature of the contemporary industrial-regulatory-welfare-warfare state seems to suggest that the very visible and at times quite heavy hand of government must pick up where its invisible mate left off. If so, it becomes important for bureaucrats to assume an aggressive stance toward the industries they regulate. They should look upon the interests of these industries, not as ends in themselves, but as instruments related to higher ends of public interest. By no means does this mean that the regulatory agencies need always and necessarily be hostile to the industries they regulate. It does mean they should be selective in the sort of activity that is encouraged, and such selective encouragement may well mean that some companies will prosper handsomely while promoting the public interest.

The ethical significance of all this is that it is not enough for the conscientious bureaucrat to adhere scrupulosuly to conflict-of-interest regulations. Although such fidelity is absolutely essential, it does no more than assure us that the bureaucrat is not the pawn of the companies he or she regulates. While this is a consummation devoutly to be wished, it ignores the more important question of how government can manipulate corporate property interests in a beneficial manner. This is the proper sphere of bureaucratic discretion in regulatory agencies. Not only must the regulatory agencies avoid being captured by the industries they regulate but they must also encourage, cajole, discipline, and exploit the acquisitive passions of the leaders of these industries in a way that will promote

higher national goals. This might well be a sound contemporary application of the principles announced by Marshall, Taney, Story, and Hughes. [28]

NEW PROPERTY

Thus far in this chapter we have stressed the relationship between property and the common good by endeavoring to show how property can at
times be directed to higher, political ends. Now it is time to examine the
opposite side of the coin of property—its centrifugal aspect that stresses
independence and individualism. It is because of its individualistic aspects
that property has been so closely associated with freedom during the modern era, and it is this historic association that accounts for the paeans to
property that one finds in such abundance in the writings of liberal philosophers and legal commentators up to at least the beginning of the present
century.

The connections between property, independence, individualism, and
freedom have not been made in a way that placed these values in opposition
to the common good. Instead, they were seen as contributing to the common good. This contribution went beyond the teleological and manipulative
ways in which invisible hands and/or government regulations channel a
person's acquisitive instincts to felicitous ends. The freedom that property
confers is itself part of the common good. It is valued not because of what
it does but because of what it is and, as such, is a constitutive element of
the common good.

This point can be seen more clearly by considering the traditional civil
liberties of religion, speech, press, and assembly—aspects of freedom
that, at least ostensibly, are only marginally related to property. We take
considerable pride in claiming that citizens of the Republic may worship as
they choose, say or write what they think, and gather together with whom-
soever they please. These are not instrumental values. These traditional
liberties extend beyond those religions, writings, speeches, and assem-
blies that hold promise of some greater good for society. We glory in the
belief and, indeed at times, the fact that our society produces men and
women who speak their minds intelligently and fearlessly. This is an
attractive part of man's nature that we have been somewhat successful in
developing. It is a particular realization of human excellence and requires
no further justification. It is constitutive of the common good because to
speak one's mind and to see others do it as well is what the poet would call
a thing of beauty, a joy forever.

At a more mundane level, property is capable of generating a type of
freedom and independence, that, while perhaps falling short of inspiring
the songs of the poet, suffices to give men and women a chance to achieve

a quiet dignity and personal security. These, too, are values that constitute rather than merely promote the common good. To see the importance
of property in promoting these human values, it is necessary to look back
in history to a period before property succumbed to the division of ownership and responsibility[29] and even to a time before it became associated
with "big business," "robber barons," and "sweatshops." There was a
time when one spoke of property in connection with "the sturdy yeoman of
the middling sort." In those days it was much easier to see the relationship between property and freedom because one's vision was not distorted
by the social outrages perpetrated in the name of property during the past
century.

The connection between freedom and property was especially clear in
the preindustrial era when so much private property was held in land.
Indeed, this connection had been clear since the break-up of feudalism
where political power and the ownership of land had been inextricably bound
together. In the middle ages, the same word, dominium, stood for both
ownership and political authority. The feudal lord exercised political
authority over his subjects because he owned the land they tilled. They
could make use of his land and in this sense they "held" it, but they did not
own it. They were entitled to the benefits the land might yield, but only on
condition that they met certain demands that the lord might impose. Thus
feudalism rested on an elaborate hierarchical structure of land "tenure"
(from the Latin tenere, "to hold") as opposed to ownership, and the "tenure" was conditioned upon the fulfillment of specific obligations owed to
one's lord.

At the upper echelons of the feudal hierarchy, the "tenure" system was
often a mere legal fiction. The king, though theoretically superior to the
great barons of the land, was often so dependent upon them for money and
supplies, especially soldiers and military equipment, that for all practical
purposes they could treat the land they "held" as their own. As one
descended the hierarchy, however, the control exercised by lords over
vassals became more effective. The end of the Middle Ages and the beginning of modernity coincided with the rise of a middle class whose wealth
was based on commerce rather than land alone. These "new men," as they
were called, found the static feudal system intolerable. Commercial
enterprises created new forms of property that could not be merely "held"
conditionally but had to be owned outright. The personal freedom of the
"new men" to pursue their commercial ventures was indissolubly linked
with the need to establish control over "property" as something that was
strictly their own.

New political and legal theories emerged to reflect the dramatic
changes of the sixteenth, seventeenth, and eighteenth centuries. Thus John
Locke could use the terms "liberty" and "property" almost interchangeably
and insist that it was to further these values that men left the state of
nature and entered civil society. In the same spirit, Blackstone could put

forth his celebrated definition of property as "that sole and despotic dominion which one man claims and exercises over the external things of the
world, in total exclusion of the right of any other individual in the universe."[30] Although these words jar contemporary sensibilities, in Blackstone's time they were accepted because of the obvious connection between
property and the supreme value of liberty.[31]

The best American expression of this sort of thinking can be found in
James Madison's Essay on Property:

> This term [property] means "that dominion which one man claims and
> exercises over the external things of the world, in exclusion of every
> other individual." But in its larger and juster meaning, it embraces
> everything to which a man may attach a value and have a right; and
> which leaves to every one else the like advantage. In the former
> sense, a man's land, or merchandise, or money is called his prop-
> erty. In the latter sense, a man has property in his opinions and a
> free communication of them. He has a property of peculiar value in
> his religious opinions, and in the profession and practice dictated by
> them. He has property dear to him in the safety and liberty of his
> person. He has equal property in the free use of his faculties and free
> choice of the objects on which to employ them. In a word, as a man is
> said to have a right to his property, he may be equally said to have a
> property in his rights. . . . If there be a government then which
> prides itself on maintaining the inviolability of property, which pro-
> vides that none shall be taken directly even for public use without
> indemnification to the owner, and yet directly violates the property
> which individuals have in their opinions, their religion, their person
> and their faculties, nay more which directly violates their property in
> their actual possessions, in the labor that acquires their daily subsis-
> tence, and in the hallowed remnant of time which ought to relieve their
> fatigues and soothe their cares, the inference will have been antici-
> pated that such a government is not a pattern for the United States. If
> the United States mean to obtain or deserve the full praise due to wise
> and just governments they will equally respect the rights of property
> and the property in rights.[32]

The close connection Madison made between property and personality
helps to explain the esteemed place enjoyed by property in the annals of
American law and tradition. It should be noted, however, that although
Madison condemns any government that violates the "property which individuals have in their opinions, their religion, their person, and their
faculties," he is even more critical of governments that violate men's
"property in their actual possessions, in their labor that acquires their
daily subsistence." It was, of course, property in the fruits of one's labor
that had been denied to the common man in the Middle Ages. Madison was

aware that Locke's definition of property as something a man "hath mixed his labor with" was a hallmark of modernity. Enlightened governments respected rights of property both in the sense of material objects and in the broader sense in which Madison used the word.

Today we feel somewhat uneasy with the language used by Locke, Blackstone, and Madison to defend the importance of property. We know all too well the story of how, during the laissez-faire era, their eloquent defense of property was applied to situations they could not possibly have foreseen. The rights of property were transformed into engines of oppression against the poor. So profound and painful was the struggle against the alleged sanctity of property rights that today we frequently make a sharp distinction between property rights and human rights.

It was in the light of these developments that Charles A. Reich wrote an article entitled "The New Property" in the mid-1960s.[33] Reich was disturbed by what he described as the emergence of a "new feudalism." By this he meant that modern governments create new forms of wealth by taxing severely and rewarding generously through a complex network of institutional and legal relationships that confer not property but "status" upon certain citizens. That is, the income of many depends upon governmental largess as manifested in Social Security benefits, government contracts, occupational licenses, business franchises, public service employment, welfare payments, and so on. The continuous enjoyment of these benefits is contingent upon one's status—that is, upon one's ability to meet certain relevant criteria. Writing in 1964, Reich claimed that the legal status of these benefits was more closely akin to a privilege than a right.[34] That is, because these benefits were based on the largess of government rather than the property rights of citizens, they could be terminated at the pleasure of the government. This was a "new feudalism" because one's security in material goods was "held" at the pleasure of the government rather than owned outright as one's own property. This "new feudalism," like old feudalism, gave those in authority considerable leverage in encouraging the kind of behavior that was officially approved. Thus the absence of property rights in government benefits created a danger of government making serious inroads on one's personal liberties.

Reich cites the Supreme Court case of Flemming v. Nestor[35] to establish this point. Ephram Nestor was an alien who came to the United States in 1913 and, after many years of hard work, became eligible in 1955 for Social Security retirement benefits. He and his employers had made Social Security contributions since 1936. From the years 1933 to 1939 Nestor had been a member of the Communist party. Years later Congress retroactively made such membership a cause for deportation and further provided that those deported for having been members of the Communist party would lose their Social Security benefits. Nestor was deported in 1956, but his wife remained here. Shortly after his deportation, all payments to his wife were terminated. Litigation ensued and the Supreme Court upheld the government's position on the grounds that Nestor had "no accrued property right" to the benefits. [36]

Reich cites several other examples to show how government uses its power of largess to discipline its citizens in areas that ordinarily would be beyond the sphere of the government's reach. The most famous illustration of this point came in a New York case in which the state denied welfare benefits to an old man who insisted upon sleeping in a barn under what the welfare officials considered unsanitary conditions. The tone of the New York court's opinion is quite instructive:

> Appellant also argues that he has a right to live as he pleases while being supported by public charity. One would admire his independence if he were not so dependent, but he has no right to defy the standards and conventions of civilized society while being supported at public expense. This is true even though some of those conventions may be somewhat artificial. One is impressed with appellant's argument that he enjoys the life he leads in his humble "home" as he calls it. It may possibly be true, as he says, that his health is not threatened by the way he lives. After all he should not demand that the public at its expense, allow him to experiment with a manner of living which is likely to endanger his health so that he will become a still greater expense on the public.
>
> It is true, as appellant argues, that the hardy pioneers of our country slept in beds no better than the one he has chosen. But, unlike the appellant, they did it from necessity, and unlike the appellant, they did not call upon the public to support them, while doing it. [37]

Had the eccentric old man been paying his own way, he could have slept wherever he pleased, but because he took the benefit of welfare he had to renounce the right to choose his own resting place.

These examples will suffice to illustrate what Reich means by the "new feudalism." His response is to call for a new understanding of property that will reestablish its old connection with personal liberty. By this he does not mean that we should simply return to the pre-New Deal days, for such a reaction would do precious little for the values Reich has in mind. Instead, he maintains, we must bring new forms of wealth and possessions under the old constitutional protection reserved for property. There is no good reason, Reich argues, why a man's home should be considered property but his Social Security benefits should not. As Reich puts it, it is now time "that largess begin to do the work of property." [38]

In the remainder of this chapter we shall examine the Court's reaction to Reich's proposal over the past decade.

Sniadach v. Family Finance Company

Sniadach v. Family Finance Company (1969)[39] involved Wisconsin's procedure for garnisheeing wages. Sniadach owed the Family Finance Corporation $420 on a promissory note. Her failure to pay prompted the company to initiate the state's garnishment procedures. Sniadach's employer was notified by the clerk of the court to withhold one-half of her wages. A court order was issued at the request of the company even though Sniadach had no opportunity for a hearing in which she might explain her failure to pay the note.

Justice Douglas delivered the opinion of the Court, which upheld Sniadach's claim to a hearing prior to garnishment proceedings:

> A procedural rule that may satisfy due process for attachments in general . . . does not necessarily satisfy procedural due process in every case. The fact that a procedure would pass muster under a feudal regime does not mean it gives necessary protection to all property in its modern forms. We deal here with wages—a specialized type of property presenting distinct problems in our economic system. We turn then to the nature of that property and problems of procedural due process.
>
> A prejudgment garnishment of the Wisconsin type is a taking which may impose tremendous hardship on wage earners with families to support. Until a recent Act of Congress, § 304 of which forbids discharge of employees on the ground that their wages have been garnisheed, garnishment often meant the loss of a job. Over and beyond that was the great drain on family income. As stated by Congressman Reuss:
>
>> The idea of wage garnishment in advance of judgment, of trustee process, of wage attachment, or whatever it is called is a most inhuman doctrine. It compels the wage earner, trying to keep his family together, to be driven below the poverty level.
>
> Recent investigations of the problem have disclosed the grave injustices made possible by prejudgment garnishment whereby the sole opportunity to be heard comes after the taking. Congress Sullivan, Chairman of the House Subcommittee on Consumer Affairs who held extensive hearings on this and related problems stated:
>
>> What we know from our study of this problem is that in a vast number of cases the debt is a fraudulent one, saddled on a poor ignorant

person who is trapped in an easy credit nightmare, in which he is charged double for something he could not pay for even if the proper price was called for, and then hounded into giving up his pound of flesh, and being fired besides. . . .

The leverage of the creditor on the wage earner is enormous. The creditor tenders not only the original debt but the "collection fees" incurred by his attorneys in the garnishment proceedings:

The debtor whose wages are tied up by a writ of garnishment, and who is usually in need of money, is in no position to resist demands for collection fees. If the debt is small, the debtor will be under considerable pressure to pay the debt and collection charges in order to get his wages back. If the debt is large, he will often sign a new contract of "payment schedule" which incorporates these additional charges.

Apart from those collateral consequences, it appears that in Wisconsin the statutory exemption granted the wage earner is "generally insufficient to support the debtor for any one week."

The result is that a prejudgment garnishment of the Wisconsin type may as a practical matter drive a wage-earning family to the wall. Where the taking of one's property is so obvious, it needs no extended argument to conclude that absent notice and a prior hearing . . . this prejudgment garnishment procedure violates the fundamental principles of due process.

Notice that Douglas bases his argument on human need and hardship. Would you find his argument more persuasive if he had stressed the fact that the case dealt with wages—something Sniadach had earned by her work? Had he done so, he would have been following more closely the influential teaching of John Locke—that property is something a person "hath mixed his labor with." If, however, he had stressed the earned character of Sniadach's property, what sort of precedent would he be creating for a case involving the termination of welfare benefits without a hearing?

Justice Black dissented in Sniadach. He maintained that the Wisconsin procedure was constitutionally sound because the kind of property involved in garnishment proceedings is somewhat different from the more conventional property that the Constitution protects. In support of this position, he cited a statement from the Supreme Court of Maine. The court's syntax is a bit garbled but the point is clear enough. "But although an attachment may, within the broad meaning of the definition, deprive one of property, yet conditional and temporary as it is, and part of the legal remedy and procedure by which the property of a debtor may be taken in satisfaction of debt, if judgment be recovered, we do not think it is the deprivation of property contemplated by the Constitution."

Does this statement suggest a two-tier theory of property? Is the property of the poor—items like garnisheed wages—less worthy of constitutional protection than the more conventional forms of property held by the more affluent? If so, would it be fair to say that American law has not been excessively dedicated to property interests but merely one-sided in the types of property it has protected?

Goldberg v. Kelly

In Goldberg v. Kelly (1970)[40] the Supreme Court declared unconstitutional the procedure used by New York City in terminating welfare benefits. Following one of several options allowed by state regulation, New York City adopted a termination procedure requiring that notice be sent to a welfare recipient at least seven days prior to the date of termination. The notice had to state the reasons for the proposed termination and also had to advise the recipient that upon request a review would be granted by an officer holding a position superior to the supervisor who had originally approved the termination. The recipient also had an opportunity to submit a written statement explaining why his welfare payments should not be terminated. Once the payments had stopped, the recipient could request a full evidentiary hearing before an independent state hearing officer. The recipient could appear personally at this hearing, could be represented by counsel, could offer oral evidence, could confront and cross-examine adverse witnesses, and could request that a written record be made.

Thus the full panoply of due process was accorded the recipient after the payments had been discontinued. If the post-termination hearing should vindicate his claim, all benefits would be restored retroactively.

The point at issue in the case was whether the truncated procedures followed by New York prior to termination met constitutional standards of due process. Welfare recipients maintained the process was constitutionally defective because prior to termination there was no opportunity for a personal appearance before the reviewing officer where oral evidence could be presented and adverse witnesses could be cross-examined. As Justice Brennan stated at the outset of his opinion: "The question for decision is whether a State that terminates public assistance payments to a particular recipient without affording him the opportunity for an evidentiary hearing prior to termination denies the recipient procedural due process in violation of the Due Process Clause of the Fourteenth Amendment."

The case came to the Supreme Court from the Federal District Court for the Southern District of New York where the termination procedures had been found unconstitutional. The Supreme Court of the United States upheld this judgment. In so doing, the Court provided a fascinating debate between Justice Brennan and Justice Black on the relationship between welfare payments and the property that is protected by the due process clause.

Justice Brennan maintained that welfare payments should be considered as property. His position on this point is stated most clearly in a footnote that quoted extensively from the writings of Charles Reich on the "new property."

> It may be realistic today to regard welfare entitlements as more like "property" than a "gratuity." Much of the existing wealth in this country takes the form of rights that do not fall within traditional common-law concepts of property. It has been aptly noted that
>
>> [s]ociety today is built around entitlement. The automobile dealer has his franchise, the doctor and lawyer their professional licenses, the worker his union membership, contract, and pension rights, the executive his contract and stock options; all are devices to aid security and independence. Many of the most important of these entitlements now flow from government: subsidies to farmers and businessmen, routes for airlines and channels for television stations; long term contracts for defense, space, and education; social security pensions for individuals. Such sources of security, whether private or public, are no longer regarded as luxuries or gratuities; to the recipients they are essentials, fully deserved, and in no sense a form of charity. It is only the poor whose entitlements, although recognized by public policy, have not been effectively enforced. Riech, Individual Rights and Social Welfare: The Emerging Legal Issues, 74 Yale L.J. 1245, 1255 (1965). See also Reich, The New Property, 73 Yale L.J. 733 (1964).

Having suggested that welfare entitlements are more like property than a gratuity, Brennan continued:

> [W]e agree with the District Court that when welfare is discontinued, only a pre-termination evidentiary hearing provides the recipient with procedural due process. . . . For qualified recipients, welfare provides the means to obtain essential food, clothing, housing, and medical care. . . . Thus the crucial factor in this context . . . is that termination of aid pending resolution of a controversy over eligibility may deprive an eligible recipient of the very means by which to live while he waits. Since he lacks independent resources, his situation becomes immediately desperate. His need to concentrate upon finding the means for daily subsistence, in turn, adversely affects his ability to seek redress from the welfare bureaucracy.

In the preceding paragraph, Brennan follows Douglas's reasoning in
Sniadach and stresses the connection between the need for due process and
the degree of hardship visited upon the person who has suffered some
deprivation. He then shifts the grounds of his argument to the question of
the government's interest in granting a pretermination hearing. This is a
bold and quite unusual argument. New York had argued that its interest in
denying a pretermination hearing outweighed Kelly's need for such a hearing. Brennan now tells New York that to grant such a hearing is in its own
best interest! Do you find the following paragraph persuasive?

> Moreover, important governmental interests are promoted by afford-
> ing recipients a pre-termination evidentiary hearing. From its found-
> ing the Nation's basic commitment has been to foster the dignity and
> well-being of all persons within its borders. We have come to recog-
> nize that forces not within the control of the poor contribute to their
> poverty. This perception, against the background of our traditions,
> has significantly influenced the development of the contemporary public
> assistance system. Welfare, by meeting the basic demands of sub-
> sistence, can help bring within the reach of the poor the same oppor-
> tunities that are available to others to participate meaningfully in the
> life of the community. At the same time, welfare guards against the
> societal malaise that may flow from a widespread sense of unjustified
> frustration and insecurity. Public assistance, then, is not mere
> charity, but a means to "promote the general Welfare, and secure the
> Blessings of Liberty to ourselves and our Posterity." The same gov-
> ernmental interests that counsel the provision of welfare, counsel as
> well its uninterrupted provision to those eligible to receive it; pre-
> termination evidentiary hearings are indispensable to that end.

Brennan goes on to state New York City's position that it would be too
expensive and time-consuming to grant full hearings prior to termination.
In the paragraph that follows he rejects this position. Is Brennan's view of
welfare administration realistic?

> We agree with the District Court, however, that these governmental
> interests are not overriding in the welfare context. The requirement
> of a prior hearing doubtless involves some greater expense, and the
> benefits paid to ineligible recipients pending decision at the hearing
> probably cannot be recouped, since these recipients are likely to be
> judgment-proof. But the State is not without weapons to minimize
> these increased costs. Much of the drain on fiscal and administrative
> resources can be reduced by developing procedures for prompt pre-
> termination hearings and by skillful use of personnel and facilities.
> Indeed, the very provision for a post-termination evidentiary hearing

in New York's Home Relief program is itself cogent evidence that the
State recognizes the primacy of the public interest in correct eligibility determinations and therefore in the provision of procedural safe-
guards. Thus, the interest of the eligible recipient in uninterrupted
receipt of public assistance, coupled with the State's interest that his
payments not be erroneously terminated, clearly outweighs the State's
competing concern to prevent any increase in its fiscal and administrative burdens. As the District Court correctly concluded, "[t]he
stakes are simply too high for the welfare recipient, and the possibility for honest error or irritable misjudgment too great, to allow
termination of aid without giving the recipient a chance, if he so
desires, to be fully informed of the case against him so that he may
contest its basis and produce evidence in rebuttal." . . .

Justice Brennan then takes up the main requirements of due process—
personal appearance, oral evidence, representation by counsel, cross-
examination of adverse witnesses—and shows why welfare recipients should
be accorded each of these before any payments are terminated. The quotation that follows deals with the presentation of oral evidence and the right
to cross-examine adverse witnesses:

The city's procedures presently do not permit recipients to appear
personally with or without counsel before the official who finally determines continued eligibility. Thus a recipient is not permitted to present evidence to that official orally, or to confront or cross-examine
adverse witnesses. These omissions are fatal to the constitutional
adequacy of the procedures.

    The opportunity to be heard must be tailored to the capacities and
circumstances of those who are to be heard. It is not enough that a
welfare recipient may present his position to the decision maker in
writing or secondhand through his caseworker. Written submissions
are an unrealistic option for most recipients, who lack the educational
attainment necessary to write effectively and who cannot obtain professional assistance. Moreover, written submissions do not afford the
flexibility of oral presentations; they do not permit the recipient to
mold his argument to the issues the decision maker appears to regard
as important. Particularly where credibility and veracity are at
issue, as they must be in many termination proceedings, written submissions are a wholly unsatisfactory basis for decision. The secondhand presentation to the decisionmaker by the caseworker has its own
deficiencies; since the caseworker usually gathers the facts upon
which the charge of ineligibility rests, the presentation of the recipient's side of the controversy cannot safely be left to him. Therefore,
a recipient must be allowed to state his position orally. Informal

procedures will suffice; in this context due process does not require a
particular order of proof or mode of offering evidence. Cf. HEW
Handbook, pt. IV, § 6400 (a).

In almost every setting where important decisions turn on questions of fact, due process requires an opportunity to confront and
cross-examine adverse witnesses. . . . What we said in Greene v.
McElroy is particularly pertinent here:

> Certain principles have remained relatively immutable in our juris-
> prudence. One of these is that where governmental action seriously
> injures an individual, and the reasonableness of the action depends
> on fact findings, the evidence used to prove the Government's case
> must be disclosed to the individual so that he has an opportunity to
> show that it is untrue. While this is important in the case of docu-
> mentary evidence, it is even more important where the evidence
> consists of the testimony of individuals whose memory might be
> faulty or who, in fact, might be perjurers or persons motivated by
> malice, vindictiveness, intolerance, prejudice, or jealousy. We
> have formalized these protections in the requirements of confronta-
> tion and cross-examination. They have ancient roots. They find
> expression in the Sixth Amendment. . . . This Court has been
> zealous to protect these rights from erosion. It has spoken out not
> only in criminal cases, . . . but also in all types of cases where
> administrative . . . actions were under scrutiny.

Welfare recipients must therefore be given an opportunity to confront
and cross-examine the witnesses relied on by the department.

Justice Black, in dissenting sharply from the Court's opinion, seemed
particularly vexed by the idea that welfare is property:

> The more than a million names on the relief rolls in New York, and
> the more than nine million names on the rolls of all the 50 States were
> not put there at random. The names are there because state welfare
> officials believed that those people were eligible for assistance.
> Probably in the officials' haste to make out the lists many names were
> put there erroneously in order to alleviate immediate suffering, and
> undoubtedly some people are drawing relief who are not entitled under
> the law to do so. Doubtless some draw relief checks from time to
> time who know they are not eligible, either because they are not
> actually in need or for some other reason. Many of those who thus
> draw undeserved gratuities are without sufficient property to enable
> the government to collect back from them any money they wrongfully
> receive. But the Court today holds that it would violate the Due Pro-
> cess Clause of the Fourteenth Amendment to stop paying those people
> weekly or monthly allowances unless the government first affords them

a full "evidentiary hearing" even though welfare officials are per-
suaded that the recipients are not rightfully entitled to receive a penny
under the law. In other words, although some recipients might be on
the lists for payment wholly because of deliberate fraud on their part,
the Court holds that the government is helpless and must continue,
until after an evidentiary hearing, to pay money that it does not owe,
never has owed, and never could owe. I do not believe there is any
provision in our Constitution that should thus paralyze the government's efforts to protect itself against making payments to people who
are not entitled to them. . . .

The Court . . . in effect says that failure of the government to pay
a promised charitable installment to an individual deprives that individual of his own property, in violation of the Due Process Clause of
the Fourteenth Amendment. It somewhat strains credulity to say that
the government's promise of charity to an individual is property
belonging to that individual when the government denies that the individual is honestly entitled to receive such a payment. . . .

The procedure required today as a matter of constitutional law
finds no precedent in our legal system. Reduced to its simplest
terms, the problem in this case is similar to that frequently encountered when two parties have an ongoing legal relationship that requires
one party to make periodic payments to the other. Often the situation
arises where the party "owing" the money stops paying it and justifies
his conduct by arguing that the recipient is not legally entitled to payment. The recipient can, of course, disagree and go to court to compel payment. But I know of no situation in our legal system in which
the person alleged to owe money to another is required by law to continue making payments to a judgment-proof claimant without the benefit
of any security or bond to insure that these payments can be recovered
if he wins his legal argument. Yet today's decision is no way obligates
the welfare recipient to pay back any benefits wrongfully received during the pre-termination evidentiary hearings or post any bond, and in
all "fairness" it could not do so. These recipients are by definition
too poor to post a bond or to repay the benefits that, as the majority
assumes, must be spent as received to insure survival.

Whose position do you find more persuasive—Black's or Brennan's?
Is welfare "property," a "gratuity," or a "promised charitable installment"? If welfare bureaucrats should agree with Brennan that welfare is
property, what practical effect might this belief lead to at the behavioral
level in a welfare agency? In the past decade we have had occasion to hear
a great deal about racist and sexist language. Is there a form of antipoor
("classist") language as well? Could there be a use of language within a
welfare agency that tends to demean the recipients in the eyes of the caseworkers and their supervisors? If so, would professional ethics suggest

that such language be avoided? If welfare is property, would it be morally and prudentially advisable for the director of a welfare office to insist that the money distributed by his office not be referred to as a "gratuity" or a "benefit"? If so, what would be a suitable substitute? Is "debt" too strong? What about the more neutral term "payment"? What other language changes might follow if welfare is property?[41]

Personal Rights and Property Rights

Earlier in this chapter, we had occasion to comment briefly on the distinction that is often made between personal (or human) rights and property rights.[42] The Supreme Court addressed this question directly in 1972 in Lynch v. Household Finance Corporation.[43] Like Sniadach, this case involved a garnishment statute, but the precise point at issue before the Supreme Court was a question of federal jurisdiction.

Dorothy Lynch, a citizen of Connecticut had directed her employer to deposit $10 of her weekly $69 wage in a credit union savings account. In 1969, Household Finance Corporation brought a suit against her in a state court for $525; the company alleged nonpayment of a promissory note. Before she was served with process, the company "garnisheed her savings account under the provisions of Connecticut law that authorize summary pre-judicial garnishment at the behest of attorneys for alleged creditors."

Lynch brought a class action in a federal district court against Connecticut sheriffs who levy on bank accounts under the garnishment statutes. She based her action on two federal statutes that give federal courts jurisdiction in cases in which a state official, acting "under color of a State law," subjects any citizen of the United States "to the deprivation of any rights, privileges, or immunities secured by the Constitution and laws" of the United States. The statute further provided that the offending parties "shall be liable to the party injured in an action at law."

The federal district court in Connecticut never reached the merits of the case. Instead, it dismissed Lynch's complaint on the grounds that it lacked jurisdiction. The court reasoned that the federal statute Lynch relied upon was not concerned with property rights but only with personal rights. The Supreme Court of the United States rejected this distinction and remanded the case to the district court for a rehearing on the merits. The Court's opinion was given by Justice Stewart:

This Court has never adopted the distinction between personal liberties and property rights as a guide to the contours of § 1343 (3)[44] jurisdiction. Today we expressly reject that distinction.

Neither the words of § 1343 (3) nor the legislative history of that provision distinguishes between personal and property rights. In fact, the Congress that enacted the predecessor of §§ 1983[45] and 1343 (3) seems clearly to have intended to provide a federal judicial forum for the redress of wrongful deprivations of property by persons acting under color of state law. . . .

A final, compelling reason for rejecting a "personal liberties" limitation upon § 1343 (3) is the virtual impossibility of applying it. The federal courts have been particularly bedeviled by "mixed" cases in which both personal and property rights are implicated, and the line between them has been difficult to draw with any consistency or principled objectivity. The case before us presents a good example of the conceptual difficulties created by the test.

Such difficulties indicate that the dichotomy between personal liberties and property rights is a false one. Property does not have rights. People have rights. The right to enjoy property without unlawful deprivation, no less than the right to speak or the right to travel, is in truth a "personal" right, whether the "property" in question be a welfare check, a home, or a savings account. In fact, a fundamental interdependence exists between the personal right to liberty and the personal right in property. Neither could have meaning without the other. . . .

Do you agree with Justice Stewart's rejection of the "personal-property" distinction? If so, can you explain why the distinction is so commonplace in ordinary parlance? Do you agree with Stewart's statement that the interdependence between the personal right to liberty and the personal right to property is so fundamental that neither could have meaning without the other? Can you think of any exceptions? Would you want to qualify Stewart's statement?

Public Service Employment

The final aspect of the "new property" we shall examine is that of employment in the public sector. Does one who works for government—state or federal—have a property interest in his job and, if so, does this mean he cannot be dismissed constitutionally without the full benefits of a due process hearing before his dismissal becomes effective? Some light was shed on this question in two cases decided on June 29, 1972—Board of Regents v. Roth[46] and Perry v. Sinderman. [47]

The cases were quite similar in that both involved the failure of state colleges to renew contracts of nontenured professors. Roth was in his first year as an assistant professor of political science at Wisconsin State University at Oshkosh. During that year he was told his one-year contract would not be renewed. No reasons were given for the decision, and no review or appeal was allowed.

Sinderman was in his tenth year as a teacher in the Texas state college system. He had taught for two years at the University of Texas, for four years at San Antonio Junior College, and for four years at Odessa Junior College. As president of the Texas Junior College Teachers' Association, Sinderman had become involved in a public dispute with the Board of Regents over the question of whether Odessa Junior College should be elevated to four-year status. Because the college had no tenure system, the Board of Regents decided not to renew Sinderman's contract at the end of the academic year in which he had publicly challenged the Board's policies. He was never given any formal statement of why his contract was not renewed, nor was he given an opportunity for a hearing to challenge the basis of the nonrenewal. The Board of Regents did, however, issue a press release charging Sinderman with insubordination.

Despite the similarities in the two cases, the Court was far more sympathetic to Sinderman's claim of a property interest in continued employment than it was toward Roth.[48] Justice Stewart delivered the Court's opinion in both cases and, in so doing, drew some interesting distinctions between Roth's situation and that of Sinderman. The two opinions together give some insight into just when, in the absence of explicit statutory provisions, one acquires a constitutionally protected property interest in public service employment.

In Roth, Stewart gave the following analysis of when one's public employment becomes property:

> The Fourteenth Amendment's procedural protection of property is a safeguard of the security of interests that a person has already acquired in specific benefits. These interests—property interests— may take many forms.
>
> Thus, the Court has held that a person receiving welfare benefits under statutory and administrative standards defining eligibility for them has an interest in continued receipt of those benefits that is safe-guarded by procedural due process. Goldberg v. Kelly. Similarly, in the area of public employment, the Court has held that a public college professor dismissed from an office held under tenure provisions . . . and college professors and staff members dismissed during the terms of their contracts . . . have interests in continued employment that are safeguarded by due process. Only last year, the Court held that this principle "proscribing summary dismissal from public employ-ment without hearing or inquiry required by due process" also applied to a teacher recently hired without tenure or a formal contract, but nonetheless with a clearly implied promise of continued employment. . . .
>
> Certain attributes of "property" interests protected by procedural due process emerge from these decisions. To have a property inter-est in a benefit, a person clearly must have more than an abstract

need or desire for it. He must have more than a unilateral expectation of it. He must, instead, have a legitimate claim of entitlement to it. It is a purpose of the ancient institution of property to protect those claims upon which people rely in their daily lives, reliance that must not be arbitrarily undermined. It is a purpose of the constitutional right to a hearing to provide an opportunity for a person to vindicate those claims.

Property interests, of course, are not created by the Constitution. Rather, they are created and their dimensions are defined by existing rules or understandings that stem from an independent source such as state law—rules or understandings that secure certain benefits and that support claims of entitlement to those benefits. Thus, the welfare recipients in Goldberg v. Kelly had a claim of entitlement to welfare payments that was grounded in the statute defining eligibility for them. The recipients had not yet shown that they were, in fact, within the statutory terms of eligibility. But we held that they had a right to a hearing at which they might attempt to do so.

Just as the welfare recipients' "property" interest in welfare payments was created and defined by statutory terms, so the respondent's "property" interest in employment at Wisconsin State University-Oshkosh was created and defined by the terms of his appointment. Those terms secured his interest in employment up to June 30, 1969. But the important fact in this case is that they specifically provided that the respondent's employment was to terminate on June 30. They did not provide for contract renewal absent "sufficient cause." Indeed, they made no provision for renewal whatsoever.

Thus, the terms of the respondent's appointment secured absolutely no interest in re-employment for the next year. They supported absolutely no possible claim of entitlement to re-employment. Nor, significantly, was there any state statute or University rule or policy that secured his interest in re-employment or that created any legitimate claim to it. In these circumstances, the respondent surely had an abstract concern in being rehired, but he did not have a property interest sufficient to require the University authorities to give him a hearing when they declined to renew his contract of employment.

In Perry v. Sinderman, decided the same day as Roth, Justice Stewart continued his analysis of when property interests emerge in public employment:

The respondent's lack of formal contractual or tenure security in continued employment at Odessa Junior College . . . is . . . relevant to his procedural due process claim. But it may not be entirely dispositive.

We have held today in <u>Board of Regents</u> v. <u>Roth</u> that the Constitution does not require opportunity for a hearing before the nonrenewal of a nontenured teacher's contract, unless he can show that the decision not to rehire him somehow deprived him of an interest in "liberty" or that he had a "property" interest in continued employment, despite the lack of tenure or a formal contract. In <u>Roth</u> the teacher had not made a showing on either point to justify summary judgment in his favor.

Similarly, the respondent here has yet to show that he has been deprived of an interest that could invoke procedural due process protection. As in <u>Roth</u>, the mere showing that he was not rehired in one particular job, without more, did not amount to a showing of a loss of liberty. Nor did it amount to a showing of a loss of property.

But the respondent's allegations—which we must construe most favorably to the respondent at this stage of the litigation—do raise a genuine issue as to his interest in continued employment at Odessa Junior College. He alleged that this interest, though not secured by a formal contractual tenure provision, was secured by a no less binding understanding fostered by the college administration. In particular, the respondent alleged that the college had a <u>de facto</u> tenure program, and that he had tenure under that program. He claimed that he and others legitimately relied upon an unusual provision that had been in the college's official Faculty Guide for many years:

> <u>Teacher Tenure</u>: Odessa College has no tenure system. The Administration of the College wishes the faculty member to feel that he has permanent tenure as long as his teaching services are satisfactory and as long as he displays a cooperative attitude toward his co-workers and his superiors, and as long as he is happy in his work.

Moreover, the respondent claimed legitimate reliance upon guidelines promulgated by the Coordinating Board of the Texas College and University System that provided that a person, like himself, who had been employed as a teacher in the state college and university system for seven years or more has some form of job tenure. Thus, the respondent offered to prove that a teacher with his long period of service at this particular State College had no less a "property" interest in continued employment than a formally tenured teacher at other colleges, and had no less a procedural due process right to a statement of reasons and a hearing before college officials upon their decision not to retain him.

We have made clear in <u>Roth</u> . . . that "property" interests subject to procedural due process protection are not limited by a few rigid, technical forms. Rather, "property" denotes a broad range of interests that are secured by "existing rules or understandings." . . . A

person's interest in a benefit is a "property" interest for due process
if there are such rules or mutually explicit understandings that support
his claim of entitlement to the benefit and that he may invoke at a
hearing. . . .

A written contract with an explicit tenure provision clearly is evidence of a formal understanding that supports a teacher's claim of
entitlement to continued employment unless sufficient "cause" is
shown. Yet absence of such an explicit contractual provision may not
always foreclose the possibility that a teacher has a "property" interest in re-employment. For example, the law of contracts in most, if
not all, jurisdictions long has employed a process by which agreements, though not formalized in writing, may be "implied." . . .
Explicit contractual provisions may be supplemented by other agreements implied from "the promisor's words and conduct in the light of
the surrounding circumstances." . . . And, "[t]he meaning of [the
promisor's] words and acts is found by relating them to the usage of
the past." . . .

A teacher, like the respondent, who has held his position for a
number of years, might be able to show from the circumstances of this
service—and from other relevant facts—that he has a legitimate claim
of entitlement to job tenure. Just as this Court has found there to be
a "common law of a particular industry or of a particular plant" that
may supplement a collective-bargaining agreement, . . . so there may
be an unwritten "common law" in a particular university that certain
employees shall have the equivalent of tenure. This is particularly
likely in a college or university, like Odessa Junior College, that has
no explicit tenure system even for senior members of its faculty, but
that nonetheless may have created such a system in practice. . . .

In this case, the respondent has alleged the existence of rules and
understandings, promulgated and fostered by state officials, that may
justify his legitimate claim of entitlement to continued employment
absent "sufficient cause." We disagree with the Court of Appeals
insofar as it held that a mere subjective "expectancy" is protected by
procedural due process, but we agree that the respondent must be
given an opportunity to prove the legitimacy of his claim of such
entitlement in light of "the policies and practices of the institution." . . . Proof of such a property interest would not, of course,
entitle him to reinstatement. But such proof would obligate college
officials to grant a hearing at his request, where he could be informed
of the grounds for his nonretention and challenge their sufficiency.

After reading these excerpts from Stewart's opinions, how would you
describe the Court's understanding of when a property interest arises in
government employment? Among the criteria Stewart mentions are the
following: (1) property is "a safeguard of the security of interests that a

person has <u>already</u> acquired in specific benefits"[49];   (2) the purpose of
"the ancient institution of property is to protect those claims upon which
people rely in their daily lives"; (3) a property interest must be more than
a "mere subjective expectancy of continued employment"; (4) the fact that
Roth had an "abstract concern" in being rehired did not give him a property
interest; (5) the complex network of informal understandings at Odessa
Junior College could add up to a property interest even in the absence of
"an explicit contractual provision."

What other criteria would you add either from the excerpts given above
or from your own opinion? Do you think the job of a career civil servant
should be looked upon and protected as a form of property? Would this
protection tend to encourage bureaucrats to use their discretionary authority in an independent way without worrying about "signals" they were
receiving from the elected leadership? If so, would this be good? If it is
true that historically property has given persons a sense of security, is it
also true that it has given some persons a sense of arrogance as well? It
is usually individuals and corporations with great property holdings that we
associate with the attitude—"the public be damned." Would the principle
that a government job is a form of property tend to create (or reinforce)
this attitude in bureaucrats? What would Andrew Jackson say about all
this?[50]

Regardless of what Andrew Jackson might say, Justice Thurgood
Marshall did not think Justice Stewart went far enough in covering public
service employment with the protective mantle of property. In his dissenting opinion in <u>Roth,</u> Marshall had this to say:

> I would go further than the Court does in defining the terms "liberty"
> and "property."
>
> The prior decisions of this Court, discussed at length in the opin-
> ion of the Court, establish a principle that is as obvious as it is com-
> pelling—i.e., federal and state governments and governmental agencies
> are restrained by the Constitution from acting arbitrarily with respect
> to employment opportunities that they either offer or control. Hence,
> it is now firmly established that whether or not a private employer is
> free to act capriciously or unreasonably with respect to employment
> practices, at least absent statutory or contractual controls, a govern-
> ment employer is different. The government may only act fairly and
> reasonably.
>
> This Court has long maintained that "the right to work for a living
> in the common occupations of the community is of the very essence of
> the personal freedom and opportunity that it was the purpose of the
> [Fourteenth] Amendment to secure." . . . It has also established that
> the fact that an employee has no contract guaranteeing work for a
> specific future period does not mean that as the result of action by the

government he may be "discharged at any time for any reason or for
no reason." . . .

In my view, every citizen who applies for a government job is
entitled to it unless the government can establish some reason for
denying the employment. This is the "property" right that I believe is
protected by the Fourteenth Amendment and that cannot be denied
"without due process of law." And it is also liberty—liberty to work—
which is the "very essence of the personal freedom and opportunity"
secured by the Fourteenth Amendment.

This Court has often had occasion to note that the denial of public
employment is a serious blow to any citizen. . . . Thus, when an
application for public employment is denied or the contract of a government employee is not renewed, the government must say why, for
it is only when the reasons underlying government action are known
that citizens feel secure and protected against arbitrary government
action.

Employment is one of the greatest, if not the greatest, benefits
that governments offer in modern-day life. When something as valuable as the opportunity to work is at stake, the government may not
reward some citizens and not others without demonstrating that its
actions are fair and equitable. And it is procedural due process that
is our fundamental guarantee of fairness, our protection against arbitrary, capricious, and unreasonable government action. . . .

It may be argued that to provide procedural due process to all
public employees or prospective employees would place an intolerable
burden on the machinery of government. . . . The short answer to
that argument is that it is not burdensome to give reasons when reasons exist. Whenever an application for employment is denied, an
employee is discharged, or a decision not to rehire an employee is
made, there should be some reason for the decision. It can scarcely
be argued that government would be crippled by a requirement that the
reason be communicated to a person most directly affected by the government's action.

Where there are numerous applicants for jobs, it is likely that few
will choose to demand reasons for not being hired. But, if the demand
for reasons is exceptionally great, summary procedures can be
devised that would provide fair and adequate information to all persons. As long as the government has a good reason for its actions it
need not fear disclosure. It is only where the government acts
improperly that procedural due process is truly burdensome. And that
is precisely when it is most necessary.

Do you agree with Justice Marshall that "every citizen who applies for
a government job is entitled to it unless the government can establish some

reason for denying the employment"? Does Marshall's view differ from
that of Stewart, who says that property rights arise only in interests that
have been already acquired? Is there any significance in the fact that
Marshall speaks of a citizen's property in a claim on a job he does not yet
have? Does this mean that by his citizenship he has already acquired a
property right to public employment? If citizenship is the basis of the
property right, does it follow that a less qualified citizen must always
be preferred to a more qualified noncitizen when the two are competing for
the same job?[51]

What significance is there in Marshall's reference to a government
job as a "reward"? A reward for what? Marshall says, "Employment is
one of the greatest, if not the greatest, benefits that governments offer in
modern-day life." Are terms like "benefit" and "reward" compatible with
his position on government jobs as property? If government employment
is a "benefit" or "reward," do we delude ourselves when we talk about
careers in public "service"? What sort of image does Marshall have of
the bureaucracy? Is his position a call for a "new patronage" instead of
a "new property"?

Some Reflections

The "new property" cases studied in this chapter have all raised procedural questions. The reason for this, of course, is that property is protected by the two due process clauses of the Constitution. Hence, once it
is determined that the goods or claims pertinent to the case are property,
the only remaining question is whether a person was deprived of this
property by a process that was "due."[52] Although it is well known
that there can be little substantive justice where unfair procedures
prevail, it is still wise to underscore the strictly procedural and therefore
quite limited nature of our investigation. Although it might improve the
tone of a welfare agency to encourage caseworkers to think of welfare payments as property, such wholesome reflections do not absolve welfare
bureaucrats from also reflecting on the more substantive question of
whether they are achieving the statutory objectives of their program.[53]

Despite its emphasis on procedure, the questions of attitude triggered
by the "new property" have the capacity to channel the thinking of bureaucrats along the lines of a substantive regime value and, hence, are useful
for our purpose. The kind of issue raised by the "new property" has something for everyone. Liberals will delight in its egalitarian and redistributive thrust, while conservatives will note with pleasure that it takes
seriously their perennial fear that the welfare state will destroy personal
liberty. Conservatives have always maintained that in a welfare state the
government will manipulate the behavior of the citizens by threatening to
withhold certain public benefits. Welfare will then become a form of

bribing the citizen into tame submissiveness, and the welfare state itself
will become a place of dull and drab conformity.

These fears are not the product of reactionary disingenuousness. The
appalling violation of the privacy and dignity of welfare recipients is all too
familiar. The "new property" takes the conservative argument seriously
and offers a serious response. In so doing, the "new property" could
broaden the sense of a "stake in society" that conservatives have always
held so dear. This would tend to build confidence in existing institutions,
and in this way the "new property," like the "old property" of contracts,
would be aimed toward higher political ends. The likelihood of such happy
results remains, of course, a matter of pleasant conjecture. It is no flight
of fancy, however, to expect that at the educational level a serious analysis
of the issues raised by the "new property" will offer bureaucrats the
basis for some solid reflection on how our traditional values can be applied
to changing circumstances. By accepting the discipline of investigating a
current problem in the light of traditional regime values, we can hope that
bureaucrats will find in these values intellectual and moral resources that
will give them sound guidance on just how the goods and services of our
society might be distributed in a more equitable way.

NOTES

1. Although the distinction between property rights and human rights has
   a decidedly contemporary flavor, it should be noted that in The Federalist Papers, No. 54, Madison distinguishes between personal rights
   and property rights. This, however, is by way of exception. It is
   more common for Publius to speak of liberty and property together.
2. Ogden v. Saunders 12 Wheat. 213 at 344-345 (1827).
3. From "General Marshall's Address to the Citizens of Richmond,
   Virginia," cited by Robert K. Faulkner, The Jurisprudence of John
   Marshall (Princeton, N.J.: Princeton University Press, 1968), p. 13.
   The entire text of the speech can be found in Albert J. Beveridge, Life
   of John Marshall, 4 vols. (Boston: Houghton Mifflin, 1919), vol. 2,
   p. 572.
4. See Faulkner, The Jurisprudence of John Marshall, for a thorough
   discussion of Marshall's philosophical and jurisprudential thought.
   The main points of his book are summarized in Faulkner's article,
   "John Marshall," in The Philosophic Dimension of American Statesmanship, ed. Morton J. Frisch and Richard G. Stevens (Dubuque:
   Kendall-Hunt, 1971), pp. 71-98.
5. 4 Wheat. 518 (1819).
6. Fletcher v. Peck 6 Cranch 87 (1810).
7. New Jersey v. Wilson 7 Cranch 164 (1812).
8. 290 U.S. 398 (1934).

9. Alfred H. Kelly and Winfred A. Harbison, The American Constitution:
    Its Origins and Development, 3rd ed. (New York: W.W. Norton,
    1963), p. 773.
10. 326 U.S. 230 (1944).
11. See pp. 136-143 above.
12. See pp. 156-159 above.
13. The doctrine has its origin in a famous footnote to Justice Stone's
    opinion in Carolene Products Co. v. U.S. 304 U.S. 144 (1938).
14. Cited by Francis S. Philbrick, "Changing Conceptions of Property in
    Law," University of Pennsylvania Law Review 86 (May 1938): 711.
15. William Blackstone, Commentaries, bk. II, chap. I, p. 11.
16. 9 Wheat. 1 (1824).
17. U.S. Constitution; Article I, Section 8.
18. Morton J. Horwitz, "The Transformation in the Conception of Prop-
    erty in American Law, 1780-1860," University of Chicago Law Review
    40 (Winter 1973): 248-290; James Willard Hurst, Law and the Condi-
    tions of Freedom in the Nineteenth Century United States (Madison:
    University of Wisconsin Press, 1964).
19. Horwitz, "The Transformation in the Concept of Property," p. 253.
20. Merritt v. Parker 1 N.J.L. 526 at 530. Cited by Horwitz, "The
    Transformation in the Conception of Property," p. 252.
21. Cary v. Daniels 49 Mass. (8 Met.) 466 (1844). Cited by Horwitz, "The
    Transformation in the Conception of Property," p. 260.
22. Horwitz, "The Transformation in the Conception of Property," p. 260.
23. Ibid.
24. 12 Wheat. 213 (1827).
25. Sturges v. Crowninshield 4 Wheat. 122 (1819).
26. 11 Pet. 420 (1837).
27. I do not believe there are any commonly accepted dates for when the
    laissez-faire era began and ended. As far as constitutional history is
    concerned, I would suggest the era began with Chicago, Milwaukee and
    St. Paul Railway Co. v. Minn. 134 U.S. 418 (1890). In my opinion,
    laissez-faire collapsed with West Coast Hotel Co. v. Parrish 300
    U.S. 379 (1937).
28. An excellent treatment of the potential of acquisitiveness to lead to
    certain forms of human excellence can be found in Martin Diamond,
    "Ethics and Politics: The American Way," (Paper delivered at the
    1976 meeting of the American Political Science Association). This
    paper was reprinted in Robert Horwitz, ed., The Moral Foundations
    of American Democracy (Charlottesville: University of Virginia
    Press, 1977).
29. See Adolph A. Berle and Gardiner C. Means, The Modern Corporation
    and Private Property (New York: Macmillan, 1932); and Adolph A.
    Berle, Power Without Property (New York: Harcourt, Brace, 1957).

30. Blackstone, Commentaries, bk. II, chap. I.
31. This sketchy discussion of the role played by property in the transition from the feudal era to modernity probably raises more questions than it answers. Those interested in pursuing this question should consult the following: Philbrick, "Changing Conceptions of Property in Law," pp. 691-732; Richard McKeon, "The Development of the Concept of Property in Political Philosophy," International Journal of Ethics 48 (April 1938): 298-374; Morris R. Cohen, "Property and Sovereignty," The Cornell Law Quarterly 13 (December 1927): 8-30; Neil Hecht, "From Seisin to Sit-In: Evolving Property Concepts," Boston University Law Review 44 (Fall 1964): 435-466.
32. Cited in Alphaeus T. Mason and William M. Beaney, American Constitutional Law, 5th ed. (Englewood Cliffs, N.J.: Prentice-Hall, (1972), p. 292.
33. Charles A. Reich, "The New Property," Yale Law Journal 73 (April 1964): 733-787. This article was followed by a sequel: "Individual Rights and Social Welfare: The Emerging Legal Issues," Yale Law Journal 74 (June 1965): 1245-1257. Reich became a well-known public figure with the publication in 1970 of his best-seller, The Greening of America. The Yale Law Journal articles, however, were certainly written in a "Consciousness II" period.
34. Since Reich's article appeared, courts have become increasingly reluctant to stress the distinction between rights and privileges.
35. 363 U.S. 603 (1960).
36. Reich, "The New Property," pp. 768-769.
37. Ibid., p. 758; citing Wilkie v. O'Connor 25 N.Y.S. 2d 617 (1941).
38. Ibid., p. 778.
39. 395 U.S. 337 (1969).
40. 397 U.S. 254 (1970).
41. For further development of the principles in Goldberg v. Kelly, see Bell v. Burson 402 U.S. 535 (1971) and Fuentes v. Shevin 407 U.S. 67 (1972). The latter, however, was severely qualified in Mitchell v. W.T. Grant Co. 416 U.S. 600 (1974). For a limitation on the reasoning in Goldberg see Richardson v. Belcher 404 U.S. 78 (1971).
42. See p. 191 above.
43. 405 U.S. 538 (1972).
44. 28 USC § 1343 (3). This section was the basis of Lynch's action.
45. 42 USC § 1983.
46. 408 U.S. 564 (1972).
47. 408 U.S. 593 (1972).
48. The Court did not actually say that Sinderman had a property interest in a renewed contract. Instead it remanded the case to a lower court with new guidelines to apply in rehearing Sinderman's claim of a property right.

49. Emphasis added.
50. See pp. 16 and 18-19 above. For further discussion of public employ-
    ment as property, see Arnett v. Kennedy 416 U.S. 134 (1974) and
    Bishop v. Wood 96 S. Ct. 2074 (1976). On the relationship between the
    due process clause and the right to a hearing prior to suspension and
    removal, see Victor G. Rosenblum, "School Children: Yes; Police-
    men: No," Northwestern University Law Review 72 (March-April
    1977): 146-170.
51. See Hampton v. Mow Sun Wong 96 S. Ct. 1895 (1976).
52. It is possible, of course, that the "new property" may contain more
    than a hint of "substantive due process."
53. On this point see Joel F. Handler, "Controlling Official Behavior in
    Welfare Administration," California Law Review 54 (May 1966):
    479-510.

Conclusion

[The responsible administrator] must be fully familiar with the difficulties and obstacles in the way of administrative achievement; he must realize how to strive for efficiency without losing sight of other and more important objectives. Above all, he must know the inherent limitations which the American Constitution imposes upon administrative work. Such knowledge and experience will make it possible for him to guide the development of American governmental services without getting them embroiled in insoluble conflicts with the American governmental tradition and Constitution as a whole.

Carl J. Friedrich

The purpose of this concluding chapter is to present a brief review of the argument of this book and then to examine in detail some important issues touched upon only in passing in the previous chapters.

REVIEWING THE ARGUMENT

The governing authority exercised by bureaucrats through their discretionary powers is the most appropriate starting point for analyzing ethics for bureaucrats. This, in brief, is the main point of the Introduction and Chapter 1 of this book. The Introduction examined and rejected as "false starts" such considerations as conflict of interest, Watergate, resignation in protest, and basic decency. Although each of these starting points was rejected for somewhat different reasons, they all failed to meet the twofold criterion of raising ethical issues that are (1) peculiar to government managers and (2) likely to occur frequently in one's own career in public management.

Chapter 1, "Stating the Problem," attempted to do what its title indicates. The ethical problem for bureaucrats is how they should use their discretionary authority to share in governing a democratic regime. The historical foundations of the present personnel system were examined to highlight the normative considerations that were raised when "merit" began

237

to displace "spoils." At issue was the argument that the "spoils system," however corrupt, was more democratic than the proposed reform. A temporary solution was found in Woodrow Wilson's famous essay on administration, which was widely interpreted as proposing a sharp dichotomy between politics and administration. To criticize the personnel system of the reformers as being undemocratic was, in terms of Wilson's analysis, to betray a misunderstanding of the scientific and therefore fundamentally apolitical character of administration. Wilson's dichotomy became high doctrine in government circles and helped to shift the focus of normative thinking about bureaucracy toward economy and efficiency and away from its character as an institution of government. Beginning in the 1940s, political scientists set out to demonstrate the inadequacy of the Wilsonian dichotomy, but, in doing so, they tended to neglect the normative dimensions of their very compelling arguments. In Chapter 1, an attempt was made to develop these normative considerations and to apply them to mid-level government managers.

Chapter 2, "Regime Values," described an educational method intended to encourage normative reflections by students and practitioners of public administration on how they should govern. Because American bureaucrats govern a democratic regime without being directly responsible to the electorate, they have a moral obligation to alert themselves to the values of those in whose name they govern. The method of "regime values" was presented with the limitations in mind that other demands of the training and educational curriculum will necessarily impose. Rather than relying upon the ultimate principles of philosophy, the method of regime values proposed the Constitution of the United States as the most appropriate focal point for normative reflection by American bureaucrats. This choice was defended on the grounds that American bureaucrats have taken an oath to uphold the Constitution of the United States and that such an act should have a moral character about it that creates a moral community. The study of Supreme Court opinions was put forth as providing the best way for the student to reflect upon the meaning of the Constitution he or she has sworn to uphold. Concurring and dissenting opinions, as well as opinions that have been overruled, were proposed for the bureaucrat's reflection along with majority opinions currently in force. The purpose of the opinions was not to instruct bureaucrats in what the law is but rather to encourage them to think about and discuss the underlying values of the regime in which they serve. All this was presented in the hope of creating within the bureaucracy a community of moral discourse centered on fundamental constitutional values.

Chapters 3, 4, and 5 applied the method described in Chapter 2 to the salient regime values of equality, freedom, and property.

CONSTITUTIONAL FOUNDATION OF
BUREAUCRATIC GOVERNANCE

Because this book has relied so heavily on constitutional questions, it is
only fitting that its conclusion should touch upon the constitutional foundations of the bureaucratic "model" suggested in these pages. The model of
American bureaucracy proposed in this essay is a "public interest" model.
Based on thirty years of research by political scientists who have demonstrated conclusively that bureaucrats do govern, the public interest model
addresses the normative question of how they should govern. What we have
neglected, however, is whether there is any normative support in the
American constitutional tradition for the empirical findings of the political
scientists. That is, granted that bureaucrats do govern, does this mean
that they should? What constitutional considerations entitle them to
govern?

Textual Considerations

It would be less than candid to hold out any serious hope that further
research might provide some evidence of an argument by the framers of
the Constitution that bureaucrats should particpate significantly in governing the Republic. The short of the matter is that bureaucrats govern today
because they must. The word "bureaucracy" was unknown to the framers,
and the word "administration," though known to them, does not appear in
the Constitution. Clearly the modern administrative state with its need for
bureaucratic discretion based on technical expertise was not foreseen by
the framers.

It does not follow, however, that the public interest model of bureaucracy is bereft of support in the American constitutional tradition. Helpful
here is the familiar consideration that the Constitution is an "organic"
instrument with a remarkable capacity to adapt itself to changing conditions. Given the practical needs of contemporary government, there is no
reason why this capacity should stop short of supporting a share for
bureaucrats in the governing of America. John Marshall's dictum is as
true today as it was in 1819: "[W]e must never forget that it is a constitution we are expounding." [1]

Although the text of the Constitution offers no direct support for
bureaucratic sharing in governance, there are a few hints and suggestions that are relevant. Chief among them is the provision in Article II
that Congress should share the power of appointment with the president.
Not only must the Senate advise and consent to certain presidential

appointments, but the Congress as a whole "may by Law vest the Appointment power of such inferior officers, as they think proper, in the President alone, in the Courts of Law, or in the Heads of Departments." The
explicit grant of power to Congress to vest certain appointments in the
heads of departments suggests an intent of the framers to prevent the
executive departments from being absolutely subjected to presidential
authority—as several presidents, notably Andrew Jackson and Richard
Nixon, were to discover. In delivering the departments from absolute
presidential control, however, the Constitution did not subject them to
Congress. Thus, the executive departments, precisely because they are
totally subjected to neither the president nor to Congress, are somewhat
independent of both. This independence, based on the framers intent to
"check" executive power, might possibly confer some textual legitimacy
upon a bureaucratic claim to govern.

The Senatorial Analogue

A more substantial claim, however, can be made from the function of
bureaucracy in contemporary American government. This claim is based
more on the reasons why the Constitution was written and adopted than on
its text. One finds in the functions of today's bureaucracy an interesting
similarity to what the framers had in mind for the Senate. As far as the
contemporary Senate is concerned, the intent of the framers is of little
practical significance. The Seventeenth Amendment nullified the original
provision that the senators should be chosen by the state legislatures and
provided instead for the popular elections we have today. This was a significant departure—at least in principle—from what the framers had
intended. For Madison, the Senate was not to be just a second legislative
body but a different legislative body—that is, it was based on a different
principle from the House of Representatives and was designed to play a
different role in formulating legislation.[2] This role included nothing less
than "to protect the people against their rulers [and] to protect the people
against the transient impressions into which they might be led."[3]
Madison's statement occurred at the Constitutional Convention of 1787 in
the context of supporting a motion that would have provided a nine-year
term for senators. The people's "rulers"—that is, those chosen directly
by the people—would serve two-year terms in the House of Representatives. The lengthy nine-year term of the senators, who would not be
directly elected by the people but chosen by the state legislatures instead,
would help to provide a "cool and deliberate sense of the community,"[4]
and this, in turn, would safeguard against the danger that the country "may
possibly be betrayed by the representatives of the people."[5]
    It is particularly interesting to note that Madison draws a distinction
between the Senate and the representatives of the people. That is, he

envisions the need for a governing body that does not represent the people
in a formal sense, but whose purpose is to protect the people against possible abuses from those who do. Although this is not exactly the function
of the bureaucracy today, there is some similarity. The bureaucracy does
not, and certainly should not, directly check the will of Congress, but
because contemporary legislation is rife with discretionary language, the
bureaucracy, through its power to interpret, decides what the representatives of the people must have intended. In this sense, the bureaucracy
rescues Congress from the necessity of speaking in a more precise way
than its limited expertise would reasonably allow and thereby delivers the
Congress from taking unwarranted risks in betraying public confidence
through unwise legislation. A bureaucracy attuned to regime values can
supply that "cool and deliberate sense of the community" that was originally to be the contribution of the Senate.

It is no coincidence that Madison should speak of the Senate's role in
"protecting the people" in a context in which he was arguing for a nine-year
senatorial term. The consideration that the senators would never be
directly elected by the people was crucial to his argument. This distance
from the electorate was put forth as supporting rather than contradicting
republican institutions. Hamilton went even further than Madison along
these lines. He wanted a Senate that would serve for life,[6] and, consequently, his model comes even closer to contemporary bureaucracy than
that of Madison. Like Madison, Hamilton was worried over the ill-
considered legislation that might come from the House of Representatives.
In addition, Hamilton looked to the Senate to serve as a "center of political knowledge," that would be able to distinguish interests that were
"apparent" and those that were "real"; interests that were "local" and
those that were "general."[7] Above all, the Hamiltonian Senate, with its
life-long membership, would provide the nation with a "permanent will."[8]
This coincides with Madison's hope that the Senate would provide a "due
sense of national character."[9] Both these terms suggested the value of the
stability that the original Senate, like today's bureaucracy, would bring to
American institutions.

Further, Hamilton stressed the close working relationship he envisioned between the Senate and the president. History disappointed him in
this regard, but the bureaucracy he did not foresee has filled this gap in
the Hamiltonian vision. Somewhat surprisingly, Madison, who would later
champion the rights of the states, supported the idea at the 1787 Convention
that the Senate should have power to veto the laws of the states.[10] Although
the contemporary federal bureaucracy does not have this power as such, its
important authority to initiate decisions as to whether state laws and regulations are in conflict with federal "guidelines" is a significant aspect of
bureaucratic governance.

If all these attributes are brought together, we find in the Senate
envisioned by Hamilton and Madison: (1) a governing body that is not

directly elected by the people; (2) whose members would serve (at least
for Hamilton) during good behavior; (3) which provides stability to republican institutions; (4) protects the people from their elected officials;
(5) works closely with but not under the president; (6) exercises some discretionary power over state laws and policies; and (7) provides the regime
with a permanent will and national character. Such an institution does not,
of course, describe precisely today's bureaucracy, but is it close enough
to warrant a claim based on the American constitutional tradition for the
bureaucracy to function as a legitimate institution of government?

STRUCTURING ADMINISTRATIVE DISCRETION

Throughout this book constitutional values have been analyzed to see what
relevance they might have for bureaucrats struggling with the moral dimensions of discretionary power. Although personal choices among regime
values have provided the focus of this study, it would be a mistake to think
that such personal choices are the only ways to deal with administrative
discretion. In his seminal book Discretionary Justice, Kenneth C. Davis
has suggested a variety of institutional methods to "structure" discretion
that raise important normative questions. Davis has pointed out that the
use of discretion is far more undisciplined—to the point of approaching
arbitrariness—in "some of the most backward agencies (e.g., police,
prosecutors, Immigration Service, parole boards, welfare agencies,
selective service boards)" than it is in "our most advanced agencies (e.g.,
SEC, Internal Revenue Service)." [11] He suggests the reason for this is
that agencies like the SEC and IRS, which must deal on a regular basis
with the great financial interests of the nation, are compelled by competent lawyers to exercise their discretionary authority in a reasonably consistent way. Similar pressures are seldom brought upon the "backward"
agencies that deal with the poor and less powerful. Consequently, the
"backward" agencies have had little incentive to develop institutional techniques to "structure" their discretion in ways that will produce a greater
evenhandedness in its exercise.

Techniques for Structuring Discretion

Davis's use of the word "structure" is significant. Although his writings
stress relentlessly the excessive discretion in American government at all
levels, it is the excess of discretion and not its existence that is his tar-
get. His books and articles are sprinkled with reminders of the need for
considerable discretionary authority to meet the particular circumstances
of discrete administrative situations. He takes considerable pains to dis-
associate his position from what he calls the "extravagant version of the

of law." His favorite example of such extravagance is Frederick A. Hayek's The Road to Serfdom, which offered the following description of the "Rule of Law":

> Stripped of all technicalities, this means that government in all its action is bound by rules fixed and announced beforehand—rules which make it possible to foresee with fair certainty how the authority will use its coercive powers in given circumstances and to plan one's individual affairs on the basis of this knowledge. [12]

Davis dismisses this viewpoint as an "absurdity." If the government "in all its action," were "bound by rules fixed and announced beforehand," mindless rigidity would replace the flexibility that common sense demands in a modern administrative state. Hence, for Davis, the task at hand is not to destroy discretion but to "structure" it, that is, to control "the manner of the exercise of discretionary power within designated boundaries, as through open plans, open policy statements, open rules, open findings, open reasons, open precedents, and fair informal procedure." [13]

For our purposes, Davis's work is of considerable interest because, under his influence, some courts have begun to compel administrative agencies to structure their discretionary power in a way that reduces the appearance of arbitrariness without destroying discretion itself. The clearest examples of this came in Environmental Defense Fund v. Ruckleshaus[14]—a case involving the discretionary authority of the secretary of agriculture to refuse to suspend summarily the registration of pesticides containing DDT. Under the Federal Insecticide, Fungicide, and Rodenticide Act, the secretary is empowered to initiate proceedings to cancel the registration of pesticides that fail to conform to statutory standards for product safety. In addition, he may summarily suspend a registration when "necessary to prevent imminent hazard to the public." The purpose of this grant of summary power is designed to get particularly dangerous products off the market while the protracted litigation concerning the ultimate fate of the pesticide is being carried out. In Environmental Defense Fund, the secretary of agriculture, pursuant to a scientifically documented complaint, issued a notice of cancellation that would initiate proceedings against DDT pesticides but refused to use his power to suspend the registration of these pesticides summarily while litigation was in progress. Thus the Environmental Defense Fund, the originator of the complaint, contended that it had been denied interim relief without a satisfactory explanation from the secretary.

Chief Judge Bazelon of the United States Circuit Court for the District of Columbia relied explicitly on Davis's writings in holding that the secretary had to give some explanation of his decision not to use his discretionary power to suspend the registration summarily. Bazelon was extremely careful not to challenge the scientific expertise of USDA in deciding what

sorts of pesticides were actually harmful. His point was rather that
because Congress had made a distinction between hazardous products that
were to be removed through the ordinary process of extended litigation and
those that were to be removed summarily, the secretary had to give some
explanation of how he decides when to follow one procedure rather than the
other:

> The Secretary has made no attempt to deal with [this] problem, either
> by issuing regulations relating to suspension, or by explaining his
> decision in this case. If regulations of general applicability were for-
> mulated, it would of course be possible to explain individual decisions
> by reference to the appropriate regulation. It may well be, however,
> that standards for suspension can best be developed piecemeal, as the
> Secretary evaluates the hazards presented by particular products.
> Even so, he has an obligation to articulate the criteria that he develops
> in making each individual decision. We cannot assume, in the absence
> of adequate explanation, that proper standards are implicit in every
> exercise of administrative discretion.
>
> Since the Secretary has not yet provided an adequate explanation
> for his decision to deny interim relief in this case, it will be necessary
> to remand the case once more, for a fresh determination on that issue.
> On remand, the Secretary should consider whether the information
> presently available to him calls for suspension of any registrations of
> products containing DDT, identifying the factors relevant to that deter-
> mination and relating the evidence to those factors in a statement of
> the reasons for his decision. [15]

The court "structured" the secretary's discretion by telling him what
questions he must ask—how to decide rather than what to decide. While
recognizing the desirability of "regulations of general applicability," the
court indicated it would be satisfied with standards developed "piecemeal."
The key point in all this is that the secretary has "an obligation to articulate the criteria that he develops in making each individual decision." This
is "structured" discretion.

In addition to compelling administrators to announce the standards by
which they exercise their discretionary authority, the courts have also
approved of efforts by administrators who have done this on their own. [16]
Such voluntary efforts to structure discretion by developing publicly stated
criteria would seem to be a form of bureaucratic behavior of considerable
ethical significance, for it would make the exercise of discretion more
regular, consistent, and evenhanded. Bureaucrats with expertise in their
areas of specialization are usually more technically competent than legislatures and courts to strike the proper balance between the arbitrariness
that comes from too much discretion and the rigidity that comes from too
little.

Unfortunately, what is often lacking is a proper sensitivity to the dangers of injustice inherent in excessive discretion. For bureaucrats sensitive to these dangers, however, there are several techniques that could be used in persuading one's agency to structure its discretion voluntarily. Agency rule making is one such technique. Because all federal agencies have inherent power to issue interpretative rules,[17] there is no reason why federal bureaucrats could not try to persuade their agencies to use this power to clarify unnecessarily broad delegations of authority.[18] Publicly announced policy statements would be another device to achieve the same purpose.[19]

Treating prior agency decisons as precedents would be still another method,[20] but here one would have to be careful that adherence to precedent did not destroy the flexibility that quite properly distinguishes the administrative from the judicial process. Administrative agencies must not be transformed into common law courts in the name of structured discretion. Adherence to administrative precedent should never assume the salience of judicial practice, but it could become operative to the extent that administrators would feel obliged to state openly their reasons for not following their own precedents.

Law Enforcement

The discretionary power not to enforce the law is a cause of considerable injustice. Although the problem appears in regulatory and other administrative agencies, it is found in its worst form in police departments and prosecutors' offices. Despite clear statutory language at the federal and state levels that police and prosecutors "shall" enforce the law against "all" offenders, the widespread practice of "selective enforcement" is well known. The exercise of discretion not to enforce the law is particulary distressing because of the finality of such decisions; they are hardly ever reviewed. The notoriety achieved in the early 1970s by the Justice Department's failure to prosecute ITT for alleged antitrust violations was due to a Senate investigation that was being carried on while Richard Kleindienst's nomination as attorney general was pending. Most decisions not to arrest or not to prosecute escape such publicity. There is no mechanism for systematically reviewing decisions not to enforce the law, and in the nature of things there probably never could be. Consider the following examples of why a policeman might choose not to make an arrest for an obvious misdemeanor: (1) the officer will go off duty in five minutes and does not want to work overtime on the paperwork that is a necessary part of making an arrest; (2) the offense is slight and the offender, youthful and repentant, convinces the policeman it will never happen again; (3) the victim pleads that no arrest be made; (4) the policeman sympathizes with the offender; (5) the offense is common and not taken seriously within a cultural subgroup; (6) more urgent duties call the policeman from the scene of the offense; (7) the policeman thinks a word of warning is a more appropriate technique in these particular circumstances; (8) the only witness to the offense makes it clear that he will not testify.[21]

Although one might question the propriety of some of these decisions, there is usually no way they can be reviewed. For all practical purposes, such discretionary decisions are final. The same is true of the prosecutor's discretion. When the present chief justice, Warren Burger, sat on the bench of the federal Court of Appeals for the District of Columbia, a case came before him in which a defendant argued that he had been denied equal protection of the laws because his partner in crime had been allowed to plead guilty to a misdemeanor but no such opportunity was offered to him, and, as a result, he was convicted of a felony. Judge Burger upheld broad discretionary authority for prosecutors in such circumstances:

> [Prosecutors] must have broad discretion. . . . [T]he existence of
> very broad discretion in the prosecutor has long been taken for
> granted. . . . [P]ublic prosecutions are within the exclusive direction
> of the United States Attorney. . . . Myriad factors can enter into the
> prosecutor's decision. Two persons may have committed what is
> precisely the same legal offense but the prosecutor is not compelled
> by law, duty or tradition to treat them the same as to charges. On the
> contrary, he is expected to exercise discretion and common sense. . . .
> It is assumed that the United States Attorney will perform his duties
> and exercise his powers consistent with his oaths; and while this dis-
> cretion is subject to abuse or misuse just as is judicial discretion,
> deviations from his duty as an agent of the Executive are to be dealt
> with by his superiors. The remedy lies ultimately within the estab-
> lishment where power and discretion reside. The President has
> abundant supervisory, and disciplinary powers. . . .[22]

In applying his method of "structuring" discretion to law enforcement agencies, Davis avoids a blanket condemnation of selective enforcement. Despite legislative mandates to enforce "all" the laws, it is quite obvious that this cannot always be done. A policeman chasing a purse snatcher in a park comes upon a minor drinking beer. He cannot arrest one violator without letting the other one go. Some form of "selective enforcement" is unavoidable.

The same principle applies when a police department is not funded at a level that will provide sufficient personnel to enforce all the laws. Some ranking of offenses is necessary. The problem in this situation is that such ranking is usually done in an informal and haphazard way. In the absence of a policy decision at the departmental level, it is quite likely that each police officer could develop his or her own "policy," which, of course, is no policy at all. If decisions are made at a departmental level but not announced publicly, we have a form of "secret law" known only to those who enforce it. An exception to the nonenforcement policy can be made without a public explanation if the police department decides it wants to make life unpleasant for a particular citizen. This, of course, is where selective enforcement can lead to real injustice. The principle of selection shifts from the best utilization of scarce resources to questions of personality, life-style, or political viewpoint.

To safeguard against these abuses without destroying the practice of selective enforcement, Davis suggests that police departments and prosecutors' offices make use of rule-making procedures to structure discretion. Open hearings could be held and written statements solicited on which laws should be enforced in a given community! Law enforcement agencies could then announce publicly their canon of selective enforcement. To safeguard flexibility for unforeseen circumstances, the rule might be prefaced with a qualifying "ordinarily" or "except when special circumstances otherwise require." Davis maintains such a procedure would be perfectly legal despite legislative mandates that all laws be enforced. Legislatures, Davis argues, speak with three voices: (1) the universal mandate of the formal legislative enactment that all laws be enforced; (2) the level of appropriation that makes universal enforcement impossible; (3) legislative acquiescence in the status quo of selective enforcement. Davis is suggesting that we trade selective enforcement that rests on "secret law" for selective enforcement in which the public participates in formulating publicly announced principles of selection.[23]

Some Reflections

Do you think Davis's proposals to structure discretion go too far? Should he have stopped short of applying his analysis to law enforcement agencies? Are federal commissions such as FTC, ICC, FCC, and SEC law enforcement agencies? If a local police department were to announce publicly the laws it will not enforce, would respect for the "rule of law" be increased or diminished? If the police in your state have an unannounced "policy" of enforcing a speed limit of 62 m.p.h. instead of the posted 55, would you like to know about it? If so, how would you like to receive your knowledge? By word of mouth; by trial and error; by formal notification from your police department? If you were a police officer and motorists asked you if a 62 m.p.h. policy were in effect, would you tell them the truth? Suppose a prosecutor's office decides that in embezzlement cases it will not prosecute anyone under thirty years of age when the amount embezzled is less than $2,500. The reason behind the policy is that such a person is likely to be punished enough by being discharged by his or her employer. Should such a policy be announced publicly?

Does Davis's allowance of a qualifying clause like "except in unusual circumstances" undercut his position? Will a new "secret law" develop around just what sorts of circumstances are deemed "unusual"? Or has some progress been made even though some room for selective enforcement remains? Can you think of specific rules or announcements your agency (or one with which you are familiar) might make to structure its discretion? Do you see this as an ethical issue in public management?[24]

POSITIVE GOVERNMENT

In the chapters on equality, freedom, and property, considerable emphasis was placed on the limited character of American government. Normative reflections were generated from constitutional principles demanding that the government avoid taking actions that inhibit speech, press, and religion or promote inequalities among the races and between the sexes. Alerting the bureaucrat to the limited dimensions of American government is time well spent if one recalls the tendency of bureaucracies to act in a heavy-handed, authoritative manner. It is important to stress the limitations on governmental power because our traditional values are liberal.

The emphasis on limitations, however, must not obscure the more fundamental point that our form of government—however liberal—is nonetheless a form of government. We are told that it is to secure certain rights that governments are instituted among men. To do this, governments must not only refrain from exercising power, but they must also use it in a positive manner to command action conducive to the ends for which they were created. Because this fundamental concept of government was not emphasized in Chapters 3, 4, and 5, it might be helpful to show in this concluding chapter how Supreme Court opinions can provide the basis for reflections on the positive uses of power.

The most interesting cases along these lines can be found in the Supreme Court's interpretation of the commerce clause—"The Congress shall have power . . . to regulate commerce with foreign nations, and among the several states, and with the Indian Tribes." Rather than quoting extensively from commerce clause cases, it will suffice to touch upon certain highlights in the development of the commerce clause as an instrument of positive government in defense of fundamental values.

The most interesting interpretations of the commerce clause center on the distinction between intra- and interstate commerce. The origins of this well-known distinction can be found in some of the less illuminating dicta of Chief Justice John Marshall's famous but somewhat confusing opinion in Gibbons v. Ogden (1824).[25] Although Marshall never explicitly made this distinction, the language of his opinion invited it and by mid-century it was solidly established in the law.[26] Throughout most of the

nineteenth century, the primary function of the commerce clause with its
intra-/interstate gloss was to prevent the states from regulating commerce
that crossed state lines. Congress showed little interest in exercising its
regulatory powers over interstate commerce. Thus what the states could
not do the Congress would not do; the result was a virtually unregulated
national economy.

All this began to change, however, in 1887 when Congress passed its
first major regulatory law—the Interstate Commerce Act which dealt primarily with the railroad industry. Subsequently, Congress moved into
such areas as the transportation of oil and gas through interstate pipelines,
the interstate movement of electric power, the trucking industry, and radio
transmission. It came as no surprise that the courts should uphold congressional authority in these areas. As early as 1878, in a case involving
the interstate transmission of information by telegraph, the Supreme Court
had said that the provisions of the commerce clause "are not confined to
the instrumentalities of commerce, or the postal service known or in use
when the Constitution was adopted, but they keep pace with the progress of
the country, and adapt themselves to the new developments of time and
circumstances."[27]

Commerce and Manufacturing

The Court was not always supportive of Congress's regulatory efforts. In
U.S. v. E.C. Knight (1895),[28] for example, it refused to apply the Sherman
Antitrust Act against a sugar monopoly on the grounds that the manufacturing of refined sugar—however monopolistic—was not "commerce." "Commerce," said the Court, "succeeds to manufacture and is not a part of it."
Interstate commerce is not underway until goods "commence their final
movement from the States of their origin to that of their destination." This
distinction between manufacture and commerce was applied to the oil, fish-
ing, and mining industries as well. It took on great political significance in
the New Deal era when a conservative Court viewed with dismay President
Roosevelt's willingness to encourage a dramatic expansion of federal intervention in the economy.

Regulating and Prohibiting

If the Court offered an impoverished interpretation of "commerce" in Knight
and its progeny, it was far more generous in its interpretation of what it
means to "regulate." A congressional act of 1895 prohibiting the transportation of lottery tickets in interstate commerce was challenged on the
grounds that the power to regulate did not include the power to prohibit.
The Court rejected this challenge and later upheld another congressional

act that banned impure food and drugs from interstate commerce and still
another that forbade the transportation of women across state lines for
immoral purposes.[29] In interpreting "regulate" to include flat prohibitions, the Court seemed to find a national police power in the recesses of
the commerce clause that enabled Congress to legislate to prevent harm to
public health and morals regardless of any effect on the safety of interstate
commerce.

In view of these solid precedents upholding congressional power to
prohibit in the name of regulating, the Court's decision in a 1918 case,
Hammer v. Dagenhart,[30] came as quite a surprise. The case involved the
Federal Child Labor Act of 1916 in which Congress prohibited the shipment
in interstate commerce of goods manufactured or mined in places of business employing on a full-time basis children under fourteen years of age.
The Supreme Court found this act unconstitutional by a vote of five-to-four.
The majority opinion, written by Justice Day, resurrected the discredited
distinction between the power to regulate and the power to prohibit. Day
attempted to square this distinction with the precedents that had clearly
rejected it by saying that the earlier cases involving lottery tickets,
impure drugs, and prostitution dealt with things or activities that were
harmful in themselves. Goods produced by child labor "are of themselves
harmless." The power to regulate includes the power to prohibit only in
situations where the items or behavior in question are per se evil. This
argument is, of course, as Herman Pritchett has said, "the purest
sophistry."[31] What it amounts to "is that Congress can prevent harm to
consumers after the interstate journey ends but cannot prevent harm to
producers [children under fourteen] before the journey begins."[32] Quite
clearly the Court's majority was scrambling desperately for some way of
legitimating its own misgivings on the desirability of Congress's efforts to
curb the abuses of child labor—regardless of what the precedents might
hold.

In an eloquent dissent, Justice Holmes stated:

> The notion that prohibition is any less prohibition when applied to
> things now thought evil I do not understand. But if there is any matter
> upon which civilized countries have agreed, . . . it is the evil of pre-
> mature and excessive child labor. I should have thought that if we
> were to introduce our own moral conceptions where, in my opinion,
> they do not belong, this was pre-eminently a case for upholding the
> exercise of all its powers by the United States.
>
> But I had thought that the propriety of the exercise of a power
> admitted to exist in some cases was for the consideration of Congress
> alone, and that this court always had disavowed the right to intrude its
> judgment upon questions of policy or morals. It is not for this court
> to pronounce when prohibition is necessary to regulation if it ever may

be necessary—to say that it is permissible as against strong drink, but not as against the product of ruined lives. [33]

Direct and Indirect Effects

Because of the difficulty in drawing a clear line between intra- and inter-state commerce, the Supreme Court in the early years of the present century gradually expanded federal authority by allowing Congress to regulate activities that were local in character but had a serious effect on commerce among the states. In this way, the Court set the stage for federal entry into the exclusive power of the states over manufacturing as opposed to commerce. The Court was reluctant to bring all manufacturing (or mining or production) that affected commerce under federal control, and, so, in good lawyerly fashion, it distinguished between direct and indirect effects on interstate commerce. Only those manufacturing concerns with direct effects on interstate commerce were subject to congressional control. Chief Justice Hughes had the good sense to recognize that it was impossible to define the difference between a direct and indirect effect with any precision. [34] The distinction was quite obviously a conceptual device for safeguarding the principle that some forms of manufacture and production were exempt from federal control.

In a 1936 case, Carter v. Carter Coal Company, however, Justice Sutherland attempted to draw a bright line between direct and indirect effects. The case involved industry codes established under the Bituminous Coal Conservation Act of 1935. The codes were found unconstitutional because they attempted to regulate activity that had only an indirect—albeit very significant—effect on interstate commerce:

The word "direct" implies that the activity or condition invoked or blamed shall operate proximately—not mediately, remotely, or collaterally—to produce the effect. It connotes the absence of an efficient intervening agency or condition. And the extent of the effect bears no logical relation to its character. The distinction between a direct and an indirect effect turns, not upon the magnitude of either the cause or the effect, but entirely upon the manner in which the effect has been brought about. If the production by one man of a single ton of coal intended for interstate sale and shipment . . . affects interstate commerce indirectly, the effect does not become direct by multiplying the tonnage, or increasing the number of men employed, or adding to the expense or complexities of the business, or by all combined. . . .

Much stress is put upon the evils which come from the struggle between employers and employees over the matter of wages, working conditions, the right of collective bargaining, etc., and the resulting

strikes, curtailment and irregularity of production and effect on
prices; and it is insisted that interstate commerce is <u>greatly</u> affected
thereby. But . . . the conclusive answer is that the evils are all local
evils over which the federal government has no legislative control.
The relation of employer and employee is a local relation. . . . And
the controversies and evils, which it is the object of the act to regulate
and minimize, are local controversies and evils affecting local work
undertaken to accomplish that local result. Such effect as they may
have upon commerce, however extensive it may be, is secondary and
indirect. An increase in the greatness of the effect adds to its importance. It does not alter its character.[35]

Sutherland's opinion was a textbook case of just how far some judges
are willing to go in cultivating sterile conceptualism. As one commentator
has noted, Sutherland's argument "illuminates as by a flash of lightening,
a judicial dream world of logical abstractions, where there was no difference between one ton of coal and a million tons of coal, where considerations of degree were not cognizable by the law."[36] Fortunately, Sutherland's reasoning did not pass unchallenged. In a carefully reasoned and
eminently sensible dissent, Justice Cardozo, joined by Brandeis and Stone,
pointed out that "a survey of the cases shows that the words [direct and
indirect] have been interpreted with suppleness of adaptation and flexibility
of meaning."[37] In brief, Cardozo held that the commerce power should be
"as broad as the need that evokes it."[38]

Sutherland's conceptualism in <u>Carter</u> proved short-lived. Within a
year, a majority of the Court backed Cardozo's more flexible understanding of the distinction between direct and indirect. The opportunity to do
this came in <u>NLRB</u> v. <u>Jones and Laughlin Corporation</u>[39]—a case that tested
the National Labor Relations Act of 1936. This act protected the right of
employees to organize themselves into unions and to bargain collectively
with their employers. It also empowered the NLRB to prevent employers
from engaging in unfair practices "affecting commerce." If the Court were
to follow Sutherland's reasoning in <u>Carter,</u> it was clear that the Labor
Relations Act could not be applied to production industries that had only an
indirect—albeit massive—effect on commerce. The Jones and Laughlin
Corporation was a leading steel producer with integrated operating facilities in a number of states. Because the specific unfair labor practices
that provided the substance of the litigation in <u>Jones and Laughlin</u> occurred
in one of the company's Pennsylvania plants, <u>Jones and Laughlin</u> maintained that the dispute was local in character and hence not subject to
federal (that is, NLRB) jurisdiction.

Chief Justice Hughes and Justice Roberts, who had supported
Sutherland's opinion in <u>Carter,</u> now joined Cardozo, Brandeis, and Stone
in rejecting the implications of the <u>Carter</u> ruling. The Chief Justice

delivered an opinion that was characterized by its flexible and pragmatic
understanding of the distinction between direct and indirect effects.

> In view of respondent's far-flung activities, it is idle to say that the
> effect would be indirect or remote. It is obvious that it would be
> immediate and might be catastrophic. We are asked to shut our eyes
> to the plainest facts of our national life and to deal with the question of
> direct and indirect effects in an intellectual vacuum. . . . .
>   When industries organize themselves on a national scale, making
> their relation to interstate commerce the dominant factor in their
> activities, how can it be maintained that their industrial labor rela-
> tions constitute a forbidden field into which Congress may not enter
> when it is necessary to protect interstate commerce from the para-
> lyzing consequences of industrial war? [40]

Hughes went on to state the underlying values the Court had always
intended to protect when it used such conceptual tools as the distinction
between direct and indirect effects on commerce. He warned that not all
forms of federal intervention into the process of manufacturing and production would be approved by the Court. Such intervention, instead of being
judged by a wooden standard of direct and indirect effects, would be
examined "in the light of our dual system of government and may not be
extended so as to embrace effects upon interstate commerce so indirect or
remote that to embrace them, in view of our complex society, would
effectually obliterate the distinction between what is national and what is
local, and create a completely centralized government." [41]

The hints of far-reaching congressional power over commerce became
quite explicit in Wickard v. Filburn[42] —a 1942 case involving the constitutionality of the Agricultural Adjustment Act of 1938. The case involved a
farmer who maintained the regulatory provisions of the act could not possibly apply to him because he planted only twenty-three acres of wheat and
his entire crop was fed to his own livestock. Hence, he argued, his wheat
had no effect whatsoever on commerce and could not be subject to federal
marketing quotas. To subject his wheat crop to federal regulation would
involve a clear violation of the distinction between production and commerce. The Agriculture Department countered this position by presenting
the regulatory system as being aimed at marketing rather than production
and arguing that wheat produced in excess of national acreage allotments—
even if consumed on the farm—could have an adverse effect on market
prices. In delivering the Court's majority opinion, Justice Jackson said:

> The Government's concern lest the Act be held to be a regulation of
> production or consumption rather than of marketing is attributable to
> a few dicta and decisions of this Court which might be understood to

lay it down that activities such as "production," "manufacturing," and "mining" are strictly "local" and, except in special circumstances which are not present here, cannot be regulated under the commerce power because their effects upon interstate commerce are, as matter of law, only "indirect." Even today, when this power has been held to have great latitude, there is no decision of this Court that such activities may be regulated where no part of the product is intended for interstate commerce or intermingled with the subjects thereof. We believe that a review of the course of decision under the Commerce Clause will make plain, however, that questions of the power of Congress are not to be decided by reference to any formula which would give controlling force to nomenclature such as "production" and "indirect" and foreclose consideration of the actual effects of the activity in question upon interstate commerce. . . .

Once an economic measure of the reach of the power granted to Congress in the Commerce Clause is accepted, questions of federal power cannot be decided simply by finding the activity in question to be "production" nor can consideration of its economic effects be foreclosed by calling them "indirect." . . .

Whether the subject of the regulation in question was "production," "consumption," or "marketing" is, therefore, not material for purposes of deciding the question of federal power before us. That an activity is of local character may help in a doubtful case to determine whether Congress intended to reach it. The same consideration might help in determining whether in the absence of Congressional action it would be permissible for the state to exert its power on the subject matter, even though in so doing it to some degree affected interstate commerce. But even if appellant's activity be local and though it may not be regarded as commerce, it may still, whatever its nature, be reached by Congress if it exerts a substantial economic effect on interstate commerce and this irrespective of whether such effect is what might at some earlier time have been defined as "direct" or "indirect."[43]

The final sentence of the previous quotation has quite properly been called the "high-water mark of commerce clause expansionism."[44] It marked the end of a long struggle to establish the supremacy of the federal government over the nation's economy.

Some Reflections

Bureaucrats, especially those in regulatory agencies, are among the heirs of the legacy of power bequeathed by the Roosevelt Court of the late 1930s and the early 1940s. In exercising this power today, do you find your

agency (or agencies with which you are familiar) struggling with the problem of putting content into a broad grant of power? That is, do bureaucrats at times face the type of problem the Supreme Court faced in trying
to decide what the commerce clause should mean? What fundamental
values would have been jeopardized had the Court not embarked on an
expansionist interpretation of the commerce clause? What values are at
stake when your agency interprets the reach of its own statutory powers?
In interpreting their powers, do agencies ever succumb to the sterile conceptualism that characterized Justice Sutherland's discourse on the meaning of direct and indirect? Can you think of any examples? Would it be
accurate to describe the Court's struggle to interpret the commerce clause
as nothing less than an exercise in making operational the nebulous but
normative standard of the public interest? Isn't this what Justice Cardozo
was really doing when he said in his Carter dissent that the commerce
clause must be interpreted to have a meaning "as broad as the need that
evokes it"?

In light of this discussion of "positive government," would you want to
rethink some of the problems we examined in the three previous chapters?
In particular, would you want to modify your opinions on Korematsu
(Chapter 4) or Blaisdell (Chapter 5)?

Before concluding this discussion, look up Heart of Atlanta Motel, Inc.
v. U.S. 379 U.S. 241 (1964) and Katzenbach v. McClung 379 U.S. 294
(1964). There you will find the Court's discussion of the famous Civil
Rights Act of 1964 that banned racial discrimination in public accommodations throughout the nation. When the constitutionality of this act was
challenged, the Court upheld the power of Congress to prohibit racial discrimination in the nation's inns, motels, hotels, restaurants, cafeterias,
theaters, and motion picture houses because these places of business
"affect commerce." There was no need, the Court held, to decide whether
the equal protection clause of the Fourteenth Amendment also would justify
this legislation. The commerce clause was sufficient. Thus the Court
held that Congress had power to pursue a policy of high moral purpose that
rested on the low but solid ground of its power over commerce. These two
cases are of particular significance for our purposes because in them the
values of freedom, equality, and property come together in a most fortui-
tous manner. Commercial need justifies high aspiration. It is all quite
American.

THE PROBLEM OF AMBIGUITY

The reader who opened this book with the hope of finding clear answers to
ethical problems in public management may well be disappointed with what
he or she has discovered. Perhaps, however, such a reader will now
understand why this original hope was illusory. As was noted in a recent

study on ethics, "the ethical argument must be cut to the size of the actual . . . debate."[45] If the breathtaking world views of the great philosophers are too large for public management ethics, the crabbed directives of the casuist are surely too small. Discussions of bureaucratic ethics must follow the contour of public management itself. The ambiguity that pervades the management process cannot be peremptorily expelled in the name of moral righteousness.

The ambiguity that inheres in ethical discourse should not discourage the manager from undertaking further thought and reflection. For years managers have rallied around the venerable standards of "economy and efficiency." These terms, like "equity" and the "public interest," are vague but not meaningless. Indeed, it is not unreasonable to conjecture that if managers did not think and talk in terms of economy and efficiency, government might well be more wasteful and less effective than it actually is. The thoughts one thinks and the discussions one takes seriously can influence behavior.[46] Managers have been made "sensitive" to the need for economy and efficiency; their consciousness has been "raised" along these lines. The same can be done along lines of equity and public interest.

As practical people, managers may understandably have a low threshhold of tolerance for ambiguity but, unless they have surrendered unconditionally to what James Carroll delightfully ridicules as the "ersatz machismo" of the "hard-nosed" image of management,[47] they will see the folly of trying to force clarity where none exists. Indeed, there is no dearth of management literature that extols the creative possibilities that arise from ambiguity. John Aram's Dilemmas of Administrative Behavior argues this point most persuasively.[48] Existentialist philosophers never cease praising the glories of ambiguity, for it provides the occasion for the sorts of choices that give meaning and purpose to one's life.

The ethical ambiguity that surfaces in this book is a structured ambiguity—a constitutional ambiguity. Such ambiguity should not be confused with the sheer indeterminacy of the philosophers. The bureaucrat's choices in the face of constitutional ambiguity are less dramatic than those of the lonely individual who struggles to define a "self" by personal choices over and against nonbeing. A vague outline of the bureaucrat's professional "self" has been given in the constitutional framework that confers meaning on his or her activity. This outline can assume a richly detailed definition through the habit of discretionary choices made within the structured ambiguity of constitutional values with the intention of promoting the common good. This possibility confers legitimacy and value on ethical reflection by public managers.

NOTES

1. McCulloch v. Maryland 4 Wheat. 316 at 408 (1819).
2. Paul Eidelberg, The Philosophy of the American Constitution (New York: The Free Press, 1968), pp. 145-146.
3. The quotation is taken from Madison's speech to the Convention on June 26, 1787. See Winton U. Solberg, ed. , The Federal Convention and the Formation of the Union of the American States (Indianapolis: Bobbs-Merrill, 1958), p. 175.
4. The Federalist Papers, No. 63.
5. Ibid.
6. See Hamilton's speech to the Convention on June 18, 1789, in Solberg, The Federal Convention, pp. 145-146.
7. From Hamilton's speech before the New York ratifying convention; cited by Eidelberg, The Philosophy of the American Constitution, p. 133.
8. Eidelberg, The Philosophy of the American Constitution, p. 136.
9. The Federalist Papers, No. 63.
10. Max Farrand, The Records of the Federal Convention of 1787, 4 vols. (New Haven, Conn.: Yale University Press, 1937), vol. 1, p. 168.
11. Kenneth C. Davis, Administrative Law and Government 2nd ed. (Minneapolis: West, 1975), p. 218.
12. Ibid. , p. 29.
13. Ibid. , p. 219.
14. 439 F2d 584 (1971). The administrator of EPA replaced the secretary of agriculture as the responsible official by Reorganization Plan #3 of 1970.
15. Ibid. at 596.
16. Fook Hong Mak v. Immigration and Naturalization Service 435 F2d 728 (1970). See also Weyerhauser Timber Company 87 NLRB 1076 (1949); Boise Cascade Corporation 148 NLRB 491 (1964); Teamsters, Chauffers, Helpers, and Delivery Drivers v. NLRB 375 F2d 966 (1967).
17. Skidmore v. Swift and Company 323 U.S. 134.
18. Fook Hong Mak v. Immigration and Naturalization Service 435 F2d 728 (1970).
19. Mystik Tape v. Illinois Pollution Control Board 16 Illinois App. 3d 778; 306 N.E. 2d 574 (1973).
20. FTC v. Crowther 430 F2d 510 (1970).
21. Davis, Administrative Law and Government, pp. 264-265.
22. Newman v. U.S. 382 F2d 479 at 481-482 (1967).
23. Davis, Administrative Law and Government, pp. 273-274.

24. For a critique of Davis suggesting that at times the more significant problem is that administrators have too little rather than too much discretion, see Victor G. Rosenblum, "On Davis on Confining, Structuring, and Checking Administrative Discretion," Law and Contemporary Problems 37 (Winter 1972): 49-62.
25. 9 Wheat. 1 (1824).
26. An excellent discussion of the commerce clause can be found in Felix Frankfurter, The Commerce Clause Under Marshall, Taney, and Waite (Chicago: Quadrangle, 1964).
27. Pensacola Telegraph Company v. Western Union Company 96 U.S. 1 at 9 (1878).
28. 156 U.S. 1 (1895).
29. Hipolite Egg Company v. U.S. 220 U.S. 45 (1911); Hoke v. U.S. 227 U.S. 308 (1913).
30. 247 U.S. 251 (1918).
31. C. Herman Pritchett, The American Constitution, 2nd ed. (New York: McGraw-Hill, 1968), p. 261.
32. Ibid.
33. 247 U.S. 251 at 280.
34. Schechter Poultry Corp. v. U.S. 295 U.S. 495 (1935).
35. Carter v. Carter Coal Company 298 U.S. 238 at 307-308 (1936).
36. Pritchett, The American Constitution, p. 269.
37. 298 U.S. 238 at 328.
38. Ibid.
39. 301 U.S. 1 (1937).
40. Ibid. at 41.
41. Ibid. at 37.
42. 317 U.S. 111 (1942).
43. Ibid. at 119-125.
44. Pritchett, The American Constitution, p. 274.
45. Albert R. Jonsen and Lewis H. Butler, "Public Ethics and Policy-Making," The Hastings Center Report 5 (August 1975): 29.
46. This belief, at least in part, accounts for the current policy of requiring agencies to issue Economic Impact Statements to accompany new proposals. The hope is that agency personnel will learn to think in cost-benefit terms. See James C. Miller, "Economic Impact Statements," Regulation 1 (July-August 1977): 14-21.
47. James D. Carroll, "Education for the Public Trust: Learning to Live with the Absurd," The Bureaucrat 4 (April 1975): 24-33.
48. John D. Aram, Dilemmas of Administrative Behavior (Englewood Cliffs, N.J.: Prentice-Hall, 1976).

Appendix

CONSTITUTION OF THE UNITED STATES OF AMERICA

We the people of the United States, in Order to form a more perfect Union, establish Justice, insure domestic Tranquility, provide for the common defence, promote the general Welfare, and secure the Blessings of Liberty to ourselves and our Posterity, do ordain and establish this CONSTITUTION for the United States of America.

ARTICLE I

Section 1. All legislative Powers herein granted shall be vested in a Congress of the United States, which shall consist of a Senate and House of Representatives.

Section 2. 1 The House of Representatives shall be composed of Members chosen every second Year by the People of the several States, and the Electors of the most numerous Branch of the State Legislature.

2 No Person shall be a Representative who shall not have attained to the Age of twenty-five Years, and been seven Years a Citizen of the United States, and who shall not, when elected, be an Inhabitant of that State in which he shall be chosen.

3 Representatives and direct Taxes shall be apportioned among the several States which may be included within this Union according to their respective Numbers, which shall be determined by adding to the whole Number of free Persons, including those bound to Service for a Term of Years, and excluding Indians not taxed, three-fifths of all other Persons.

The actual Enumeration shall be made within three Years after the first
Meeting of the Congress of the United States, and within every subsequent
Term of ten Years, in such Manner as they shall by Law direct. The
Number of Representatives shall not exceed one for every thirty Thousand,
but each State shall have at Least one Representative; and until such
enumeration shall be made, the State of New Hampshire shall be entitled to
chuse three, Massachusetts eight, Rhode-Island and Providence Planta-
tions one, Connecticut five, New-York six, New Jersey four, Pennsylvania
eight, Delaware one, Maryland six, Virginia ten, North Carolina five,
South Carolina, five, and Georgia three.

4 When vacancies happen in the Representation from any State, the
Executive Authority thereof shall issue Writs of Election to fill such
Vacancies.

5 The House of Representatives shall chuse their Speaker and other
Officers; and shall have the sole Power of Impeachment.

Section 3. 1 The Senate of the United States shall be composed of two
Senators from each State, chosen by the Legislature thereof, for six
Years; and each Senator shall have one Vote.

2 Immediately after they shall be assembled in Consequence of the
first Election, they shall be divided as equally as may be into three
Classes. The Seats of the Senators of the first Class shall be vacated at
the Expiration of the second Year, of the second Class at the Expiration of
the fourth Year, and of the third Class at the Expiration of the sixth Year,
so that one-third may be chosen every second Year; and if Vacancies
happen by Resignation, or otherwise, during the Recess of the Legislature
of any State, the Executive thereof may make temporary Appointments
until the next Meeting of the Legislature, which shall then fill such
Vacancies.

3 No Person shall be a Senator who shall not have attained to the Age
of thirty Years, and been nine Years a Citizen of the United States, and
who shall not, when elected, be an Inhabitant of that State for which he
shall be chosen.

4 The Vice President of the United States shall be President of the
Senate, but shall have no Vote, unless they be equally divided.

5 The Senate shall chuse their other Officers, and also a President
pro tempore, in the Absence of the Vice President, or when he shall
exercise the Office of President of the United States.

6 The Senate shall have the sole Power to try all Impeachments.
When sitting for that Purpose, they shall be on Oath or Affirmation. When
the President of the United States is tried, the Chief Justice shall preside;
And no Person shall be convicted without the Concurrence of two-thirds of
the Members present.

7 Judgment in Cases of Impeachment shall not extend further than to
removal from office, and disqualification to hold and enjoy any Office of

honor, Trust or Profit under the United States; but the Party convicted
shall nevertheless be liable and subject to Indictment, Trial, Judgment
and Punishment, according to Law.

Section 4. 1 The Times, Places and Manner of holding Elections for
Senators and Representatives, shall be prescribed in each State by the
Legislature thereof; but the Congress may at any time by Law make or
alter such Regulations, except as to the Places of chusing Senators.

2 The Congress shall assemble at least once in every Year, and such
Meeting shall be on the first Monday in December, unless they shall by
Law appoint a different Day.

Section 5. 1 Each House shall be the Judge of the Elections, Returns
and Qualifications of its own Members, and a Majority of each shall constitute a Quorum to do Business; but a smaller Number may adjourn from
day to day, and may be authorized to compel the attendance of absent
Members, in such Manner, and under such Penalties as each House may
provide.

2 Each House may determine the Rules of its Proceedings, punish its
Members for Disorderly Behavior, and, with the Concurrence of two-
thirds, expel a Member.

3 Each House shall keep a Journal of its Proceedings, and from time
to time publish the same, excepting such Parts as may in their judgment
require Secrecy; and the Yeas and Nays of the Members of either House on
any question shall, at the Desire of one-fifth of those Present, be entered
on the Journal.

4 Neither House, during the Session of Congress, shall, without the
Consent of the other, adjourn for more than three days, nor to any other
Place than that in which the two Houses shall be sitting.

Section 6. 1 The Senators and Representatives shall receive a Compensation for their Services, to be ascertained by Law, and paid out of the
Treasury of the United States. They shall in all Cases, except Treason,
Felony and Breach of the Peace, be privileged from Arrest during their
Attendance at the Session of their respective Houses, and in going to and
returning from the same; and for any Speech or Debate in either House,
they shall not be questioned in any other Place.

2 No Senator or Representative shall, during the Time for which he
was elected, be appointed to any civil Office under the Authority of the
United States, which shall have been created, or the Emoluments whereof
shall have been encreased during such time; and no Person holding any
Office under the United States, shall be a member of either House during
his Continuance in Office.

Section 7. 1 All Bills for raising Revenue shall originate in the House of Representatives; but the Senate may propose or concur with Amendments as on other Bills.

2 Every Bill which shall have passed the House of Representatives and the Senate, shall, before it becomes a Law, be presented to the President of the United States; If he approve he shall sign it, but if not he shall return it, with his Objections to that House in which it shall have originated, who shall enter the Objections at large on their Journal, and proceed to reconsider it. If after such Reconsideration two-thirds of that House shall agree to pass the Bill, it shall be sent, together with the Objections, to the other House, by which it shall likewise be reconsidered, and if approved by two-thirds of that House, it shall become a Law. But in all such Cases the Votes of both Houses shall be determined by Yeas and Nays, and the Names of the Persons voting for and against the Bill shall be entered on the Journal of each House respectively. If any Bill shall not be returned by the President within ten Days (Sundays excepted) after it shall have been presented to him, the same shall be a Law, in like Manner as if he had signed it, unless the Congress by their Adjournment prevent its Return, in which Case it shall not be a Law.

3 Every Order, Resolution, or Vote to which the Concurrence of the Senate and House of Representatives may be necessary (except on a question of Adjournment) shall be presented to the President of the United States; and before the same shall take Effect, shall be approved by him, or being disapproved by him, shall be repassed by two-thirds of the Senate and House of Representatives, according to the Rules and Limitations prescribed in the Case of a Bill.

Section 8. The Congress shall have Power

1 To lay and collect Taxes, Duties, Imposts and Excises, to pay the Debts and provide for the common Defence and general Welfare of the United States; but all Duties, Imposts and Excises shall be uniform throughout the United States;

2 To borrow Money on the credit of the United States;

3 To regulate Commerce with foreign Nations, and among the several States, and with the Indian Tribes;

4 To establish an uniform Rule of Naturalization, and uniform Laws on the subject of Bankruptcies throughout the United States;

5 To coin Money, regulate the Value thereof, and of foreign Coin, and fix the Standard of Weights and Measures;

6 To provide for the Punishment of counterfeiting the Securities and current Coin of the United States;

7 To establish Post Offices and post Roads;

8 To promote the Progress of Science and useful Arts, by securing for limited Times to Authors and Inventors the exclusive Right to their respective Writings and Discoveries;

9 To constitute Tribunals inferior to the supreme Court;

10 To define and punish Piracies and Felonies committed on the high Seas, and Offences against the Law of Nations;

11 To declare War, grant Letters of Marque and Reprisal, and make Rules concerning Captures on Land and Water;

12 To raise and support Armies, but no Appropriation of Money to that Use shall be for a longer Term than two Years;

13 To provide and maintain a Navy;

14 To make Rules for the Government and Regulation of the land and naval Forces;

15 To provide for calling forth the Militia to execute the Laws of the Union, suppress Insurrections and repel Invasions;

16 To provide for organizing, arming, and disciplining, the Militia, and for governing such Part of them as may be employed in the Service of the United States, reserving to the States respectively, the Appointment of the Officers, and the Authority of training the Militia according to the discipline prescribed by Congress;

17 To exercise exclusive Legislation in all Cases whatsoever, over such District (not exceeding ten Miles square) as may, by Cession of particular States, and the Acceptance of Congress, become the Seat of the Government of the United States, and to exercise like Authority over all Places purchased by the Consent of the Legislature of the State in which the same shall be, for the Erection of Forts, Magazines, Arsenals, dock-Yards, and other needful Buildings;—And

18 To make all Laws which shall be necessary and proper for carrying into Execution the foregoing Powers, and all other Powers vested by this Constitution in the Government of the United States, or in any Department or Officer thereof.

Section 9. 1 The Migration or Importation of such Persons as any of the States now existing shall think proper to admit, shall not be prohibited by the Congress prior to the Year one thousand eight hundred and eight, but a Tax or duty may be imposed on such Importation, not exceeding ten dollars for each Person.

2 The Privilege of the Writ of Habeas Corpus shall not be suspended unless when in Cases of Rebellion or Invasion the public Safety may require it.

3 No Bill of Attainder or ex post facto Law shall be passed.

4 No Capitation, or other direct, Tax shall be laid, unless in Proportion to the Census of Enumeration herein before directed to be taken.

5 No Tax or duty shall be laid on Articles exported from any State.

6 No Preference shall be given by any Regulation of Commerce or Revenue to the Ports of one State over those of another; nor shall Vessels bound to, or from, one State, be obliged to enter, clear, or pay Duties in another.

7 No Money shall be drawn from the Treasury, but in Consequence of Appropriations made by Law; and a regular Statement and Account of the Receipts and Expenditures of all public Money shall be published from time to time.

8 No Title of Nobility shall be granted by the United States; And no Person holding any Office of Profit or Trust under them, shall, without the Consent of the Congress, accept of any present, Emolument, Office, or Title, of any kind whatever, from any King, Prince, or foreign State.

Section 10. 1 No State shall enter into any Treaty, Alliance, or Confederation; grant Letters of Marque and Reprisal; coin Money; emit Bills of Credit; make any Thing but gold and silver Coin a Tender in Payment of Debts; pass any Bill of Attainder, ex post facto Law, or Law impairing the Obligation of Contracts, or grant any Title of Nobility.

2 No State shall, without the Consent of the Congress, lay any Imposts or Duties on Imports or Exports, except what may be absolutely necessary for executing its inspection Laws; and the net Produce of all Duties and Imposts, laid by any State on Imports or Exports, shall be for the Use of the Treasury of the United States; and all such Laws shall be subject to the Revision and Controul of the Congress.

3 No State shall, without the Consent of Congress, lay any Duty of Tonnage, keep Troops, or Ships of War in time of Peace, enter into any Agreement or Compact with another State, or with a foreign Power, or engage in War, unless actually invaded, or in such imminent Danger as will not admit of delay.

Article II

Section 1. 1 The executive Power shall be vested in a President of the United States of America. He shall hold his office during the Term of four Years, and, together with the Vice President, chosen for the same Term, be elected, as follows.

2 Each State shall appoint, in such Manner as the Legislature thereof may direct, a Number of Electors, equal to the whole Number of Senators and Representatives to which the State may be entitled in the Congress; but no Senator or Representative, or Person holding an Office of Trust or Profit under the United States, shall be appointed an Elector.

3 The Electors shall meet in their respective States, and vote by Ballot for two Persons, of whom one at least shall not be an inhabitant of the same State with themselves. And they shall make a List of all the Persons voted for, and of the Number of Votes for each; which List they shall sign and certify, and transmit sealed to the Seat of Government of the United States, directed to the President of the Senate. The President of the Senate shall, in the Presence of the Senate and House of

Representatives, open all the Certificates, and the Votes shall then be counted. The Person having the greatest Number of Votes shall be the President, if such Number be a Majority of the whole Number of Electors appointed; and if there be more than one who have such Majority, and have an equal Number of Votes, then the House of Representatives shall immediately chuse by Ballot one of them for President; and if no Person have a Majority, then from the five highest on the List the said House shall in like Manner chuse the President. But in chusing the President, the Votes shall be taken by States, the Representation from each State having one Vote; A quorum for this Purpose shall consist of a Member or Members from two-thirds of the States, and a Majority of all the States shall be necessary to a Choice. In every Case, after the Choice of the President, the Person having the greatest Number of Votes of the Electors shall be the Vice President. But if there should remain two or more who have equal Votes, the Senate shall chuse from them by Ballot the Vice President.

4 The Congress may determine the Time of chusing the Electors, and the Day on which they shall give their Votes; which Day shall be the same throughout the United States.

5 No Person except a natural born Citizen, or a Citizen of the United States, at the time of the Adoption of this Constitution, shall be eligible to the Office of President; neither shall any Person be eligible to that Office who shall not have attained to the Age of thirty-five Years, and been fourteen Years a Resident within the United States.

6 In Case of the Removal of the President from Office, or of his Death, Resignation, or Inability to discharge the Powers and Duties of the said Office, the Same shall devolve on the Vice President, and the Congress may by Law provide for the Case of Removal, Death, Resignation, or Inability, both of the President and Vice President, declaring what officer shall then act as President, and such Officer shall act accordingly, until the Disability be removed, or a President shall be elected.

7 The President shall, at stated Times, receive for his Services, a Compensation, which shall neither be encreased nor diminished during the Period for which he shall have been elected, and he shall not receive within that Period any other Emolument from the United States, or any of them.

8 Before he enter on the Execution of his Office, he shall take the following Oath or Affirmation:—"I do solemnly swear (or affirm) that I will faithfully execute the Office of President of the United States, and will to the best of my Ability, preserve, protect and defend the Constitution of the United States."

Section 2. 1 The President shall be Commander in Chief of the Army and Navy of the United States, and of the Militia of the several States, when called into the actual Service of the United States; he may require the Opinion, in writing, of the principal Officer in each of the executive Departments, upon any Subject relating to the Duties of their respective

Offices, and he shall have Power to grant Reprieves and Pardons for Offences against the United States, except in Cases of Impeachment.

2 He shall have Power, by and with the Advice and Consent of the Senate, to make Treaties, provided two-thirds of the Senators present concur; and he shall nominate, and by and with the Advice and Consent of the Senate, shall appoint Ambassadors, other public Ministers and Consuls, Judges of the supreme Court, and all other Officers of the United States, whose Appointments are not herein otherwise provided for, and which shall be established by Law; but the Congress may by Law vest the Appointment of such inferior Officers, as they think proper, in the President alone, in the Courts of Law, or in the Heads of Departments.

3 The President shall have Power to fill up all Vacancies that may happen during the Recess of the Senate, by granting Commissions which shall expire at the End of their next Session.

Section 3. He shall from time to time give to the Congress Information of the State of the Union, and recommend to their Consideration such Measures as he shall judge necessary and expedient; he may, on extraordinary Occasions, convene both Houses, or either of them, and in Case of Disagreement between them, with Respect to the Time of Adjournment, he may adjourn them to such Time as he shall think proper; he shall receive Ambassadors and other public Ministers; he shall take Care that the Laws be faithfully executed, and shall Commission all the Officers of the United States.

Section 4. The President, Vice President and all civil Officers of the United States, shall be removed from Office on Impeachment for, and Conviction of, Treason, Bribery, or other high Crimes and Misdemeanors.

Article III

Section 1. The Judicial Power of the United States, shall be vested in one supreme Court, and in such inferior Courts as the Congress may from time to time ordain and establish. The Judges, both of the supreme and inferior Courts, shall hold their Offices during good Behaviour, and shall, at stated Times, receive for their Services, a Compensation, which shall not be diminished during their Continuance in Office.

Section 2. 1 The Judicial Power shall extend to all Cases, in Law and Equity, arising under this Constitution, the Laws of the United States, and Treaties made, or which shall be made, under their authority;—to all Cases affecting Ambassadors, other public Ministers and Counsuls;—to all Cases of admiralty and maritime Jurisdiction;—to Controversies to which the United States shall be a Party;—to Controversies between two or more

States;—between a State and Citizens of another State;—between Citizens of different States;—between Citizens of the same State claiming Lands under Grants of different states, and between a State, or the Citizens thereof, and foreign States, Citizens or Subjects.

2 In all Cases affecting Ambassadors, other public Ministers and Consuls, and those in which a State shall be Party, the supreme Court shall have original Jurisdiction. In all the other Cases before mentioned, the Supreme Court shall have appellate Jurisdiction, both as to Law and Fact, with such Exceptions, and under such Regulations as the Congress shall make.

3 The Trial of all Crimes, except in Cases of Impeachment, shall be by Jury; and such Trial shall be held in the State where the said Crimes shall have been committed; but when not committed within any State, the Trial shall be at such Place or Places as the Congress may by Law have directed.

Section 3. 1 Treason against the United States, shall consist only in levying War against them, or in adhering to their Enemies, giving them Aid and Comfort. No Person shall be convicted of Treason unless on the Testimony of two Witnesses to the same overt Act, or on Confession in open Court.

2 The Congress shall have Power to declare the Punishment of Treason, but no Attainder of Treason shall work Corruption of Blood, or Forfeiture except during the Life of the Person attainted.

Article IV

Section 1. Full Faith and Credit shall be given in each State to the public Acts, Records, and judicial Proceedings of every other State. And the Congress may by general Laws prescribe the Manner in which such Acts, Records and Proceedings shall be proved, and the Effect thereof.

Section 2. 1 The Citizens of each State shall be entitled to all Privileges and Immunities of Citizens in the several States.

2 A Person charged in any State with Treason, Felony, or other Crime, who shall flee from Justice, and be found in another State, shall on Demand of the executive Authority of the State from which he fled, be delivered up, to be removed to the State having Jurisdiction of the Crime.

3 No Person held to Service or Labour in one State, under the Laws thereof, escaping into another, shall, in Consequence of any Law or Regulation therein, be discharged from such Service or Labour, but shall be delivered up on Claim of the Party to whom such Service or Labour may be due.

Section 3. 1 New States may be admitted by the Congress into this Union; but no new State shall be formed or erected within the Jurisdiction of any other States; nor any State be formed by the Junction of two or more States, or Parts of States, without the Consent of the Legislatures of the States concerned as well as of the Congress.

2 The Congress shall have Power to dispose of and make all needful Rules and Regulations respecting the Territory or other Property belonging to the United States; and nothing in this Constitution shall be so construed as to Prejudice any Claims of the United States, or of any particular State.

Section 4. The United States shall guarantee to every State in this Union a Republican Form of Government, and shall protect each of them against Invasion; and on Application of the Legislature, or of the Executive (when the Legislature cannot be convened) against domestic Violence.

Article V

The Congress, whenever two-thirds of both Houses shall deem it necessary, shall propose Amendments to this Constitution, or, on the Application of the Legislatures of two-thirds of the several States, shall call a Convention for proposing Amendments, which, in either Case, shall be valid to all Intents and Purposes, as Part of this Constitution, when ratified by the Legislatures of three-fourths of the several States, or by Conventions in three-fourths thereof, as the one or the other Mode of Ratification may be proposed by the Congress; Provided that no Amendment which may be made prior to the Year One thousand eight hundred and eight shall in any Manner affect the first and fourth Clauses in the Ninth Section of the first Article; and that no State, without its Consent, shall be deprived of its equal Suffrage in the Senate.

Article VI

1 All Debts contracted and Engagements entered into, before the Adoption of this Constitution, shall be as valid against the United States under this Constitution, as under the Confederation.

2 This Constitution, and the Laws of the United States which shall be made in Pursuance thereof; and all Treaties made, or which shall be made, under the Authority of the United States, shall be the supreme Law of the Land; and the Judges in every State shall be bound thereby, any Thing in the Constitution or Laws of any State to the Contrary notwithstanding.

3 The Senators and Representatives before mentioned, and the

Members of the several State Legislatures, and all executive and judicial
Officers, both of the United States and of the several States, shall be bound
by Oath or affirmation, to support this Constitution; but no religious Test
shall ever be required as a Qualification to any Office or Public Trust
under the United States.

Article VII

The Ratification of the Conventions of nine States, shall be sufficient
for the Establishment of this Constitution between the States so ratifying
the same.

Amendments

Amendment I

Congress shall make no law respecting an establishment of religion,
or prohibiting the free exercise thereof; or abridging the freedom of
speech, or of the press; or the right of the people peaceably to assemble,
and to petition the Government for a redress of grievances.

Amendment II

A well regulated Militia, being necessary to the security of a free
State, the right of the people to keep and bear Arms, shall not be
infringed.

Amendment III

No Soldier shall, in time of peace be quartered in any house, without
the consent of the Owner, nor in time of war, but in a manner to be prescribed by law.

Amendment IV

The right of the people to be secure in their persons, houses, papers,
and effects, against unreasonable searches and seizures, shall not be violated, and no Warrants shall issue, but upon probable cause, supported by
Oath or affirmation, and particularly describing the place to be searched,
and the persons or things to be seized.

Amendment V

No person shall be held to answer for a capital, or otherwise infamous
crime, unless on a presentment or indictment of a Grand Jury, except in
cases arising in the land or naval forces, or in the Militia, when in actual

service in time of War or public danger; nor shall any person be subject
for the same offence to be twice put in jeopardy of life or limb; nor shall
be compelled in any criminal case to be a witness against himself; nor be
deprived of life, liberty, or property, without due process of law; nor shall
private property be taken for public use, without just compensation.

Amendment VI

In all criminal prosecutions the accused shall enjoy the right to a
speedy and public trial, by an impartial jury of the State and district
wherein the crime shall have been committted, which district shall have
been previously ascertained by law, and to be informed of the nature and
cause of the accusation; to be confronted with the witnesses against him:
to have compulsory process for obtaining witnesses in his favor, and to
have the Assistance of Counsel for his defence.

Amendment VII

In suits at common law, where the value in controversy shall exceed
twenty dollars, the right of trial by jury shall be preserved, and no fact
tried by a jury shall be otherwise re-examined in any Court of the United
States, than according to the rules of the common law.

Amendment VIII

Excessive bail shall not be required, nor excessive fines imposed,
nor cruel and unusual punishments inflicted.

Amendment IX

The enumeration in the Constitution, of certain rights, shall not be
construed to deny or disparage others retained by the people.

Amendment X

The powers not delegated to the United States by the Constitution, nor
prohibited by it to the States, are reserved to the States respectively, or
to the people.

Amendment XI

The Judicial power of the United States shall not be construed to
extend to any suit in law or equity, commenced or prosecuted against one
of the United States by Citizens of another State, or by Citizens or Subjects
of any Foreign State.

Amendment XII

The Electors shall meet in their respective states, and vote by ballot
for President and Vice-President, one of whom, at least, shall not be an
inhabitant of the same state with themselves; they shall name in their ballots the person voted for as President, and in distinct ballots the person
voted for as Vice-President, and they shall make distinct lists of all persons voted for as President, and of all persons voted for as Vice-President,
and of the number of votes for each, which lists they shall sign and certify,
and transmit sealed to the seat of the government of the United States,
directed to the President of the Senate;—The President of the Senate shall,
in the presence of the Senate and House of Representatives, open all the
certificates and the votes shall then be counted;—The person having the
greatest number of votes for President, shall be the President, if such
number be a majority of the whole number of Electors appointed; and if no
person have such majority, then from the persons having the highest numbers not exceeding three on the list of those voted for as President, the
House of Representatives shall choose immediately, by ballot, the President. But in choosing the President, the votes shall be taken by states;
the representation from each state having one vote; a quorum for this purpose shall consist of a member or members from two-thirds of the states,
and a majority of all the states shall be necessary to a choice. And if the
House of Representatives shall not choose a President whenever the right
of choice shall devolve upon them, before the fourth day of March next
following; then the Vice-President shall act as President, as in the case
of the death or other constitutional disability of the President. —The person
having the greatest number of votes as Vice-President, shall be the Vice-
President, if such number be a majority of the whole number of Electors
appointed, and if no person have a majority, then from the two highest
numbers on the list, the Senate shall choose the Vice-President; a
quorum for the purpose shall consist of two-thirds of the whole number of
Senators, and a majority of the whole number shall be necessary to a
choice. But no person constitutionally ineligible to the office of President
shall be eligible to that of Vice-President of the United States.

Amendment XIII

Section 1.   Neither slavery nor involuntary servitude, except as a
punishment for crime whereof the party shall have been duly convicted,
shall exist within the United States, or any place subject to their
jurisdiction.

Section 2.   Congress shall have power to enforce this article by appropriate legislation.

Amendment XIV

Section 1. All persons born or naturalized in the United States, and subject to the jurisdiction thereof, are citizens of the United States and of the State wherein they reside. No State shall make or enforce any law which shall abridge the privileges or immunities of citizens of the United States; nor shall any State deprive any person of life, liberty, or property, without due process of law; nor deny to any person within its jurisdiction the equal protection of the laws.

Section 2. Representatives shall be apportioned among the several States according to their respective numbers, counting the whole number of persons in each State, excluding Indians not taxed. But when the right to vote at any election for the choice of electors for President and Vice President of the United States, Representatives in Congress, the Executive and Judicial officers of a State, or the members of the Legislature thereof, is denied to any of the male inhabitants of such State, being twenty-one years of age, and citizens of the United States, or in any way abridged except for participation in rebellion, or other crime, the basis of representation therein shall be reduced in the proportion which the number of such male citizens shall bear to the whole number of male citizens twenty-one years of age in such State.

Section 3. No person shall be a Senator or Representative in Congress, or elector of President and Vice President, or hold any office, civil or military, under the United States, or under any State, who, having previously taken an oath, as a member of Congress, or as an officer of the United States, or as a member of any State legislature, or as an executive or judicial officer of any State, to support the Constitution of the United States, shall have engaged in insurrection or rebellion against the same, or given aid or comfort to the enemies thereof. But Congress may by a vote of two-thirds of each House, remove such disability.

Section 4. The validity of the public debt of the United States, authorized by law, including debts incurred for payment of pensions and bounties for services in suppressing insurrection or rebellion, shall not be questioned. But neither the United States nor any State shall assume or pay any debt or obligation incurred in aid of insurrection or rebellion against the United States, or any claim for the loss or emancipation of any slave; but all such debts, obligations and claims shall be held illegal and void.

Section 5. The Congress shall have power to enforce, by appropriate legislation, the provisions of this article.

Amendment XV

Section 1. The right of citizens of the United States to vote shall not be denied or abridged by the United States or by any State on account of race, color, or previous condition of servitude.

Section 2. The Congress shall have power to enforce this article by appropriate legislation.

Amendment XVI

The Congress shall have power to lay and collect taxes on incomes, from whatever source derived, without apportionment among the several States, and without regard to any census or enumeration.

Amendment XVII

The Senate of the United States shall be composed of two Senators from each State, elected by the people thereof, for six years; and each Senator shall have one vote. The electors in each State shall have the qualifications requisite for electors of the most numerous branch of the State legislatures.

When vacancies happen in the representation of any State in the Senate, the executive authority of such State shall issue writs of election to fill such vacancies: Provided, That the legislature of any State may empower the executive thereof to make temporary appointments until the people fill the vacancies by election as the legislature may direct.

This amendment shall not be so construed as to affect the election or term of any Senator chosen before it becomes valid as part of the Constitution.

Amendment XVIII

Section 1. After one year from the ratification of this article the manufacture, sale, or transportation of intoxicating liquors within, the importation thereof into, or the exportation thereof from the United States and all territory subject to the jurisdiction thereof for beverage purposes is hereby prohibited.

Section 2. The Congress and the several States shall have concurrent power to enforce this article by appropriate legislation.

Section 3. This article shall be inoperative unless it shall have been ratified as an amendment to the Constitution by the legislatures of the several States, as provided in the Constitution, within seven years from the date of the submission hereof to the States by Congress.

Amendment XIX

The right of citizens of the United States to vote shall not be denied or abridged by the United States or by any State on account of sex.

Congress shall have power to enforce this article by appropriate legislation.

Amendment XX

Section 1.   The terms of the President and Vice President shall end at noon at the 20th day of January, and the terms of Senators and Representatives at noon on the 3d day of January, of the years in which such terms would have ended if this article had not been ratified; and terms of their successors shall then begin.

Section 2.   The Congress shall assemble at least once in every year, and such meeting shall begin at noon on the 3d day of January, unless they shall by law appoint a different day.

Section 3.   If, at the time fixed for the beginning of the term of the President, the President elect shall have died, the Vice President elect shall become President.   If a President shall not have been chosen before the time fixed for the beginning of his term, or if the President elect shall have failed to qualify, then the Vice President elect shall act as President until a President shall have qualified; and the Congress may by law provide for the case wherein neither a President elect nor a Vice President elect shall have qualified, declaring who shall then act as President, or the manner in which one who is to act shall be selected, and such person shall act accordingly until a President or Vice President shall have qualified.

Section 4.   The Congress may by law provide for the case of the death of any of the persons from whom the House of Representatives may choose a President whenever the right of choice shall have devolved upon them, and for the case of the death of any of the persons from whom the Senate may choose a Vice President whenever the right of choice shall have devolved upon them.

Section 5.   Sections 1 and 2 shall take effect on the 15th day of October following the ratification of this article.

Section 6.   This article shall be inoperative unless it shall have been ratified as an amendment to the Constitution by the legislatures of three-fourths of the several States within seven years from the date of its submission.

Amendment XXI

Section 1. The eighteenth article of amendment to the Constitution of the United States is hereby repealed.

Section 2. The transportation or importation into any State, Territory, or possession of the United States for delivery or use therein of intoxicating liquors, in violation of the laws thereof, is hereby prohibited.

Section 3. This article shall be inoperative unless it shall have been ratified as an amendment to the Constitution by conventions in the several States, as provided in the Constitution, within seven years from the date of the submission hereof to the States by the Congress.

Amendment XXII

Section 1. No person shall be elected to the office of the President more than twice, and no person who has held the office of President, or acted as President, for more than two years of a term to which some other person was elected President shall be elected to the office of the President more than once. But this Article shall not apply to any persons holding the office of President when this Article was proposed by the Congress, and shall not prevent any person who may be holding the office of President, or acting as President, during the term within which this Article becomes operative from holding the office of President or acting as President during the remainder of such term.

Section 2. This Article shall be inoperative unless it shall have been ratified as an amendment to the Constitution by the legislatures of three-fourths of the several States within seven years from the date of its submission to the states by the Congress.

Amendment XXIII

Section 1. The District constituting the seat of Government of the United States shall appoint in such manner as the Congress may direct:
A number of electors of President and Vice President equal to the whole number of Senators and Representatives in Congress to which the District would be entitled if it were a State, but in no event more than the least populous states; they shall be in addition to those appointed by the States, but they shall be considered, for the purposes of the election of President and Vice President, to be electors appointed by a State; and they shall meet in the District and perform such duties as provided by the twelfth article of amendment.

Section 2. The Congress shall have power to enforce this article by appropriate legislation.

Amendment XXIV

Section 1. The right of citizens of the United States to vote in any primary or other election for President or Vice President, for electors for President or Vice President, or for Senator or Representative in Congress, shall not be denied or abridged by the United States or any State by reason of failure to pay poll tax or other tax.

Section 2. The Congress shall have power to enforce this article by appropriate legislation.

Amendment XXV

Section 1. In case of the removal of the President from office or of his death or resignation, the Vice President shall become President.

Section 2. Whenever there is a vacancy in the office of the Vice President, the President shall nominate a Vice President who shall take office upon confirmation by a majority vote of both Houses of Congress.

Section 3. Whenever the President transmits to the President pro tempore of the Senate and the Speaker of the House of Representatives his written declaration that he is unable to discharge the powers and duties of his office, and until he transmits to them a written declaration to the contrary, such powers and duties shall be discharged by the Vice President as Acting President.

Section 4. Whenever the Vice President and a majority of either the principal officers of the executive departments or of such other body as Congress may by law provide, transmit to the President pro tempore of the Senate and the Speaker of the House of Representatives their written declaration that the President is unable to discharge the powers and duties of his office, the Vice President shall immediately assume the powers and duties of the office as Acting President.

Thereafter, when the President transmits to the President pro tempore of the Senate and the Speaker of the House of Representatives his written declaration that no inability exists, he shall resume the powers and duties of his office unless the Vice President and a majority of either the principal officers of the executive departments or of such other body as Congress may by law provide, transmit within four days to the President pro tempore of the Senate and the Speaker of the House of Representatives their written declaration that the President is unable to discharge the powers and duties of his office. Thereupon Congress shall decide the issue, assembling within forty-eight hours for that purpose if not in session. If the Congress, within twenty-one days after receipt of the latter written declaration, or if Congress is not in session, within twenty-one days after Congress is required to assemble, determines by two-thirds vote of both Houses that the President is unable to discharge the powers and duties of his office, the Vice President shall continue to discharge the same as Acting President; otherwise, the President shall resume the powers and duties of his office.

Amendment XXVI

Section 1.   The rights of citizens of the United States, who are eighteen years of age or older, to vote shall not be denied or abridged by the United States or any state on account of age.

Section 2.   The Congress shall have the power to enforce this article by appropriate legislation.

Amendment XXVII (Proposed)

Section 1.   Equality of rights under the law shall not be denied or abridged by the United States or by any state on account of sex.

Section 2.   The Congress shall have the power to enforce, by appropriate legislation, the provisions of this article.

Section 3.   This amendment shall take effect two years after the date of ratification.

ADDENDUM

As this book was in the final stages of its production for publication, the Supreme Court announced its long-awaited opinion in Regents of the University of California v. Bakke (Docket No. 76-811; decided June 28, 1978). Initial reaction to the decision was that it contained something for everyone. Allan Bakke, the white plaintiff, was to be admitted to the medical school of the University of California at Davis but the principle of affirmative action was upheld at least to the extent that under certain circumstances universities may take race into account in designing their admissions programs. Despite the Court's opinion, the legal future of affirmative action is not entirely clear. This is due primarily to some uncertainty as to how the Court in future cases will interpret the crucial "swing" opinion of Justice Powell. Powell found that, although racial quotas are impermissible, race may be considered as a "plus" in weighing the various factors that go into making admissions decisions at universities. This statement is a virtual invitation to further litigation especially in the areas of employment and government contracts.

As a study in constitutional values, Bakke is quite interesting. Five of the six opinions address the theme of the colorblind Constitution and therefore have a direct bearing on our discussion in this chapter of benign racial classifications. For our purposes, however, the most important aspect of the case is its ambiguity. In upholding affirmative action in principle while banning the rigid quotas of the Davis plan, the Court introduced considerable flexibility into just what affirmative action will mean at various institutions. On this point the noted constitutional scholar, Philip Kurland, observed: "The Bakke decision leaves much discretion to admissions officers to determine how they may secure whatever diversity they deem appropriate for their student bodies without resting solely on racial categories."

This is perhaps as good an example as one could find to illustrate the moral significance of discretionary authority exercised by mid-level bureaucrats. The ambiguity of Bakke will allow those seriously committed to the goals of affirmative action to pursue an aggressive program of minority recruitment. The same ambiguity will protect those for whom tokenism is quite enough. Addressing this point the day after Bakke was decided, a New York Times editorial quoted from the opinion of Justice Blackmun: "The ultimate question, as it was at the beginning of this litigation, is: among the qualified how does one choose"? The editorial replied, "The ultimate answer remains: with conscience."

Case Index

Name Index

Appleby, Paul H., 43n, 50, 76n
Aquinas, Thomas, 11n, 83n
Aram, John D., 256, 258n
Aristotle, 11n, 59, 81n, 82n, 83n

Bailey, Stephen K., 13n, 76n
Baker, Gladys, 45n
Ball, Howard, 46n
Beaney, William M., 188n, 235n
Berger, Peter L., 57, 81n
Berle, Adolph A., 234n
Bickel, Alexander M., 68, 73, 84n, 85n
Biller, Robert P., 81n
Blackstone, William (see Index)
Blackwell, Kate, 13n
Bloom, Allen, 78n
Branch, Taylor, 13n, 47n
Butler, Lewis H., 83n, 258n

Carey, George W., 84n
Carroll, James D., 256, 258n

Chitwood, Stephen R., 78n
Cleveland, Harlan, 10n, 81n
Cohen, Morris R., 235n
Commager, Henry S., 84n
Cox, Harvey, 81n
Crenson, Matthew A., 41n

Dahl, Robert H., 43n
Davis, Kenneth C., 29-31, 45-46n, 242-248, 257n
Diamond, Martin, 11n, 234n
Dickson, William M., 19
Drucker, Peter, 77n
Dworkin, Ronald, 78n

Easton, David, 27, 44n
Eidelberg, Paul, 85n, 257n

Farrand, Max, 257n
Faulkner, Robert K., 233n
Frank, Thomas M., 13n

Index